HUMANIST
WITHOUT PORTFOLIO

*An Anthology
of the writings of
Wilhelm von Humboldt*

HUMANIST

WITHOUT

PORTFOLIO

*Translated from the German
with an Introduction
by Marianne Cowan*

Detroit 1963
Wayne State University Press

CONTENTS

v

MAN IN THE PHYSICAL UNIVERSE 101

MAN AS A BEING WHO CAN BE EDUCATED 125

MAN IN THE REALM OF SPIRIT 145

MAN'S INTRINSIC HUMANITY: HIS LANGUAGE 235

INTRODUCTION

I

Wilhelm von Humboldt (1767–1835) lived a century before psychoanalysis was discovered as the most influential modern technique for knowing oneself. Indeed, of the three great modern revolutions which have limited Western humanity's exalted opinion of itself and driven man out of his central position in the universe, Humboldt knew only one, the Copernican displacement of humanity's abode. The other two, the Darwinian devaluation of man's uniqueness (together with the devastating Nietzschean corollary that man is not only an animal, but *the* diseased animal), and the Freudian disorientation of man's conscious opinion of himself: these still lay in the future when Humboldt lived. The collective ideas which fell to his experience were comprised in the shift, during his lifetime, from rationalistic enlightenment through the cult of sentiment to the romantic discovery of the "night" aspects of the human soul. Humboldt stood, in other words, at the very beginning of the psychic drama whose climax we may have experienced and to whose end we look with such nightmarish feelings of helplessness. Will man, having rendered himself increasingly insignificant, displace himself altogether out of his universe, grown increasingly vast and alien?

In the face of such prospect, it is very natural that each of these three revolutionary upheavals should have produced diverse counterrevolutionary phenomena. At present there are, for example, a number of voices raised in criticism against the values inherent in the psychoanalytical concepts. Many young intellectuals currently seem to feel that depth analysis is but a new and insidiously virulent form of authoritarianism and far indeed from the liberation that their fathers believed it was and lauded or attacked accordingly. It is not yet clear whether analysis as such is the hated object, or analysis of the unconscious, or analysis of one person at the direction of another, or analysis by a professional who earns his living by this task, or a combination of some or all of these. What seems plain, however, is that deep and important human values are felt to be at stake. The word "humanism," several times a battle cry in modern times, once again seems to tremble in the disturbed air.

If the current protest is essentially a humanistic one—and it seems wisest to take it as such—then Humboldt's voice is a timely one. He is innocent of all partisanship, yet he saw many of the problems and tasks of our today and tomorrow with astounding clairvoyance. If humanism has any meaning it must be so all-encompassing a concept that no person's view or definition of it, however strained or one-sided, will entirely miss the sense of it. But no amount of viewing of humanism as an "ism" can create meaning for it unless it is expressed as the total way of life of a real person, a humanist. If we were to set out to invent a humanist whose entire life orientation suggested an approach to our contemporary problem of disorientation, we could scarcely come up with a better model than that provided by Wilhelm von Humboldt.

But what, one might ask, is Humboldt's specific relation to us? He was by no means in any existential situation comparable to our own. And yet, by nature and temperament he sought what we do: the orientation or reorientation of man in a universe from whose center he has displaced himself. In the welter of psychological notions, then as now emerging, he sought to clear the ways to the wellsprings of the living self. By accident of birth he was un-aided—and unburdened—by the modern tools and techniques for attaining his goals. He invented his own, and each reader may judge by the light of his own insights and prejudices how like or unlike Humboldt's are to those that we now take for granted and are free to accept or reject. Self-knowledge and insight into others, self-acceptance and tolerance of others, complete self-orientation in his contemporary universe and a diligent lifelong preparation for a death that should be appropriate for his life: these were the values to which Humboldt with remarkable single-mindedness applied the acts and thoughts of his life. And lest such a formulation of his goals sound all too German and programmatic, we had better state it in his own words right at the outset.

To carry life lightly and have the capacity for enjoying it deeply is . . . the sum of all wisdom.[1]

This calls for reading between the lines if not outright explication, but it should serve to counteract the shadow of pedagogic pedantry which a certain type of editor is apt to project upon the author.

Humboldt's name has never really disappeared anywhere it was once heard, though this is certainly partly due to the eminence of his brother Alexander, whose travels and discoveries were directly responsible for the great number of places in North and South America which bear the family name. Wilhelm founded the University of Berlin which today, in East Berlin, bears his name—divested of its "von" to be sure. During their own time the two brothers, Wilhelm and Alexander von Humboldt, were of equal and practically world-wide renown. In Wilhelm's case this did not rest on any written works. Very few of his writings were published during his lifetime and of those that were, none by the

---

[1] To Caroline v. Humboldt, June 1804. For the explanation of all bibliographical references, see p. 421.

remotest stretch of good will could be called popular in any sense. Nor did his fame rest on any public acts of consequence. His public life was that of a career diplomat during some of Prussia's most troubled times, and his political achievements, if any, were never before the public eye.

Humboldt's position in posterity is strongly reminiscent of that of his American contemporary, John Quincy Adams. He too wrote voluminously and is scarcely read. He too was something of an anonymous diplomat for much of his life. Of his diligent poetic efforts it has been said that "while they are mechanically perfect as to meter and rhyme, there is nothing in them to lead even the most friendly critic to the conclusion that the poetry of the world suffered great loss when John Quincy Adams devoted his life to statecraft." [2] This would be a most apt comment on Humboldt's poetry as well. Humboldt wrote a paragraph in which he noted the ineffable quality of the kind of renown that seems to be based almost solely on the quality and variety of a man's living contacts with his contemporaries.

> There is a fuller and more immediate effectiveness of a great spirit than that possible through his works. These show only a part of his being. The entirety flows pure and whole through his living personal self. In a way which cannot be proved in detail, nor investigated, nor even wholly thought, his real self is taken up by his contemporaries and handed on to the generations to follow.[3]

Humboldt wrote this in connection with Schiller who was his close friend and associate, but the description, seen in retrospect, fits him (as well as Adams) better than Schiller in whose case it turned out to be the work, after all, rather than the human being which was primarily transmitted to posterity. Humboldt did, however, undergo a wave of popular posthumous acclaim in Germany that was directly due to his written work, but this was by a curious and

[2] Bennett Champ Clark, *John Quincy Adams: Old Man Eloquent* (Boston, 1932), p. 94.
[3] See below, p. 164.

4

totally unpredictable accident, the tale of which is worth recounting here because it illustrates certain sides of Humboldt's personality with which we are particularly concerned. While vacationing in a small resort Humboldt met, as a young man of twenty or so, a young girl with whom he walked and talked a number of times during the three days they knew each other. In the fashion of the day, he wrote a word of salutation in her souvenir album when they parted. Their paths never crossed again until, twenty-five years later, he received through the mails that souvenir page together with a story-length letter from the lady, one Charlotte Diede, which told the sad tale of her personal life during the intervening years, assured him that the three days of his presence in their youth had left her with an ideal of noble manhood never since forgotten, and asked the now internationally famous and presumably influential diplomat to intercede in her behalf so that a small part of her lost moneys might be restored to her, since she was alone and financially in desperate straits.

Humboldt wrote back that he remembered her well, asked her to accept some money to tide her over, saw to it that they should not meet, except for an hour's visit on his part once or twice years later, discouraged in no uncertain terms her greatest desire which was to occupy some sort of position in his household, and seized the opportunity to engage in a full-scale experimentation with a human personality, or rather two of them, since it was quite clear to him that his own would be involved as well as hers. He proposed a bargain to her that he would do what he could to help her straighten out the outer difficulties of her life, never deviating from his high regard for her and his gratitude for her affection and loyalty, while she, in turn, if she so wished, might show her gratitude by simply writing to him regularly, regardless of whether he should have time or even inclination to answer. Further, she should follow his advice whenever she conscientiously felt she could, and should begin these spiritual exercises by writing and sending him in installments the complete history of her early life, omitting nothing that she might remember and could bring herself to write

5

down. She in turn asked, and received, the promise not only that the correspondence would be entirely private but that all her letters to him would be destroyed. This promise Humboldt kept. Her letters were destroyed and no one in his family even knew of the correspondence which they kept at first intermittently, then quite regularly on both sides for over twenty years, till his death put an end to it. She, however, had not been able to bring herself to destroy his letters and had received from him a somewhat grudging permission to keep them always with her, since she would not be vouchsafed his own physical presence during their lifetimes.

When some years after his death she published them anonymously in edited form under the title *Wilhelm von Humboldt's Letters to a Woman Friend,* the volume (containing some 400 pages of letters and excerpts from letters) became something of a best seller. The first interest in them must naturally have been due to the fact that many people who had known Humboldt and his family personally or by hearsay hoped for intimate revelations of a possibly shady side of the great man's personal relationships. But the letters turned out to be impeccable, nor did the editing hint of any lapses or indiscretions, and a Victorian Europe (they were widely translated, including into English) bought them as the perfect gift for a "lady's library," full of good advice and uplift and encouragement for underprivileged but genteel females. We should call them rather stiff and didactic, especially as contrasted to Humboldt's subsequently published correspondence with his wife and daughters, although toward the end of his life, particularly during the last six years after his wife's death, they take on some of the unusually spontaneous and totally uncontrived tones which are the mark of his family letters. The very frank and really quite curious avowals of his psychological experimentation seem not to have been felt as a jarring note.

In Humboldt's posthumous fragments there is an outline plus a few introductory sentences for a project which interested him all his life but which he never carried out, aside from some partial treatments of a fictional character that he incorporated into several narrative poems. He called it "A History of Dependence in the Human Race," and its scope may be briefly indicated by the main divisions of his outlines of projected chapters: I. History of the Feminine Sex (Philosophical elucidation. Basic principles. General legislation. Bodily condition. Dress. Spiritual condition. Marriage. Condition of the unmarried; Widowhood. Historical events.) II. History of the Sex Impulse (Philosophical elucidation. Basic principles. General legislation. Nature of sex in general. Intercourse between the sexes. Intercourse within each sex. Intercourse with animals. Intercourse with one's self. Historical events. Hetaerae.) III. History of Servitude (Philosophical elucidation. Basic principles. General legislation. Types of servitude. Condition. Types of labor. Chastisements. Historical events.) IV. History of Dependence Within Masculine Freedom (Labor. Suffering. Historical events.) [4]

Within the framework here suggested Humboldt's initial interest in the letters that Charlotte Diede might be expected to write him becomes quite readily comprehensible.[5] In the end it is obvious that she became what she called herself, a woman-friend, no more and no less, and it turned out that he was to give of himself much more than he asked of her. And although he wrote a good deal during his life on the subject of liberty, he never did write on dependence, feeling perhaps that even his lifetime of effort had not quite sufficed to bring this subject wholly out of the shadows for him. This, however, belongs to a realm of speculation which it is best here to avoid. The point I wish to make is simply that Humboldt's intensive search for insight into the human condition was able to take him into, and cleanly through, commitments of his personality and character without in any way damaging commitments of himself in other directions, and without either youth or personal impulsiveness or private discontent to propel him.

Humboldt's second claim to fame through his written works did not reach public notice until the twentieth century. It is the full

---

[4] VII, 653 f.
[5] See below, pp. 378 f.

correspondence with his wife, both her letters and his, which he left to each of his surviving three daughters in turn, asking only that it not be destroyed and that it remain in the hands of further female descendents, for them to do with as they wished. This correspondence was published by one of these descendents, Anna von Sydow, beginning in 1907.[6] Most readers of Humboldt undoubtedly feel and shall continue to feel that these seven volumes contain not only the "most genuine" Humboldt but a great deal of his finest writing. Quite literally, one might say, they contain his legacy to our century. He meant them to be a living monument to his wife in the hearts of her daughters and daughters' daughters, as well as the record, one must suppose, of a most remarkable lifetime marriage. They are all this and much more besides—and there is no conceivable substitute for reading them in their entirety.

Having thus touched upon Humboldt's posthumous career, as it were, it now seems desirable for us to review what this humanist did in the sixty-eight years of lifetime. He was born at Potsdam (Berlin) in Prussia in 1767, into a fairly well-to-do family of the minor nobility, of mixed Prussian and French Huguenot ancestry. He was the oldest son of his parents; two years later his brother Alexander was born. There was also an older half brother from a previous marriage of his mother. She was twice widowed; Wilhelm and Alexander, too, lost their father before they reached their teens. All three boys were educated privately by tutors. Their consensus in later life seems to have been that their home life had been dull and rather cold in the tone set by their mother and various elderly relatives who made their home with her. Nonetheless Humboldt, in discussing the near-tragedy for a girl to lose her mother early in life, has this to say about sons who lose their father:

> Any feeling son will deeply and seriously mourn the early death of his father. . . . But this event is seldom dangerous to the development of character. If fate preserves his mother, the son is able to rescue the ties of filial love which bind him—not exactly more intimately or even more naturally—to his mother, but which are ren-

<hr/>

[6] See below, p. 421.

8

dered somehow different and more tightly encompassing by the inexpressible elements which are part of the feminine character. Thus a father may influence his sons more deeply by the image intensified by reverence and love that his wife preserves of him than by his immediate presence. Circumstance and accident are better educators, anyway, than the definite guidance which even a sensible and reasonable father seldom can refrain from at least wishing to impart.[7]

One can hardly help feeling that the mother archetype here alluded to received at least a share of its endowment from the woman who guided the young Humboldts through circumstances similar to those here described.

Wilhelm attended a course in Natural Law in Berlin and subsequently attended the universities at Frankfurt a.O. and Göttingen, none too diligently, one gathers. He became an intimate of the famous Berlin salon of Henriette Herz where he could talk poetry and philosophy and tender sentiments by the current rules of the game. He took at least part of the grand tour, to Paris and to Switzerland, and at the age of twenty-three took a post as an apprentice or junior judge at the Prussian High Court which should have been the first stepping stone to a distinguished public career. But at this point his youthful conventionality gave out altogether. He met and married (at the age of twenty-four) a girl as conventionally brought up and as inwardly independent as himself and with her encouragement and aid decided to fashion a personal life for them which should be truly one of their choice. He felt himself emotionally unsuited for the work of being a judge, being inclined to try and sentence himself in every criminal case that came before him.[8] After a year's try he simply gave it up, to the somewhat appalled wonder of his mother and his bride's father who had expected a brilliant career and the assurance of financial security for the young couple in accordance with their class.

Instead, Wilhelm and Caroline retired to the country, each with a small parental allowance, to see what they might discover

[7] XV, 539.
[8] See below, pp. 38 f. and 409.

about themselves. The first project was to teach Caroline Greek and to have as many babies as possible. She learned the Greek readily, and there were, eventually, eight babies. After a year or two of secluded honeymoon they set up housekeeping in the small university town of Jena in order to live in close communion with Schiller and—as they got to know him—Goethe, to both of whom they remained bound in cordial friendship as long as they all lived. This living arrangement was eventually broken into by the necessity for moving in with Humboldt's dying mother.

After that, with somewhat more private income at their disposal, they traveled. They lived in Paris and in Vienna and traveled in Spain where Humboldt established, by studying the dialects of the Basque country, the interest in linguistics which was to be the major task of his mature life. All in all, Humboldt's first retirement lasted ten years, a period reminding one in every respect, except for the physical, external situation, of Thoreau's two years at Walden Pond. Humboldt, too, went to the "woods" to "transact some private business with the fewest obstacles," and to "see if I could not learn what [life] had to teach, and not, when I came to die, discover that I had not lived." And he, too, left the woods because it seemed to him that he had several more lives to live and could not spare any more time for that one. If Thoreau's meditative sojourn has come down to us as a more inspiring example, this is due in part to its clear-cut romantic appeal to a nature- and contemplation-starved posterity, but also and mainly because he had the gift to articulate its meaning within the confines of a single artistic production. This talent Humboldt did not possess, though he knew that it was lacking.

A glance at the titles of his writings between 1791, the year of his retirement, and 1801, the year he returned to public life, will indicate perhaps more clearly than anything else what he was trying to do. It will show, also, why, even aside from his self-critical temperament, he was bound to remain dissatisfied with his writings. Of this list, some few titles were published; most remained in the archives. It does not include his letters, diaries, poems, attempts at translation, revision of lecture notes, and so on, which of course increase the bulk of his actual written meditations and communications to several times the volume here indicated.

"Ideas on government, occasioned by the new French Constitution" (1791, 8 pp.)

"On the developmental laws of human energies" (1791, 10 pp.)

"An attempt to define the legal limits of government" (1792, 157 pp.)

"About classical studies, particularly concerning the Greeks" (1793, 26 pp.)

"A theory of the developmental organization of man" (1793, 5 pp.)

"Review of Jacobi's *Woldemar*" (1794, 22 pp.)

"About sexual differences and their influence on organic nature" (1794, 23 pp.)

"On masculine and feminine form" (1795, 34 pp.)

"Review of Wolf's edition of the *Odyssey*" (1795, 6 pp.)

"Plan for a comparative anthropology" (1795, 33 pp.)

"Pindar" (1795, 18 pp.)

"The eighteenth century" (1796–97, 112 pp.)

"On Goethe's *Hermann und Dorothea*" (1797–98, 210 pp.)

"On the spirit of humanity" (1797, 10 pp.)

"Review of *Agnes von Lilien*" (1798, 9 pp.)

"Musée des petits Augustins" (1799, 31 pp.)

"On the contemporary French theater" (1799, 23 pp.)

"Review of his own work on Goethe's *Hermann und Dorothea*" [written in French, for Parisian friends and acquaintances] (1799, 29 pp.)

"Montserrat near Barcelona" (1800, 29 pp.)

"On the antique theater in Sagunt" (1800–01, 53 pp.)

"Cantabrica" [small essays on Spain] (1800, 21 pp.)

"The Basques: Observations made during a trip through the Spanish and French Basque country in the spring of 1801" (1801, 196 pp.)

Such were the subjects which came to articulation during this period. They revolve basically around his lifetime interests: human beings, with particular emphasis on the female sex; language and origins of the human race; and the attempt to orient himself in the times in which he lived. His dearest project, in many ways, is for the first time represented in the fragmentary work he entitled "The Eighteenth Century." He was fascinated by the symbolic experience of living through the turn of a century, as he was by the "January" feelings that each year would revive in him. He never ceased to speculate on where he had been and where he was going, and with him the whole human race. In his whole subjectively felt orientation he was ever a spectator, an onlooker, a man who could quite properly say of himself that he was "a thoroughly inward-oriented person whose entire effort goes to transform the world in its most manifold shapes into his own solitude." [9] But he also never underrated or undervalued the manifold shapes of the world; his contemporaries saw him, also properly, as a thoroughgoing activist, even a manipulator, a man who lived with singular vivacity for the moment and the moment's enjoyment. Nietzsche once expressed the wish to see—or better yet to be—that kind of complex, highly individuated character.

"One thing is needful: to fashion a style for one's character: a great and rare art! It is practiced by him who has an over-all view of what his nature provides by way of strengths and weaknesses. Such a man may then adapt them to an artist's plan, until each facet seems to partake of both art and reason, and even the weaknesses will delight the eye. Here we see added a large mass of second nature, over there a piece of original nature removed: both the result of long practice and daily effort. Here, something ugly which could not be carried off has been camouflaged; over there it is reinterpreted into something sublime. Many a vagueness, many a form-resistant trait has been carefully saved and is used for a lookout upon a distant view —a view made to invite us to contemplate open space and immeasurability." [10]

[9] See below, p. 399.
[10] Nietzsche, *Fröhliche Wissenschaft* in Karl Schlechta (ed.), *Friedrich Nietzsche: Werke in drei Bänden* (Munich, 1956), II, 168 f.

The paragraph might have been written of Humboldt, or even by Humboldt. Such, at any rate, were the subtle arts which he practiced while he tried to find out whether he was a writer or a thinker or a doer, whether he was a child primarily of the outgoing or of the incoming century, whether he was meant to stay on or leave his native soil in self-imposed exile like his brother Alexander. It might be said, incidentally, that he found answers to all these questions, but not a single answer was clear-cut in terms of the original either-or of the question.

If we ask, then, what the accomplishments of his ten years' retirement were, we might say that he learned to come to an understanding of himself as a subtle, complicated character destined for a great degree of individuation. He learned that he would undoubtedly think *and* do *and* write with considerable ability, but that he would do none of these with the singleminded devotion of a great specific talent. He was to find out that he was primarily a man of intuitions and feelings. (He had long designated himself inwardly much more womanlike than manlike and had speculated much on this strange division in himself.) He learned that he would always lean toward the times and places of man's origins, as showing the purity and simplicity and archetypal grandeur that he missed in the world around him. He also learned that what interested him most profoundly and absorbingly in all times and all places was a science (as well as an art) whose day had not yet dawned: psychology, and especially psychological insight into the unconscious. And finally he learned that, subjective certainty to the contrary, he was not to be an exile, though most assuredly a cosmopolite. As for his writings during this period, they were the conscientious and painstaking record of his apprenticeship years.

Humboldt put an end to these years by accepting, at the age of thirty-five, the post of Prussian Resident to the Vatican (the duties not being important enough to warrant a full ambassador) and moving his family to Rome where he was to reside for six years and his family, with some interruptions, for even longer. When he did this he felt he was continuing or even deepening his retire-

13

ment. He and Caroline had long wanted to live in Rome but had not been able to afford the move; they both felt that Rome would hold the very epitome of the contemplative life for them. His official duties would be light, largely social, and they were ready to do some entertaining. He must have felt, also, that here, if anywhere, he might come to the flowering of his creative talent, if there were to be any. And Rome did turn out to be the great central experience of his and Caroline's life; he never ceased looking upon the city and its environs as composing the landscape of his soul.[11]

But it was also to be the turning point of his life. He was, after all, nearing forty, and life had all the things to teach him to which he had not been receptive hitherto. It started with the death of his oldest son, at the age of ten, when they had been in Rome scarcely a year. The boy was an unusually healthy and brilliant child, and his father's favorite; his death was sudden, leaving no one time to prepare for it: It put an end to Humboldt's youth, to his unspoken assumption that he was fortune's darling. He did not break down or even interrupt his daily affairs, but something in him forever shifted gears, so to speak. Years later he could still write to his wife on the anniversary of the boy's death that it marked "the first unhappy day of our life together." [12] "The holy part of happiness is gone . . . and ever after, each impulse of happiness is mixed. . . ." [13]

The deaths of two other children followed. Though both were but infants, and Humboldt had never even seen one of them, he never ceased to mourn them; especially, in fact, the little one who was born and died while Caroline was on a visit in Paris. Many years later Humboldt sought out her burial place, still feeling deeply grieved that he had never seen this departed piece of himself and that she should have to lie so far from them all, even from the graves of her unknown brothers in Rome. The untimely death of Schiller during this same period further provided Humboldt with

[11] See below, pp. 156–59.
[12] See below, p. 392.
[13] See below, p. 393.

the darker aspects of fate that were now to receive unstinting response from him.

> "It is terrible," he wrote to his wife shortly after he had left Rome, "that so few people live with an acceptance of their own feelings and fewer still with those of another. To most people only their youth, with its first upwelling of feelings which cannot be ignored only because they are like the germination of a plant or the spring-stirring of the sap, gives to their love its humanity. . . . For most people the heart's youthfulness in the midst of life's transitoriness remains forever a riddle. Nor can it be denied that it must usually be bought at the price of sacrificing one's peace of mind. One must intervene more deeply in one's inner life and make one's heart sorer than even the world's rough handling prepares it for. But joy mingled with sadness, even with grief, is the deepest human joy. It winds itself about the soul with indescribable sweetness, with a dim but unerring sense for what will some day be born of it." [14]

Humboldt left Rome as he had entered it, changed but as yet unaware of the consequences of the change. He left on what he thought was a brief furlough, to straighten out some business in connection with his wife's inheritance. He was never to return. The call to a truly responsible public office reached him exactly as the call to war reaches many a man. He was not eager, he was not the reverse of eager; he felt his own basic values did not include the experience, but he went. "All this . . . is terribly sad for us," he wrote. "But I do believe that I cannot withdraw right now from the duty to act." [15] His stay in Rome, it turned out, had intensified or possibly even evoked strong feelings of responsibility toward his native country. He suddenly found that his children ought perhaps to find a home in the country of their ancestors and learn to speak what would have been their native tongue if their parents hadn't dragged them all over Europe. He was not to learn until considerably later that he himself was not merely a man of some intellectual loyalties and moral responsibilities, as he now discovered

[14] See below, pp. 309.
[15] See below, p. 389.

himself to be, but actually a man so deeply tied to his native soil in the narrowest sense that he would have to end his life exactly where it had begun, in the family home at Tegel a few miles outside Berlin. But this he was not yet ready to believe when he found himself exiled from his beloved Rome, back in the cold muddy-skied north.

Meanwhile off to the wars he went, successively as Privy Councilor of State, Minister of Worship and Public Instruction in Prussia, Ambassador to the Austrian Court, Privy Minister of State, negotiating diplomat at the Peace Congress of Prague, at the Congress at Chatillon, at the Congress of Vienna, member of countless territorial settlement commissions, Ambassador to London, and finally Co-Minister of the Interior. Counting the first post in Rome, he had twenty years of political action during which he became famous for his indefatigability, his shrewdness in practical manipulations, his wit, his apparent cold intellectuality.

From the very beginning he never sought to hide from himself or from others his instant realization, once he was involved in public life, that he found it utterly engrossing. He did, in a very genuine sense, live for the moment. He loved the life in which he now found himself without ever ceasing to love the life he had given up. He was saddened by the many months—at times years —of separation from his wife and children, but he found warm friends among both men and women and enjoyed life fully, as before. He had fabulous clear-sightedness and good judgment of people and of situations coupled with genuine disinterestedness in all outcomes. The work turned out to mean a great deal to him, the results nothing. He was, in other words, a natural diplomat, with a clear understanding of his own value. Hence he was cool, fearless, and flexible, hardly ever encountering the situation so common among politicians and statesmen, of having to project his own uncertainties upon his opponents or his own emotionality upon his co-workers. Needless to say he was valued and feared, celebrated and detested. Among all his traits it was perhaps only his undeviating uprightness which did not receive full recognition.

Eventually, after some years of bickering and hedging in obvious fear of Humboldt, his bosses succeeded in having him summarily fired by the King. This was in 1819, with the onset of a period of reaction in Prussia which wiped out for a time all the progress that the reform ministers, among whom Humboldt had worked, had made. Only when it became clear that he did not intend to return to public office or to discuss any scandals, was his name more or less cleared by the awarding of one or two decorations and his reinstatement in a titular office or two. Humboldt accepted these favors with amused grace, but refused to take any pension. His second retirement was to be his own, as the first had been. A year before his forced retirement he had written his wife, "For long now I have felt a longing to withdraw myself from [active life] without violating it . . . I am now at a point where outer circumstances will perhaps permit of it, and I am therefore stepping delicately in order not to tie any new knots as I try to loosen the old ones." [16]

His dismissal was thus obviously no surprise for him, and it seems to have come as a genuine relief. In any event he issued not a word of recrimination or in any way sought to vindicate his activities. He settled down to his wife and children and his studies as though the day he had been interrupted had been but yesterday. More than nineteen years had passed since he had accepted the first job at Rome; he was a healthy active fifty-two; he had financial independence; and he was free. He settled at Tegel, as we have mentioned, imagining at first that he was merely putting the old house to rights, in order to be able to sell it. It was not until the death of his wife, ten years later, that he fully understood that all his wanderings had brought him to his roots again and that he would never leave this home but be buried in its garden, alongside his wife.

Meanwhile he started once again to write, and this time he did not have to cast about for a proper vehicle in which to launch his never-ending inquiries into the conditions of the human spirit. Perhaps he had shed the youthful longing to make something of him-

[16] See below, p. 411.

self through his writings. He was now ready to record simply what he knew and what he was thinking on a subject that he was coming to know, exactly in the spirit of any worker in a scientific field. His subject of competence had turned out to be language—and languages. During his period of active life he had managed a number of translations from the Greek including Aeschylus' *Agamemnon*. He had, of course, also written countless political papers including some of more general interest such as the discussion of administrative problems at the University of Berlin.[17]

Beginning with 1820 we find titles such as "On the Sanskrit verbal forms formed by the suffixes *tva* and *ya*"; "On Comparative linguistics with special reference to the various periods of linguistic development," "Attempt at an analysis of the Mexican language," "On the development of grammatical forms and their influence upon the history of ideas"; "On the most general principles of word accent, with special consideration of Greek accentuation"; "On the national characteristics of languages"; "On the relationships between writing and language"; "On the grammatical structure of the Chinese language"; "Essays on the American language"; "Basic characteristics of linguistic types"; "On the dual form"; "On the languages of the South Sea Islands"; "On the relationship of the Greek Past Perfect, the reduplicating Aorist, and the Attic Perfect, with Sanskrit tense development"; "On the differences in human linguistic structure."

Some of these titles were published; again many were not or remained fragments, some of considerable size. But this partial list shows quite clearly that Humboldt had found his work in the world, and had found it without giving up anything which had interested him previously. Indeed this would have been impossible, because his life and work were so related that he never did anything which did not seem wholly characteristic of him. "Only what we are is our property"; he once wrote, "what we do depends on chance and circumstance. Each man, one justly says, is more than his work, because he never manages to attain the ideal that he

---

[17] See below, pp. 126–35.

18

carries in his head. In another sense, however, a man's work is more than he is, for it is the fruit of his collected and distilled energies that, in his life, lie diffused and less active." [18] In his own case, what he was and what he did are to an unusual degree of a piece.

Not much remains to tell of his life. Death seems again to have played the role of the great transmuter for him. Just as he reached maturity upon the death of his children, so the death of his wife, in 1829, very rapidly brought old age upon him. All of a sudden many of his physical powers failed him. His hand would no longer write, and his eyes would no longer see. But his mind and his spirit did not fail; he dictated what he could not manage with his own hand, and his ever clearer inward vision compensated the blurring of the outer. The final seven years of his life were spent putting his thoughts on language together in the monumental *Kawiwerk*, a comparative study of the Malayan-Polynesian Kawi dialects. Humboldt himself was able to see its first volume through the press; the remaining two came out four years after his death. Into the general introduction to this work, taking up some 350 pages, he incorporated all of his insights into the history and philosophy of human language that he had garnered during a lifetime and which in turn were a distillation of his insights into human personality, conscious and unconscious, individual and social.

But, characteristically, he could not terminate this period of his life with a mere objective, scientific work, however broadly conceived. In addition, he undertook a final and most personal experiment which is perhaps the most interesting of all his humanistic projects. He determined to keep a record of each day's inward image for the four years which he thought might be his final ones. He decided to keep this record in sonnet form in order to check the resultant flood, and possibly also because he knew the record would have to be dictated each night to a stranger, or because he continued to yearn for a formal artistic product from his hands. His estimate of four years proved to be a slight miscalculation. He

[18] II, 69.

began on January 1, 1832 intending to write until the end of 1835, 1,461 sonnets in all. Actually he stopped on March 28, 1835, having written 1,183. On April 8 he died. Many of them remain unpublished; less than 500 are reprinted in his collected works as of now; the content of the remaining ones is indicated by a brief phrase.

No one but the secretaries to whom they were dictated saw these sonnets during Humboldt's lifetime; there is no indication that he ever intended them for publication. They are simply his final attempt at understanding himself as a human being. They take up many of the dark strands of his inner life since childhood days. A great number of them try to formulate the essence of the persons he had known. Some of these are easily recognizable; about others there is bound to be eternal speculation and disagreement on the part of interested persons. He once wrote that the archetypes and images of his early life, down to his childhood dreams, had remained ever with him; that he recognized in many of them the living persons who had contributed to their color and structure, but that many others were works of fantasy which he had recognized to be such even in childhood and had worked on intermittently throughout his life. What Humboldt himself learned from his experiment can only be surmised. Since he left no directions for the poems to be destroyed, we may justly assume that he wished them read at least by his descendents. They were surely to be read, however, not for their content to which he quite purposefully (as appears in several of the poems themselves) left no key, nor for their poetic value which, as might be imagined, is not notable, but simply as another evidence of what he was and what he did. Unanalyzed, they provide a tremendously moving experience for the reader, suggestive of the final scene in Hermann Hesse's story "Klein und Wagner" where the hero, while drowning, sees floating past him all the terrible and beloved shapes of humanity, its monsters, its gods, and its plain people, until at last he recognizes that this same current is sweeping him out to sea and that the myriad faces and bodies may be called those of humanity or those of the self: he has come to the place where this difference no longer has any meaning.

II

A word must be said on the selections of which this anthology is made up. Someone has remarked that Humboldt is one of the most widely quoted but least read of German authors. From my vignette of his life and works it should be clear that not many of his works lend themselves well to a complete reading if the object of the reading is a first introduction to Humboldt. This makes him the perfect candidate for anthology-making and prey to all the dangers inherent in that project. There are obviously at least as many Humboldts as there are readers who pick and choose the bits that suit them from among his writings. It is therefore an almost meaningless sentiment to hope that this particular selection has done him no violence and utterly absurd to imagine that it may have done him justice.

Fortunately Humboldt himself provides a criterion for translating with which I wholeheartedly agree, and which may be stretched to cover the principle of selection as well. The best purpose of a translation, he says, is to acquaint those who are about to read an author in the original with the manner and spirit of his writing. That translation is therefore most useful which stimulates the reader to throw it away and reach for the original. That this is not merely a pretty conceit has been proved countless times by the thousands of people (Humboldt, incidentally, being among them) who have undertaken to learn a language precisely in order to read the original of something of which a translation could give but the barest glimmer.

Certain selections in this volume were not excerpted but rendered completely or almost completely. They were chosen with special care for representing a well-rounded Humboldt, and a word of explanation regarding them is in order.

There is, first of all, a fragment called "On the proper conditions

for science and art." [19] This was a little work begun and left un-
finished in the midst of his diplomatic career, around 1814. It was
conceived by Humboldt in the nature of a warning to the German
people not to expect a flowering of either the arts or the sciences
in the wake of the momentous political and patriotic movements
which they had undergone during the period of the wars of liberation—a sound enough prediction, as it turned out. But typically,
Humboldt reflected at the very beginning of his essay, that as a matter of fact art and science could hardly be lumped together in such
a prediction, even if what he were saying should turn out to be
true for both. And so he wrote a little classic on the different psychic
and social conditions necessary for the fundamentally different endeavors of art and science and, also typically, never returned to his
original main topic.

Another selection from the same, primarily nonliterary, period
of Humboldt's life is the somewhat technical one entitled "On the
inner and outer organization of the higher institutions of learning
in Berlin." [20] This too was not completed by Humboldt, although
the draft as it stands was turned over to the Berlin Academy of
Sciences for whose reorganization, in connection with the newly
founded University of Berlin, it was written. It is included here
partly to provide a sample of Humboldt's writing in his professional capacity as Minister of Worship and Public Instruction,
partly because the thinking on the fundamental questions of educational administration seems so sound that one can easily conceive
of its continuing usefulness. We do not have academies at war with
universities, to be sure, but we have graduate schools and professional schools and so-called institutes, often at considerable odds
with the colleges and universities of which they claim to be cooperating parts. And we certainly have professors who teach and professors who do research, with all the problems attendant upon dividing these functions up among separate human beings or encourag-
ing them to struggle within a single person.

[19] See below, pp. 103–07.
[20] See below, pp. 132–140.

22

Section E of our anthology contains a major and fairly long work, entitled "On the episode from the Mahabharata known as 'Bhagavad-Gita.'"[21] Humboldt read this as a lecture before the Berlin Academy of Sciences in 1825. The inclusion of this work may initiate some surprise at first reading. On the face of it, it is little more than a detailed summary of the philosophical thought contained in that book, written at a time when interest in the languages and literatures of the Far East was first sweeping Germany and when most Germans, even members of the Academy, had little access to the works if they did not read the original languages. But even if it were not for the most interesting fact that our current generation feels an equally strong impulse toward enriching itself with the "wisdom of the East" it would be highly desirable to read this work of the mature Humboldt. For through its unassuming purpose of simply conveying some significant information shines what seems to me the most valuable of all of Humboldt's thought: his essentially religious turn of mind.

This may take a little explaining. There was probably never a "Minister of Worship" who was less interested in the work of any church or even the history of religious thought. Nor is there any evidence that he was even a prayerful man or one who performed any private acts of worship, not to mention public ones. For a long time in his life Humboldt himself would have denied that he had anything whatever to do with religious thinking, any more than his cultural heroes, the classical Greeks, would normally be considered religious thinkers in any Christian sense. For a long time, in fact, he resisted reading any pre-Greek documents for this very reason and had, on first reading, a very low opinion of the ancient Hindu writings. But the course of further years and persistent studies brought home to him that it was precisely in India, and most of all in the *Bhagavad-Gita* where his own spiritual ancestors could best be found. By the time he wrote his two lectures on that work (the first of which is presented here) he himself knew what is also quite clear to his readers: that there is scarcely an aspect of

[21] See below, pp. 168–213.

religious thinking in the *Bhagavad-Gita* which he had not already long ago come to accept for himself. Basically it comprises what Aldous Huxley has referred to as the Perennial Philosophy, with its four interrelated tenets of an ideal ground of the universe, man's ability to participate in it through exercising his intuitive function, man's identification of his spirit-self with the spirit of the universe, and his spiritual-moral responsibility to come to represent this self as the highest step of his self-education. This of course comprises the essential message of all mysticism, Eastern and Western, past and present.

That Humboldt's spiritual orientation belongs in this framework is most easily recognizable if one asks oneself what the primary difference was that set him apart in his self-chosen intellectual environment from the secular idealism of Goethe and Schiller. It is that Goethe and Schiller belong to the universe of discourse that we label "art," Humboldt to "religion." It also explains why Humboldt's frequently startling resemblance to certain aspects of the thought of C. G. Jung is not an accidental one nor one to be explained by my predilection to translate such words as *Ideal* with "archetype" or *Gemüt* with "psychic constitution" wherever the modern, "Jungian" word speaks for the precise psychic content which Humboldt was describing within the vocabulary at his disposal. The Perennial Philosophy speaks vividly out of the works of both.

Finally there have been included substantial whole portions of the aforementioned Introduction to the *Kawiwerk* as incorporating Humboldt's final thoughts on language,[22] and his entire autobiographical fragment[23] of 1816 which forms perhaps the best introduction of all to the qualities of his mind and heart as looked upon from the point of view here emphasized, his exemplary humanism. To sum it up once more, in Humboldt's words,

> Man stands in such close contact with his whole environment that many of his actions exert a great and visible, and all of his actions

[22] See below, pp. 251–298.
[23] See below, pp. 395–403.

some, even if weak, influence on the remotest corners of human activity. He cannot loosen the bonds that connect him with all his fellow creatures; he cannot prevent the seismic impulses that his actions impart to the body of mankind. Whatever his objections, his sphere of influence is infinite; even if the active part of his existence should finally pass away, just as a stone thrown in water forms visible circles only up to a certain point, yet he can never calculate the point of his disappearance and, to avoid dangerous error, must assume himself to form much wider circles than he thinks.[24]

M. C.
April 1961

[Note.—The translator has supplied the subheadings for this translation, except those appearing on pp. 253, 260, 267, 276, 278, and 286, which are Humboldt's].

---

[24] II, 7.

Part I

FIRST PERSON
PLURAL

POLITICAL PRINCIPLES

The relationship between world affairs and individuals

All things called world or state affairs have tremendous significance for much external life. They may found or destroy in a moment the happiness, often the life, of thousands upon thousands of individuals. But when the tidal wave has passed and the storm dies down, their influence is lost sight of; often it disappears without a trace. Many other matters, those for example which noiselessly determine human thoughts and feelings, last much longer and have much deeper effects. Man can in fact keep himself relatively free of everything that does not directly involve his private life, and this is a wise arrangement of providence, because individual happiness stands an infinitely greater chance under it.

But the more a man includes in his individuality, the more there emanates from him what may bless the hearts and the inner happiness of many others. These observations are very different from current opinion on what is right and what is not, because what is considered most important is here deposed to the point of indifference, and great weight is attached to the seemingly insignificant. But they are nonetheless true and will be felt as true, I believe, by all those whose inner sense has not been completely deadened by public opinion. Of course age has much to do with a change of opinion in such matters, also. In youth and early adulthood we find agreeable whatever removes us to a larger scene of action; in advanced age the false splendor fades, but the objects once invested with it do not therefore pale into significance, nor do they turn empty and hollow. We learn instead to esteem them for the purely human archetypes contained in them, and this esteem can last forever, as long as we retain the capacity to place ourselves in contact with them. [To C. Diede, October 1827]

The human need for freedom

Whatever one may cite against it, the human spirit is, in itself and of its very essence, more at home in ideas and in the feelings related to ideas than it is in worldly doings and their needs and inclinations. It does take freedom from the constant battle with nature which through labor and worry has a depressive effect on us, however, to develop the human spirit. . . . And so the human race needs not merely time to attain intellectual power but also freedom from disturbing influences. [V, 342]

Freedom of thought permits of no limitations

How manifold are the pernicious results of limitations upon freedom of thought surely needs no lengthy analysis from me, it being implicit in all I have said. I have likewise often discussed and implied the harm done if the government takes a positive promoting hand in the business of religious worship. If the harm were limited merely to the results of inquiry and investigation, if it merely produced incompleteness or even error in our scientific knowledge, there might be some show at least of reason in an attempt to weigh the possible utility for character-building that may be implicit in censorship. But the harm is more serious and far-reaching. The uses of free inquiry extend not only to our ways of thinking but to our whole way of life. A man who is accustomed to judge truth and error without regard to outer circumstances as they affect him or others, and who is accustomed to openly hearing them thus judged, is quite a different person from one whose inquiries and investigation are always guided by situations which are not intrinsic to the things investigated. All the principles of action of the former will be better thought through, more orderly, and originate from a loftier point of view. Inquiry and investigation and the conviction which grows from them is a spontaneous, independent activity.

Faith, on the other hand, is the trust in someone else's power, someone else's intellectual or moral perfection. Hence there is far more independence, firmness, and spontaneity in the inquiring mind; more weakness and inertia in the trusting believer. It is quite true that faith, where it dominates completely and is able to choke down all doubt, produces even more dauntless courage and more enduring strength than freedom of thought can. We see it in the history of all fanaticisms. But this sort of strength is desirable only where we are interested in a definite external result for which a mechanical action is demanded, never where we expect individual decisions, thought-through actions based on reason or—most of all—inner perfection. For the strength induced by faith rests only on the suppression of all individual activity of reason. Doubts torment only the believer, never him who goes where his own free inquiry leads him. Results, generally, are far less important to the latter. During the process of his free inquiry he is conscious of the active strength of his psyche; he feels that his true consummation, his very happiness, rests on it. Instead of feeling oppressed by doubting what were hitherto truths for him, he rejoices in his new-found growing strength of thought which allows him to see error where before it was hidden. Faith, on the other hand, can be interested in results only, for a truth once recognized as such puts an end to the believer's thinking. If his reason stirs up doubts nonetheless, they torment him. For they are not—as they are to the other—new means for reaching truth; they merely take away certainty without giving a hint as to how to regain it in some other way.

A further consequence of these matters is that it is never good to grant too much importance to individual results, to believe too implicitly that either many other truths or many outer or inner useful consequences depend on them. It too readily brings about a standstill of all inquiry and investigation; many a time the freest and most enlightened assertions work quite properly to contradict the foundations without which they could never have arisen. Thus important is freedom of thought; thus harmful any restriction upon it. The state does not lack the means for upholding law and preventing crime. Let it plug up as tightly as possible the sources of immorality which are to be found in its own administration; let it sharpen the eyes of the police with reference to crimes actually committed; let it attend to reasonable and purposive punishment, and all its proper aims will be fulfilled. Do we forget that freedom of thought and the enlightenment which flourishes only under its safeguards is the most effective of all the means that promote security? All other means merely suppress outbreaks of civil strife, but freedom of thought operates on men's preferences and sentiments; all others produce but a uniformity of external activities, freedom of thought creates the inner harmony of will and endeavor. But when shall we cease esteeming the external consequences of an action more than the inner spiritual mood from which they flow? When shall we see the man who will accomplish for the law what Rousseau did for education, namely withdraw our gaze from external physical effects and redirect it to the inner organic development of man?

Let no one believe, furthermore, that freedom of thought and enlightenment are for the few in any nation; that the many are so exhausted by activities dictated by the need for earning a living, that freedom of thought is useless to them, or even disturbing. Or that they can best be activated by the diffusion of principles handed down from on high, while their freedom to think and to investigate is restricted. There is something utterly degrading to humanity in the very thought that some human being's right to be human could be abrogated. No one stands at such a low level of culture that he is incapable of reaching a higher one. Even if the most advanced and enlightened religious and philosophic ideas could not reach a large part of the citizenry directly, even if it proved to be necessary to clothe the truth in such a way that it could find a point of contact, even if one were forced, in other words, to speak more to their hearts and their imaginations than to their cold reason, nonetheless the widening of horizons of scientific knowledge which is the result of freedom of thought reaches them as well, and the beneficent consequences of free unrestricted inquiry stretch over the spirit and character of a whole nation, down to its last and least knowing individual. [I, 160–62]

Bread cast upon the waters

[Before the French Revolution] mankind suffered from an extreme; it had to seek its salvation, likewise, in an extreme. Will this new form of government last? No, to judge by historical analogy. But it will clarify our ideas anew, it will kindle all active virtues anew, and thus it will spread its blessings far beyond the borders of France. It will reassert the age-old course of human events which shows that the good never has its maximum effect where it happens, but only at long distances of space and of time, and the spot thus seemingly left bare in turn receives its blessing from far-off events. [I, 84]

Governmental structure fails if it is planned in accordance with reason alone

The Constituent National Assembly has undertaken to erect a completely new governmental structure, solely according to the principles of reason. This must be conceded as a fact by everyone and by itself, as well. But no state constitution can possibly succeed just because it has been planned according to principles of reason—even assuming that it gets unlimited powers to give reality to its projects; the only way a new governmental structure can flourish is if it results from the struggle between mightier chance and ever-resisting reason. This proposition is so self-evident to me, that I should like to extend it not merely to state constitutions but to all practical undertakings of any sort whatever. But it may not have equal self-evidence for so hearty a proponent of reason as you are, and I shall therefore explain myself at greater length.*

Before I look at the principles involved, let me say a few words by way of closer definition. First of all, as you see, I shall grant that the plan of the National Assembly for new legislation is actually a plan drawn up by the principles of reason. Secondly, I do not charge it with being too speculative, too little aimed at actual execution. I shall even grant that all the legislators involved have a truly realistic view of the condition of France and its inhabitants and have adjusted the principles of reason so far as feasible and as would not violate the ideals of reason, to that condition. Finally, I do not wish to speak of the difficulties of putting the plan into practice. However true and witty it may be, *qu'il ne faut pas donner des leçons d'anatomie sur un corps vivant,* nonetheless only the successful results could show whether the undertaking will actually be permanent and whether the passing evils affecting individuals

---

* This essay grew out of an annotated letter to a friend. Footnotes are Humboldt's, except where marked *Tr.* for translator.

are not after all to be preferred in favor of the properly established welfare of all. For all these reasons, I proceed only from the following simple assertions: 1) the National Assembly wanted to found a completely new constitution of government; 2) it wanted to form it in accordance with pure principles of reason, however adapted to the individual situation of the French nation. For the moment I accept this constitution as totally capable of execution, or, if you wish, as actually executed. Nonetheless, I say, such a constitution cannot prosper.

A new constitution should follow the one before it. In place of a system which was solely calculated to withdraw as many means as possible from the nation in order to satisfy the wastefulness and ambition of a single person, there is now to arise a system which aims only at freedom, tranquillity, and the happiness of every individual. Two wholly opposed conditions are therefore supposed to follow one upon the other. Where is the bond that relates them? Who may trust himself with sufficient inventiveness and skill to weave such a bond? Regardless of how carefully we study the present condition, regardless of how painstakingly we calculate what shall be made to follow it—none of it is enough. All our knowledge and insight rests on collective (i.e., if we speak of objects of experience), incomplete, half-true ideas; we are able to grasp only very few individuated objects and processes, and yet everything depends on individuated energy, on individuated activities, sufferings, and joys. The situation is completely altered if chance acts and reason strives to reorient it. Then the consequences will spring from the entire individuated nature of the present—for these constellations unconscious to us are what we call "chance"; the plans which reason then tries to put over receive, even if reason is successful, much of their form and their modification from the objects which they concern. Thus they can attain permanence and become useful. If they are applied by reason in a vacuum, they remain forever sterile, even if they are carried out. Whatever is supposed to flourish in human affairs must spring from the inmost heart of human beings, not be imposed upon them from the out-

35

side, and what else is a state but the sum of humanly active and humanly passive powers.

Besides, every action demands a re-action which is its equal; every act of generation a correspondingly active receptivity. The present must therefore be already oriented toward the future. That is why chance has such a powerful effect. In it, the present violently embraces the future. If the future is still alien to it, all remains cold and dead. And cold and dead remains everything that conscious intention is supposed to produce. Reason, to be sure, has the ability to form materials already there, but it does not have the energy to produce new ones. This energy rests solely in the nature of things; these act; all reason does, if it is truly wise, it stimulates them into activity and then seeks to guide them. With this, it is modestly satisfied. State constitutions cannot be grafted onto people like buds onto trees. Where time and nature have not done their prior work, it is as though one tied blossoms on with string. The first noonday sun scorches them.

Now you may well ask whether the French nation is not, as a matter of fact, sufficiently prepared to accept a new state constitution. The answer is that no nation is ever ripe for a constitution systematically outlined according to the principles of reason. Reason demands a joint and proportioned operation of all energies. It looks not only for perfection in individuals but also for the firmness of their association, and the proper degree of relationship between individuals. If, however, reason is satisfied on the one hand by the most diverse activity, the lot of the human race, on the other hand, becomes complete uniformity. Each moment exercises only one form of energy in one method of expression. Frequent repetition is transformed into habit, and this one expression of one type of energy sooner or later becomes characteristic. However man may try to arrange to have the single active power of any given moment modified by the cooperation of all others, he never reaches this goal; what he snatches from uniformity, he loses in energy. If he spreads himself over many objects, he weakens his ability to deal with any of them. Thus energy and organic development into a

culture stand forever in inverse proportion. The wise man follows neither wholly; each is too dear to sacrifice entirely to the
other. Even in the highest ideal type of human nature that ardent imagination is able to project, each present moment is a
beautiful blossom—but only one. Only memory may twine the
wreath which joins the past to the present. As with individuals, so
with nations. They pursue only one direction at any one time.
Hence the differences from one nation to the next, and the differences within them from one epoch to the next. What does the wise
legislator do, therefore? He studies the present direction and then,
according to his findings, he either promotes it or he works counter
to it; thus it receives a modification, which is modified in turn,
and so on. He rests satisfied with forever approaching the goal
of perfection. But what will and must be the result if he suddenly
works at the entire ideal at once, according to the plans of sheer
reason, if he no longer pursues a single excellence worth promoting
but all of them simultaneously? Laxity and inertia! Everything
that we seize upon with warmth and enthusiasm is kin to love.
But when our soul is no longer oriented toward a single ideal, cold
takes the place of warmth. In general, no one can act with any
energy who tries to act evenly all at once with all his powers. But
the loss of energy brings about the loss of all other virtues. Without
it, man turns into a machine. We may admire what he does; but
we despise what he is. [I, 78–81]

Ancient policy strove for humanistic development
of individuals, modern political theory for
the happiness of the greatest number

There is one vast difference be-
tween ancient and modern governments. The ancients sought to
develop the energy and development of men as men; the moderns
are concerned with their welfare, their property, and their ability
to earn a living. The ancients sought virtue; the moderns seek

happiness. For this reason, all limitations and restrictions upon free-dom in the ancient states were, on the one hand, more oppressive and more dangerous. For they attacked directly what constitutes the inner life of man, his whole inner existence. This is why all ancient nations exhibit a one-sidedness which (quite aside from any possible lack of a sophisticated culture and the dearth of general communications) was produced and nourished largely by the gen-eral public education which was introduced almost everywhere and by the intentionally communal life of citizens in general.

On the other side, however, these state institutions also pre-served and heightened the active energy of mankind. Even the point of view that was never lost sight of: to form energetic and self-sufficient citizens gave a considerable verve to spirit and char-acter. Compared with this, we limit men not so much directly, but give to everything surrounding them a constricting form, and there-fore it seems possible to us to begin the struggle against external bonds with inner strength. But the very nature of the modern states' restrictions upon our freedom—the fact that their intention to in-fluence goes far more toward what men have than toward what they are, and even there they do not cause men, as did the ancients, to exert their physical, moral, and intellectual powers but merely force their laws on them—suppresses all the energy which is the source of every active virtue and the necessary condition to a higher and more diverse development. If therefore in the case of the an-cient states a greater degree of energy made up for the one-sided development, then in the modern states the disadvantage of less energy is actually heightened by one-sidedness. This difference be-tween us and the ancients is everywhere unmistakable. If our atten-tion is drawn to the rapidity of progress in the last few centuries, to the number and ready distribution of inventions, and to the great-ness of newly founded establishments, and when we then contem-plate the ancients, we find instead of progress that greatness which departs from the earth each time a single of their individuals de-parts from it. We find the flower of their creative imagination, the profundity of their spirit, the strength of their will, and the wholeness of the entire human being which alone gives worth to his life.

It was man in his energy and his organic development, among the ancients, who mobilized all activity; with us it is all too often only an ideal collectivity in which we almost forget the presence of individuals, or at least notice not their inner being but their peace, their welfare and their happiness. The ancients sought for happiness in virtue; we moderns have tried all too long to develop virtue out of happiness, and even he who saw and represented morality in its greatest purity [Kant] believes he has to provide his ideal man with a happiness wrought by a most artificial machinery, more as a reward from without than as a personally earned good. [I, 103–05]

What government may and may not do:

*It may not make the positive welfare
of its citizens the object of its solicitude.*

I consider the following maxim as amply demonstrated: *That true reason cannot desire for man any condition other than that in which not only every individual enjoys the most absolute, unbounded freedom to develop himself out of himself, in true individuality, but in which physical nature, as well, need receive no other shaping by human hands than that which is given to her voluntarily by each individual, according to the measure of his wants and his inclinations, restricted only by the limits of his energy and his rights.* From this maxim, in my estimation, reason may never yield more than is essential for its own preservation. It must therefore be at the foundations of . . . every political policy.

Expressed in a completely general formula, one might call the true extent of state operations all those things which the government may do for the well-being of society, without violating the above maxim; and from this maxim we may derive the even more definite restriction that any state interference in the private affairs of its citizens is to be condemned, wherever it is not strictly occasioned by the interference with one citizen's rights by another.

Meanwhile it will be necessary, in order to solve our entire problem, to examine carefully the various aspects of the state's usual or possible activity.

The aims of a state may be twofold: it may promote happiness or it may merely prevent evil, and, in the latter case, either evils of nature or evils of mankind. If it restricts itself to the latter, it aims merely at security. This security I wish to oppose to all other possible aims that are considered under the name of positive state welfare. The variety of the means employed by the state, moreover, affects the extension of its activities. It either seeks to attain its aims directly, either by coercion—laws and punishments—or else by encouragement and example; or it may work indirectly, by an attempt to shape the citizens' external lives in such a way that they fall in with its desires, or it prevents them from acting otherwise. Finally, it may actually seek to sway their preferences by exercising an influence upon their thoughts and feelings. In the first case, it supervises only single actions; in the second, the citizens' whole way of life, and in the third, their character and modes of thinking. Likewise, the effect of the state's restriction is least in the first case, greater in the second, and greatest in the third, partly because it affects the source of a number of actions, partly because the very possibility of such influence means that a number of separate agencies must be at work. However separate the various aspects of governmental operations look, there is hardly an institution of government which does not pertain to several at once, since for example security and welfare are very much dependent on one another, and since even single acts lead to habits which in turn influence character. It is therefore extremely difficult to find a proper systematic division of our subject. It will probably be best, first of all, regardless of whether the state is to promote the positive social welfare of the nation, or merely maintain its security, to look at all its institutions in line with what is their main object or their main consequence, and to examine in connection with each aim those means which the state may allow itself.

I shall speak here, then, of the entire effort of the state to elevate the positive social welfare of the nation, its solicitude for population, for the subsistence of its inhabitants, whether manifested directly through its poor laws, or indirectly through the encouragement of agriculture, industry, and commerce, for all its finance and currency regulations, trade regulations, etc. (insofar as they have the above aim); finally for all its measures for the preventing or remedying of natural catastrophes—in short, for every arrangement and institution of the state which has as its purpose the maintenance or promotion of the physical well-being of the nation. Since its moral well-being is usually not so much promoted for its own sake as for the sake of security, I shall take it up later.

Now all these aforementioned social institutions, I assert, have disadvantageous consequences and are inappropriate to true political policy which proceeds from the highest but always human points of view.

1) The spirit of the government pervades every institution of this kind, and—regardless of how wise and salutary this spirit may happen to be—it produces monotony, uniformity, and alienates people's actions from their own character. Instead of human beings socializing themselves in order to sharpen their energies, even at a loss of some part of their exclusive possessions and enjoyments, they now attain *goods* at the cost of *energy*. The very diversity which is the result of the communion of men is the highest good that society can offer; it is sure to get lost in the same degree that the state intervenes. It is now no longer the individual members of a nation who live in communion with one another, but instead the isolated subjects of a state which stand in a certain relation to the spirit which rules it, a relationship which is predetermined by the greater power which the state exerts over the free play of individual energies. Like causes produce like effects. The more the state cooperates, the more uniform grow not only the operators but the materials they operate with. And this, of course, coincides with the state's purposes. The state desires well-being and tranquillity. These are always to be had where there is least contention between individuals. But what human beings are after, and should be after, is

diversity and activity. Only they will yield many-faceted and strong characters, and surely we human beings have not sunk so low that we actually prefer welfare and happiness to greatness for ourselves, as individuals. But if we reason that we want them for others, not for ourselves, then we ought justly to be suspected of failing to recognize human nature for what it is and of wishing to turn men into machines.

2) The second disadvantage, then, is that the social institutions of a state weaken the energies of the nation. For material substance is annihilated by externally imposed form, though strengthened in fullness and beauty by that form which grows out of itself. For what is matter other than the union of opposites, a union which constantly requires the finding of new combinations, hence whole new series of discoveries, which constantly increase the tension between themselves and those that have gone before. But if external form is superimposed upon matter, a something is being suppressed in favor of a nothing. Everything intrinsically human means organization, organic life. What is to flourish, must first be sown. All energy presupposes enthusiasm, and only a few things so nourish enthusiasm, as to consider its object as a present or future possession.

Now man does not so much regard what he *has* as his property as that what he *does,* and the worker who plants a garden is its owner in a truer sense than the idle consumer who enjoys it. Perhaps such a line of reasoning seems too general to permit of specific application. Perhaps it will even seem that the extension and propagation of many sciences which we owe to these and other social institutions of the state, which is the only agency able to carry on vast experimentation, actually increases our intellectual powers and thereby culture and human character in general. But we must remember that not every enrichment of knowledge signifies refinement, not even of the intellectual energies as such, and whenever such refinement does as a matter of fact take place through state agency, it does not take place in the nation as a whole but only in those members who have directly to do with governmental operations. Man's understanding, like all his other energies, is cultivated only by each human being's own activity, his own inventiveness, or his own utilization of the inventions of others. Governmental regulations all carry coercion to some degree and even where they don't, they habituate man to expect teaching, guidance and help outside himself, instead of formulating his own.

The only method of instruction that the government has available is that it declares certain procedures to be best, as the result of its investigations, and then orders them to be followed either by law or by some other institution binding upon its citizens, or else stimulates them by the backing of its own prestige, or reward, or other means of encouragement, or even only recommends them by argumentation. But whatever method the government chooses, it will be very far from a good method of instruction. For sound instruction undoubtedly consists of spreading out before the person to be instructed various solutions, and then preparing him to choose the most appropriate, or, even better, to invent his own solution by simply arranging before him all the difficulties to be conquered. This method of instruction can be followed by the state, in connection with its adult citizens, only negatively, namely by allowing them complete freedom, permitting obstacles to rise which in turn produce strength and skill for their removal, or positively in connection with its youthful citizens alone, who are partaking of a genuine national [public] education. Subsequently we shall deal with the objection that might be advanced in favor of social state institutions, namely that in connection with such important projects as the ones under discussion it is of much greater importance that the thing be done than that the person doing it shall understand it, that the land be tilled rather than that the tiller be an especially skillful agricultural economist.

Through too much solicitude on the part of the government, active energy in general, and the whole moral character of a nation with it, suffers. This hardly needs further explication. Whoever is easily and often guided, easily reaches the point of sacrificing his entire active spontaneity of his own free will. He fancies that he is free of the cares which he sees in someone else's hands, and his conscience is satisfied when he expects and follows outside guidance; thus gradually his notions of deserts and guilt become distorted. The former no longer motivates him; the torments of the latter affect him less and less often, since it now becomes easy to blame one's position and the agency which forms it. If to this is added the feeling that the state's motives are not wholly pure, the belief that he is not the main object of the state's concern but plays second fiddle to other purposes, then we find not only the individual citizen's energies flagging, but also the morality of his good will. He now believes himself not only free from all duties toward the government except those expressly commanded, but actually relieved from all responsibility for bettering his own condition since he might come to fear of any improvement that it too will redound to the state's credit. As for the laws actually enjoined, he seeks loopholes as avidly as he can and considers each evasion a personal gain. If we reflect that for a large portion of the nation, the laws and institutions of government coincide with its morality, it is a depressing spectacle to hear the holiest injunctions and most ridiculous arbitrary regulations pronounced by one and the same agency and their violation all too often punished with the same measures of punishment. No less obvious is the bad influence in the behavior of citizens toward one another. As much as each person relies on the solicitous care of the state, just so much does he yield the fate of his fellow citizens to it, in fact more. This in turn weakens his sympathies and renders him idle and careless so far as assistance to others is concerned. This much is true, at least: mutual assistance must be most active where the feeling of individual responsibility is most lively. And experience shows that the oppressed parts of a nation, abandoned by the protection of their government, are all the more firmly interconnected and supported among themselves. And where one citizen is cold to another, there too is one spouse toward the other, and the head of each household toward his dependents.

If men were left completely to themselves, cut off from all external aid which they did not themselves procure, they would often, by their own fault or not, fall into embarrassment and misfortune.

But the happiness meant for man is nothing other than that which is promoted by his own energies, and it is precisely the unfortunate situations which sharpen his wits and form his character. And where the state cuts off active spontaneity through specific interventions— do not the same evils arise there? They do arise and leave man to a far more hopeless fate, accustomed as he is to leaning on external strength. For as constant wrestling with problems and activities lightens misfortune, so, and ten times more so, does hopeless or delusive expectation make it hard to bear. Even at best, the governments of which I here am speaking are like physicians who play along with a disease and put off death. Before there were physicians, there were only two forces: health and death.

3) Everything toward which man directs his attention, whether to satisfy his physical needs directly or indirectly, or to attain any external ends whatever, is most closely related with his inward sensations and feelings. Sometimes there is an inner aim which runs parallel with the outer and sometimes the inner is the one really intended, and the outer merely accompanies it, by necessity or by chance. The more harmonious and at one with himself a human being is, the more freely does his chosen external activity spring from his inner being, and the more frequently and firmly his inner being relates itself to his outer activity, if the latter was not a chosen one. That is why an interesting human being is interesting in all situations and all activities; that is why he blossoms into enchanting beauty when his external way of life can be in keeping with his character.

In this way, perhaps, all peasants and craftsmen could be transformed into *artists,* i.e., people who love their craft for its own sake, who refine it with their self-guided energy and inventiveness, and who in so doing cultivate their own intellectual energies, ennoble their character, and increase their enjoyments. This way humanity would be ennobled by the very things which now, however beautiful they might be, degrade it. The more a man is accustomed to live in ideas and feelings, the stronger and subtler his intellectual and moral energies, the more he seeks to choose only

45

those external situations which at the same time afford substance for his inner humanity, or see those aspects in the situations into which external fate casts him. It is impossible to estimate the magnitude of man's possible harvest as to beauty and greatness when he incessantly strives to maintain his inner existence in control of his outer, to let it be the first source and the ultimate aim of all his operations, and to render everything corporeal and external as but its instrument and veil.

To give but one example: how strikingly all-of-a-piece is the character of a people, throughout history, when undisturbed cultivation of the soil is its main occupation. The labor which such a people devotes to the soil, the harvest with which the soil rewards them, bind them sweetly to their fields and their firesides; participation of all in the blessed toil and communal enjoyment of its rewards wind loving bonds around each family, not excluding the ox who did his share. The fruit which must be sowed and reaped, but returns year after year, only seldom deceiving hope, makes them patient, trusting, and frugal. The fact of their receiving what they do directly from nature, the ever insistent feeling that, even if the hand of man scatters the seed, it does not control growth and harvest, the everlasting dependence on weather—all these impart to the basic psychic constitution of workers on the land the at times terrible, at times happy intuitions of the existence of higher beings; they impart alternately hope and fear, leading most naturally to prayer and to gratitude. The living image of the simplest grandeur, the most undisturbed tranquil order, and the deepest goodness forms their souls so that they can be simple, great, gentle, and gladly submissive to morality and to law. Accustomed to produce and never to destroy, the tiller of the soil is peaceable; his mind remote from insult or revenge, but deeply imbued by a feeling for the injustice of an unprovoked attack, and animated by courageousness in the face of any disturber of his peace.

Naturally, freedom is the necessary condition without which even the most soul-satisfying occupation cannot produce any wholesome effects of this sort. Whatever task is not chosen of man's own free will, whatever constrains or even only guides him, does not become part of his nature. It remains forever alien to him; if he performs it, he does so not with true humane energy but with mere mechanical skill. The ancients, particularly the Greeks, considered every occupation which concerned the exercise of bodily strength, or the pursuit of external goods, anything that did not aim at the development of the inner man, harmful and degrading. Their philanthropic philosophers, therefore, approved of slavery, while at the same time recognizing it as an unjust and barbaric means for assuring to one part of humanity, by sacrificing another, the highest degree of power and beauty. Reason and experience, to be sure, easily point out the error at the bottom of that argument. Every occupation may ennoble a man; any may give him a well-rounded, dignified stature. It all depends on the spirit in which it is performed, and the only rule here could be that an occupation will have a wholesome effect if it, and the energy applied to it, wholly fills the soul. It will be less beneficial or downright harmful if one looks only to its results and considers the activity as only a means to an end. For everything which is worthwhile in itself, awakens love and respect; whatever promises to be useful as a means, merely arouses interest. And man is as ennobled by being loved and respected as he stands in danger of being degraded by being interested. If the state, now, exercises the kind of positive solicitude that I am here talking about, it can only fasten its view on the results to be obtained, and establish the regulations whose observance will be most conducive to such results.

This limited point of view undoubtedly does the most severe damage wherever the proper aim of man is totally moral or intellectual, or where some end is regarded in itself and not for the sake of any consequences to arise from it, or where such consequences at any rate are merely necessarily or accidentally connected with it. This is the case with all scientific experiments, with religious sentiments, with all interpersonal relations among human beings and particularly with the most natural of these which is the most significant for the individual as well as for the state: the relationship of marriage.

A union of two persons of opposite sex, founded upon their sexual difference (as marriage might perhaps most correctly be defined) may be thought of as diversely as there are diverse people to think of it, and as the inclinations of the heart and the objects which they present to reason, assume diverse forms; each person will demonstrate his whole moral character, and most especially the strength and the type of his feelings and sensations in this relationship. Whether a person pursues external ends or prefers to occupy his inner being, whether his reason or his feelings are more active, whether he takes a lively interest which soon flags or penetrates slowly and remains faithful, whether he ties himself and others with loose bonds or tightly, whether he retains more or less independence in the most intimate of all relationships—these and an infinite multitude of other considerations modify in many, many ways his relations in married life. But however it is formulated, its effect upon his nature and his subjective happiness is unmistakable, and the highest perfection or the deepest failure of his life depends largely on whether his attempt to find a reality to suit his inner mood is successful or not. Its influence is especially strong in the case of those interesting people who are most delicately and easily receptive and most deeply retentive. In general, one must reckon the feminine sex as belonging to this group, more than the masculine, and this is why the female character is very much dependent on the type of family relations which exist within a nation. Wholly exempt as women are from many external occupations, living for the most part in an environment which leaves their inner natures undisturbed, stronger through what they can be than through what they can do, more expressive in their quiet feelings than in their uttered ones, more richly endowed with all the signs of direct, indefinable expressiveness such as a quicker eye, a more moving voice, a more delicate bodily structure, more meant for expectancy and acceptance in their relationship to others, less aggressive, weaker in themselves and more intimately clinging, but not for reason of their weakness so much as for their admiration of the strength and greatness of others, in their union with another incessantly striving to be receptive with all their unified being, and to form within themselves the thing received in order to return it organized anew, at the same time inspired with that high courage which comes only from solicitude of love and a feeling of strength, a strength which does not defy resistance but which does not succumb in endurance— being all these things, women are intrinsically closer to the ideal of humanity than are men. And if it is not untrue that they more seldom reach it, it may well be because it is always more difficult to walk the direct, steep path, than to ascend by switchbacks. We need hardly describe how deeply such a being . . . may be disturbed by external unfortunate relationships. And yet so very much in society depends entirely on the harmonious development of the feminine character. If it is not incorrect to say that each species of excellence is embodied by some sort of being which best represents it, then surely the feminine character preserves our entire storehouse of morality.

Nach Freiheit strebt der Mann, das Weib nach Sitte.*

If, according to this deeply and truly felt expression of the poet [Goethe, in *Torquato Tasso*], man strives to remove the external limitations which hinder human growth, the careful hands of women prescribe the beneficent inner restraints only within which the fullness of energy may come to its flower, and prescribe it all the more delicately because women feel the inner existence of human beings more deeply; they see through their diverse circumstances more subtly, and each of their senses is more at their command, obviating that rational sophistication which so frequently obscures truth.

If it were necessary to pursue this argument further, history too, we should find, establishes its confirmation and exhibits everywhere a close connection between the moral level of nations and the es-

* Man strives for freedom, woman for the moral order. *Tr.*

teem in which the feminine sex is held. The foregoing considerations, therefore, illuminate for us the following: the effects of marriage are as diverse as the character of individuals; the consequences can only be most harmful if the state attempts to regulate by law a union so inextricably bound up with the unique qualities of individuals, or seeks to make it dependent on any consideration other than the personal preference of those individuals. This must be all the more true, since the state can only be interested in the consequences of such union, i.e., population figures, instruction of the children, etc. Of course it can be asserted that the highest solicitude for a beautiful inner life will lead to precisely the same concerns and results. For mankind has experimented sufficiently often to have found that the single enduring union of one man with one woman is on the whole the best arrangement, and it is undeniable that no other arrangement springs equally from true, natural, unspoiled love. Moreover this love leads to precisely those secondary institutions which law and custom in our culture approve of: children, their education, community living, community property (to some extent, at least), business arrangements being made primarily by the man, domestic ones primarily by the woman. But the great mistake seems to me to lie in the fact that the law *orders* these institutions, since the basic relationship can come about only through preference and not through external regulations, and wherever guidance or coercion contradict personal preference, they cannot possibly have other than ill effects. That is why, it seems to me, the state should not merely loosen the bonds, but (if I may be permitted to decide solely in line with my previous argument, and to speak not of marriage in general but of one of the many harmful consequences of state intervention which is here particularly noticeable) withdraw all intervention whatsoever from the institution of marriage, leaving it wholly in the hands of the individuals concerned and whatever contracts they may see fit to enter into. The objection that all family relationships would be disturbed by such a course, or perhaps not even come into existence any longer—however well founded in certain local situations such an objection might be—would not deter me. For experience shows rather frequently that morality often binds what is left loose by law. The idea of external coercion is totally alien to a relationship which rests entirely, as does marriage, on personal preference and inner sense of duty; and the consequences of coercive arrangements simply do not correspond to their intentions.*

*   *   *

. . . In the moral and, generally speaking, practical life of man, insofar as he observes the rules (which probably should be limited to the fundamental principles of law only) [he must] ever keep in sight the highest point of view as regards his own development and that of others, must everywhere be guided by this pure motive, and subordinate all other interests to this law which is recognized without the aid of any shallow sense-motivations. But all the sides in himself which a man may cultivate stand marvellously interwoven and interrelated, and if the intellectual universe produces connections which are far more intimate than physical ones, then the moral universe does so far more still. This is why human beings must join together in mutual dependence, not in order to lose their individuality, but to lose their exclusive isolation; their union must not transform one being into another, but open up approaches between two individuals. What each individual possesses, he must compare with that which he receives, modifying it but not allowing it to be suppressed. For as one truth in the realm of intellectuality never truly fights another, neither does one human value in the realm of morality. Another reason, therefore, for close and diverse relationships between characters of high individuality is that whatever cannot coexist will be destroyed, and only coexistence can lead to greatness and beauty, each leaving the other undisturbed but sustaining him, nourishing him, and fructifying him to produce ever newer, more beautiful offspring. This is why the greatest—and perhaps most neglected—principle of the art of social inter-

* Section 4 is missing in Humboldt's manuscript. What follows is presumably Section 5. *Tr.*

course is the incessant striving to comprehend the inmost individuality of another, to utilize it, to seek its response while wholly steeped in sincerest appreciation of its individual qualities—an appreciation which will hardly ever utilize a method other than to exhibit one's own individual qualities, to compare oneself with the other in the presence of the other.

It may be argued that we have properly neglected this art because social intercourse is meant to be recreation, not hard labor, or we may excuse ourselves on the ground that it is unfortunately extremely difficult to see anything individually interesting in a great many people. Yet each of us should have too much respect for himself to seek recreation other than that afforded by a change of interesting occupations, or to seek it in a way which leaves exactly one's most valuable energies out of account. And each of us likewise should have too much reverence for the human race to declare even a single one of its members as good for nothing whatever, incapable of being turned to good account or of being modified by outside influence. Least of all may that agency overlook this point of view which makes the dealing with human beings and its influence upon them its business. Since, therefore, the state when it exerts positive social solicitude simply cannot help being a hindrance to individual development, since care for physical well-being is always bound up with inner existence, we see a further reason why we should permit no such solicitude except in cases of absolute urgent necessity.

These then may constitute the principal harmful consequences which spring from the positive solicitude of the state for the well-being of its citizens. They may be particularly strong in the case of certain governmental institutions and regulations more than of others, but in my estimation they are also inseparable from the whole adoption of such a policy. I had been going to speak of solicitude for physical well-being alone, and everywhere did proceed from that standpoint and tried to separate it from moral considerations. But as I said at the beginning, physical and moral welfare are very difficult to separate, and I should like to cite this once more as serving to excuse the fact that many of my arguments so far advanced apply to the entire field of positive social welfare. So far, however, I have been assuming that the state institutions of which I have been speaking are already established, and I must therefore speak now of some obstacles which present themselves in the very framing of such institutions.

6) It would seem most important, in this connection, to weigh the advantages which are intended when such institutions come under consideration against the disadvantages which are always connected with them, most particularly the restriction of freedom. Yet such a balance can hardly be drawn up, certainly never with any completeness. For every limiting arrangement collides with the free and natural utterance of energies, thus bringing about an infinitude of new combinations. Hence the full measure of consequences (even assuming a normal course of events and discounting important and surprising developments which, of course, always happen) can never be predicted. Anyone who has ever had occasion to occupy himself with governmental administrative procedures knows from definite experience that very few regulations have an immediate, absolute necessity underlying them, and that most of them are relative, indirect, and depend mostly on equally uncompelling rules which have preceded them. Hence an enormous number of means becomes necessary and these very means are therefore preventative of the true ends. Not only does a highly administrative government need more revenue, but it demands greater artifices to secure its political stability; its departments are very loosely interconnected, and the solicitude regarding everything, including itself, has to keep multiplying. From this there results a difficult calculation—unfortunately all too often neglected—whether or not the state's natural resources are sufficient to produce all the means of intervention, and if this calculation turns out to be wrong, or if a genuine misproportion is present, then new artificial devices overstrain the already taxed energies. This is the evil from which (though not from this cause alone) all too many modern states are suffering.

We must not overlook one particular manifestation of this disease, since it affects so very closely the individual human being and his development, and that is that the administration of government becomes increasingly so complicated and overburdened that it requires, to save it from complete chaos, an unbelievable number of detailed arrangements, institutions, and regulations, and a like number of persons to handle them. But most of these persons operate directly only with mechanical and automatic formulae, not with the objects for which they stand. In this way a great many, in some cases perhaps excellent, heads are prevented from doing their own thinking; worse yet, their entire spiritual energy suffers from their partly empty, partly far too one-sided occupation. Many hands which might otherwise be performing useful work are likewise idled. A new source of earning one's living now becomes established, that of civil service, and this makes the civil servants much more dependent on the governmental administrative agencies that pay them than on the nation as a whole. As for the further harmful consequences, the tendency to wait for the state's aid, the lack of independence, the false vanity, and finally the idleness and want of spirit—all these are recorded by incontrovertible experience. And the same evil which gives rise to these conditions is in turn brought about by them. Those who have long engaged in governmental administration tend to forget more and more the substance of their work and to devote themselves increasingly to its necessary forms; they tend to keep improving the formal aspects—possibly quite honestly so—but it is work done at the expense of the substance and can therefore only worsen matters. Hence there arise new forms, new complexities of operation, often new restrictive regulations, from which of course grow a new crop of civil servants.

In most of our governments there is a noticeable increase, from one decade to the next, in the number of personnel, the number of licenses and registrations, and a corresponding decrease in the freedoms of the governed. A busy administration naturally requires close supervision and the most punctual and honest discharge of its duties, since there are so many more opportunities for shortcomings. It seems therefore quite justified to have every piece of business go through as many hands as possible, and to try to sift out all possibilities for errors or shady dealings. This, however, makes the processes involved almost wholly mechanical and the men involved into machines; genuine skill and honesty decrease with decreasing trust. And in the end there results a distortion of all points of view, since the occupations of which I have been speaking have to be considered of utmost importance in order to be maintained at all. Finally no one any longer has a feeling for what is important and what is not, for what is honorable and what is contemptible, for which aims are ultimate and which merely expedient. And since the necessity for occupations of this sort also has a number of beneficial by-products—quite obvious ones, in fact—which might be thought to compensate for the disadvantages, I shall dwell no longer on this part of the subject and shall proceed instead to that for which all the foregoing has been but the preparation: a discussion of the basic distortions in point of view which all positive governmental solicitude necessarily brings in its wake.

7) Human beings—in order to conclude this part of my investigation with some universal considerations from an elevated point of view—human beings are neglected in favor of objects; energies are neglected in favor of results. A state which operates under such a system is more like a garbage heap of lifeless plus living instruments of operations and pleasures than like a multitude of active energies which are enjoying themselves and their work. The price of apparent happiness and enjoyment is the neglect of the spontaneous active energies of the acting members. But even if this calculation were correct—since only the feeling of the consumer thereof can decide whether or not happiness and enjoyment has been achieved—it would still be far removed from human dignity. Where else could be sought the reason for the fact that this system which aims primarily at peace and quiet and safety voluntarily renounces the highest human pleasure? For man most enjoys himself during those moments in which he feels the highest degree of energy and wholeness in himself.

Of course these moments are also the closest to complete misery.

For only an opposite tension can follow moments of tension, and the direction toward enjoyment or deprivation lies in the hands of invincible fate. And yet, if the feeling of what is highest in man deserves the name of happiness, we gain an altered point of view toward pain and suffering, as well. Man in his inmost nature becomes the seat of happiness and unhappiness; he does not alter with the shifting waves that carry him. The above outlined system leads, in my estimation, to a fruitless striving to escape pain. Whoever really understands pleasure, tolerates pain which willy-nilly catches up with everyone; his superior pleasure lies in the contemplation of the appointed operations of fate. All vistas of greatness sweetly bind him, whether it be greatness that is just developing or greatness that is perishing. In such ways man comes finally to a feeling (but, unless he is a fanatic, only at rare moments) that even his own destruction may be a moment of ecstasy.

It may be that I shall be accused of having exaggerated the disadvantages of governmental solicitude; yet I had to describe the full effects of state intervention, and it is obvious that the disadvantages will vary considerably with the degree and the method of the intervention. In general, I desire that all the generalities contained in these pages be viewed apart from direct comparisons with reality. In reality one seldom finds a clear-cut case, and even if one finds one, one does not see it exclusive of its relationships to many other things. On the other hand, neither may one forget that *if* harmful influences are present, the ultimate ruination toward which they work is considerably accelerated. Just as great energy coupled with greater energy produces doubly great energy, so inferior coupled with more inferior produces most inferior. How dare we, even in thought, accompany the rapidity of such deterioration! And even if we admitted that the disadvantages were far less great than we have described them, I still believe my above maxim would far outweigh all benefits to be had on the other side—assuming it could be put into effect completely, which to be sure, leaves room for doubt. For the always active, never idle energy inhabiting all objects is in constant opposition against all arrangements hostile to it and promotes all those which further it, so that in a certain high sense it is true that even the most diligent effort can never produce as much evil as the spontaneous generation of good can everywhere effect.

I might now draw the agreeable picture of a nation existing in highest and most boundless freedom, in the greatest diversity of its own internal relationships and those with others surrounding it. I might demonstrate how out of such a people would arise even more beautiful, great, and marvellous configurations of diversity and originality than arose in antiquity, so rich in this respect. . . . I might show what abundant strength could flourish when each being organizes himself with a view to only his own, intrinsic nature, when each is free to realize in himself the archetypes of beauty and grandeur that freely surround him, with the aid of unlimited spontaneous activity ever encouraged by his freedom. How delicate and subtle would be the inner development of such human beings; how such development would become their main occupation; how all things physical and external would flow over into things internal, moral, intellectual; how the bond which allies these two aspects of human nature would gain in endurance if nothing were allowed to disturb the free reaction of all human occupations upon spirit and character; how no one would be sacrificed to anyone else; how each person would be able to retain his entire strength, which would in turn inspire in him a beautiful willingness to give it a direction that would bless others as well as himself; how, if each person could advance in individuation, far more diverse and subtle nuances of beautiful human character would arise, and one-sidedness, always a consequence of weakness and destitution, would lessen; how each person, as soon as the external compulsion toward artificial equality were removed, would be inwardly compelled far more urgently by the very nature of human interdependence to modify himself in his responses to others; how in such a nation no energy and no working hand would be lost to the heightening and the enjoyment of human existence. And I might finally show how even a point of view which was merely oriented toward all these aims would lead to their actual pursuit and thereby serve to lessen the power of all less worthy or downright false objectives. I might then conclude by calling attention to the fact that the consequences of such policy within a single nation, whichever one it might be, would lead far beyond its borders and take a great deal of the terror from the to some extent inescapable misery of mankind, the catastrophes of nature, the evil of human hostilities, and the excesses of too great a concentration of material riches and pleasures. But I rest content with having described the opposite situation; it is enough for my purposes to toss out some suggestions, to be investigated by a maturer judgment.

If, then, I attempt to draw the final conclusion from my entire argument thus far, my first principle must be the following: *Let the state abstain from all solicitude for the positive welfare of its citizens, and let it proceed not a step further than is absolutely necessary for its internal and external security; let it limit the freedom of its citizens for no other purpose whatsoever.* [I, 111–29]

Government may not seek to influence the manners and morals of its citizens

The state must wholly refrain from any and all endeavor to influence directly or indirectly the manners and morals of a nation, except insofar as this is a natural and unavoidable consequence of its necessary regulations. Everything, however, which may promote such intention on the part of the government, especially its supervision over education, religious institutions, sumptuary laws, etc. is to lie absolutely and wholly outside the limits of its legitimate activity. [I, 177]

It may restrict such acts on the part of its citizens as interfere with the rights of others

In order to provide for the security of its citizens, the state must forbid or restrict those acts, referring immediately to the agent, which imply the violation of the rights of others, i.e., which en-

croach upon their freedom or their property without or against their consent. It must do so even when such encroachment is only a probability, but the probability must be weighed against the extent of the probable damage and against the restriction of personal freedom. Any further restriction of personal freedom, from whatever motive, lies beyond the bounds of legitimate governmental activity. [I, 187]

Government may maintain external and internal security

I believe that I can assert as a positive . . . maxim that *the maintenance of security both as over against external enemies as well as against internal discord constitutes the proper aim of the state and must occupy its activity.* . . .

This assertion is affirmed by history, by the fact that the kings in all earlier nations were nothing other than leaders in war and judges in times of peace. I say: kings. For—if I may be permitted a digression—history shows us nothing but kings and monarchies, however strange this may seem to us, in those periods when the feeling of liberty was dearest to man, having as he did as yet little property and knowing and valuing only his personal strength, finding the highest enjoyment in its unhindered exercise. Thus all the governments of Asia, the oldest governments of Greece and Italy, and those of the most freedom-loving peoples, the Germanic tribes. If we look for the reasons behind this paradox, a certain truth takes us by surprise, as it were. It turns out that the choice of monarchy is a highest proof of the freedom of the ones making that choice. The thought of a chief ruler arises, as I say, only through the feeling that a military leader or else an umpire is necessary. Now a single leader or judge is obviously the most efficient answer to this need. The truly free man simply does not know the apprehension that this one leader or judge might become an autocrat; he has no inkling of the possibility even, for he cannot imagine any man with so much power that he would be able to suppress his, the chooser's freedom, nor can he imagine a free man who is possessed by the will to rule. And indeed it is true that whoever is ambitious for power is not receptive toward the beauties of liberty, but loves slavery instead, with the only reservation that he not be the slave. Thus, as morality grows at an equal rate with vice, and theology with heresy, politics does with servitude. [I, 134 f.]

It may neither promote wars nor prevent wars in which its citizens believe

I wish to limit my views on war to its effect on national character. . . . Looking at it with that viewpoint in mind, war seems to me to be one of the most wholesome phenomena in the educational development of the human race, and I dislike seeing it gradually disappear from the scene. It is the—frightful to be sure—extreme situation in which all active courage is tested and steeled against danger, toil, and discomfort, a courage which is afterward modified in so many diverse nuances of human life and which alone can give to human beings the strength and diversity without which their flexibility is weakness and their inner unity, but emptiness. People will answer that there are plenty of other means to bring about these results—physical dangers in many occupations and . . . moral ones of several varieties which may test the firm statesman in his cabinet as much as the fearless thinker in his lonely cell. And yet it is impossible for me to rid myself of the notion that as everything spiritual is but a subtler blossoming of the body, so is this matter of war and courage. The stem on which this particular blossom grows, to be sure, lies in the past. But our memory of the past is ever receding; the number of people whom it affects grows fewer, and even on the few who remember, the effect grows weaker. Other equally dangerous occupations—seamanship, mining, etc.—lack, to various degrees, the idea of greatness and glory which is so closely bound up with war. And this is not a chimerical idea. It rests on the conception, a perfectly realistic one, of superior power. So far as the elements are concerned, we seek more to escape their blind force, or to learn to endure their repeated onslaughts, than to overcome them—

mit Göttern
soll sich nicht messen
*irgend ein Mensch.**

Deliverance is not the same as victory. What fate kindly grants and human courage or inventiveness simply utilizes is not the fruit or the proof of superior power. Everyone involved in a war believes right is on his side, believes he is avenging an insult. Natural man, with a depth of feeling which even the most cultivated cannot wholly deny, deems it a higher thing to redeem his honor than to accumulate the means for subsistence. No one can accuse me of considering the death of a fallen warrior more glorious than, say, the death of a bold Pliny . . . and yet, examples of the latter are fewer, and who knows whether they would exist at all without the archetype of the former. Nor have I chosen a particularly favorable position for war. Take the Spartans at Thermopylae. Let me ask any reader what the effect of such an example is on a nation. I know very well that exactly such courage and such selflessness may be shown in any walk of life, and in fact are shown. But shall we blame sense-bound man if he is most carried away by the most vivid utterance? Can we deny that an utterance of this sort carries the most universal authority? And although I have *heard* much of various fates which are said to be worse than death, I have yet to *see* a man, loving and enjoying the fullness of life, who—unless he were a fanatic—could afford to be contemptuous of death. Least of all should we find such people in antiquity, where the thing was still greater than the name, and the present more esteemed than the future. What I am saying here about warriors does not apply to those who are trained, as in Plato's *Republic,* to take life and death as they come, with a feeling of indifference, but to those who with

* Against the gods no man should measure himself. Goethe, *"Grenzen der Menschheit." Tr.*

their eye on the highest aim risk the dearest and best they have. All situations in which the interrelationships between extremes are involved are the most interesting and instructive. But where is such a situation better to be found than in war, where preference and duty seem involved in the most violent struggle, likewise one's duty as a human being and one's duty as a citizen? And yet, when justified defense gives the signal, all these antagonisms find their full resolution.

The very point of view from which I consider war as wholesome and necessary, should show how the state, in my opinion, should make use of it. The spirit which war invokes must be left free to inspire all members of a nation. This alone speaks against the idea of a standing army. I am well aware that standing armies, as well as modern warfare in general, are very remote indeed from the ideal which would be most useful for the development of mankind. If any warrior, at any time, must become something of a machine as he sacrifices his freedom for subordination, he must do so in a far greater degree in our type of warfare where so little depends on the strength, bravery, or skill of the individual. What a vicious system, therefore, it is, to keep considerable numbers of men in a nation not only for a few years but perhaps for their whole lifetime chained to a totally mechanized existence, and this in peacetime, with a mere view toward the eventuality of war! This is a notable instance of the fact that as the theory of human undertakings is developed, their practical utility vanishes for the ones who are their agents.

Undoubtedly the art of warfare has advanced tremendously among us moderns, but equally certain is that the noble character of warriors has become a rarity. Its greatest beauty is visible nowhere except in the history of antiquity. If this statement is felt to be exaggerated, we may modify it somewhat. But this much of it is true: the warrior-like spirit in our times has very frequently only harmful consequences for the nations, whereas in antiquity we see it very often accompanied by wholesome ones. Our standing armies bring war into the very womb of peace. A warlike spirit is honorable only in connection with the fairest peaceable virtues, military discipline only with the loftiest feeling for freedom. Separate the two—and see how easily they are separated by the presence of armed soldiers in time of peace—and discipline degenerates into slavery and a warlike spirit into ferocity and unbridled excess. I wish to remind the reader, however, that my condemnation even of standing armies extends no further than is prescribed by my immediate point of view here, as outlined. Their great undoubted utility—with which, like all other earthly things, they balance off their failings which would otherwise hurry them into oblivion— is well recognized by me. They are a part of a whole which was not formed by any planning on the part of vain human rationality but by the sure hand of fate. . . . Nor am I of the opinion that the government should from time to time whip up a war.

The government is to give freedom, and all its neighboring governments are to enjoy similar freedom. Men are men in all periods of history and do not lose their original passions. War will come of itself, and if it does not come of itself, one may then at least be certain that the peace was neither coerced nor produced by an artificial paralysis of powers. In that case peace will be a far more blessed gift to a nation, just as the peaceful plowman is a far lovelier sight than the bloody warrior. And if we think of the advance of humanity from one generation to the next, then we may expect the future to be increasingly peaceful. But if this happens, peace shall have grown out of the inner strength of human beings; men —free men—shall themselves have become peaceful. Right now—as any year of modern European history amply demonstrates—we enjoy the fruits of peace, but not those of peacefulness. Human energies, striving incessantly for infinite activity, contend with one another or else join one another when they meet head-on. What shape the battle shall assume, whether that of war, or of competition, or whatever nuance may work itself out in the future—this depends first and foremost on their degree of refinement.

If I am now to postulate another maxim . . . it can only be that *the state must in no wise promote war nor, on the other hand, forcibly prevent war when necessity demands. It must allow perfect freedom to the diffusion of a warlike spirit throughout the spirit and character of the entire nation. It must above all refrain from all positive institutions which educate a nation for war. Insofar as these may be absolutely necessary, such as the training of citizens in the use of arms, it must give its training such a direction that it imparts to citizens not merely the bravery, skill, and ability of soldiers, but inspires them with the spirit of true warriors —which is no more than that of noble citizens who are ever ready to take up arms in defense of their country.* [I, 136–40]

MAN IN HIS SOCIAL
ENVIRONMENT

Sociality is not derived from mere need

Sociality . . . cannot be derived from mere need, without one's idea of it being one-sided. Even in animals it does not rest on need. No animal is so self-sufficient in its superior strength as the elephant—who by preference lives in herds. In animals, too, the inclination to sociality, which is found in greater or lesser degree in various species, springs from far deeper-lying causes. We find it impossible to fathom them only because we have no concept for the nonetheless undeniable capacity of animals to perceive, to sense and feel, and to combine perceptions. But thinking in man is bound essentially to social existence; man needs, quite aside from all bodily and sentient relationships, for his thinking alone a "thou" corresponding to his "I." Concepts attain their definition and clarity only by being reflected against the thinking capacity of another. They are begotten by being torn loose from the moving mass of representations and being formed into objects as they are confronted by subjects. It is not sufficient, however, that this splitting off should occur in the subject alone; objectification is not complete until the representor really sees the thought outside himself, which can only be in another being who, like himself, is a representor and a thinker. [V, 380]

What can an individual do in times of social upheaval?

It is, first, the homely simplicity of the objects described and, second, the grandeur and depth of the resultant effect, that cause the reader to admire Goethe's *Hermann und Dorothea* so profoundly and overwhelmingly. . . . The poet tells of the connection of a son of a prosperous middle-class family with an emigrant girl; he does nothing more than spread before us the various aspects of the action, . . . developing the circumstances as they naturally and necessarily follow each other. . . . All his means for evoking the sympathy of his readers are contained within this narrow sphere. The poet never once appears before us in his own individual person; he never comes up with an observation or feeling of his own. But to what a lofty standpoint does he thereby elevate the reader! Life in its greatest and most important relationships, man in all the significant moments of his existence: suddenly they stand revealed; we look through them with vivid illumination.

What is dearest to the reader's heart, what busies his thinking and his powers of observation most enduringly, he sees described in this work with a few, masterly strokes drawn with astonishing truth: the changes from one generation to the next, the changing times with their changing opinions and customs, the main levels of human culture, and, above all, the relationship of middle-class virtue and domestic bliss to the fate of nations and the current extraordinary events. Though the reader seems to be listening to the tale of events that occurred in a single family, he feels his mind steeped in serious, general reflections, his heart torn with melancholy emotion, his total psychic life, on the other hand, calmed by a simple tried and true wisdom. For the question which is so important to all of us today, the question of what an individual can do in times of complete social upheaval, when opinions, customs, constitutions and whole nations are torn loose from their moorings —this he finds not merely posed by the various characters of this book, but also answered in such a way that the answer breathes into his soul the strength to act as well as the courage to endure. [II, 123 f.]

We must strike a balance between operating in our narrow sphere and being citizens of the world

We cannot exclude from the demands that reason makes on us the adaptation of our activities to the whole of humanity, to be not merely citizens of our state and our time but also to be citizens of the world.

It has been found with considerable frequency, to be sure, that such a comprehensive and lofty point of view, however it may broaden the mind and elevate the disposition, yet renders one cold and indifferent to that which is truly necessary, one's nearest duties. Hence the most fruitful and simple wisdom limits the number of our duties to a narrow, easily comprehended circle. But that high command of reason of which we speak does not demand that we should directly and with specific intention work on a progress plan for the whole human race. On the contrary, such a gigantic undertaking, one which would scarcely leave the end within sight, much less afford any certainty in calculating the means, should without fail appear too foolish and presumptuous to even be euphemistically described in terms of noble and pure enthusiasm for virtue and universal human welfare. It is our spirit that should be steeped in the lofty thought of universal cooperation of all creatures and all energies. It is the over-all orientation-principles of our actions that we should test on this thought, in order to be sure of their own universal cooperativeness. Our imagination should be inspiringly busied by this great image—and then be active in the limited sphere which accords with our own capacity. One can never sufficiently recall man's outward activity into the bounds of necessity, just as one can never sufficiently invite his spirit to dwell in the fields of infinity. If the improvement of our outward circumstances has been so severely out of step with the broadening of our spiritual horizons, we may primarily blame it on a double error of ours. At times we have tried to adapt our immediate practical activities to ideal models far beyond the borderline of possible execution; at other times we have sought to enclose the bold flight of our spirit within the narrow restrictions of practical reality. Not the quickest, but the surest and most lasting improvement begins with the education of the spirit. The form which the spirit, and through it one's entire character, thus receives, imparts itself in a manner unnoticeable at any given moment but ultimately decisively effective to one's acts and all one's external doings. And thus nature herself, without being influenced intentionally or by force, of her own accord accepts, through man's gentle but incessant influence upon her, the stamp of his inmost individuality. By changing himself, man changes nature as well, and his power over her depends on his character and the consistent efforts of his own activities.

Here, too, we demand no more of man than that he regard mankind as a whole, and himself as a part of it, with the help of his spirit; that he espy its broad course with the help of his thoughts; and for the rest, that he keep walking on his own narrow footpath, in modesty as before, but with firmer steps and greater understanding of where and how his steps are going. [II, 12–13]

There are times for public participation
and times for personal development

[Upon rereading my correspondence with Schiller] I do not know whether people still exist nowadays who will speak so openly about themselves and delve so deeply into their individuality. I doubt it. One no longer has the time, either, to be so concerned with oneself. I noticed in particular, in a whole set of letters covering more than a year's time, that there wasn't a single mention of public affairs. Do we nowadays ever write a single letter (even when one's job, as is mine, isn't part and parcel of public matters) without alluding to them? I don't want to say which is better, now or then. In the old days one looked upon everything that tended toward public affairs as being business, separate from the life of the mind and disturbing to it. Nowadays one believes that a human being cannot attain true completion, or inmost worth, if he does not take a lively interest in whatever happens to the state, regardless of whether his share is an active one. There is no question that science and literature and the thinking spirit of the nation benefited more in the old days. On the other hand, our time may really make other claims; the nation may have gained in character, and the fruits for science may yet be harvested. One thing is certain: one cannot turn back the stream. It is flowing with a strong current, and one must find the proper means to direct it worthily as it is, without letting all the old benefits go. To suppress anything now, to lament the lost good old days (no matter if I do consider them as such) would be to choke off the efforts of the present. Nor would it bring back the past. The past is past, and no one can bring it back by magic. What consoles me personally is that oneself is receding with the past. [To Caroline v. Humboldt, January 1818]

There are mysterious relationships between individuals and nations

The most important things, also the most mysterious, are the relationships between an individual and his nation. About the mysteries of individuality in which (as even the most abstract philosophy has to keep recognizing) the characteristics and the fate of human nature lie buried, no real clarification can be had within the barriers of earthly existence. But this much our feeling and our reflection make very plain: man's individuality lies within the single individual in only a very narrowly conceived sense. For man stands before us not so much as a single isolated creature but more like an offshoot from a larger whole, his entire existence closely bound up with that whole. His feelings demand response, his insight affirmation by others; self-confidence in his capacities needs inspiring example. His whole inner being calls for consciousness of a corresponding being outside him, and the more his capacities grow, the wider the circle with which he needs to keep in contact. At the same time his nature is predetermined by all who have preceded him, and shaped by all who exist around him, so that even the operations of whatever truly and absolutely free powers he may have are variously limited and determined. This dependence of man on his fellow creatures springs simultaneously from an earthly and a super-earthly source. The former is found in heredity and in the necessity for social connections. The latter in the fact that consciously or unconsciously, in philosophical thought or in inspired sentiments and actions, urged by a higher urge or aware of an inferior goal, man really does strive for something which is infinite. He feels that his existence without this striving, even if it continued in the best regulated social order, would not be truly human and that therefore the demand indwelling in his nature cannot be vain. Since his individual strength nonetheless is incommensurate with it, he recognizes that this striving was placed into all humanity and is felt by him only because he is a part of humanity.

On the other hand, a nation lives and operates only through its individuals. However close its communal living, it comes into existence only within individuals. How remote an individual may be from his nation, how much of an independent advance he may make beyond its circle, cannot be decided, since it is fortunately impossible to place a preknown limitation on a man's allotment of independence. At all times there have been individuals . . . who have redirected their nations in art, science, and wisdom; there have arisen reformers who have caused a sudden overthrow of religions, governments, or morals. In the Americas we see such men in the persons of Quetzalcoatl, Bochica, Amalivaca, and Manco Capac, and we shall have to return to the question of whether they were genuine strangers or whether their contemporaries merely looked upon them as such because of the suddenness of their appearance and their tremendous effect. On the other hand it is certain, and demonstrable by historical example, that the capacity of an individual may be weakened both by too close a communal life and by lack of cooperation from his fellow nationals. [V, 29–30]

The tendency to form large social groups is limited by imagination and feeling

It seems an inevitable arrangement in the course of human culture that on a certain level of development the differences which divide small nations must dissolve, and only large masses can enter into communal relationships. To stimulate whole nations to significant intellectual advances, and particularly to secure them against relapses into barbarism and ignorance, requires great political means. The diversity of resultant new conditions produces diversity and infuses new elements into opinions and ideas; the human spirit would perhaps never have attained some of its sublimest insights without the stimulating spectacle of violent and almost universal friction between various human powers. Whether there is not a limit to this as well, however, whether development does not reach another point at which it is just as necessary to contain imagination and feelings within a circle as tight as that of rationality must be wide, in order to retain for character that warmth and inner strength without which it cannot bear fruit—this is a different and surely not unimportant question. [XIII, 10]

Man is both individual and social, and nations
are both individuals and groups

Living means preserving, as the legislative ruling power, a thought-form in a mass of raw material, by means of a mysterious energy. In the physical universe this form and this legislative power is called organization; in the intellectual and moral universe, character. To generate means to permit that mysterious energy to begin or, in other words, to kindle an energy which suddenly tears a certain quantity of raw material, in an absolutely definite form, away from the total mass, and to place this form in all its unique individuality in opposition to all other forms. True individuality, in short, grows from the inside outward, unexpectedly and suddenly, and is so little developed by life that it merely comes to a state of consciousness in life, and often enough to a consciousness confused or misinterpreted. But because man is a social animal (and this is his distinctive character), because he needs other creatures like himself not for protection, not for help, nor for procreation nor for his life of habit and custom (all of which a number of animal species also do) but because he reaches consciousness of self, because an "I" without a "Thou" is unimaginable to his reason and his senses—for this reason does the individuality of his sociality (his Thou) tear itself off simultaneously with that of his own individuality (his I). And so a nation too is an individual, and the individual human being is an individual of an individual. [III, 355]

The greatest genius for living is possessed by
the genius inherent in a nation

Life may well be considered an art, and living characters, works of art. As only the artistic genius finds the indivisible point in which, after mighty striving, the in-visible is wedded to the visible, and finds it for the sake of its ob-jectification, so in life too, only genius does this—the greatest of all geniuses, the genius of a whole, living, cooperating nation. [VII, 610]

The highest ideal of coexistence depends on individual development

The highest ideal of coexistence among human creatures to my mind would be the development of each one for himself, out of himself, and for his own sake. Physical and moral nature would see to it soon enough that such people came together. Just as the battles of war are more honorable than those of the arena, and just as the struggle of impassioned citizens yields a greater fame than those of organized, mercenary soldiers, so the contention and struggles of such human beings would dem-onstrate and at the same time produce the highest energies. [I, 109]

The art of social intercourse demands freedom and a spirit of playfulness

The strongest influence upon the education of individual character is free and daily social intercourse in the widest and narrowest possible spheres: in marriage, in friend-ships, in small and not so small social circles. The art of social living, if it is not to be demeaned to a mere talent for pleasing and for gaining personal profits, as has too often been done, rests en-tirely upon psychology (knowledge of character) and education (formation of character).

The first attempt of the art of sociality is always to make each relationship as important as possible for the culture and for the individual character, to infuse into it as much soul as it can hold.

This accomplished, it attempts to place the individualities and the groupings within each relationship in such a fashion that to an observer they will form an instructive image of variety in functioning, and at the same time make the people involved in them both more receptive and more individuated. But none of these purposes is to be achieved under conditions other than those of utmost freedom, avoiding even all semblance of intent. All shall happen as though of itself; all shall be play and recreation; nothing serious, nothing businesslike. All these things make the art of social intercourse into a truly fine art. [I, 382 f.]

The question of the extent of man's equality cannot be settled by reference to either heredity or environment

Whether men are unequal (precisely and strictly speaking) or whether an originally quite equal endowment of all is merely altered and individualized by the different positions that each man finds himself in, is a question which lies wholly outside our experience and our insight. We have not seen any human beings who have not completed a considerable stretch of their course, if not a long one measured in time, then certainly a significant one measured in terms of progress. And since all things about which we are capable of judging are always results of the working together of environment and inner capacity or energy, we can never completely distinguish these two forces which are always simultaneously operative for us.

All that we may say with any certainty is that some sort of capacity, equal or unequal (the latter, if one is to permit oneself an impermissible guess, having the greater probability) is present from the start, independent of all environmental circumstances, for without such initial presence there would be nothing for the environment to act upon. Further, for us the differences that we note between people might as well be in them originally and by nature. For a baby, even before he leaves his mother's body, is in a spe-

74

cific, unique situation, which situation, plus his specific physically determined heritage, exert their influence upon his character for life. But since the entire series of events comprising this aspect of human uniqueness lies beyond the realm of experience for us, we quite justly look upon these differences, determined though they be by outside forces, as though they were original and essential. [II, 91]

Human beings of greatest refinement most need constant contact with simple fellow-beings

In the very highest culture there is undoubtedly a point where the most delicate and subtle stirrings of refined sentiments return by themselves to the simple pourings-out of natural feelings, and where the most carefully developed and educated individuals stand in constant and mutual contact with the plainest but healthy segments of the common people. [XIII, 11]

*   *   *

I wrote you yesterday about Böttcher, the foundry foreman. He fell ill on Monday and said instantly that he would not get up again. The evening of his death he foretold its hour, midnight, correctly. He took leave of everyone and sent messages to all his workers that he was thinking of them at the hour of his death. The courage and loyalty of such ordinary people at such moments always moves me tremendously. It proves that such moments bring out human nature at its purest, but also that the best and noblest parts of man depend precious little on culture, education, and whatever else it is called. One can never have enough respect for true humanity as it is visible in the persons of the totally uneducated classes, and never enough humility if one sometimes believes one is superior to them. The relationship of all these single, unnoticeable traits to each other is the true substance of a people; it forms the foundation of the highest conceivable national development. All culture and education would wither like a wreath wound around a pole if there were not the living trunk which keeps all blossoms alive through its invisible powers. [To Caroline v. Humboldt, November 1824]

We neglect the forces of nature, individuality, and particularity in our view of world history

The errors in our present view of world history are the following:

We look almost exclusively to culture and civilization, having in mind a progressive perfectibility. Hence we automatically preconceive various levels and steps of progress and overlook the most important nuclei from which great things will develop, just as they have similarly developed from earlier nuclei.

We look upon the generations of men too much as though they were beings composed of reason and understanding, too little as though they were products of nature.

We seek the consummation of humanity in attainment of a general, abstractly conceived perfection, rather than in the development of a wealth of great individuated forms. [III, 358]

Human history has meaning only in its connectedness with all existence

In each period of history there have been things, harmful in themselves, which saved for mankind an invaluable good. What preserved liberty during the Middle Ages? The feudal system. Who preserved enlightenment and the sciences and scholarship during barbarian times? The monks. What kept alive a noble love for the opposite sex at a time when this sex was demeaned among the Greeks—to choose a domestic example? Pederasty. We do not even need any demonstrations from history; the very course of human life is the best example. At each age one aspect of existence plays the main role, all the others subordinate ones. And at the next age the main role is transferred to one of the previously subordinate ones.

Thus we owe all carefree serene pleasure to childhood; all enthusiasm for the beautiful, all scorn for the toil and dangers undergone in order to attain the beautiful, to late youth; all careful reflection, all diligence for reasons of prudence, to maturity; all preparedness for death, all melancholy joy at what has been and will be no more, to old age. In each of these epochs the human being exists as a whole. But in each of them only one spark of his nature flames bright and luminous; the others yield only the soft glow of half-extinguished or not yet flaming light. The same thing is true of each individual human being, with each individual ability and sensation. A single individual of one particular type does not exhaust all possible feelings, no matter how many circumstances calling for feelings befall him. . . .

What now follows from all this? That no single condition of people or things deserves exclusive attention upon itself alone, but only in its connection with all existence preceding it and following upon it; that results are nothing, and the energies which produce them and which again spring from them are everything. [I, 84 f.]

The German character is marked by inner-directedness

The deepest and truest orientation of that which we call German lies in its great inner-directedness. It retains Germans close to the truth of nature on the one hand, and gives them their tendency to occupy themselves with ideas and idea-directed sentiments and with everything else related to ideas, on the other. Here lies the difference between Germans and most other modern nations, and also between Germans and the ancient Greeks. The German seeks both poetry and philosophy; he does not wish to separate them, but on the contrary, strives to unite them. . . . [VI, 505]

What Germans owe to the Greeks

But as the sense of a language is extended, so is the sense of a nation. To cite only one example: how much has the German language gained since it began to imitate the Greek meters, and how much has the German nation developed —by no means only its learned representatives but its masses, down to its women and children—due to the fact that the Greeks, in a genuine and undisguised form, have truly become part of the nation's reading matter. [VIII, 131]

The one-sidedness of modern times forms a necessary step toward the maturity of the human race

The sensitive lover of antiquity who admires with joyous wonder the Greeks for harmonious development of all their powers, for the noble freedom of their whole disposition, for the distance they kept between themselves and all menial tasks, for their distinguished indolence and their high esteem of the inner man, notices not without shame and dejection that almost all of us, by contrast, develop only a few talents and those one-sidedly, that our freedom of thought tolerates many a shackle, that laborious sociality lays waste a great part of our lives, and that we often reject our inward development in favor of the outward influence we may come to exert. On a wave of noble zeal such an observer will condemn the orientation of our age and wish back those happier times. But if he carefully studies the step by step development of the human spirit, from its first beginnings, he will find that man must necessarily always make his way from that character-unity which belongs solely to imagination and inward sensation, through a one-sided development of individual capacities, up to fully rounded maturity through reason. And he will then come to recognize the use, as well as the measure, of the seeming lopsidedness with which our age is so often reproached. [II, 14]

On the ideal, as opposed to the historical, view of the Greek influence on modern times

Our time finds itself in a situation regarding antiquity which was quite foreign to antiquity itself. In the Greeks we have a nation before our eyes in which, according to the criterion of our own most fervent inward feeling, all that which preserves the highest and richest forms of human existence had already ripened to a final perfection. We look upon them as though they were a human type made from a nobler and purer stuff than ourselves; we look upon the centuries of their efflorescence as though it were a time when nature, freshly emerged from the workshop of creation, had maintained a yet undiluted relationship with the creative powers. To us it seems as though, hardly looking backward or even forward, the Greeks planted and founded everything anew, and in unassuming simplicity, relaxedly pursuing their way, exhaling with each breath a natural yearning of their bosom, they erected for us models of everlasting beauty and grandeur.

Our study of Greek history is therefore a matter quite different from our other historical studies. For us, the Greeks step out of the circle of history. Even if their destinies belong to the general chain of events, yet in this respect they matter least to us. We fail entirely to recognize our relationship to them if we dare apply the standards to them that we apply to the rest of world history. Knowledge of the Greeks is not merely pleasant, useful or necessary for us—no, in the Greeks alone we find the ideal of that which we ourselves should like to be and produce. If every other part of history enriches us with its human wisdom and human experience then from the Greeks we take something more than earthly—something almost godlike.

For what other name shall we give to a sublimity whose unattainability, instead of discouraging us, raises us up and spurs us to do likewise? If we compare our constricted, narrow-hearted situation, oppressed by a thousand shackles of caprice and habit, splintered and scattered by countless petty occupations which nowhere deeply reach into life with the Greeks' free activity, their pure striving for the highest in humanity; if we compare our works, painfully and slowly maturing by constant trial and error with theirs, streaming forth from their spirit as though from the fullness of freedom; if we compare our gloomy brooding in ascetic solitude or else our thoughtless drifting on the loose connections of sociality with their serene joyousness in their citizens' community, joined together by the holiest bonds—any such comparisons, one should think, would make us sad and downcast, like the prisoner's recollection of unhindered joyous freedom, the sick man's of sound health, or the northerner's memory of an Italian spring.

But the contrary is true. Only our ability to transfer our spirits into those times of antiquity can lift our hearts and widen our mind's horizon and recreate for us our original, not so much lost as never possessed, human freedom, so that we can return with fresh courage and renewed strength to our own, so very different situation. Only from their never-drying wellspring can we take our true inspiration. And it is precisely our deep insight into the chasm that fate has placed evermore between them and us that incites us to reach our own proper stature, aided by wings lent us by our contemplation of them. We imitate their models in full consciousness that they are unattainable; we fill our imagination with the images of their free, richly gifted life, knowing that such life is gainsaid us, just as the effortless existence of the inhabitants of Olympus was gainsaid them.

And perhaps this may do for a proper analogy of our relationship to them. Their gods, like themselves, incorporated the human form and were formed from human material; the same passions, joys and griefs, moved their breasts; the trials and tribulations of daily living were no stranger to them; hatred and persecution reared their violent heads in the halls of the divine mansions. Mars lay dying among slain warriors; Hermes painfully wandered over the solitary wastes of the ocean; Latona felt all the afflictions of the mother-to-be, Ceres all the terrors of the mother bereaved. So likewise do we find in Hellas all life's unevennesses; not only the tribulations which befall individuals and nations, but the most violent passions, deviations, and crudities of untamed humanity. But just as the unique splendor of cloudless Olympus melted and dissolved those darker colors, so do we find something in the Greeks which never lets down the life of the feelings, which erases the harshness of earthliness, transforms the overflow of energy into exuberant play, and gentles the brass-hard pressure of fate to a mild earnestness.

This something is the ideal-oriented quality of their nature. Their whole unique appearance, their deep impressiveness which the coldest, most objective comparison of them with the works and nature of other peoples cannot erase, stems from the fact that the Greeks touch just that point in us which is the ultimate goal of all our own strivings. We are left with a vivid sense that they reached the summit in their own way, that they have attained the goal which enables them to rest at the end of their appointed course. But their greatness is so pure and true, its origins so genuinely rooted in nature and humanity, that they move us, not with compulsion to be more like them, but with inspiration to be more ourselves. They attract us because they heighten our independence and relate themselves to us only in the idea of ultimate perfection of which they are an undeniable model, permitting us to work toward it ourselves, although in different ways and by a different route.

It requires perhaps a very intimate acquaintance with the works of the ancients not to consider the assertion of their superiority and its unattainability a biased exaggeration. One fact about them which very easily produces a bias in their favor is precisely that it takes neither a scholarly mind nor long study to develop a taste for their works. They leave the deepest impression in the most naïve hearts, those as yet unburdened with any philosophic or esthetic considerations. And it is notable that they find entry into any nation, any age, and any psychic constitution, in contrast to modern works which, springing as they do from a less universal, less objective mood, demand also a more individual and subjective reception. Shakespeare, Dante, and Cervantes will never produce such a wide-spread general influence as Homer, Aeschylus or Aristophanes.

To compare modern works of any genre (except from the point of view of progressively advanced information or mechanical skill) demonstrates a view of antiquity as erroneous as the esthetic one which attempts to compare the beauty of real objects with the beauty of art objects. For, just as art and reality lie in two different spheres, so do antiquity and modernity. Nowhere, in the realm of phenomena, do they touch. And in the realm of truth they touch only in that place where idea, but never perception, reaches, in the reservoir of the archetypal energies of nature and humanity. Of this, art and reality are two different images, just as antiquity and modernity are two different efforts of dealing with existence.

Surely reality is not a whit less noble than art, for reality (which is to say truth and nature herself) is itself the model of art. And its character is so great and sublime that, in order to draw at all close to it, we can only do with it what art does: embark on our own incomprehensible way. For the tiniest object of reality is completely drenched by and expressive of the entire character of reality as such. It is quite incorrect to assume that nature in its completeness exists only in all its particular objects taken together, or that the totality of its living energy is met only in the sum of all the particular movements of its existence. They may appear in this fashion, to be sure, but we cannot imagine the one divided and separated in space, nor the other in time. Everything in the universe is one, and one is all; else there is no uni-verse. The energy that pulses in the plant is not merely a part of, but the whole energy of nature; else there opens up an unbridgeable gap between it and the rest of the world, and the harmony of organic forms is thereby irreparably destroyed. Each present moment comprises within it all the past and all the future. For there is nothing for the transitoriness of the past to fasten onto except the durability of that which now lives.

But reality is not the vessel which can transmit to us its own character. Or better, the character of reality never reveals itself in reality itself, except as an archetypal truth. And truth in that form is inaccessible to us. Since we do not comprehend the existence of real objects by means of their own inner life, we try to explain it through the influence of external forces and thereby fail to recognize both its completeness and its independence. Instead of believing in an organic form of a real object, conditioned by its inner content, we believe it to be constricted by its outer boundaries—an error which we do not make in the case of art, because art represents the character of nature not as it is in itself, but as it is comprehensible to our sense organs, harmoniously predigested for them.

It must be remembered, however, that our human life is not such a stepchild of fate that it too, at its very core and quite aside from the realm of art, doesn't contain something by means of which we may draw close to the character of nature herself. This something I call passion. Let us not throw the word away on the inferior affects by means of which we ordinarily love and hate, strive and despise. Deep and rich psychic constitutions know a desiring for which the word "enthusiasm" is too cold, "yearning" [*Sehnsucht*] too quiet and mild, yet in the throes of which a human being nonetheless remains in perfect harmony with the whole of nature; a state in which urge and idea in a manner incomprehensible to cold prosaic thought are merged, bringing forth the loveliest offspring. Caught up in passion in this sense, we truly experience a more correct recognition of the idea which appears in reality, and one may say truthfully that friendship and love, in their lofty, pure inspiration, contemplate their object with more seeing, more holy—as it were—eyes than does art. But such is reality's fate that it places its objects before us sometimes too high, sometimes too low; it never permits the full and beautiful balance between the phenomenality of the object and the perceptive capacities of the observer which results from the inspired and fruitful, yet always peaceful and quiet enjoyment of art. It is not nature's fault, therefore, but our own, that nature seems to lag behind art. And if a high valuation upon art is the sign of an era of human advance, then a high valuation upon reality is even more so.

But we meet with that full and beautiful balance only in antiquity, never in modern times. The ancients had a way of looking at and dealing with life, whereby the pure and original natural energy of humanity seems to have burst all its shells so happily, that it presents itself to our eyes in clarity and simplicity, completely visible at a glance, like a half-opened blossom. The humanity of the Greeks did not seem to have to peer painfully at the road it wanted to take; it did not seem anxiously concerned over what it might be leaving behind. Instead, yielding itself trustingly to an unrestricted longing for measureless fullness of life, it expressed what it longed for in myriads of images, always happily chosen. We moderns engage in endless search and research; we wrestle and do battle; we often know bloody sweat, but seldom the joyous ease of victory; we deplete ourselves by our lonely, scattered, and solitary existence; we never know the well-being, the buoyancy, that lifts the heart of each citizen when he knows himself a part of a congenial people, on a soil richly sown with monuments of its fame and its art, beneath a serene and smiling sky.

And so we can find just the same characteristics which, in our contemplation, differentiate reality (in its particular, restricted aspects) from art, also differentiating modernity from antiquity. Like art, everything ancient is the pure and full expression of a spiritual quality: it leads to the universality of ideas; it invites us to immerse ourselves ever more deeply in each of its particular aspects; bound voluntarily by its magic, our spirit confines itself to definite boundaries which alone enables it to widen these to infinity. Our modern style, on the other hand, like reality itself, provides more of an intimation, a hint, of the spirit rather than a real, unmediated and spontaneous expression of it; it frequently knows no unity other

84

than that upon which feeling, moved by reality, concentrates and focuses; it often exerts its best and loftiest effects only by leading us beyond itself and its own horizons. And even when it is suffused by the same spirit as that of antiquity and exerts similar effects, it leaves something out, as on a cloudy day there is missing from a landscape that luminousness which alone fuses all objects together, melting and blending them indissolubly with its own clarity and splendor.

For let man worry and choose and try as he may—the tenderest and the sublimest works of his hand, those that stream from the artist without his knowing it and flow over into the observer without his being able to give an account of them—he owes only to a happy constitution of his nature and to the favorable mood of the moment. Let man be armed with as much genius and as much will power as human nature may ever produce—yet what shines resplendent from him is just that which he himself is not: the hereditary reservoir of strength that produced him, the soil which carries him, the nation whose language echoes round about him. Man belongs to nature; he is not meant to stand alone and segregated; the word of his mouth is an element in or an echo of nature's sound; the image he casts carries the outline of that mold in which nature, too, poured her images; man's entire faculty of willing takes its impulse from nature's creative powers. This does not lessen his independence, for, in the totality of reality, nature's energy is his own, and in the world of phenomena, everything—nation, soil, sky, environment, past and present—is closed off to him, speechless and dead, except insofar as he unlocks it by his own inward energy that knows how to perceive these things and infuse them with life. That is why it is the surest mark of genius to draw attention, everywhere, in every expression of energy, but especially in that most complicated one, life itself, by means of admiration, of contempt, love or hatred, to that which inspires, admonishes, and urges. And where reality yields no such element, genius evokes a new and more beautiful world out of the past. But these are aids to which we moderns are compelled to take recourse; the ancients met everything they needed close to home, and their environment corresponded perfectly to their innermost desiring.

Be that as it may, a modern sculptor (to mention the field where competition with antiquity presents the greatest difficulties) might well vie with the works of the ancients, so far as excellence is concerned. Genius can still occur, as formerly; technical studies have advanced on a long, painstaking road since ancient times, and skill, enriched by this and by centuries of accumulated experience, has made great progress. But what can never be attained, what divides antiquity from modernity by an unbridgeable chasm, is the breath of ancient days that covers the simplest potsherd, as it does the perfect masterpiece, with an inimitable magic. It is not the property of any particular sculptor; it is not part of a certain technique, nor even of art itself: it is, rather, the reflected glow, the flowering, of a nation and an era. And since these shall not return, it too is irreparably lost with them. For it is the melancholy yet proud prerogative of living things that they never reproduce themselves in the same way again, that the past in them is forever past.

All works, naturally, that have even the slightest degree of individuatedness, are similar in that they express more than the object they immediately represent. But what differentiates antiquity over and above this are two further considerations. One, that the mood of the moment and the character of the artist (and through him, that of his environment, his era, and his nation) are dominated by a wondrous, magic harmoniousness. Two, that all these things are so at one with the idea-to-be-expressed, that they do not, personality-like, oppose it in the work, but merge with it to a greater effectiveness. The peripheral factors, thus, with their subjective power, make the work more objective. This could not be the case if the humanity which speaks to us from ancient times were not a clearer, purer, or at least a more easily recognizable expression of those archetypal ideas for which each genuinely human bosom longs, or if these ideas did not inflame and inspire them more ardently than we are ordinarily justified in even intuiting.

That "breath of ancient days," then, is the breath of a lucent humanity, irradiated by godliness (for what is godlike if not the archetypal ideas), and it is such humanity that testifies through the works of art, the poetry, the constitutions, the battles, sacrifices, and festivals of the ancients; testifies against our dullness and half-heartedness, but at the same time testifies loudly and spiritedly in behalf of that which human beings might become and toward which, by our different, own, appointed way, we too may strive. For it would be unfortunate if the superiority of antiquity communicated itself only in dead marble instead of—equally elevating and inspiring—in customs, attitudes and deeds. . . .

The real superiority of the Greeks over us, whether by merit or by accident, wherein we cannot possibly undertake to vie with them, is . . . their inborn, as it were, sense for the most lucent, most particularized, and richest revelation of the highest sum of human life in their individual as well as their national character.

That they found this highest of all achievements, they owe to the simple constitution of their nature; their success in the most difficult of all the arts, the art of life itself, they owe to a natural instinct-like urge to which they yielded themselves freely and without reservation.

All individuality rests upon, or rather expresses itself in, an urge and is one with that which is peculiar to itself. We recognize each creature in its totality, in the concept of its nature, from the lowest through the highest forms of life, less by its way of being than by its way of striving. Only in the latter state do all its past, present, and future cohere in a single unity. As we can imagine life neither standing still nor moved by an external mover, so does the whole universe subsist only in urge; nothing lives or exists except insofar as it strives to live or exist, and man would be indisputable lord and master of his life and his whole existence in time if, by an order of his will, he were able to destroy his life-urge. This urge is, of course, determined and itself determines the forms of life. All differences among living creatures, among plants and animals, among the manifold species of the latter, among nations and individuals in the human species, rest solely upon the differences in their life-urge and its ability to work through, and against, whatever resistances it finds. . . .

What is here called "urge" [*Trieb*] should perhaps more correctly be called "self-acting, or spontaneous, idea" [*selbstthätige Idee*]. But I avoided this otherwise synonymous expression because it may lead to the misapprehension that the idea lies ready and waiting only to carry itself out gradually, in time. According to my conviction, however, the workings of nature's fundamental energies, the epitome and the norm of all ideas, consist in activity which defines and determines itself only through its own operations. . . .

That irresistible urge which yet springs from that part of the psychic constitution which is ruled by self-given law, is called, by Germans, *Sehnsucht* [yearning]. It is a term duplicated by no other nation (and the German language is by preference at home in that realm which, in order to be fully surveyed, requires the aid of feeling and sensation); according to it, man has a definite character only insofar as he knows a definite *Sehnsucht*. Such a one stirs in every human being, but few are so happily constituted that they are able to reveal it, pure and well-defined, not diffused by contradictory affects, and still fewer that they advance on a genuinely ideal course toward the archetypes of humanity. Rarest of all is the good fortune that comes when these two conditions are fulfilled and the external environment as well fully accords with man and enables him to gain new strength from his satisfaction with this state of accord.

The ideality of a character depends on nothing so much as on the depth and the kind of *Sehnsucht* that inspires it. For the expression of ideality adds something to morality (something other, not greater, for morality itself always remains at the highest level of all), something more comprehensive, since an ideal character does not merely subordinate itself to a single idea (as the simple moral character does to duty), but rather forms itself to be a fitting accompaniment to all ideas, to the entire invisible world. For, as the artist strives to produce an object of art, the ideal character strives to produce an attitude which (as art does beauty) should represent all humanity (in its nobility and its dignity) within the confines of one particular case. Such a character is, in the true sense, creative, because it transforms the idea of highest humanity, ordinarily only intuited by thought, into a fact of nature. For this one needs more than correct thinking or practiced will power; for this, the entire psychic constitution must be made capable of something which far outreaches concepts or sensations; something which, when it seems to freely form the imagination, is taken creatively out of the depths of nature. The archetypal idea, in other words, which makes up the soul and the life of nature, from which comes all meaning and all form, must appear to our whole feeling-life and awaken that love whose spontaneous, unmediated, natural fruit is that high and godlike *Sehnsucht.*

Sehnsucht may sound to many people like the trifling, dallying expression of a sentimental era, and they may wish to substitute the more directly vivid, active term *Streben,* striving. But *Sehnsucht* and striving, even if both are taken in their most elevated context, are by no means synonymous. *Sehnsucht* expresses also the unattainability of that which is yearned for, and the mystery of its origin; striving, on the other hand, suggests the road between a clearly thought out concept and a definite aim. Striving may be weakened or thwarted by difficulties and obstacles; in *Sehnsucht* there lies a magic which casts all shackles, broken, to the ground. The artist when he invents or plans *yearns* to reach that beauty which hovers in a yet unfixed form before his imagination; after formulating his notion he *strives* for its faithful execution. The Roman felt a zealous, earnest, powerful striving from which grew connected activities and sure, progressive results. The Greek was inspired by *Sehnsucht;* his intentional and worldly activity was often very diffuse and not all of a piece, but, on the side, unsought, there germinated the heavenly, enchanting blossom of his *Sehnsucht.* There are many aspects of *Sehnsucht.* There is its relationship to the world, the way in which the greatest undertakings (whether directed toward the freedom and fame of a fatherland or toward the well-being of humanity in general) are ennobled by *Sehnsucht* because *Sehnsucht* above all else enables us to catch a glimpse of the archetype which . . . is to be the cast of reality. There is the fact that no man deserves being called great, though he were the greatest benefactor of mankind, if the breath of *Sehnsucht* has not somehow touched him. All these aspects would have to be delineated in some other place if they were not already self-evident.

If one carries these ideas over into an attentive observation of daily life, one soon becomes aware, mostly by one's own example, that there are three educational forces operating on human beings. These are, first, the clarification of understanding, second, the strengthening of will power, and third, the inclining to that which is never expressed and forever inexpressible, of whose general nature are physical and spiritual beauty, truth in its ultimate foundations, and the freedom by which, in lifeless nature, form overcomes inert mass and, in living nature, free thought overcomes blind force. This third educational force might be called the education of the feeling-life toward religion if the term "religion" were not at the same time so noble and so ill-used that one must constantly fear that either one is desecrating it by one's own use or else desecrating what one has in mind by using the word "religion" for it. The first two educational forces can be the work of instruction and example; the third, however, is of the soul alone, and of the whole life experience. Above all it demands the happy tendency to let the world have an effect upon one and then to digest this effect in self-created solitude. Here is revealed what a properly attuned psychic constitution, mild and strong at the same time, may make of the manifold emotions that, like desire, love, admiration, adoration, joy, grief, and by whatever names they may be known, sometimes pay friendly calls, sometimes make violent visitations upon the human heart. For these and all the other affects are the true awakeners of that high and noble *Sehnsucht,* just as *Sehnsucht* may be looked upon as the cleansing agent of the affects, purifying and clarifying by its strength. In whose breast the affects have raged most frequently and mightily, in him (or her, for women are usually better attuned and in a better position for this than men) does *Sehnsucht* mature to its noblest and most beneficent powers.

Every worthy character demands strength and energy of will, but an ideally oriented character demands, in addition, that the intellectual urge inhabiting every human being become such a definite and predominant *Sehnsucht* in him that it gives to a particular human being his individuated, unique configuration, which at the same time to a greater or lesser degree widens the horizon of humanity as a whole. As life in general must be looked upon as a partly successful battle of the spirit against the body, so the forming of individuality by the rule of the basic urge which guides it, must be looked upon as the highest summit of life's victory. And just through this, it becomes the ultimate purpose of the universe. Take one's eye off it, and every effort, however apparently noble, turns into something low, mechanical, and earth-bound. The investigated, recognized, surveyed universe, the fathomed depth of truth, the self-attained height of feeling—all are vain showpieces of toying, wasted energies, unless they ultimately reveal themselves in the thinking, speaking, acting human being; unless they reflect back from his eyes what they have worked in him; unless his words and deeds bring tidings of them.

In each person there indubitably dwells such a definite character, just as there dwells a definite physical organization-urge. The difference between them is only that the latter (except in a few instances) always attains its end, whereas the former only rarely, at least to the degree that its raw material, completely subjugated, takes on its form, true and pure. It cannot even be properly assumed that—regardless of whether one believes that in some epoch of creation there had been a chaotic flood of forms-to-be-organized, and the outlines of present configurations and the present organs of life had for long seesawed back and forth before settling themselves into the present boundaries of species and sex—even so, I say, we cannot assume that there exists now a similar epoch of moral forms-to-be-organized, in spite of the fact that truly ideal-oriented characters do have the privilege of becoming, individually, representative of a species. Rather, throughout all time, their number will be small, and the smallest number of these will be those who appear in active life, such as Aristides, Socrates, Epaminondas, Philopomenes and others among the Greeks, Scipio and Cato among the Romans, Luther and Frederick in modern history. A somewhat greater number will reflect in their works, as do so many poets and wise men, a form transfigured more into attitude than into action, and the far greatest number will exhibit only single, predominantly worked-out features, mere elements of ideality, not ideality itself. And similar will be the distribution of character among nations. . . .

Nature and archetypal idea (if one may use the word "idea," taken as an absolute, for the archetypes in the universe which, gifted with independent energy, slowly and gradually organize and reveal themselves) are one and the same thing. Nature is idea seen as active force; idea is nature seen as reflected thought. In single human individuals both occur only separately; idea as mind, nature as desire. They can be related only imperfectly by means of will power (always within anyone's reach) or by happy genius. All type, or ideal, forms are more readily revealed where, as is true in the character of whole nations, nature plays a more predominant role.

Before an ideal-oriented character comes into actual existence, no one can guess what it will be or that it will be. It is a pure and new creation, not synthesized out of already known elements. Rather, a forever young, forever fresh, inexhaustible energy transforms its elements into a new configuration. To take, for example, some poetic characters: who could have imagined an Oedipus before Sophocles gave birth to him, who an Othello before Shakespeare? Or who could have believed a nation even possible, such as history shows us the Greeks to have been! But this is true of every individuated creature. Its idea becomes possible only by appearing as fact. . . .

But if individuality is to receive its ideal orientation, it must surprise by more than mere novelty; it must reveal a great, worthy, universal idea of humanity in such a way that it seems comprehensible only in this particular form, seeming to have been created by it. An ideal-oriented character must have enough verve and vitality to propel itself and its observers out of the narrow realm of reality into the wide one of mind. It must see life's serious side only in the seriousness of ideas which it awakens; it must rescue its horrors and griefs by transmuting them into sublimity, widen its joys and pleasures into gracefulness and intellectual serenity and cheer, appear, in all life's battles and dangers, as the protagonist who is meant to gain for humanity all that is great, noble and imperishable in it, and vanquish all that is low, limited and transitory. For these reasons, the least dispensible condition of life for the ideal-oriented character is freedom in every best sense of the word; profound love for wisdom and art its faithful handmaidens; gentleness and grace its unmistakable characteristics. . . .

Two reasons made it necessary, even at the risk of diverging from our main topic, to steep ourselves in the foregoing reflections. Otherwise neither the most essential trait of the Greek character nor our view of its relation to our times could have been clearly recognized.

If we had not properly touched upon the existence of deep and pure *Sehnsucht* in each human breast that lays claim to any nobility, if we had not drawn attention to this *Sehnsucht* as the principle through which each individuality receives its proper roundedness, we should never have seen clearly how the ideality of the Greek character was made possible only by these incessantly blazing, forever warming and inspiring flames. We have, in the above, seen the peculiar characteristic of the Greeks in a certain impulse which animated them to represent, as a nation, the highest form of human life. And we have said, further, that a native inclination led them, that their striving to be nothing more or less than complete, rounded human beings was inwardly most well-defined and outwardly extremely favored by circumstance.

But this striving, from the remotest times that we know anything of, already carries the stamp of that higher *Sehnsucht*. For the more the Greeks were complete human beings, the more they touched the ground with their feet only, as it were, in order to soar above it with their spirit. Everywhere they found their point of contact with the superterrestrial realm; beginning anywhere at all, they created for themselves an independent sphere of thought and imagination. Their dearest pleasure was sociality, communication of ideas and feelings; in their work they preferred processes to results. Too mobile to be tied down, they carried an amount of freedom into both their family and their public life that would be forever incompatible with complete stability of either; their very patriotism was based more on their love for the fame than for the prosperity or preservation of the fatherland.

Several of these traits, particularly the latter few, are usually found only in savage nations before their civilization; after their entry into civilized society such traits become obscured. But the Greeks are characterized precisely by the fact that, in the midst of civilization, they retained and developed them, their natural character thus turning directly into their ideal character. And this is again evidence of that *Sehnsucht* which faithfully accompanied them, at their archaic as well as their more civilized level, the aim of which was intellectuality and superterrestriality and, among these, specifically that which by creative imagination could be formulated in sound and in shape. Thus they had the happy fate of being able to strive for the ultimate goal possible to a nation, without inner contradiction or battle—instinctually as it were. For destiny rules nations as it does individuals; it gives richly to some, sparsely to others, and only a very few are privileged to become conscious, straightforwardly and without obscurity and confusion, of the efforts which they are destined to perform.

Secondly, a somewhat careful illumination of the nature of individuality was necessary because the investigation of destiny's economy with respect to individuality (if such an expression may be permitted), and the investigation into whatever character the nation and the centuries that we are here looking at have produced, and how much we may save for ourselves from its ruins, shall always be in the direct line of interest for a work such as this one. For since the goal of all human endeavor lies in the realization that the passing of centuries gradually builds up, in the realm of factuality, a progressively higher concept of humanity, no investigation which touches even remotely on history can afford to turn its gaze elsewhere, least of all one which involves the Greeks who undeniably form our link between ancient and modern times. And this is the view from which we proceed. Life should, through the fullness of its events, crystallize and create the archetypal ideas which are elevated above itself and above any reality. Man should possess the power, gained both by his own efforts and by a favorable destiny, to give birth to spiritual phenomena which, measured by the past, are new and, with reference to the future, are fertile. Just as art seeks—or better, generates—in ideal beauty a pure, uncorporeal archetypal idea, so should philosophy be capable of generating truth, and active life greatness of character. All things should evermore abide in activity—creative activity. All things should amount to the fathoming of the now unknown, to the birth of the now unseen. Each of us should believe that he is now standing at a point which he is about to leave far behind.

Whoever does not agree with these "oughts," whoever imagines that superior art consists only in the attainment of amiable truth, superior philosophy only in the ordering of clearly developed concepts, superior moral worth only in orderly happiness or in private and social perfection attainable to law-abiding citizens; whoever does not sense that beauty, truth, and depth of character spring from efforts which in their nature and methods are incomprehensible to us, which cannot be judged by existent standards but themselves, by their acts and deeds, provide the standards for being judged and judging themselves—all such people will have to part company with us right here. Everything we have already said about the Greeks and their relationship to us must seem to them exaggerated and chimerical, and since the point at which our truth begins exactly marks the end of theirs, our paths obviously cannot coincide at any step.

After we have thus—not proved, for no proof is required—but . . . shown that the Greeks have an ideal-oriented character, and after we have thus indicated where, in general, it lies, we shall now have to define the nature of its ideality more precisely, especially in contrast with ours. For it is not our intention to describe the Greek character as such, but only to shed some light on its ideality, to answer the questions: Is it truly so? Or does it only look that way to us? What are its foundations? And how shall we treat it, to best benefit by it?

Enthusiasm is kindled only by enthusiasm. The Greeks have such a wondrous effect on us because the celestial *Sehnsucht* flaming through them expresses itself so vividly. Otherwise it would be completely beyond understanding how often even insignificant fragments of theirs utterly overwhelm our souls, and how whatever contradictions or lacks or failings we note in them never disturb that basic impression. It has long been, and frequently still is, our blunder to compare their works with the genres among which science may classify them instead of with one another; and to search for rules and theories in them, instead of gathering from them, pure and clear, the great and graceful spirit of their creators. As long as a nation looks upon the ancient Greek works as though they comprised a technical literature, created with the intention of producing a scientific esthetic . . . just so long shall it erect a wall of brass between itself and the genuine Greek spirit, and thereby silence Homer and Pindar and all the heroic figures of Greek antiquity.

Only the spirit, only the way of thinking, only the view of humanity, of life, and of destiny, is what fascinates us in the remains of that era which was in possession of the marvellous secret of simultaneously unrolling life in all its multiplicity, convulsing the breast in profound upheavals, and controlling the flood of imagination, feeling, and sensation thus aroused by a rhythm at the same time stimulating and pacifying. One must to some extent be attuned to their mood in order to understand them, to recognize now their depth, now their delicacy. But it is notable that nothing hinders our understanding of them so readily as a one-sided, illiberal education, and nothing is less essential to it than technical knowledge or scholarship. . . .

Whatever interests man in man, it is not his bodily pleasure or pain, his external doings, that require the participation of his deepest, best feelings, but the extent to which he partakes of universal human nature, the interplay of its energy in action and reaction. When history attracts us, we do not demand to know how this or that mass of people pushed or was pushed, won or lost something, but we wish rather to see, experientially, as though in a panoramic painting . . . what fate can do to man and, even more, what man can do to fate. Nothing is more tiring than the multiplicity of reality, the countless number of its chance events, if at the end there does not shine through it an Idea. But even the greatest number of details seems little to us when our mind, guided by objects, discovers its way to an Idea. For the simplicity of an archetypal idea can be recognized, like a many-faceted mirror, only in the manifoldness of appearances. Wherever a human being, a human activity, or a human event, carries visibly, as though under a light cover, the archetypal idea which corresponds to it, it seizes most vividly our feeling life and reacts most beneficently upon our entire psychic constitution.

And such is the case with the Greeks. The Greeks treated all things symbolically, and by re-forming everything that drew near them into a symbol. They themselves became a symbol of humanity —humanity in its most delicate, pure, and perfect configuration.

The term "symbol" is not always correctly interpreted and is often mistaken for "allegory." Both allegory and symbol express, to be sure, an invisible idea in a visible form, but they do it in very different ways. When the Greeks surnamed Bacchus for his wings, or pictured Mars in shackles, these were allegorical ideas, as was the Diana of Ephesus. For these were clearly thought out ideas purposely attached to an image. But Bacchus himself, or Venus, or

Sleep as the pet of the Muses, as well as so many figures of antiquity, are true and genuine symbols. For, starting with simple natural objects—a youth in the full swing of his strength, a girl in her first bloom and her first consternation at becoming conscious of her bloom, the freedom of the soul in sleep, relieved from all care, roaming through the loosely interwoven realm of dreams—starting, I say, with these objects, the Greeks found themselves with ideas they never had before; ideas, in fact, which will always remain incomprehensible, which can never be understood if they are separated from their sensuous form, or which, if felt to be understood, are robbed of their individuality and their unique nature. . . . For the unique nature of a symbol consists in the fact that the representation and the object represented alternately invite the spirit to tarry and to seek ever deeper insight. An allegory, on the other hand, once its core of idea has been ascertained, is like a solved riddle, leaving us with cold admiration or with the easy, inconsequential pleasure we take in a gracefully successful form.

Mere allegory is quite alien to the Greeks; where it is found, it generally belongs to a late period. For where the sense for recognizing symbols has departed, it becomes easy to demean them with allegorical explanations. [III, 188–218]

Fairy tales and fantasies rest on human archetypes

It is very marvellous but very true that fables and fairy tales are by no means accidental or arbitrary products of the imagination of individuals; it always seems to me as though the nations and in fact the whole human race carried these materials within themselves in the form of a predisposition, and as though they were urged by something like an instinct to spin them out. This seems demonstrated by a certain monotony of content which all such creations carry within themselves and with which they continue to branch out. It would account also for the fact that the various tales appear in series, fitting into each other, thus making up a whole universe which runs along beside history and seeks to interweave itself with it. . . . Since my earliest childhood I have experienced configurations of men and of women, many of whom had no foundation whatever in my real experience, and others of whom only the palest reflection in reality which has since then disappeared entirely. When I was a child, into my fourteenth or even sixteenth year, I lived within their sphere until life shooed them into the background, but they still appear to me at times. [To Caroline v. Humboldt, March 1818]

MAN IN THE PHYSICAL UNIVERSE

Man must be looked upon as a product of nature

One must always contemplate man, even in his loftiest endeavors, as a whole product of nature, one of whose sides he shares with the animal world. [V, 378]

Poor reasoning may be forgiven or corrected; a faulty view of objective nature is fatal to the scientific spirit

No treatment of philosophical objects is more harmful to the establishment of truth than when one overlooks the true and original nature of things and fancies that one has surveyed and even exhausted with one's concepts that which in its true configuration can never be wholly realized. No blame is more properly depressing for an author than that he has burdened his material with the limited horizons of his head. Loose reasoning, faulty proofs, gaps in the chain of conclusiveness—all these can in time be corrected or filled in. Whoever is guilty of them demonstrates his unsystematic, possibly even his confused brain, but by no means proves that he has not the sense and the spirit to see and to discover truth, merely by lacking the ability to represent it adequately or to prove it. He will never clean house in the field of his science, but he is not thereby proved incapable of extending its frontiers. Whoever, on the other hand, denies real, incontrovertibly existent objects, thereby removes from reflection its true object; he closes off the paths on which we might find it and, robbing us of content, gives us empty words instead. [II, 87]

Physics and astronomy have made progress because they rest largely on speculation; sociology and psychology lag behind because true empiricism is needed for them

Assuming we had some sort of rational truth which would lead us to the necessity of uniform (moral or social) laws, we should nonetheless expect no clarifications about their nature or characteristics. Only observation of the operative energies and their effects, only experience in other words, whether it be the inner experience lying in self-consciousness or the outer experience lying in observation, tradition and history, may here be our teacher. The human mind has discovered the laws that govern the earth's movements, and the positions and various orbits of the planets of our solar system, and with exactitude and reliability it foretells the events which depend on these. All the more marvellous then that, familiar as man is with the revolutions of spheres millions of miles away, he remains a stranger to the changes that surround him, on which he himself has such tremendous influence, and which react back upon him. But these "laws of nature" rest, as does almost everything about which we possess reliable theories, on universal ideas about the extent and conditions of space and time, and on so-called observations which usually amount to the same thing in another guise. Whereas in the psychological and social field we are in a realm of knowledge in which everything depends on real, actual energies and on the nature of objects. Here only the insight of a particular individual may approach truth, and all universal ideas grow remote from truth in exactly the same ratio as the number of individuals from which they are abstracted grows. [I, 88 f.]

The conditions for a flowering of the sciences vary from those for a flowering of the arts

There is a tremendous but not always sufficiently heeded difference between the flowering of the sciences and that of the arts, between the flourishing of a true scientific spirit and that of a genuine esthetic sense. A period of flourishing science often owes its passing existence to accidental and external causes; a period of art springs only from an indigenously powerful or happily constituted nature. In the former, genius usually remains a stranger; in the latter, mere talents often appear in unabashed mediocrity. A period of science leaves us, at best, with materials for future research; art, when it is predominant, spreads light, warmth, and energy. To differentiate between all these matters which are often mixed up, to trace down that spirit from whose breath alone the dead letter of science may receive its living soul, is one of the prime reasons for this present paper.

The realm of science is so immense that it can be worked over in its most diverse parts and each part by most diverse methods. None of it is useless; on the contrary, everything contributes to the whole, provided it does not add false assumptions and thereby hinder clarification of other issues. . . . The spirit of true science by no means rests exclusively on high standpoints or comprehensive views. It is the spirit of truth, and honors equally the simple view, proceeding from perception and association, the sublime view, which relates all details to archetypal ideas, and the pure view, which looks for fundamental energies. The scientific spirit in its comprehensiveness embraces all three, but it does not feel alienated by any single one.

And now we have already expressed what we were searching for. True science must be imbued and animated by an intuition of a fundamental energy whose nature reflects itself, as though in a mirror, in an archetypal idea, and it must relate the total sum of appearances to it. The way into these depths, the impulse which leads to these heights, need not always be ventured upon; the entire circle need not always be run through. But the orbits must remain open, the sense for striving onward must be present, and false, conceited pride in a worthless possession must make way for modest search for a genuine one.

These concepts need further development, and the easiest way of clarifying them would be to stop a moment and look at their opposites. Now what resists and contradicts the true spirit of science is, on the one hand, one-sided clinging to experience and, on the other hand, mere logical analysis of concepts. Both tendencies displace genuine philosophy, and without the striving toward philosophy, no flourishing of science is complete, nor, for any length of time, pure and true.

We by no means wish to censure the endeavor to clarify and widen experience within its own rights. All experiential sciences, historical and natural, should proceed on their way undisturbed. Even if in their purely experiential form they do not comprise true science, they nonetheless contribute infinitely to the over-all structure of true science. Blameworthy is only the attempt to cut off all possibility for progress which lies beyond the realm of experience, or to apply experience as the only standard where man's spiritual and moral nature enters another sphere. Where such a view gains mastery over a nation, one is forced to give up the dimensions of depth and purity in science, many happy partial successes notwithstanding. For everyone then merely aims at the applicability of science. Since, however, human feelings and human actions are a part of life and of experience, they may be of considerable help in replacing some of the missing elements. For even if its sources are impure, the scientific spirit may still be felt properly through instinctive comprehension.

Such help is much less forthcoming where philosophy neither steeps itself in the fundamentals, nor spreads itself among experiences, but stops at mere logical development of concepts. This narrow circle is soon exhausted. Singled out, it rests on nothing and leads to no discoveries. A worthless pseudo-wealth in method hides sterile poverty, and the kind of analytical philosophy which does injustice to every substance it touches, above all to language which seems to be its very life element, can at best lend a hand to the formal tasks of the sciences. But it never reaches life itself, since it does not even fully permit the feelings their rights.

Mathematics, by its peculiar and admirable nature, can well help overcome both these erroneous approaches. It yields itself absolutely to the application to experience without running the danger of becoming impure thereby; it also analyzes each of its concepts down to the last particle while always remaining conscious (at least dimly) that its nature consists of something quite other than the transformation of one concept into another. On the other hand, the aforementioned erroneous approaches exert an influence on mathematics as well, not precisely harmful to its techniques but bad in the sense that mathematics lowers its own value, that it chokes out what would ordinarily be its natural yearning for true philosophy and, through conceit in its own infallibility and clarity even helps along the general intolerance which persecutes philosophy.

This is not how the Greeks pictured mathematics when they looked upon it as an indispensable exercise on the road to philosophy. The pure flame of the one should kindle the pure flame of the other. Their youthful sense, more unselfishly receptive for the inner harmony of the forms of thinking, helped along by a more leisurely life . . . was pleased by the admirable correspondence of mathematical concepts, as though by a true harmony of the spheres. They regarded it as a revelation of a much greater and more magnificent harmony, one which held the universe together and ruled the destinies of men.

Here we have the central point. Where thought enchants for thought's sake, there true scientific sense can lead thinking until it is close to its primordial source. Where it is used for purposes which do not lie in itself, there science may exist, but its spirit will not be alive. The demand of science, in all its manifold appearances, is always the recognition of the invisible in the visible. Beyond this there is nothing thinkable, but less than this science may not engage in, at least not for long. That such is its truest nature is best shown by the fact that only from this point of view can sense be made of it, and only on this path is it capable of inner growth. Only in this way does it accord with the needs of man, for whom it is not the final aim but a step to the ultimate and the highest aims.

But these are the very basic assertions which are denied not only by individuals but by whole respectable nations. The sciences are zealously confined to the collection and classification of facts and kept within the confines of their applicability. Speculation is considered dangerous for them, also hollow and empty in itself, and is therefore rejected. Or else it is restricted to being a brain exercise, or to clothing the more substantial and necessary sciences in appropriate garb. Hereon has rested for a long time the never wholly settled quarrel between Germans and other nations; and the same difficulty has become a source of division and conflict among Germans themselves. But speculation nonetheless retains its rights; only through it can each science attain its character of necessity, and only through it can there be such a thing as the scientific spirit, encompassing all individual sciences.

The objects of the sciences, the extent of their frontiers, can be measured not only in terms of the thinkable materials with which they work, but also in terms of the mental activity that they set in motion, and this latter way is doubtless the more correct one. Now reason can divest appearances of everything which belongs to them; it can confront a naked object with a naked subject. With this, however, and with the subsequent unavoidable questions

(Which of the two is now independent of the other? How is the subject its own object in consciousness? Is there, then, a subject which can never become an object?) we have metaphysics, the speculative science as such. Even if the mental mood which is directed toward the answering of such questions might be called an aberration, nonetheless the organization of a brain incapable of it would be as unnatural and unhealthy as the organization of a body incapable of running a fever. It is so much a part of the mind's health that, whenever the mind relieves itself of the turmoil of its senses, of the confused pressures of its business activities, of the sterile burden of its knowledge, it returns to these objects as though to its home. But even the desire for knowledge of phenomena leads to the same result. For the particular phenomena tend to guide the mind to the more general ones, in search for fundamentals, and so the very inadequacy of all finiteness so far as containing explanations is concerned, compels the mind to transcend its own frontiers. [III, 345-49]

Scientific methodology must draw upon experience which always includes both empirical observation and speculative philosophy

Upon comparing the manifold judgments that human beings make about actions and characters, one finds everywhere two totally opposed parties, each of whom denies correctness or fundamental dependability as regards knowledge of human nature to the other. There are those who appeal to actual observation, others who appeal to philosophical analysis; the former cite successful experiments and happy results as proof of their superior method, the latter a sure-fire, and in their opinion incontrovertible method of reasoning. To the first party belong those who are generally counted as men of the world, or businessmen, particularly those who transact important public matters in respected posts of authority, or else those who have sharpened their knowledge of people by extensive travel and observation of foreign customs. To the second belong the lonely thinkers who have, however, not specialized in a particular scientific field but who have chosen the same subjects as the others, only with a view to theoretical treatment rather than active intervention. Since most authors precipitate out of the second party, it explains the disadvantageous and strongly felt opposition between the two parts of public opinion: those who only act, and those who only think and write. The politician and businessman object to the theoretician on the grounds that the latter is ignorant of the world of realities; the man whose private life has involved him in various complicated, interesting, and subtle relationships objects to the poet on the grounds that the latter makes up such relationships merely in his head. The writers and poets, in turn, with equally proud contempt, reply that the active one may indeed know the fads of the day and the evils of the times, but they do not understand the inner, true, better, and higher man.

Doubtless there is much truth and much falsity mixed up in such mutual recriminations. But each, by uncovering correctly the failings of the other, hides therewith his own one-sidedness. True knowledge of human beings rests on experience. But experience presumes a twofold activity of the soul: observation of what is there or what has occurred, and the digestion of this observational material into an understandable result. A single phenomenon is always incomplete, torn out of context, unexplained, and ununderstood. Only through being related to other phenomena or to concepts can it receive the theoretic or practical formulation which enriches our knowledge or our wisdom. Insofar as an individual accords more emphasis to one or the other of these two basic activities of the mind, he departs from the course of true experience, either in a too empirical or a too speculative manner. This is the reason why the aforementioned warring parties can everywhere be found, especially in all the experiential sciences, and most particularly in those that deal with physical nature. [II, 146–47]

Comparative anthropology, in particular, demands the twofold methodological approach

Human beings develop only in relation to the physical things that surround them. Conditions and events which at first glance seem wholly heterogeneous to them, such as climate, soil, occupation, external arrangements of all sorts, combine in them to bring forth the subtlest and highest moral phenomena. Their once acquired moral nature is handed down and transmitted by physical means, by heredity, family, and race, and thereby their intellectual and moral progress acquires a share in the steadfastness and permanence of physical nature. . . . In other words, man's physical attributes play a considerable role in the formation of his character.

This is more plainly seen by looking at the human race as a whole than by looking at individuals. Great masses of people, tribes, and nations retain a common character sometimes for centuries, and even when alterations occur in it, the traces of its origins may still be visible. . . . Everywhere the acts of individuals reveal arbitrary will and preference, whereas the destinies of groups carry the unmistakable imprint of nature. How much clearer and better defined this would be if we did not have such a very short time of observation at our disposal and were not constantly hindered even in this by our lack and incompleteness of information.

For this reason, comparative anthropology is not only obliged to begin with experience, but to exhaust it as profoundly as possible. It must search out the permanent character of the sexes, the various age levels, the temperaments, and the nations, as carefully as the zoologist determines the races and species of animal life. Though all it ultimately cares about may be the type differences, anthropology must proceed as though it wished to determine solely the differences between actual individuals in reality.

It therefore characteristically treats empirical materials speculatively, historical objects philosophically, and the real qualities of people genetically and with a view to their further development.

The purpose of comparative anthropology is to measure out in their whole ideality the possible differences of human nature or—which is the same thing—to investigate how the human ideal type, which no individual is ever adequate to represent, can be represented by many.

What this science is seeking, in other words, is not a natural object but something unconditioned: ideals, or types, which are however referred entirely to individuals, to empirical objects, so that they can be looked upon as aims which individuals may approach.

If anthropology could fulfill this purpose without empirical observation of real nature, it would remain a purely philosophical and speculative science. In a certain sense, to be sure, this is just what it is. It can stop at the universal human types; it can analyze them and form single ideal configurations out of the single virtuosities thus discovered; it can collect around its constructs all the other characteristics without which man does not form a whole, and place them in the proper order and interrelationship. . . .

But in order to fulfill its purpose wholly, as outlined above, comparative anthropology must necessarily accustom itself to the strict observation of reality and even employ it as its starting point. Because

1) the more speculative methodology carries with it the great disadvantage of meagerness, both as to variety of forms as well as to the definition of each factor. Even the luckiest effort would not suffice to acquaint it with an individuality of any magnitude.

2) the positing of any ideal or type requires conscientious observation of reality. For an ideal or a type is nothing other than nature extended in all directions, freed from all limitations.

3) it can be applied to practical life only if it hews to empirical observation. It is vain to set up high ideals if there are no means for relating them to reality.

When scientific and philosophic methods are used in combination, the scientific method usually suffers; in this case, however, considerable danger threatens the other, as well. Since comparative anthropology seeks generic or type characters, it is easily persuaded to take them as partly more defined, partly more permanent, than reality shows them to be and human dignity permits. Such a tendency must be highly ruinous to the future development of human nature, whose whole nobility rests exclusively upon its possibilities of free individual development. This is the dangerous reef in connection with any judgment about human nature in general or in particular: one must take man both as a creature of nature and at the same time not altogether a creature of nature. [I, 388–91]

The scientific study of man demands the natural scientist, the historian, and the philosopher

When the individuality of human character, with the view to setting up its typology, is investigated, and the resulting materials are to be worked on not only as individual histories but theoretically, the methodology must partake of all the ways of nature study: it must be scientific, historical, and philosophical.

Man, individually or generically, is obviously a link in the chain of physical nature. Like other animals, he contains racial characteristics, and these races may continue pure or mixed. In this, and in other respects, man obviously shows predeterminable natural operations which cannot be in any way rejected, but only used and possibly guided. He is a part of nature and subject to her. He can be observed like her and—this being the distinguishing mark—he can be experimented with.

What stands most opposed to this natural, determined character in man is his free will. With it he may initiate or terminate actions without being driven either by natural necessity or by the exigencies of reason. He follows what we call chance, outward influences, or inner momentary impulses. What he does this way is also frequently physical, or subject to nature, since it does not proceed from any anti-natural principles, but it is the result of physical or other changes upon a free nature and therefore not admissible to calculations of natural laws nor capable of sustaining experimentation. From this side man must be treated historically. This is how he is; that is how he was. "Why" does not permit of a satisfactory answer.

Nature and free will are bound up together in a genuinely human freedom by reason. For reason brings about as much lawfulness as nature, but it does not affect freedom since it gives itself its own law. Here now we have laws again, but laws which emanate from an independent power outside the realm of phenomena. This is the proper field for philosophic and esthetic judgments.

Any theoretical treatment presupposes judgments according to laws and only insofar as human character is thus judgable, is it fit for scientific treatment.

Organic human nature, to be sure, exhibits laws which are effectuated regularly and unfailingly. It is a law, for example, that a part of the parents' individuality comes down to the children. But the complicated economy of the human body, its as yet incomprehensible connection with moral character, and the great difficulties standing in the way of experimentation in this field are the cause of those laws being as yet and possibly always very imperfectly understood. It has not been possible to determine, to return to our previous example, what is passed on through heredity, to what degree, and under what conditions there might be more or less of it. Or to mention something relatively simple, we have no general method or formula which enables us to be acquainted with the physical and physiological qualities of an individual taken as a whole. We observe and know only isolated traits and features which allow us to draw no or few conclusions.

The greatest amount of discipline and lawfulness may be found in a philosophical treatment, but even here more where it legislates man's behavior, relatively little where it seeks to find the real connections and relations between his various capacities and functions, in the interest of science alone. It can and will define and clarify single relationships, but since they never exist in completely isolated instances, since the cases as they are investigated are never the cases as they are given, man's inner intellectual and moral conditions will never be faultlessly represented nor completely exhausted.

The smallest amount of lawfulness goes into a historical treatment. All historical detail seems as accidental and arbitrary as the accident and arbitrariness which produce it. Yet if one looks at large groups from a historical point of view, certain events will recur, though less regularly and extremely difficult of observation.

The materials of comparative anthropology, therefore, are not wholly suited to scientific treatment, in fact hardly to theoretical consideration. However empirical the approach has to be, the individual phenomena do exhibit a certain steadfastness, sequence, and lawfulness, and the latter especially may be expected to increase with our widening knowledge, with the refinement of human nature, and with the simple lapse of time. Hence today's observer must stay as close to empirical reality as possible, but must constantly keep in mind a philosophical methodology, to be applied strictly whenever possible, partly in order to organize the facts he will have amassed, partly to be able to make decisions about the characters obtained through observation.

Whoever wishes to do this successfully and would thus truly extend our knowledge of human beings, must unite in his person the various spirits of the natural scientist, the historian, and the philosopher. Like the natural scientist, he must proceed from the concept of organization, presuppose complete functioning in accordance with natural laws, explain everything out of the inner capacities of each individual under observation, look upon every capacity thus found as both cause and effect in one, and never take refuge in any but physical explanations. Like the historian, he has the duty to ask with complete, objective indifference what happened here, and no more; to look upon the single facts under his observation neither as though they were natural products nor as

though they were products of will; to avoid all temptation to proceed from causes and laws to phenomena rather than the other way
around, as is proper to him. For this is what distinguishes the historian over against the natural scientist and the philosopher: he
limits his dealings to that which has happened, and looks upon his
field as neither nature nor will, but fate and accident, for whose
individual caprices, at least in their detail, no one is responsible.
Like the philosopher, finally, our would-be anthropologist must not
forget that the object of his observations is a free and independent
being, for whom he must presuppose first principles, lying outside
the realm of phenomena, and who must be judged strictly in accordance with a certain kind of law, namely the ideals of reason. . . .

To find just the right mixture of these three totally unlike
methodological natures with any regularity, or worse, to form them
by some specific kind of artful education, should prove impossible.
In fact one almost always finds observers who are either too empirical or too speculative. The best school for psychological insight,
therefore, is life, and the greatest success will be had by him whose
own character is in a state of high cultivation, who is himself many-
faceted and also accustomed to judge himself in accordance with
principles. For whoever combines the necessary freedom with the
necessary lawfulness within himself, will not lack the receptivity for
grasping the given material, nor the strength to subject it to strict
tests in accordance with laws. [I, 394-99]

Each nation differs in its concept of what is nature

Each nation has its own concept
of nature. It calls "nature" what seems easy and customary to itself.
There is no concept equally important if one would know national
differences, and there is no other, perhaps, which should be defined
with equal care for the sake of character building. For whoever has

accepted and made his own the purest and worthiest concept of whatever may be called nature, is indubitably the man of greatest substance. . . . [II, 387]

Physical nature and moral nature form two halves of a whole

For the exploration and refinement of his moral nature, man needs a thorough and serious consideration of the physical nature which is all around him. This has been made easy for him by nature herself. For in the bodily part of his own nature he finds unmistakably expressed everything that he is supposed to strive for in his moral life. The eye of the average observer, to be sure, rests only rarely on the characters of this script, so close to him. A cautious fear of being deceived by empty fantasies often draws his attention away, and even more frequently, a lack of sensitivity prevents him from even noticing it. And yet it cannot be denied that physical nature is but the other half of moral nature and that events in either half of this whole obey but one set of laws. [I, 314]

The symbolic meaning of landscape: climate, sky, ocean, rock, trees

For some time I could not tear myself away from the summit of this marvellous mountain. For a long time I looked alternately at the wide landscape before me, bounded on one side by the sea and by a snow-covered mountain range, and on the other by infinity, and at the wooded depths below me whose profound stillness is from time to time interrupted by the chimes of a hermit's chapel bell. I could not keep from looking upon this place as *the* haven of quiet refuge where the human yearning, surely alien to only a very few, to live alone with oneself

and with nature, might find its complete and undisturbed fulfillment. And is it not reasonable to believe that nature has consecrated
a particularly favorable spot for each purely human feeling, one
spot to which a man can repair, if not with his physical self, at
least with his imagination and his thoughts? [III, 34]

*　　　*　　　*

The weather is so beautiful, far
more so than usual in our northern climate. One feels spiritually
and physically serene and inclined, more than usual, to spiritual
activity. It is surely an enviable advantage of the southern climate
to enjoy a relatively even temperature. In a way, however, this
sameness of nature has a joyless aspect, and is perhaps less conducive to spiritual activity. The arrival of spring is not such a
deeply and impatiently awaited event when the preceding winter
is very much like it. This of course affects the soul and if one may
assume, as I surely do, that every passionate or at any rate profound
sensation has its original basis in an impression of outward nature,
whether conscious or not, then one may well believe that yearning
cannot drive roots as deep into the soul and the sentiments of the
southern peoples as it does in ours, where since the earliest days of
our childhood every year we experience the great and deep yearning for the green and burgeoning awakening of nature after the
gloomy locked-up rigidity of winter. And since nothing in the soul
remains unrelated, this must have a deep effect on our whole way
of sensing and feeling. In our poetry, too, everything is done with
contrasting hues, with deep shadow masses that oppose the light;
and so many things are gloomier and darker, but also deeper and
more moving. The smallest occasion seems to give rise to the contrast between a light in outer nature and a darkness and solitude in
the inner feeling life. The strength of feelings and passions which
in the south flames with a bright blaze, is here more like a secret,
inward boiling and slow consuming. This sensation of longing in
us is emphasized and increased by our constantly looking upon the

southern skies, from our uncharming gloomy ones, as though they were our lost paradise, forever denied to us as a steady habitation. [To C. Diede, Summer 1826]

*   *   *

It is such a lonely, quiet, and yet heart-lifting and busy life [that of watching the heavenly bodies]. They are a visible bond with those who are far from us, and I could imagine nothing sadder than the earth if one had to do without them, if the sky were merely blue or black, if warmth and light emanated from the earth instead of from the sky. One doesn't readily think of it, but we would be in an absolutely desperate condition if the earth had nothing to be grateful for in the heavens. [To Caroline v. Humboldt, December 1817]

*   *   *

Those enormous masses of rock in the Pyrenees, not covered by any amiable green, often took me back to the earliest ages of cosmology. They are the image of ever-lasting inertia, of a load pressing forever on its own center of gravity. It threatens to collapse but actually clings ever closer and tighter to itself. What, on the other hand, tenses the imagination to the point of horror as much as the sight of the sea, its terrifying mobility, transmitting itself simultaneously in all directions with incredible swiftness, experiencing monstrous upheavals as the result of a seemingly insignificant impulse, threatening the entire globe with destruction! The everlasting inertia of the one—the everlasting upheaval of the other—both obeying blind laws, both bound up with dead, undifferentiated, enormous massiveness and materiality, both the wild, desolate elements of chaos: they are the archetypal figures with which nature demonstrates her sublimity to us. A dark, ununderstood energy moves them. Beside it, all spiritual energy grows silent and vanishes.

Like the plant which twists itself out of a cleft of rock, clinging to the harsh bluffs, living organization maintains itself in the midst of desolation, and like the spark hidden in stone, the urge to developmental organization leaps from it.

In every sensitive sketch-artist of nature one of these two elements—the dead or the animating power—visibly outranks the other. Homer and the Greeks preferred to describe nature in the multiplicity of her configurations and the fullness of her mobility. Ossian's nordic imagination tarried by preference at description of the raw, desolate, gloomy masses. But what we miss even yet is a poet who, with deeper insight than either, truly weds the formless mass to the developmental urge; one who, forever giving up dull description of any sort, will introduce us instead to the battle and the reconciliation of these creative energies themselves.

Such a poet might lead cosmogony onward by a few steps, but his main contribution would be the enrichment of our least fertile genre, that of didactic poetry, with some hitherto unknown models. For his poetic imagination would not primarily seek to kindle worlds with other worlds, or to string mythical fable upon fable. Rather it would wish to stimulate such powers in man that he might comprehend creation outside himself and learn to recreate similar structures within himself.

For in man, too, formless matter, undefinable striving, and indefinite urge struggle with ordering thought and configurating perception; in himself too does man comprehend these struggling elements only when they are separate. And through his imagination alone is it given him to relate them, at least for a moment's duration, in their original oneness. [III, 115-17]

*   *   *

I have a very special love for trees and do not like to have one cut down or even transplanted. There is something so sad about bringing a poor tree which for many years has been at home in one place to another plot of soil which, however unwell it may feel, it can never leave but must languish there and await its slow end. There is in trees such an unbelievable quality of yearning, anyway. They stand so steadfast and limited in the ground and move their branches as far outward from their roots as they can. I know of nothing in nature better qualified to be a symbol of yearning. Basically, of course, man is no better off, for all his mobility. However far he may roam, he too is bound to a bit of space somewhere. At times he may not even leave it, which is often the case with women. The same tiny spot sees their cradle and their grave. Or he leaves, but affection or need draw him back from time to time, or he stays away altogether and his thoughts and wishes remain bound and turned in the direction of his original habitation. [To C. Diede, September 1824]

On extrasensory perception

That a beloved person at the moment of his departure, or even later, might gain enough power over the elements and the world of the senses to appear to his loved ones cannot be understood with any concepts we now possess. Yet the human soul does feel some things which let us conceive such a possibility, though dimly as through a veil. Anyone who has ever been moved by yearning understands that it can be possessed of a strength which by itself breaks through the barriers of nature. It may well be that a certain receptivity is necessary to be aware of the presence of spirits and perhaps many of us are surrounded by spirits without ever knowing or guessing that we are. Why people nowadays see fewer ghosts and hear less about apparitions than did previous generations, can be more readily explained. Many of the stories formerly told were very likely false; not exactly invented but uninvestigated or based on unununderstood natural events. People had greater faith in many things, including such; they were more inclined to fear the supernatural; the notion of an evil spirit who torments and leads people astray was taken more literally and materialistically. But it may well be true, nonetheless, that genuine tales, truly supernatural events such as the one observed by you, were more frequent in the past. If that is so, an explanation is difficult, especially where such an event affected a number of very different people such as the ones in your household at the time. For an apparition or vision to one person might be more easily accounted for. I have said that a certain receptivity is necessary for the perception of extrasensory events. Perhaps it was easier for people to have this when they lived less wrapped up and involved in world events, when their psyche was more focused on inner happenings, and oriented more devoutly and earnestly toward a realm of being which lies outside earthly bounds. This might well have been the case with as worthy and deeply religious a character as your father. However it may be, he apparently accepted the matter properly, without undue fear or disbelief. [To C. Diede, April 1823]

*   *   *

[On Charlotte's having heard the warning voice of her mother] Of course you really heard yourself spoken to; that much is undeniable. It is equally certain that no mortal person spoke to you in the total solitude in which you say you heard the warning voice. You heard the voice *within yourself,* even if your outer ear seemed to do the hearing, and within yourself did the voice resound. There are many people who would explain this as necessarily being a self-delusion. They think that in a perfectly natural way, without any connection with a spirit realm, a person may well believe that he hears something which is actually present only in his mind, in his emotions, in his imagination, or perhaps in his blood. That this may also be so, in fact may often be so, I should not deny. But I should deny that this has to be the explanation and that there can be none other, or that with certain people and under certain conditions something else did not actually occur. . . . There is undeniably a quiet, mysterious realm which lies outside sensory perception; it surrounds us, and we have no inkling of it. Why should not the veil tear at moments and that be perceived to which no perceptible trace leads in ordinary life? You were being warned at a moment when you were about to write a thought down which was known only to yourself, when by the stroke of your pen you were undertaking something which proved to have many unhappy consequences for your entire life, and you were warned by a voice which would soon be altogether silent. In order to fasten your attention more surely, furthermore, the moment of warning came at what proved to be exactly one week before the moment of your mother's death. This experience was surely not of this world. It was one of the signs that happen rarely but do happen, to show us what ordinarily is divided from us by an unbridgeable chasm. I am very grateful to you for not having withheld this incident. [To C. Diede, September 1826]

* * *

It is a strange thing about so-called intuitions and premonitions. Sometimes they come true, sometimes not. We don't want to look upon either result as accidental, thus depriving them of any credit, if earned. Everything that rests upon inward consciousness of self partakes of this fate. It may deceive us, and one may take for omens what are not omens at all, or one may fail to recognize the genuine ones. There are no objective assurances. There can be no sure outer signs of insight into truth. There are always only hints, often slight ones; they may have lain long dormant in the psyche or they may be produced by a temporary condition of uncertainty, where the soul hovers between fear and hope. In the first instance one may depend on them, in the latter instance one may not. The wisest course remains never to tease them out of their hiding places, to remember always the possibility of error when they do appear, and to be prepared for their accuracy if their prognosis looks bad. [To C. Diede, November 1824]

On current estimates of rationalism and mysticism

It is remarkable how everywhere here [in England] there is a decided feeling to treat magnetism, mesmerism, and everything pertaining to it as though it were nothing but lies, deceit, and imagination. The cold—and more than cold, one might say crude and coarse—realism which is the order of the day hereabouts doesn't even permit inquiry into anything that cannot be touched with hands and explained with rationality. All experimentation and investigation is cut off, because the English start with the certainty that they are being deceived, and so it is not with this one thing alone but with everything. On the other hand, these same people permit quacks to treat them with universal remedies. One can make unbelievable fortunes here with these. [To Caroline v. Humboldt, December 1817]

*   *   *

It is remarkable: the time seems to be at hand for regressing to all the hidden and mystic matters which the recent past has found contemptuous and ridiculous. What actually might prejudice one in favor of such regressing is that the recent era of clear, pure, but by no means deep rationality really was blameworthy in many respects and is largely responsible for the weaknesses and excesses of the present.

Mysticism of course may easily go too far, but nonetheless there is more truth in it than in shallow rationality. The real truth of things always lies deep; it cannot be easily or clearly demonstrated and can only be found through a genuine and pure attunement of our entire psychic constitution, just as a pure tone can only be produced in a purely tuned instrument. [To Caroline v. Humboldt, May 1809]

The true nature of matter remains unknown

It seems as though nature wishes to do justice to the great physiological and elemental considerations before she can think of the flourishing, much less the happiness, of her sentient creatures. It is the same way in our domestic life: not only must high-level spiritual occupation yield to ordinary physical daily tasks, but the occupation with one's daily business is by most of us better thought of than our inner preference for reflection and the enrichment of knowledge. Obviously the same sense pervades both nature's and our housewifeliness: through physical and outward circumstances the soil is supposed to be prepared and secured before the spiritual and inward inhabitants may come to live there and blossom without danger. In manmade, imperfect arrangements this is very sensible. Human reason and human strength would not be enough to attain their main purpose without some sacrifice of better things. This explanation does not seem proper to us, however, when it is applied to a cosmic arrangement originating in the highest wisdom and power. Whatever we may say about the favor shown to physical rather than spiritual development seems insufficient. There must be something in it, as yet totally ununderstood by us, perhaps something founded on a totally unknown relationship between body and spirit. For even if we know very little that is certain about spirit or soul, the true nature of the body, of materiality, is totally unknown and incomprehensible to us. [To C. Diede, August 1834]

MAN AS A BEING WHO CAN
BE EDUCATED

Self-education is vital and depends on mutual tolerance

To form and educate and organize human beings is not only a task meant for teachers, religious advisors, and lawgivers. As man always remains a human being in addition to everything else he may become, he always has the duty, no matter what business he may engage in, to take practical consideration of his own and others' intellectual and moral education.

The universal law, not to be disregarded or violated, that reason dictates to all human community is this: each man and each community must respect the morality and the culture of the other; never violate them, but, where it can be done, aid in their refinement and intensification. [I, 380 f.]

Self-knowledge is the aim of education

In order for an individual to extend and individuate his character (and this is what all character building comes down to), he must first know himself, in the fullest sense of the word. And, because of his intimate contact with all of his environment, not only know himself but also his fellow citizens, his situation, his era. In this wondrous way, now, does the whole business of education simplify itself, even if taken in its widest extent. For it is only our own self that we may work on, only our own present situation that we may learn to know and to let such knowledge bear fruit in us. [II, 15 f.]

Education can only be stimulated, never produced, by external institutions

The means which are legislatively applied to promote the moral education of citizens are appropriate and useful only to the degree to which they favor the inward development of people's capacities and inclinations. For all educational development has its sole origin in the inner psychological constitution of human beings, and can only be stimulated, never produced by external institutions. [I, 70]

Any study, properly undertaken, may lead to education

Each properly undertaken course of study has an effect, aside from one's material enrichment in knowledge, on one's mind and spirit. It enlivens us, encourages us, opens new vistas and new directions for us. And this is its most essential usefulness. [VI-1, 137]

The education to be derived from travel

With today's means of communication, travel is seldom necessary in order to amass actual information about foreign countries. This can generally be done better and more comfortably at home, with a stack of good books. But travel introduces the mind directly to the various situations of the various countries, familiarizes it with their customs and their way of life (even if one already knows all about them) and is even useful if one goes to a place quite different from that which one wishes to study, because it furthers one's skill of adapting oneself to many different external circumstances. This is why travel is after all indispensable to any close observer of human beings, but only an already knowledgeable person travels with genuine benefit to himself. Whoever wants to learn as he travels is lost in every respect; one should only go see what one already knows. [II, 81 f.]

The benefit of the education that missionaries may provide

The great business of educating and converting savage nations, important as it may be from the point of view of that love which seeks to make all men one, has nonetheless had very little philosophical examination. Yet it really demands it, because religion too can be implanted in mind and heart only according to the basic principles of all instruction and education. Both Catholic and Protestant missionaries have hitherto believed that they had to uproot the old cults completely; and they offer the new without sufficient preparation. Or else they encourage the seeing of similarities between the old and the new dogmas and leave old errors standing under the name of truth. The latter can only result in pseudo conversion; the former too is harmful. By forcing a sudden transition from one extreme to another, it blocks the natural development of [Christian] ethical capacities which is so necessary for the consolidation of religious ideas, and thereby destroys the unique character of the nation. All savages have a concept of a Highest Being, and even in the crudest languages there is evidence of that Love which comprises the nature of divinity. The natural way would be to purify gradually the primordial religion of the savages, without moving them by either force or persuasion to disloyalty and ingratitude toward the faith of their fathers which—after all—includes their noblest feelings and their most subtle character inclinations. They should be shown, rather, little by little, that divine goodness has scattered everywhere the sparks of truth, but that there exists a religion in which its source never dries but flows forever, unclouded by error. And they should see for themselves that other human beings, impelled by no interests other than that for truth and for human happiness, have set out over distant seas and have braved countless dangers, so that they might bring these insights to them. [IV, 238 f.]

Children should receive early religious instruction

I spoke with Türk [his youngest son Hermann's teacher] about Hermann. He tells me that you wrote and recommended that he start religious instruction with him. . . . He continues to be of the opinion that one must not let prayer and everything else connected with the subject of religion turn into thoughtless habit which is what happens when one starts such instruction too early. He believes it is better to wait for specific occasions that might arise, which one can then use to awaken and stimulate religious ideas. There is much to be said for that point of view, yet also much for an early habituation of a child's thoughts to God. Even if the concept of the Being to whom the child directs his prayers is not quite clear or pure, yet what gets across and remains with him is the feeling of love, gratitude, and trust toward a highest unknown power. Naturally, no religious instruction, whenever given, can turn a character and mind into anything different from what it is. I remember my own and Alexander's very well. From a very early age we both had the same instruction in religion, and a good deal of it. I should say that it never, in any way whatever, "took" with Alexander. He didn't believe, and he didn't worry about not believing. In my case it was different, at least after the age of twelve or so. I reacted quite strongly against belief in any of the dogmas that were taught me, but I was, for quite a long time, quite pious toward whatever in religion seemed to me amenable to nature and to reason. I always applied the Bible verses to my daily life, too, and they still come to mind on suitable occasions. [To Caroline v. Humboldt, May 1817]

*   *   *

I am very glad that Türk has started Hermann's religious instruction at last. Last year, when I spoke about it several times, he always had objections, but I am not at all of the opinion that one should make a point of waiting for a favorable time to make religious impressions upon children. It is said, to be sure, that children do not understand religious ideas and that they treat religious exercises, if they are given too early, like mere habits, without any living sense. But even for grownups there is no such thing as understanding religion by understanding its concepts, unless one means by religion a certain rationalized deism, devoid of power or spirit, which was unfortunately the fashion for some time. On the contrary, a certain very simple understanding is possible to the tiniest child, I feel. That preoccupation with matters religious becomes a habit does no harm whatever; don't our dearest and deepest feelings become habits without in the least losing by that? And mere dead habit it need never become. Everything here depends on the manner in which it is done. It is really easy to miss the simple and good by vainly seeking an alleged higher and best; and it is a simple necessity for heart and mind—particularly under someone's instruction—to occupy and test themselves with religious ideas and feelings. It will not in the least prevent the later adult from going his own, possibly very different way, but it prevents him from going it inconsequentially or recklessly or, what is worse, from never experiencing subordination to invisible powers. How man stands toward the forces that are invisible to him determines and solely determines his entire inner fate, everything that can give him peace in the world, content for his solitude, and strength to bear misfortune and difficulties. It constitutes the knot in which life and death, time and eternity are bound up together, and whose efficacy will not be proved until one stands alone with the invisible powers at that last moment and sets one's foot across the threshold where no one follows. I myself am sometimes seized by a sort of longing for that moment, not that I wish to escape life, for I live gladly and happily, not that I expect some sort of wondrous bliss for I never particularly sought happiness here either, nor peace, for I have not been plagued by great restlessness, but because a spiritual yearning drives me, containing all the deep and overwhelming demands of passion but devoid of passion's tormenting unrest and its confused violence. It is the yearning to step, with serene mind and measured pace, unobscured and unshaken by illness if there is any strength left at all, out of a condition which one knows so well, in which one has many times tested oneself, and which one continues to embrace with love and gratitude, into another one, related to it, but totally new, where an entirely different and marvellous vista must open up before one. One steps into eternal darkness and presumably thereby experiences the genuine light; one leaves all and presumably only then becomes truly related. There is no more sublime sight than the sky, nothing more homelike than the earth and death unites us to both. [To Caroline v. Humboldt, May 1818]

On the necessary limitations of successful educators

He [a certain educator] has something womanish and at the same time coarse about him and is no good at educating the young. . . . I too have no skill whatever at educating, and as painstakingly as I have written on the subject, and despite the fact that some good things have come of it, I never had any real love for it. To be an educator at any level (and even the Minister of Public Instruction is an educator if he is right for his job) one needs a certain pedantic, complacent credulity as to the good results to be had from education. No one can get very far in the field who, like me, has a firm belief in the strong tendency of nature to care very little for education and to pursue its own ways instead. [To Caroline v. Humboldt, June 1806]

It is easy to do injustice to youthful individuality

If injustice toward completely mature characters is harmful, it is downright dangerous to fail to appreciate those who are only on their way toward full development. That is why it is so necessary but also so difficult for an educator to recognize true individuality. For youth, just like old age, . . . shows a considerable number of chance manifestations, some of which are merely passing but others of which are rooted very deeply in their nature. [II, 102]

There is a saddening and inevitable distance between parents and children

A dim sense that one isn't meant to go through life together with his children gives the relationship between parent and child a unique and poignant cast, often without one's being aware of it consciously. As long as the children are small, one doesn't feel it at all. But afterward the mood is that of the farewell hours before a long journey. It is something that each would like to conceal from the other. The wishes of the heart and the dictates of nature are no longer in harmony. I feel quite well that one doesn't always make this kind of sense of it. But there are moments in which one has the sense of total happiness and unhappiness, and existence continues to have worth only as long as one is capable of such moments. [To Caroline v. Humboldt, May 1801]

On the relative merits of higher institutions of learning

The concept of higher institutions of learning as the summit where everything that happens directly in the interest of the moral culture of the nation comes together, rests on such institutions being designed as places where learning in the deepest and widest sense of the word [*Wissenschaft*] may be cultivated, and where the contents of learning, produced not with the intention of serving education, but being naturally best suited for it, may be given over to the nation's mental and moral education.

Their function therefore consists in the inward relating of objective learning to subjective education, and in the outward connection of a student's completed schooling to his independent study —or rather to aid in the transition between them. But the main standard of reference remains learning itself. For if it remains pure, it will be properly applied as a whole, disregarding individual deviations.

Inasmuch as all such institutions can attain their purpose only by continual confrontation with the pure idea of learning, the principles ruling their administration are isolation and freedom. Since, however, human spiritual activity, like any other, only flourishes under cooperation . . . the inward organization of these institutions must produce and maintain an uninterrupted cooperative spirit, one which again and again inspires its members, but inspires them without forcing them and without specific intent to inspire.

It is a further characteristic of higher institutions of learning that they treat all knowledge as a not yet wholly solved problem and are therefore never done with investigation and research. This in contrast to the schools, which take as their subject only the completed and agreed upon results of knowledge and teach these. This difference totally changes the relationship between teacher and student from what it was when the student still attended school. In the higher institutions, the teacher no longer exists for the sake of the student; both exist for the sake of learning. Therefore the teacher's occupation depends on the presence of his students. Without them he could not pursue his work with equal success; if students did not assemble around him, he would have to seek them out just so that he might come closer to his own goal. He wishes to join his more practiced (but therefore more easily overspecialized and less spontaneous) abilities to their weaker (but therefore less prejudiced and bolder and more varied) ones.

What are called higher institutions of learning are therefore, if we divorce them from the outer form they assume in their relation to the government, nothing other than the spiritual life of those human beings who are moved by external leisure or internal pressures toward learning and research. Even if they did not exist formally, one person would privately reflect and collect, another join himself to men of his own age, a third find a circle of disciples. Such is the picture to which the state must remain faithful if it wishes to give an institutional form to such indefinite and rather accidental human operations. The government, when it establishes such an institution, must:

1) Maintain the activities of learning in their most lively and vigorous form and

2) Not permit them to deteriorate, but maintain the separation of the higher institutions from the schools, not merely the general theoretical schools, but particularly from the various practical ones.

At the same time the government must always remain conscious that it really neither brings about such results, however desirable, nor can it bring them about. It must remember, in fact, that its intervention is invariably an obstruction to attaining the desired results, that everything would proceed infinitely better without its help, and that the true situation is really as follows:

Since, in an established society there must be external forms and means for all sorts of general operations, it is the duty of the state to provide them for higher learning as well.

It must recognize, however, that not merely the way in which it provides these forms and means may be harmful to the nature of the thing it is supposed to foster, but the very fact that there *are* such things as forms and means is a disadvantage which serves to pull something lofty and spiritual down to a level of low and materialistic reality.

Therefore it is all the more the state's duty to remember the inward nature of the thing, and to make good what by its very intervention, even without evil motives, it has already spoiled or obstructed.

It may be argued that this is only a verbal viewpoint about certain governmental activities. But even just stating it will prove beneficial because under the influence of such views, the state will intervene more modestly and humbly than it would without them. It is a general practical truth, anyway, that any incorrect theoretical views the state may hold will never go unpunished, because there are no purely mechanical activities of government.

This much agreed upon, it is easy to see that in the inner organization of higher institutions of learning everything depends on the preservation of the principle that knowledge is to be regarded as something not wholly found and never wholly findable, but as something ever to be searched out.

As soon as one stops searching for knowledge, or if one imagines that it need not be creatively sought in the depths of the human spirit but can be assembled extensively by collecting and classifying facts, everything is irrevocably and forever lost, lost for learning which soon vanishes so far out of the picture that it even leaves language behind like an empty pod, and lost for the state as well. For only that learning which comes from the inside and can be transplanted into the inside can transform character; and the state, like humanity in general, cares little about knowledge and talk but a great deal about character and actions.

In order to prevent this error once and for all, one need only maintain alive and vigorous a threefold effort of the human spirit:

1) To derive everything from one original principle (which will progressively raise the mechanical explanation of nature, for

example, into a dynamic, an organic, and finally a psychic inter-
pretation, in the widest sense of the word).

2) To approximate all things to their ideal.

3) To relate such an original principle and such an ultimate
ideal within an idea.*

This is an ideal which cannot exactly be promoted, but everyone knows that among Germans especially, it will hardly need to
be promoted. The intellectual national character of Germans contains these tendencies, and one need only prevent their being suppressed, either by force or by antagonism toward them (which of
course also exists in Germany).

Since all one-sidedness must be banned from higher institutions
of learning, there will naturally be many people active in them to
whom the above triple endeavor is alien, as well as some to whom
it is actually objectionable. Such endeavor in its full and pure functioning can only be the work of a very few, anyway, and it does
not need to shine forth except rarely, for when it does, its influence
is felt far away and long after. The principal consideration must
be that those who have an inkling of its power respect it, and those
who would like to see it destroyed, fear to do so.

With this we rest our demands so far as the inner nature of the
institution is concerned.

As regards its outward, formal relationship to the government,
we ask that the state assure it an abundance (both as to strength
and variety) of spiritual energy by its choice of men, and guarantee
them their freedom to do their work. This freedom is threatened
not only by the state itself but by the very nature of institutional organization which, as soon as it is under way, takes on a certain
color and spirit and likes to choke out anything not in keeping with
it. This too the state must try to obviate.

The main thing is always the choice of men. Corrective measures against one-sidedness, insofar as such choice is concerned, will
be discussed in connection with the various internal sections of the
institution.

* For Humboldt's definition of "Idea" see pp. 145–47. *Tr.*

After choice of men, the next consideration is that there be few and simple but profoundly interdependent organizational laws, which again we shall take up in connection with specifics.

Finally, the aids to learning must be considered. Here we can only make the general observation that the heaping up of dead collections must never be taken for the important thing. In fact it must be remembered that it may readily contribute to a dulling and deteriorating of the spirit of an institution. The richer academies and universities have by no means always been the ones where the various disciplines enjoyed the greatest and most spirited treatment.

Something can be said specifically, however, about the relationship of higher institutions to the schools, and their pure as opposed to practical learning.

The government must treat its universities neither as though they were secondary schools nor as though they were special training institutes. And it must not make its Academy of Sciences serve as a technical or scientific (in the narrower sense) consulting committee. On the whole (some exceptions to this in the case of the universities will be discussed below) the state must demand nothing of them which directly concerns itself or its own operations, but must hold fast to the inner conviction that if the higher institutions reach their ultimate aim, its own aim, too, will be thereby fulfilled, and from a much loftier point of view than any that could have been arranged directly by the state itself.

On the other hand, it is up to the state to organize its schools in such a way that they work properly into the hands of the higher institutions of learning. This must be founded on correct insight into their interrelationship. The conviction must flourish that the schools are not called upon to anticipate the instruction given in the universities, nor are the universities to be the complement and completion of the schools—a postgraduate course, as it were—but that the transition from school to university is a division in the life of a youth which the school, when successful, produces so purely and clearly that first the young man may be given his physical, moral, and intellectual freedom and independence, and second, that he has acquired a yearning which makes him long not for idleness or for immediate practical activity when the compulsion of school is lifted, but for elevation to that spirit of learning which has previously revealed itself to him only from afar.

A young mind, thus prepared, will come to higher learning of itself. An equivalent bundle of zeal and energy, if its preparation were different, will bury itself in practical pursuits, thereby rendering itself unfit even for practical pursuits, or else scatter itself among unrelated facts without making a directed effort toward higher learning.

PRINCIPLES OF CLASSIFICATION OF
HIGHER INSTITUTIONS OF LEARNING

Usually one means by higher institutions of learning the universities and the academies of the sciences and of the arts. It is not difficult to describe these historical forms as though they were necessarily derived from principles intrinsic to them, but this kind of derivation, very popular since Kant, either leaves a lopsidedness or else is simply useless.

Very important, on the other hand, is the question whether it is today still worth the trouble to found or maintain an academy side by side with a university. And what sphere each of them, as well as both together, should occupy if each is to be activated to its greatest possible degree.

If one limits the university to instruction in and communication of learning, and the academy to research, one obviously does the university an injustice. Surely all the disciplines have been extended as much (more, in Germany) by university professors as by members of academies, and these men made progress in their studies just because they also occupied teaching positions. For free oral expression before listeners, a significant number of whom are also thinking heads, surely inspires a man who is accustomed to this type of work as deeply as solitary leisure may inspire another —that of an author, for example, or loose association with a number of academic fellow researchers. The course of learning is obviously quicker and livelier at a university where it is constantly rolled around in a large number of energetic, sturdy, and youthful heads. In any event, knowledge as knowledge cannot be properly presented without having it independently and spontaneously accepted, and it would be incomprehensible if a great many discoveries did not stem precisely from such direct interaction. Furthermore the task of teaching at a university is not so time-consuming and difficult that it could be taken as a troublesome interruption of private studies. It may rather be taken as an aid toward them. Besides, any large university contains some men who lecture very little if at all and only do research. For all these reasons, one could surely dispense with the academies and entrust research to the universities, provided they are properly organized toward this end.

The social, cooperative aspects of academic associations, which to be sure are not necessarily very strong among university professors, should hardly be considered a sufficient reason to found such expensive institutions as academies. On the one hand, such association is very loose even in an academy, and on the other hand it really serves a useful purpose only in those experimental sciences where ready communication of current facts and findings is useful. But for such subjects there will always be private associations which present us with no difficulties and which are totally removed from the intervention of the state.

If one pursues the matter somewhat more closely one finds that academies have flourished mainly in countries other than Germany, at a time when universities in those countries stood at a low level, and, within Germany, in locations where there were no universities nearby, or at times when our universities, too, were lacking a more liberal and many-sided spirit. In recent times, no academy has particularly distinguished itself, and in the recent progress of German science and art the academies played little if any part.

In order to retain both types of institution alive, it is necessary to connect them in such a fashion that, although their functions remain separate, their members do not belong to one or the other exclusively. This is where their separate existence can be of new and excellent benefit. . . .

A university always stands in a somewhat closer relationship to practical life and to the needs of the state than an academy does, since a university conducts one of the state's principal tasks: the guidance of youth. An academy, on the other hand, has to do purely with knowledge alone. University professors stand in a very general relationship, insofar as they share with each other the problems of outer and inner institutional discipline, but as regards their specialized work, they communicate with each other only at random, as individual preference may dictate; other than this they go their own way. An academy, on the other hand, is made for subjecting the work of each of its associates to the judgment of all.

Because of this function of an academy, its idea must be retained as the highest and last sanctuary of learning and as the body most independent of the state. We must risk the possibility that such a body by activities which are too few in number or too one-sided in quality will demonstrate that the right things do not always flourish best under most favorable external conditions. I say we must risk it, because the idea of an academy itself is beautiful and beneficial, and there may always come a moment when it shall also be implemented in a worthy manner.

Meanwhile there will be some rivalry and antagonism between university and academy, and the resultant interaction should provide an automatic balance between too much activity in the one and too little in the other.

The first aspect of the antagonism will be the choice of members in both institutions. For every academician should have the right to conduct lectures, with or without formal habilitation, without thereby necessarily becoming a member of the university. A number of scholars must be both university members and academy members, but both institutions must contain others who are members of only one.

The appointment of university professors must be exclusively reserved to the state, and it is surely not good to permit the various faculties more influence in this matter than an understanding and fairminded administrative body will do of its own accord. For antagonism and conflicts within a university are salutary and necessary. But the disagreements among professors on their specialties can, even unintentionally and without ill will, distort completely their point of view as to what is good for the whole. Furthermore, the quality of the universities is closely related to the immediate public interest of the government.

The choice of members of an academy, however, must be left to themselves, subject only to confirmation by the King which should present no difficulties. For the academy is an association in which the principle of internal unity is far more important. Also its purely scientific or artistic purposes are less closely connected with any interests of the state.

Here however arises the above mentioned corrective in the membership of higher institutions of learning. For since state and academy thus share the responsibility of appointments (the state for the university, the academy for itself), it will soon be evident what sort of spirit moves them, and public opinion will judge both impartially where they err. But since both will hardly fail simultaneously and surely not in the same direction, not all appointments are threatened at all times, and the total institution, comprising both academy and university, is safe from one-sidedness.

The variety of all the men working in all parts of both institutions should be very great, since a third class is added to those appointed by the state and those elected by their peers: the *Privatdozenten* who are carried, at least at the beginning of their career, solely by the approval of their listeners.

The academy may perform a unique function in addition to its academic studies by organizing laboratory research and experimentation in a systematic fashion. Some of these projects should be instigated by itself, others received in the form of commissions, and such commissions should be influenced by activities of the universities. . . . [X, 250–60]

Both heredity and environment are more influential than education

Important as the influence of education may be on the course of a man's life, the hereditary and environmental conditions which accompany him throughout his life are far more so. Where these three forces do not work hand in hand, education alone can make no dent whatever. [I, 145]

Formal instruction often provides more indirect than direct education

The story of your educational development interests me greatly. You comment quite correctly that the strong and lasting effect of certain experiences which came to you accidentally in contacts with adults rather than in the course of your regular instruction made their great impression because there were relatively so few of them and because they fell upon a mind starved for more adequate instruction. . . . I should not wonder, just the same, if just the instruction you got had not contributed more and better to making you what you are than if it had been a finer and more systematic one. One mustn't think of education as being only direct guidance to sensible behavior, good character, and sufficient knowledge. Often it works mainly by a concatenation of circumstances the intended effect of which never takes place, but which, by opposing the individuality of the pupil, brings about the results which direct influence never would have been able to achieve. For the results of education depend completely on the capacity of a person to work on himself at the instigation or through the influence of the educational force. [To C. Diede, November 1823]

Public education, being interested primarily in civic virtues, produces monotony

Any form of public education, since the spirit of the government always exists in it, gives people a certain civic form. Wherever such a form is well-defined and, aside from its inevitable one-sidedness, beautiful (as we find it in the ancient city-states, for example, and perhaps today in some republics) . . . it is not so very harmful. But in our monarchic states there is no well-defined form of civic virtue, and this is lucky for our humane education. . . . As long as a subject obeys the laws, keeps up a certain standard of living for himself and his family, and does not engage in harmful activities, the state does not care about other aspects of his existence. For this, public education— which to begin with aims at the civic person or the subject of government rather than the human being—needs no special virtue or aim. It seeks merely a balance, since balance is most conducive to the peace and quiet that the state is zealously seeking to establish. But such efforts . . . either produce a standstill in progress or a lack of energy, whereas the pursuit of individual traits and talents, made possible by private education, produces quite another balance, one brought about by the various conditions and relationships of life itself, and without sacrifice of energy. [I, 144 f.]

The most educative influence on human beings is variety of life situations

The true aim of man—not any which is suggested by changing preference but that which is prescribed by forever unchangeable reason—is the highest and best proportioned development of all his capacities, in order to form a wholeness of himself. Freedom is its first, indispensable condition.

But it demands something more than freedom, something which is connected with freedom, to be sure, and that is: variety of situation. The freest, most independent human being cannot develop properly if he is placed into a monotonous situation. [I, 106]

All progress of the human race depends on the education of its individuals

All reflection upon ultimate or distant aims invariably leads us back to the investigation of our present condition. For since such aims may be found in the highest, most definite, most harmonious development of all human capacities, they always lead back from the general to the individual, from the future to what is needful right now. Any attempt to promote the progress of the human race which does not emanate from the organic development of its individuals is barren and chimerical; if, on the other hand, the individual's education is attended to, its influence upon the totality follows of itself, and without specific intention. [II, 15]

Even more important than moral education is education for individuation

It is a prerogative of noble natures that the splendor which irradiates their inner self communicates itself to everything which they may call their own. Their subtlest and their sublimest opinions and sensations show in unadulterated purity through their acts, their speech, and their gestures, even through their very bodies and outward appearance, as through a very fine medium. To be developed in such a way—subtly, delicately, and meaningfully—takes a person who is not merely concerned with the lawfulness of his way of life, as is the duty of everyone, but one who thinks of and works on his own character as though it were a free-standing work of art. Such a person is suf-fused by a deep feeling for his own individuality, and deeply fa-miliar with the universal ideal of humanity. He creates an image in the depths of his creative imagination which he then works to give validity to in his inner and his outer life alike. It is this truly ideal-oriented developmental education which far surpasses even moral education. For it does not seek to bring about morality as such (morality being quite independent of all efforts, in any case), but rather strives to attune morality, along with all the other ca-pacities and functions of the psychic constitution, to a pure, total harmoniousness. But such education demands, quite aside from the necessary exercising of the will, a naturally favorable fate so far as both inner organization and outer circumstance are concerned. Of all the things which man pursues as aims of his life, this is the highest and the ultimate one. For it alone makes the sublimest human force, morality, at home in human nature, thereby lifting it to hitherto unknown heights. It is the one human effort that we should work hardest to support, for it is self-generative wherever it appears. Working upon feeling and imagination, it awakens the burgeoning that produces its like wherever its traces are felt. And if there is anything that one generation should hand on to the next, it should surely be that which is most delicately and pro-foundly interwoven with our inmost and subtlest organic natures. [II, 343 f.]

All development depends on maturity; there can be no skipping of stages

All attainment of a different men-tal condition can only be founded on one already fulfilled. We can only reach that for which we are ripe. There is no skipping in the development of one's spirit or one's character. [To C. Diede, Jan-uary 1834]

MAN IN THE REALM OF SPIRIT

Ideas and ideals:

What ideas are and are not

You ask me what I mean by ideas when I say that they are the only permanent thing in man and that they alone deserve one's lifetime attention. The question is not easily answered, but I shall try to make myself plain. Ideas are first of all opposed to ephemeral external things and to the sensations, desires, and passions directly referring to them. Everything which aims at selfish intent and momentary pleasure fights ideas by its very nature and can never be transformed into them. But many higher and nobler things as well, such as doing good, providing for one's family, all sorts of other actions, deserving though they be, are not to be counted as ideas. They may occupy a person whose life rests on ideas, but only insofar as they are something he does; other than this they do not concern him. They could of course themselves be founded on an idea, and in an idea-oriented and organized person they always are. This idea would be the one of universal good will, accompanied by a feeling that the lack of good will is a disharmony or an obstacle which makes it impossible to join the order of higher, more perfect spirits, the benevolent sense which infuses all nature. Such actions may also spring from a feeling of duty; and duty, if it originates in a pure feeling of "ought" without the least consideration for preference or divine reward, is one of the loftiest ideas. One must also separate from ideas what is mere knowledge of the intellect and of the memory. This may lead to ideas but does not itself deserve the name. You can begin to see now that "idea" aims at something infinite, at an ultimate relatedness, at something which would still enrich the soul if it were free of all earthbound connections. All great and essential truths are ideas in this sense. But there are very many things which cannot wholly be grasped or measured by thoughts and which nonetheless are true. This is where the artist's creative imagination enters the picture. For this faculty has the gift of representing the sensuous and the finite—physical beauty for example, even aside from beauty of countenance and its soulful expression—in such a way that it seems to pertain to the infinite. Art, including poetry, is therefore a means of transforming much into ideas that originally and in itself could not be placed there. Even truth, though it lies primarily in the realm of thought, needs such an addition in order to reach its consummation. Thus far we have looked at ideas from the point of view of their objective content; we may also describe them in accordance with the psychological mood they call for. Just as, measured by their objective content, they are an ultimate relatedness, so they demand, in order to be grasped, a wholeness of psychological attunement, i.e., a united effectiveness on the part of all psychic capacities. Thought and feeling must unite intimately and since feeling, even if its object is the soul itself, always carries something of materiality, it is only the artist's creative imagination which is capable of effecting feeling's union with thought as without this intervention thought objects to the admixture of materiality. Whoever has no sense for art, or no genuine feeling for music or poetry, will find it very difficult to grasp an idea and feel its intrinsic substance. Such a difference between people is founded in their original psychic constitutions. Education avails nothing here. It may add something, but it cannot create what isn't there, and there are hundreds of artistically and technically knowing and trained people who plainly demonstrate with every word they say that their natural receptivity toward ideas doesn't exist—which is to say, they lack everything that is needed. The great value of ideas is primarily recognized in this way: man leaves behind him everything when he departs this earth, everything, that is, which does not belong wholly, exclusively, and independently to his soul, disconnected from all earthly relationships. But that is just what his ideas are, nothing else besides his ideas, and that is their genuine mark. Whatever doesn't have the right to occupy the soul during those moments when it of necessity renounces all earthly matters, cannot be counted as ideas, either. But to reach that moment, enriched by purified ideas, is a beautiful aim and end, worthy of our hearts and souls. In this connection, and for this reason, I called ideas the only permanent things because nothing else can grow where earth itself vanishes. You will perhaps counter with love and friendship. But these are ideas in themselves and are founded wholly on ideas. Of friendship this should be quite clear. Of love, permit me not to speak. It may be a weakness of mine, but I dislike speaking the word and equally dislike having it spoken to me. There are so many curious notions about love. People imagine that they loved more than once; then they claim they found out that it was the real thing only once, after all; then they say that they deluded themselves about love or were deluded. I do not wish to depreciate anyone's sentiments. But what I call love is something totally different. It appears in life but once; it does not delude, and it is never deluded. It rests totally and utterly upon ideas. [To C. Diede, March 1833]

The spirit of humanity

The man who feels the need for observing in his thinking as well as in his actions some consistency and unity cannot rest satisfied by observing merely conditional considerations when he seeks to judge the objects of his activities or the choice of his means. For his standards of what is good and desirable, he cannot accept merely those things which have value only in relation to other things. He must seek an ultimate aim, a first and absolute standard, and this ultimate that he seeks must be closely and directly related to his own inner nature.

Even if he might have set more narrow limits to his spirit of investigation if he had lived in another time, it is impossible for him to do that now. As long as there is a great deal of stability in the external situation of mankind, everything may be compared to something that already is. The only question that need be raised directly is: Does any danger threaten the basic pillars of human welfare? But when, as is true now, everything external to man is shaken to its foundations, then his only refuge lies within. Since a complete inversion of all social circumstances has, as a matter of fact, taken place in one of the most important and cultivated parts of the world, it remains doubtful how much might endure anywhere else, particularly since this revolution is being represented, in our philosophical age, as being the proper consequence of a natural law, as being an absolute moral necessity, even.

But the human striving for some ultimate and unconditional aim has yet another necessary reason for being. Everything conditional, everything that is merely a means, can only satisfy one-sidedly either our reason or our feeling. Only that which closely touches our true and inward being can be what our best, our truly human nature warms to.

Man must look for a something to which, as to an ultimate aim, he can subordinate all else and by which, as by an absolute standard, he can judge all else. But such a something cannot be found except within himself, since it is the essence of all creatures to believe that everything refers ultimately to themselves alone. But man can neither refer this something to his momentary pleasure nor to his happiness in general, since it is a noble prerogative of his very nature to be capable of rejecting pleasure and dispensing with happiness. Therefore what he is looking for can lie only in his inner values, his loftier fulfillment.

It is human worth, or dignity, then, which he is to seek. And the questions he must answer are: What is it, that by a universal standard could measure the value of things for man, and the value of one man for another? How do I recognize it? Where do I find it? How do I bring it about when it does not seem to be present?

Since it is supposed to apply to all men, it must be something general, but since it cannot be anyone's serious intention to make all the different human natures over into a single model, it must not violate the difference between individuals. It must therefore be something which always remains one and the same, but which may be carried out in manifold ways.

While he searches for this unknown something—or for the means of finding it—as long, in other words, as his method is theoretical, man, proceeding from the possibility of universal co-operation, must direct his attention to everyone, i.e., to the ennoblement of the entire human race. But as soon as he wishes to apply whatever means he has found and practice them, he must limit himself to himself. For it would be foolish to take into a definite plan factors which are not at his definite disposal. Reason seeks its totality in the universe and demands no restrictions other than universal ones, but the will finds its bounds in the individual person and never transcends him.

But if these two are not to stand in contradictory opposition, we must solve our problem in such a way that our own approach toward a solution advances at the same time as the general approach of others toward theirs, and this not incidentally, simply because one is part of everyone, but straightway and directly. One's own development must necessitate that all others make progress in theirs, whether willingly or not, and progress, further, which accords with one's own. The radical interaction of theoretical reason and practical will always produces a mode of action by means of which, with full use of our individual energies, we only carry out our individual role in a general plan.

What we are seeking cannot be granted to us by morality alone, and we cannot look upon it as something already known and familiar. For although moral worth alone determines human dignity, it is limited to only a part of our nature: our disposition and attitudes. But here we are demanding self-organization as well; in fact we are demanding something so general that it should comprise the whole of man, with all his energies and all his utterances.

For this is the differentiated character of that which we are seeking: that it should ultimately decide the value of every human energy, every human work. It must decide with equal authority whether or not a poem is genuinely poetic, a philosophic system genuinely philosophic, a character genuinely human.

For there is an imprint with which all great things that emanate from man are of necessity stamped, because it is the imprint of great humanity itself. To find it and recognize its features everywhere is the business we are here seeking to transact.

To get there, man may take two roads: that of experience and that of reason.

The road of experience: A man looks around, picking out those individuals who supply him with the best and highest sense of well-rounded humanity. Since he cannot look at the ideal itself, he keeps to its most faithful copies. From the wealth of times and nations he picks the poets, artists, philosophers, and scientists who have worked in a truly grand manner, those who have represented the genre in which they worked in its best, most characteristic light. Above all, he does not neglect those people who in his own life sketch for him most visibly the image of grand and noble humanity, by their inner qualities as well as by their outer form.

All these he compares carefully, especially noting whatever it is that they have in common which placed them on such a high level of inner value for him. Thus gradually he arrives at the following points:

The unknown something is 1) nothing mechanical. It cannot be produced by merely following a complete set of rules. It cannot, in fact, be understood by reason. . . . Whoever has no sense for it, doesn't see it. Whoever sees it cannot utter what he has seen.

So far as art is concerned, this is perfectly plain. No one has yet comprehended or explained how a genuinely artistic notion originates, and still less how it is executed, although almost everyone has a dim intuition of these things, and many people feel them quite plainly.

No less plain is the case of practical life. The energy with which we fulfill our duties simply because they are duties cannot be made clear in words. Our nature wants it thus; that is why it is thus! Such a sentence seems perfectly clear to unspoiled feeling, but trite and ridiculous to perverse feeling. How much less is it possible to express the more delicate stirrings of the feminine soul—and just these reveal the greatest subtleties and beauties of character. The soul itself feels the inadequacy so much that it unfolds only toward someone who understands it and instinctively retires from the gaze of the profane.

The philosopher may be followed step by step for a much more considerable distance by means of mere operations of reason. But it is an infallible sign that his philosophy does not ascend to first principles if at last there does not come a point where analysis cannot operate and where only the experiment can decide whether one was born to be a philosopher or not.

In the case of a natural scientist, it is hardest to make out. . . . The difficult points here are the concept of life for the observer of living nature, the concepts of motion in dynamics, and of relationship in chemistry, for the observer of inorganic nature.

Even mathematics is not exempt—it perhaps least of all. For its whole foundation, construction, can only be shown and imitated, never explained. There is more in it than a mere concept and this more was not taken from sensuous nature.

There are only two ways of making anything really comprehensible. One, by actually pointing to it as it lies outside us in nature. Two, by demonstrating the concepts on which it depends as a necessary consequence of them. That of which we here speak comes under neither of these categories, thereby showing that it is a) the fruit of spontaneity (not merely something taken from external nature) and b) a primordial archetypal activity, thereby leaving nothing which came prior to it, on which it might depend and through which it might be comprehended.

Since it must be possible to follow the course of any purely mental activity back to an act of primordial spontaneity, there must necessarily be one incomprehensible point in such activity beyond which the operations of mere reason no longer suffice.

The unknown something is 2) nothing which affords mere usefulness or pleasure; nothing which merely places certain means at man's disposal or merely flatters his senses. Rather, it intervenes deeply in mankind and strengthens its energies.

Thus we differentiate between a genuine poet who opens up a profound vista for us, into ourselves as well as into the world, and a merely pleasant or eloquent one; between an ideally organized person and a merely useful man of business or a merely good-hearted husband and father, or a merely entertaining host.

Our something is 3) of such character that whoever has it becomes through it the bearer of a higher humanity. Even if such a person has a one-sided education, even if true greatness has not completely established authority over him, he will nonetheless fit into the framework of any image of fulfilled humanity and always nourish and strengthen such an image in his effect upon others.

Only the true poet has a beneficent influence upon character. Any other is either ruinous or else of no consequence for man's inward education. To be moral in this sense is the first demand upon every artist. If the great artist is not always also a great man it is only because he is not, in all the corners of his nature and at all the moments of his life, an artist.

On this kinship of excellence of whatever sort with excellence of humanity in general rests the possibility of finding a single standpoint from which all things may be compared and judged. Without such a standpoint, man could neither assimilate what surrounds him, nor react organically back upon it; he could neither carry the world over into his own individuality nor imprint the world with that which he has made his own. But only such twofold activity can be the ultimate aim of his efforts and the single source of truly human pleasure.

It is a mistake, therefore, to legislate separately for the various genres and types of human activity and expect that through observance of such laws they will remain faithful to the general dignity and worth of humanity. Quite directly, only through art being true art, and philosophy being true philosophy, do they exert their beneficent influence upon human character.

Those persons of excellence whom we have picked to be our models show 4) always a decisive and original individuality. If one develops oneself organically into a full human being, one will surely appear a unique being, and likewise it is with the artist, the philosopher, the natural scientist. . . .

What makes those men into great men knows 5) no limitation upon its perfectibility. It develops into infinity. There is no point at which perfectibility reaches its ultimate aim or exhausts its measure; it has the energy of a living power and life grows through living.

It is, finally 6) fruitful and inspiring to things outside itself. Itself living, it sends out living sparks, and in its effectiveness it shows the following three characteristics:

First, it does not work by planning, by intentional change, or by any activity directed specifically and purposely toward others. Only through its beings, its actions, and the fact that it is perceived, does it exert its educative power.

Second, it affects men of various stages and types of individuality. Any similarity to itself is enough; the slightest glimmer perceivable under the coarsest slag causes it to awaken the half-extinguished spark, to fan it into the flames that will warm the whole.

Third, it does not equate its own individuality with that of the others upon whom it acts; it gives them no definite form, but moves them to find their own organic form. For it awakens their inner spiritual life energy and this is what develops organically the character proper to them.

The most eloquent proof of this assertion is love. Nowhere else does that of which we speak act so powerfully and plainly. That is why true love never brings about equality but always an ideal-oriented harmony of the characters involved. Both lovers together, each in the individuality of his own character, advance toward the ideal which weds them into a single concept and, in the mirror of their passion-inspired imagination, into a single image.

Any person exerts his influence either through his person or through his work. A great man imprints his person upon his work, thus preserving his existence far beyond the span of his lifetime. Hence one can divide all books and works of art into the living and the dead: only the living educate us by developing us, the dead only by instruction.

When a man, therefore, as he investigates the ultimate aim of his moral striving, compares those individuals who have afforded him the best and loftiest concept of well-rounded humanity, he finds something which has a similar effect everywhere he looks. This suggests to him that its very nature contains the qualities of sameness and harmony.

He sees that it simultaneously elevates humanity in general and strengthens each particular individuality, and does this in all men, regardless of character differences. He sees, further, that it deepens the individuality of those who possess it and simultaneously nourishes the individuality of those who approach it. By this he knows it to be the center from which all humanity may be recognized, judged, and developed. But just such a center is what he has been seeking to occupy.

In order to make ourselves better understood in what follows, we wish now to give our something a provisional name. We shall call it "the spirit of humanity"—a name which may be justified since it stands indeed for that quality through which our most esteemed individuals also seem humanity's best and highest representatives.

The road of reason: We are supposed to find the meaning of man as the ultimate aim of his striving and the highest standard for judging him. But the meaning of man, as a free and spontaneously acting being, is contained within himself alone.

The greatest human being is consequently he who represents the concept of humanity in its greatest strength and its widest extent. To judge a man means nothing other than to ask: What content does he give to the form of humanity? What concept should we have of humanity if he were its only representative?

But the concept of humanity is nothing other than the living power of the spirit which animates it, which expresses itself through it, which proves dynamic and active within it.

The object of our task therefore is the investigation of the spirit of humanity and in three subsequent books we shall have to answer the following three questions:
In what does this spirit consist?
Whereby is it recognized?
How can it be developed? [II, 324–32]

The Eternal City

The only true life lies, after all, in ideas and ideals and—if it didn't sound so pious—in God and in heaven. And back there [in Rome] one lives purely and without requiring the intervention or mediation of the painstaking steps up the ladder of so-called intellectual individuality. Harmony and beauty in lifeless nature and in man—not where it rests on specific ideas, but where it expresses itself in bodily forms and in a whole humane way of life—is what transports us, without the mediation of mind. [To Caroline v. Humboldt, April 1809]

*   *   *

One likes to hold back with the old cliches about Rome the eternal and Rome the unique. But as one reads these letters [Goethe's *Zweiter Römischer Aufenthalt*] again and sees the great and lasting influence which Rome exerted on Goethe, first in his yearning to go there and then in its living presence, one is forced back more strongly than ever upon one's own old conviction: that these walls do have something that touches the heights and the profundities of the human spirit and which no other place on earth, no other monument of antiquity, possesses. Though the most obvious nourishment Rome provides is the study of the plastic arts, it nonetheless remains undoubted that the effect Rome has on people is by no means limited to this, but is of a far more general sort. Whatever resounds humanly in us, by whatever clue of human or world destiny it is awakened in us, it is echoed back to us more strongly and more purely here. The spirit of antiquity found in Rome a power which carried it for centuries and, instead of oppressing it with sheer weight of worldliness, itself was radiant with a spiritual power and in its numerous and enormous upheavals mingled the images of death and rebirth. . . . Our present state of spiritual development rests in its most essential points upon the foundations laid in antiquity: the art and science of

Greece and the laws and institutions of Rome. Countless objects surrounding us every day have their roots in both. No epoch known to us has experienced the formative contrasting power of a former one as strongly as has ours, of a former one, moreover, which, although it was a historical one, has so many real links with us missing or else purposely overlooked, that it rises before us much more like a figment of the creative imagination. We obviously look upon antiquity as more ideal than it was, and we should do this, since we are being driven by its form and its relation to us to find ideas and influences in it which transcend all life, including our own. Now Rome has remained for us as the sensuous image of our ideally viewed antiquity. In this it is different from all other cities, even other cities founded on classical soil. History owes us an explanation of how it was that the ideal characteristics of antiquity developed from historical reality, . . . yet no history of Greece has ever done this for us completely. Yet we must expect it from that quarter. For whatever in antiquity works on us most inwardly and most spiritually was first moved by the spirit of Greece which, rising like a natural blossom from the land and the people, seems intended by cosmic destiny to carry the spiritual development of future millennia. . . . But Greek culture did not merely receive from Rome an admirable addition, but without Rome would hardly have gained its power, permanence and extension. The reasons for this lie in history. At this point of world history there seems to be one of the most enormous and complex concatenations of spiritual purposes and worldly ambitions.

And the foremost thing to be remembered about Rome is— Italy. Modern culture had to entwine itself about the spirit of antiquity before it could arch independently as a many-sided whole of powers, and in this crucial transformation, fascinating to behold from whatever angle, Italy, this marvellous land, favored by the heavens, the lie of the land, the natural products, its beauty, and the temperamental constitution of its inhabitants, played the first and most significant role. In most of the artistic, philosophic, civic, political advances of human activity, then finally in the great international developments led by the spirit of trade and of exploration, Italy led the rest of the occidental countries in those notable centuries in which modern times first began to confront antiquity with a worth and a dignity of their own. Nor can any other country show as many remarkable men, and it is particularly notable that art and natural studies, in combination, and in all of their branches, flourished more in Italy than elsewhere. The most significant discoveries in physics, anatomy, etc. had their origin here. But the language, too, shows better than any other daughter language of Latin, by its tone, its dignified power, its rich, graceful, poetic verve, an unexampled development in cultural history. Words and forms mingle and get exchanged in the turmoil of wandering hordes and nations. But a new language grows up only where a new spirit flames up in a people. Language is an organism which needs a unity-creating principle, an archetypal form around which to crystallize. . . . Now in none of the Romance languages has the new spirit, while maintaining complete independence and individual characteristics, preserved a more faithful affection for antiquity than in Italian. Even today one feels that in Rome one can hear the ancient Roman sounds, and a totally different, unique world is revealed. . . . Thus Rome has become one for us with the two greatest events of our spiritual existence, with classical antiquity and the growth of modern greatness inspired by the antique model. This is not a question of pedantic concepts, reasoned out and accepted by our understanding. Everything in Rome overwhelms us with this truth: the enormous ruins, the soul-substance of the arts, the memories flooding in upon one, wherever one sets foot. It is perhaps also a breath of the creative imagination, a poetic glow, that surrounds this city for us, a luminosity that disappears like the mists of morning before a certain type of sober consideration, but a luminosity, all the same, which, like the luminosity of art and poetry, carries truth more soundly and purely than ordinary so-called reality. [VI, 547–50]

*　　　*　　　*

There is no place so little suited to the tourist's otherwise quite admirable ability to see everything notable, take away with him the instruction it affords him, and feel that he is through with the place, as Rome. Rome demands peace and quiet and leisure. It demands that one keep all memory of the necessity of one's return trip as far from one's mind as possible. Before one can live for Rome, one must live for oneself within its boundaries, giving oneself over quietly and undisturbedly to its impressions. In no other physical surroundings does one's pure, true receptivity go over so directly into one's proper and appropriate activity, whether it be new studies, or a continuation of one's former work, meditations upon the thoughts, feelings, and images which had most moved one's soul before one entered Rome. Even in the latter case one is in a way transformed and reborn into a new, more stimulating element. The pure nature which surrounds one, the sound, substantial contours before one's eyes make the dark, the dim, the uncertain, the formless and insubstantial old atmosphere in which one had hitherto lived, simply vanish. [VI, 528–29]

The creative imagination:

Imagination and reality

The realm of imagination is directly opposed to the realm of reality, and equally opposed is the character of whatever belongs to one of these realms to anything within the other. Part and parcel of the concept of reality is the segregation of each individual phenomenon; none stands in causal relationship to any other. . . . As soon as one walks over to the realm of possibilities, on the other hand, nothing exists except in a state of dependency upon everything else. Everything, in fact, which cannot be thought of as other than in a condition of inner interaction *is ideal* in the simplest and strictest sense of the word. For it is wholly opposed to reality. [II, 128]

*   *   *

However incomprehensible the art process, however certainly there is something which the artist himself does not understand and the critic can never utter, this much is known: the artist begins by transforming something real into an image. But he soon finds out that this cannot be done except by a sort of living communication, by somehow letting an electric spark of his imagination leap over to the imagination of others, and this not directly but through the mediation of an object into which he breathes his own living soul.

This is the only way open to the artist. And without in any way wanting it, but just by fulfilling his calling and leaving the execution of his task to his imagination, he lifts nature over the boundaries of reality and leads her into the land of ideas, recreating her individuals as ideals. [II, 132]

*   *   *

If we survey the path that a poet (and every artist) takes, we are overwhelmed by the realization with what a simple aim he starts and what incomprehensible heights he reaches as he executes that aim.

He starts by turning a real object, almost playfully, into an imaginative one, and ends with the greatest and most difficult task which gives to human beings their ultimate meaning: to relate himself intimately to the whole external world and this to him; to accept the world at first like a foreign object but then, in his own fashion and with the organs at his individual disposal, to return it to itself, free and organized.

For all the materials of his observation are organized by him into an ideal form for the imagination. The world around him appears to him like a completely individual, living, harmonious, nowhere restricted or dependent, self-sufficient totality of manifold forms. Thus has he transferred his own inmost and best nature to it, turning it into a creation with which he can then completely sympathize. [II, 142]

*   *   *

The concept of ideality, as being something which lies above reality, is reminiscent of the rule that art is imitation of nature, a rule which for a long time we have commanded the artist to follow. It has even been considered a good definition of art itself. It does contain the two main concepts of art, namely reality (here called nature) and imitation (that which does not permit a total identity with its model). But it contains a vagueness or looseness which can be avoided only by the realization (hitherto not often felt) that the essence of art does not lie in the nature of its objects but in the mood of the imagination. . . . Since the artist makes nature (by which we mean everything that can have reality for us) into an object of the imagination, we may call art *the objectification of nature by the imagination.* [II, 132 f.]

What artists do

The field which the poet tills as his property is the field of imagination. Only his preoccupation with it, and only insofar as he is strongly and exclusively at work on it, gives him the right to his name. He must transform nature, which ordinarily yields objects for sensuous perception only, into materials for the imagination. *To transform reality into an image* is the most general task of all art, to which all other tasks in art are more or less directly subordinated.

To be successful, the artist need only pursue one path. He must wipe every memory of reality from our soul and preserve only our imagination mobile and alive. He cannot change his object a great deal, in its content and even its form. If we are to recognize reality in the image, he must imitate strictly and faithfully. So he must turn to the subject who receives his art and work on that. For even if he produced his work exactly as he found it in nature, down to the tiniest detail, he would nonetheless have changed it entirely, simply by virtue of having placed it in an entirely different sphere. In reality, one condition excludes another; what an object possesses by its positive qualities, it lacks by their exclusiveness. But in imagination this barrier, which arises from the very nature of reality, drops away. The soul, inspired by the imagination, can raise itself beyond reality. [II, 126]

*   *   *

To accomplish the transition from finiteness to infinity, which is always only an ideal one, the creative powers of man are exclusively adapted, and these creative powers are imagination, reason, and feeling. They in turn adapt certain forms to their use, which forms accept only enough materiality to remain sensuous. They stand in precise relationship with archetypal ideas and despite therefore being totally definable always create the impression that their definitude is not a restriction.

They are configuration [*Gestalt*], rhythm, and inward sensation [*Empfindung*]. A fourth, difficult to define or even name, might be added: one that hovers before genuine philosophy in the same way in which a certain meter hovers before an unborn poem.

Configuration operates under the eternal laws of the mathematics of space. Its basis is all of visible nature, and it speaks to the feelings in many different ways.

Rhythm springs from the mysterious but essential relationships of numbers; it rules all of nature's sounds, and is the never-departing, invisible companion of the feelings.

Inward sensation adds to the forms of the foregoing the power of feeling, and follows the leading ideas of the entire psychic constitution. [III, 140 f.]

*   *   *

In a beautifully painted fruit we may see a swelling of contour, a delicacy of meat, a downy softness of skin, a glow of color which . . . nature is never capable of reaching. We may not therefore say that the painted fruit is more beautiful than a natural one. Nature is never beautiful except when represented in imagination. One cannot say that the contours in nature are less perfect, the colors less vivid. The difference is only that reality appeals to the senses, art to the imagination. Reality yields harsher and more decisive outlines; art always definite ones, but those which are at the same time infinite. [II, 130 f.]

What art philosophers do

Philosophy of art is never primarily meant for artists, and certainly never for their moments of artistic creation. It is an advantage and a misfortune of philosophy that its direct ultimate aim is always the human being, never the practical execution of anything. Artists can be artists without it, statesmen likewise, and the virtuous can be virtuous. Only the individual, particular human being needs philosophy in order to enjoy and use what he receives from artists, statesmen, and so forth; in order to know himself and nature, and to make his knowledge fruitful. Artists, on the other hand, need it only when they want to understand themselves as human beings, when their reason wants to catch up with the flight of their genius; practical men when they want to approach with their minds the profundity and correctness of their practical sense. Thus esthetics is meant only for such people as wish to develop their taste by works of art and their character by a liberated and purified taste. But the artist himself can use it only for attuning, or reorienting himself after he has abandoned himself to his genius; he can use it to determine his position and his goal. But it cannot give him any advice on how to proceed: only his own and other artists' experience can do that. [II, 119 f.]

*   *   *

Whoever works in the field of art theory is exactly in the same position as a natural scientist. What nature is to the latter, the artistic genius is to the former. As long as he is certain that the artist has operated with all the full and pure powers at his disposal (and as to this he must be allowed free and arbitrary judgment), he can do nothing more than take his off-spring as it comes, describe it simply, and—if it resists his classification—extend his system in accordance with its need. [II, 121]

*　　*　　*

To speak or write about a poet is never anything other than finding circumlocutions for the inexpressible. [VI, 545]

The relationship between artists and their works

There is a fuller and more immediate effectiveness of a great spirit than that possible through his works. These show only a part of his being. The entirety flows pure and wholly through his living personal self. In a way which cannot be proved in detail, nor investigated, nor even wholly thought, his real self is taken up by his contemporaries and handed on to the generations to follow. It is this quiet and—it cannot be otherwise described—magical effect of great spiritual natures that carries an ever growing thought from generation to generation, from nation to nation, and allows it to rise with ever greater might and extension. Written works—literatures—then take it mummified, as it were, over those gaps which the living effectiveness can no longer leap. [VI, 494]

*　　*　　*

The less able a person (especially a woman) who is otherwise intelligent and educated and who has everything in her power to create the greatest, most beautiful relationships—the less able she is to articulate those powers in words, the deeper and more steadfast they appear in her life and in the truth of her feelings. . . . Even Schiller, good man that he was, sometimes hurt me in this connection, not on my account but on his. However great certain thoughts and works might be, it is hard to bear when the human being seems to disappear in them, when the truth of feeling is sacrificed to the artistic product, when the person yields himself completely to his work with an egoism that can't be gainsaid. Even more horrible, it seems to me, is when the same thing happens to a public figure. [To Caroline v. Humboldt, October 1809]

*   *   *

I too am terribly upset about young Körner's death. Yet I cannot be sorry that he went to war. . . . I would always try to hold back a person of fully matured talent. Such a one's nature no longer hangs in balance; it has made its decision, and the person's share in active life can contribute nothing, or little, to his gifts. The question of his participation stands separate on its own merits, as the simple fulfillment of his duty as a citizen. But where the balance of maturity is not yet attained, the creative gift also suffers irreparable loss if the human being neglects to engage in the human pursuits proper to him. . . . [To Caroline v. Humboldt, September 1813]

*   *   *

I have heard people criticize and deplore Körner's death. A man with creative gifts should not have to risk himself, they say. One couldn't speak more shabbily of creativity. . . . The true talent and the true spirit that every poet, every genuinely great author needs, stem from his character and are nourished by it. Whatever is not thus integral remains more or less mechanical in its science and shallow and insignificant in its art.

The ancients never felt otherwise; Aeschylus would have found it very odd if they had tried to prevent him from fighting at Marathon, in order that he might finish a couple trimeters more. For the essence of man's value is that he can risk himself and, when necessary, play freely with his own life. [To Caroline v. Humboldt, December 1813]

Some types of poetic greatness:

Pindar and sublime serenity

The feeling of greatness communicated by the creation of a poet is not exactly greatness of attitude, or of feelings, or of deeds—it is a greatness of existence, of life itself. Whoever possesses it enjoys unclouded peace; he is related to everything morally and physically great and luminous; he is alone with the gods and with his fate. Hence the peace, the serenity, the radiant sublimity which so especially characterize Pindar, and which are so different from that other type of sublimity, often achieved by lyric poets, which presents moral greatness in its opposition to physical greatness. [I, 422 f.]

Schiller and intellectuality

Schiller's poetic genius announced itself in his very first works. Regardless of all sorts of errors and deficiencies of form, regardless of many things which must have seemed crude to the mature artist, *Die Räuber* and *Fiesko* bear witness to an unmistakably great natural ability. Afterward it revealed itself through . . . a yearning for poetry which was kin to a feeling of homesickness. Finally it was made manifest in the virile strength and clarified purity of those dramas which will be the pride and reputation of the German stage for a long time to come. But this poetic genius was related most closely to the power of thinking, in all its depths and heights; it really appears only against the background of an intellectuality which wanted to fathom all, divide all, and—relating all—combine all into a new whole. Herein lies Schiller's uniqueness. He demanded from poetry a deeper share of thought. He subordinated it strictly to his sense for the oneness of all spiritual activities; he bound it to a firm art form, and he treated each poetic work so that its substance had to yield all its individuality in favor of the wholeness of an idea. Upon such characteristics rest the excellences which comprise Schiller's unique work. . . . They also explain the criticism of those who deny that Schiller had the free gifts of the Muses, who see in his work less the easy, happy birth of genius and more the self-conscious toil of an intellect. The kernel of truth in their judgment is that Schiller did possess a true intellectual greatness. [VI, 495]

Goethe and original genius

A great man in any field and any era is a phenomenon for which we can hardly ever, and usually never, account. Who would undertake to explain how it was that Goethe suddenly appeared in the fullness and depth of his genius, equally visible in his early as in his later works! And yet he founded a new era of poetry among us, transforming the very shape of poetry itself; he imprinted his own form upon the language, and gave certain decisive impulses to the spirit of his nation for all time to come. Genius is always new and original; it always makes the rules; it always announces its presence upon its arrival only. Reasons for its existence cannot be found in anything prior, anything already familiar; as it appears it imparts its own direction to itself. [VI, 511]

Slow growth vs. dialectical flexibility

Your poetry always did originate in your total view of nature and the world. That this view in your case could only be a poetic one, and that your poetry had to be determined by the whole fabric of relationships within nature and the world: therein consists your individuality. I should like therefore to characterize your poetry as the kind that could develop only relatively slowly out of the wealth of its materials which at no period of your life you could resist trying to render understandable to yourself. For even if you did not direct this sort of attention to your poetry itself, you had to direct it, compelled by your own nature, to the still deeper and more tremendous element which lay at the bottom of your poetry, within yourself. You see, my dearest friend, that I am speaking here of the nature of poetic production in general, not of the formal aspects of actual works though they depend on it, of course. A clearer conscious realization about the latter may have come to you, and undoubtedly did, later on in time—though it need not have necessarily. For during those happy days when I lived together with you and Schiller it always seemed to me that you were no less a philosophical and pensive nature than he. . . . Only he was also a dialectical nature, and it is a particularly strong mark of your nature, to consider nothing accomplished by dialectics. In Schiller, opinions, maxims, principles, theories were rapidly formed, rapidly verbalized, soon transformed into others. You, with similar purposes deep in your nature, experienced blockages of the dialectical process because you demanded something quite different, something harder to attain; in fact, never to be attained but always to be reached for. [To Goethe, January 1832]

The Bhagavad-Gita and religious poetry *

The god Krishna, the true and complete incarnation of Vishnu, accompanies as charioteer, according to the poem Maha-Bharata, Arjuna, third and most excellent son of Pandu (really begot by the

* The present essay has no purpose other than to give as briefly as possible a faithful and complete notion of the above poem, especially of the philosophic system presented in it, in order to render it understandable to readers who do not read the original Hindu language. I have therefore rarely allowed myself any comparison of the teachings of the Bhagavad-Gita with any Hindu doctrines known from other sources. A work which is so rich in philosophic ideas deserves to be treated as a separate whole. Additionally, I believe that there is hardly a better way of elucidating the various obscurities that remain for us in Hindu mythology and philosophy than to first quote widely from the works which may be looked upon as major sources, treating each of them completely and separately before drawing comparisons with others. Exacting and thoroughgoing treatments of all the major Hindu works, the Vedas, the Code of Manu, the two great heroic epics, the eighteen Puranas, and the best philosophical commentaries, made with the simple intent of faithful and complete presentation of their mythological and philosophical contents, would provide us with a basis for comparing all Hindu philosophical and mythological systems without danger of confusion. One could then proceed safely to the other writings and documents. Whatever has been done from this point of view, and however inestimably valuable particularly Colebrooke's excellent excerpts from the Vedas and their most important commentaries are, there is obviously much room for a far greater completeness of these indispensable preliminary studies. We are still forced

god Indra), into battle against his close relatives, the sons of King Dhritarashtra. When Arjuna recognizes within the enemy's host his own family, his religious teachers, and his friends, he falls into doubt as to whether it is better to vanquish those without whom life itself would have no value, or be vanquished by them. He falls into hesitation and despondency, drops his bow and arrow, and asks Krishna for counsel. The god encourages him for philosophical reasons to enter upon the battle and, in sight of both armies, there develops between them a conversation which in eighteen cantos (about 700 distichs) traverses an entire system of philosophy.

Colebrooke, to whose latest essay in the *Transactions of the Royal Asiatic Society* we owe the first definite and detailed information about the various Hindu philosophical systems, does not mention this episode of the Maha-Bharata, presumably because it was his intention to excerpt only from genuine philosophic textbooks and their commentators (these textbooks, however, in accordance with Hindu custom are likewise composed in verse). Krishna's doctrine seems on the whole to agree with Colebrooke's presentation of Patandshali's system, but it develops in such a peculiarly individual way, it is, so far as I can judge, so much less burdened with sophistry and mysticism, that it deserves our special attention, standing as it does as an independent work of art which is interwoven into one of the two great ancient Hindu heroic epics.

I shall attempt to summarize it briefly here, without feeling bound by the sequence of the original, and without now considering what connections these doctrines have with those Greek philosophic systems with which I am familiar.

to relate all sorts of source materials, when we seek to give a connected presentation of Hindu philosophy and mythology, for whose completeness we cannot vouch, and without full knowledge of each one in its characteristic individuality. One must openly confess, furthermore, that in most cases one has to be in the position of being able to compare the presently known excerpts and translations with the original. At present this is in part impossible, in part uncommonly difficult. For a long time to come, therefore, translating, editing, and above all publishing of the various documents will have to take precedence over general evaluations. [Here follows a brief note about the system of accent marks used in the publication of the speech. Humboldt read this essay before the Academy of Sciences in Berlin, on June 30, 1825. *Tr.*]

The two main dicta around which the system contained in this poem pivots are, one, that the Spirit, being simple and imperishable, is by its very nature separate from the body which is complex and perishable and, two, that he who strives for consummation must perform any and all acts without regard for their consequences and with perfect equanimity.

Both of these doctrines have a most natural reference point in Krishna's intention to move his heroic friend to do battle. For death and actions lose their weight; they become inconsequential, as it were, if death concerns only a body which is perishable in any case and if actions, freed from passion and intention, are merely products of nature or precepts of duty. Through the definitive separation of the spiritual and the corporeal, and the constantly counseled disinterestedness of actions, pure intellectuality becomes the foundation of the whole system and, as we shall see in greater detail, insight [*Erkenntnis*] the foremost of all human efforts.

The bodies of the souls which inhabit them are finite and changeable, like the forever flowing elements of which they are made (II, 14, 18); the soul itself is everlasting, indestructible, steadfast and unchangeable (II, 24–25). It may combine with other bodies as a man may put on other garments (II, 22), or as, within the body itself, childhood, youth, and old age succeed one another (II, 13). This unchangeableness is true eternity, without beginning and without cessation. For the impossibility of a transition from being to non-being and vice versa is a major doctrine of Hindu philosophy. No fundament is really a cause; each one contains its effect, forever equal to itself, within itself.

From non-being there is no being. Non-being is not from being.
The separateness of the two is discerned by those with insight.
(II, 16) *

* All English translations are from Humboldt's German translation. The citations are to canto and line of the original. Since these have remained substantially the same in modern English translations of the Bhagavad-Gita, I have left them in for anyone who may care to compare the spirit of Humboldt's translation with that of more modern ones. *Tr.*

In this, Krishna the god declares himself the equal of man.

At no time was I not, nor you, nor these princes
And never shall I be not; from now on forever we are.

(II, 12)

It is part and parcel of this idea that to the inevitability of death corresponds the equal inevitability of rebirth. The dead cannot remain dead. It is therefore a matter of indifference whether one thinks of the soul as imperishable or as ever dying and ever becoming anew.

Even if you think of it as becoming, and again as dying,
Even then, Great-armed One, you must not lament it.
For death is certain to those becoming, birth certain to the dead.
Destiny's lot is not to be changed, hence you must never lament it.
Creatures are of invisible origin; they have a visible middle,
And then invisibly exit. Why then mourning, Bharata?
Miraculously one looks at one, miraculously thereupon speaks the other,
Miraculously another hears him, but no one, though hearing one, knows him.
The Soul is inviolable always in the body of each, Bharata.
Therefore you too need never lament the numberless creatures.

(II, 26–30)

Spirit is invisible, unrepresentational, all-penetrating (II, 25); body has the opposite characteristics. To the simplicity and indivisibility of Spirit we shall return when we discuss the nature of divinity. For the Spirit which everywhere holds sway is one and the same (VIII, 20, 21; XIII, 27).

Action fetters Spirit by subordinating it to the conditions of reality and taking it away from pure reflection. Hence there have been in the world since ancient days two systems, that of action and that of insight (III, 3), and the observance of right in reference to action is difficult because one must pay heed not only to action but also to non-action (IV, 17). Men have sometimes preferred the one, sometimes the other (XVIII, 2, 3). The truth is that action is to be preferred to non-action (III, 8; V, 2). What counts is to free oneself from the fetters of action (II, 39), which one can do by leaving aside all considerations of success and failure and acting only in order to act. Thus one combines both systems; one destroys action, as it were, by robbing it of its binding nature. In action's midst, one does not really act at all (IV, 20; XVIII, 17). This is necessary because it always remains true that action stands far below insight (II, 49).

But any attempt to totally give up action would be vain, to say the least. There is no moment at which man can be without actions; they occur independent of his will, originating in nature and her qualities (III, 5). The wise man lets nature hold sway in them and looks upon them as occurring only in her, divorced from himself (IV, 21; XIV, 19; XIII, 19; III, 28; V, 8–10). This assertion of the unavoidability of acting rests on the fact that what this system understands by action is every bodily process, really every material change. This, in turn, has to do with the consummate wise man, as we shall see, being placed in the highest state of rest, the immersion in and transition to the godhead. Another element of action's inescapable nature arises from the variously divided duties of the castes to which each person must remain faithful, even if guilt is bound up with being thus (XVIII, 47, 48). Finally there lies in this doctrine a necessary fatalism, since nature, equal in everlastingness to the godhead, must forever and incessantly roll the wheel of her changes. Thereby the godhead which encompasses each separate being becomes, strictly speaking, the only true doer. This is why it is proper for Krishna to tell Arjuna:

> Hence up and to battle now! Gain fame, be victor, enjoy fullness of rule!
> By me were these slain long ago. Be but my instrument, Ambidextrous One!
> Drona, Bhisma, Jayadratha, Karna, and all the heroes of battle
> Whom I have slain, now slay them without hesitation. Fight! Victory is yours.
>
> (XI, 33, 34)

Only those who are blinded by earthly considerations fancy themselves the causes of their actions. The modest wise man never considers himself the doer (XVIII, 16; XIV, 19; XIII, 29).

Renunciation of the fruits of action is also expressed by the grounding of all actions in the godhead (XII, 6; III, 30; XVIII, 57). It liberates us from the shackles of action (IV, 41), and whoever practices it remains untainted by sin, just as the lotus leaf swimming on the water is not wetted (V, 10).

Several times in almost every canto the poet returns to the necessity of renouncing the fruits of action, and of equanimity, in fact indifference, toward success and failure. Bound up as this is with an equally strongly repeated insistence upon action, this theme designates in an undeniably philosophic manner a psychic mood bordering on sublimity. In addition, it has tremendous poetic effectiveness.

The simplest expression of the task of renunciation might be found in the following verses:

In action let there be appreciation of value; never, never in its fruits.
Be not one whose aim is action's fruit, nor one who seeks non-action.
With Spirit immersed, free of yearning, thus act, oh Despiser of Gold,
Indifferent to failure and success; equanimity is what immersion is.

(II, 47, 48)

In this way acting and nonacting dissolve into the same concept when seen from the point of view of Spirit.
Whoever sees in action nonaction and in nonaction action
He among men is wise, immersed, at the goal of all action.

(IV, 18)

Equanimity is designated by a special word which means freedom from the opposites, from success and failure alike. It is the blind involvement in the opposites, springing from desire and revulsion, that produces all the confusions among creatures (VII, 27). The wise man frees himself from them; for his equanimity there cannot be found a term strong enough. Not only must heat and frost, pleasure and pain, success and failure, fortune and misfortune, victory and defeat, honor and dishonor be the same to him, but he must stand without taking sides among friend and foe, good and evil. He must esteem equally soil, stones, and gold (II, 38; VI, 7–9; XII, 17–19). This abstractedness from the motions of earthly existence, this opposition in which he stands to the great mass of people, is described in several images of this poem in which images are scarce.

> Who, like the turtle its members, everywhere withdraws
> His senses from sense stimuli, his Spirit stands fast in wisdom.
>
> (II, 58)

> Who, like the never-filled undisturbed quiet ocean, though waters stream into it,
> Collects into himself the fullness of desire, attains peace; not the greedy.
>
> (II, 70)

> When for all creatures night falls, then wakes the collected wise man;
> When creatures are awake, then is it night for the discerning wise man.
>
> (II, 69)

The clear separation between Spirit and body and the nullification of action both lead, the first positively through the self-sameness of all pure Spirit, the second negatively through the removal of the disturbances in which action involves man, to insight and to the perception of the godhead from whence springs ultimate consummation. It is therefore necessary at the outset to have a proper understanding of the concept which Krishna proposes of the godhead, since his teaching is not merely a philosophical but also a religious one.

Here too, I shall attempt to illustrate all the main dicta with references to the original. I have purposely chosen them with great care and greatly desire that those who devote some attention to these matters might take the trouble to look them up. Those who do not read Sanskrit have an excellent Latin translation by Schlegel, appended to his edition of the Gita, at their disposal. This translation is so masterly and at the same time so conscientious and faithful, it treats so intelligently the philosophical content of the poem, and is such good Latin besides, that it would be a great pity if it were used only for a better understanding of the text and not read for its own sake as well, by all those who are interested in philosophy and archeology.

Where I myself have tried to translate the lines metrically, I must ask indulgence. We know far too little of the peculiarities and subtleties of Hindu prosody, only its meters and stanza forms, whereby the successful translation of a verse form can make little progress. So far as the lines themselves are concerned, I have not chosen the most beautiful or pleasing, about which judgment would vary in any case, but, in accordance with the purpose of this paper, those which best exemplify the characteristics of the philosophic system. For the same reason I have attempted to give a word-for-word rendering as accurate as possible. I should have dispensed with meter altogether if it were not for the fact that even an unsuccessful rendering of meter into meter always give a more vivid sense of the original than does a rendering into prose. Also our language is such that a metric translation may gain in faithfulness by virtue of its being metric. The translator is moved by the rhythm into a mood similar to that of the original, the binding laws of syllabic number and length make dragging prosaic paraphrases impossible and blessedly cut off the frequently too far-reaching indecisiveness as to choice of expression. The names of Arjuna occurring in direct address (Bharata, Partha, Kaunteya) are Sanskrit forms of surnames, derived from Arjuna's ancestors.

For the understanding of certain lines to follow I must note that whenever Krishna (who is usually the speaker) speaks of himself, his reference is to the highest godhead or, in better accordance with the purity of this doctrine, to absolute divinity. Krishna accompanies Arjuna in the shape of a man (IX, 11), as one of the descendants of old King Yadu, and Arjuna, after he has recognized him as God, asks his forgiveness (XI, 41, 42) for the familiarity with which he has been treating him. According to Hindu mythology, Krishna is the eighth of the ten incarnations or manifestations (*avataras*) of Vishnu. There is nothing of these revelations of divinity in various animal and human figures in our poem, which is generally quite free of mythological elements, but Krishna does mention that he returns to earth in each of the world-cycles (IV, 6–8). Since Krishna is an emanation of the godhead, the godhead—or rather Krishna in it—remains in its eternal realm of being, and in this connection Krishna speaks—but only once so far as I have been able to discover—of himself and God as though of two separate beings. He says,

> To this primordial Spirit I turn, from whom all creatures' ancient stream flows.
>
> (XV, 4b)

God then is the everlasting, invisible, undivided, hence simple principle, differentiated from all perishable, visible creation which is divided into individuals (XII, 3; VII, 24, 25).

> Differentiated from the visible is an invisible everlasting Being,
> Which shall not be destroyed if every creature is destroyed,
> The invisible Indivisible, so that praised as the loftiest path
> Is that from which there need be no rebirth, there where my highest dwelling is.
>
> (VIII, 20–21)

> Indestructible that—you must know—which has unfolded the universe:
> Destruction of this Primordial, no one, nothing can effect.
>
> (II, 17)

God is omniscient, all-penetrating, capable of no growth, lord over all things; there is nothing above him; he is one and must be worshipped in oneness (VII, 26; III, 15, 22; XI, 19, 20; IX, 11, 17, 18; VII, 7; VI, 31). Of him, Arjuna says:

Not end, not middle, nor any beginning see I in you, All-ruler, All-creator.

(XI, 16)

Of the world, of the firm, of the mobile the Father, the highest, most honorable Teacher, are you;
Nothing your equal, immeasurable Ruler. Who higher than you in the threefold world?

(XI, 43)

God's abode is beyond and outside of all creation.

Not suns, not discs of moons, not fires shed any light
Where, once there, no one returns, my highest abode.

(XV, 6)

God is the creator of the world. Everything exists only through him; he is the imperishable origin of all things (IX, 4, 10, 13; VII, 6, 7, 10).

What is every creature's life germ, that am I, Arjuna;
Nothing without me in the world, nothing fast, nothing mobile.

(X, 39)

Adoring in his way him, from whom all creatures flow,
Who has unfolded this universe, man strives for consummation.

(XVIII, 46)

As God has brought everything forth, so is he all, and all is in him. This is a main doctrine of this system, one which is implemented in various ways. It seems to be connected on the one side with the concept of divine infinity which comprises all within itself, on the other side with the peculiar Hindu philosophic notion of how one thing originates from another. Since, as we saw before, there is no transition between being and non-being, but both form two parallel lines running into infinity, all creation from nothing is impossible. Every effect must be in its cause and occur simultaneously with it since all eternity. (Colebrooke in the *Transactions of the Royal Asiatic Society,* Vol. I, Part I, p. 38.) If therefore God is the creator of all things, then all things must already have been in him before he created them. This conclusion is not explicit in our poem, but since the premise (II, 16) is clearly and definitely stated, the conclusion is self-evident.

All things spiritual are related to one another. They are one and the same, and man can recognize in himself, i.e., in his spiritual self (since the language connects within the same word [atman] the concepts of Spirit and of self) all other creatures, and God within them all. But while the divine Spirit in separateness is divided into various individuals, it is at the same time present in oneness; invisible, imperishable, and undivided, and this, its undivided nature, is the true primordial source of all existence.

That which gives to each thing its characteristic excellence is God: the splendor of the constellations, the light of the flame, the life of the living, the strength of the strong, the reason of the reasonable, the insight of the discriminating, the saintliness of the saints (VII, 8–11; X, 38). Whatever relation between him and the world may be imagined, he occupies. God is father, mother, preserver, refuge, etc. He is the teaching, the purification rite, the sacred writing, the silence of the mystery (IX, 16–18; X, 38), never ceasing time (X, 33). In the tenth canto Krishna goes through all creation (19–42) from the fish in the waters up to the gods, through mountains, oceans, winds, the seasons, the time units, through leaders of armies, wise men, saints, poets, generations of heroes. In each class he calls that which is the most excellent, himself; Narada among the saints, Vyasa among the hermits, Usana among the poets, and so on. Even the grammatical forms and the letters of the alphabet are not forgotten. Among conjunctions he is the "and," among letters, "A," which presumably has a mystical meaning if it does not merely designate the esteem in which the invention of writing was held. I stress this particularly because it proves that, if this distich (X, 33) is not a late interpolation, an alphabet already existed when the poem was made. For the plain isolation of a vowel from the forms of inflection can hardly be separated by any sort of interval from the designation thereof. All these individually numbered things, however, says Krishna in conclusion, are only cited as examples, for there is no end to the number of substances in which God appears through his miraculous power. Whatever is great, excellent, and superior participates in his splendor, and he has invested this whole universe with a part of his nature (X, 40, 42). From this we can see more plainly still in what sense he calls himself one with the objects of nature.

What is listed separately in the above-noted lines is summarized in another place (VII, 19) in the brief sentence: "Vasudeva (i.e., Krishna, the son of Vasudeva) is all."

The divine nature must accordingly contain opposites whose contradiction only dissolves in the universality of its nature. In the same distich Krishna says of himself.

Strength I am in the strong; free from desires and passions;
Desire am I, halted by no law, in the creatures, Bharata.

(VII, 11)

A god who contains within himself the raging of the untamed forces of nature and the peace which hovers above all finiteness with the pure authority of Spirit, such a god stimulates all the images in the imagination which are capable of bringing forth tremendous poetic effects.

This likewise accords with the bodily form which is ascribed to God. It is nothing other than a sense-translation of spirituality, according to which he comprises all individuals within himself, again pours himself into all individuals, and yet, at the same time, stands alone in his unity, a true monad. One must distinguish this imaginative representation of a divine body from that of a human one which the mythology of other peoples and, in another context, even of the Hindus themselves, imputes to their gods. In this philosophical, not mythical, system the entire world of bodies becomes the body of the infinite, and this not gradually, by development and growth of specific powers, but in its archetypal manifestation which comprises simultaneously all past, present, and future.

Arjuna asks Krishna (XI) to show himself as he has hitherto

described himself (in his essence, for up to then there has been no mention of his bodily form). Krishna grants this favor. He lends him a divine eye since Arjuna's human eyes would not suffice, and reveals himself to him in his splendor-shaped, all-encompassing, infinite, archetypal shape, a shape never before seen by anyone. Arjuna sees him towering toward heaven, without beginning, middle, or end, with many heads, eyes, and arms, comprising within himself thousands of divine forms, each different in color and shape, warming the universe with his luminosity, and within him all the gods, beginning with Brahma sitting in the lotus cup, all the wise men, and all the hosts of creatures of whatever sort.

If high in the heavens suddenly from a thousand suns
Light flamed, its radiance would be like the Lofty One's splendor.
The universe standing as one, and yet manifoldly divided,
The son of Pandu saw in the body of the God of gods.
(XI, 12, 13)

This is what Krishna had promised him when he said,

The universe standing as one, whatever moves and moves not, you shall see
In my body, Wavy-haired One, and whatever else you desire to see.
(XI, 7)

and whoever attains this view reaches the highest consummation.

Who sees, standing as one the divided being of creatures,
Spreading out from the one, he has raised himself to the godhead.
(XIII, 30)

The lowest level of insight is that upon which one contemplates particulars, divided from their origin, as though they were the whole. On the middle level one sees only particularity in particulars, without rising to universality (XVIII, 20-22).

But it is noteworthy that Krishna expressly says (XI, 47) that he has shown Arjuna this highest manifestation of himself through the *creativeness of his self,* i.e., through the magic power * of which more later, with whose help God and men are said to be able to transform their natures and bring about the impossible, by the exercise of abstraction and concentration on a single point and immersion into their own depth. One may perhaps conclude from this that the poet really wants Krishna's manifestation interpreted as mere semblance, since his system, infused as it is by genuine spirituality, does not need the representations of sun-splendor, manifold members, etc. Also, as we saw before, the divine being is in all other places pictured by him as invisible and undivided.

But God does not merely comprise all the modes of being, but also those of non-being.

Immortality am I and death, what is, and what is not, Arjuna.

(IX, 19)

In Manu's Code (I, ii) the eternal invisible fundamental cause from which everything even Brahma, originates, is likewise simultaneously called being and non-being. I do not believe that this should be understood (as it has been) to signify God's being as "being" and our incapacity for perceiving it with our sense limitations "non-being." If one fully participates in the way of thinking that is here represented, one realizes that with being and non-being one and the same, the last barrier before God's universality is torn down. All-being would not comprise all, would not be infinite, if a non-being could be distinguished from its being. Besides, in a higher and purely philosophical sense it is quite correct to say that the godhead, by comprising the fundaments of being, necessarily contains also the fundaments of non-being. In any event, a being which divides itself into countless individual creatures and at the same time is the universal being which unites them all within itself

---

* This power is described as a true magic (*maya*) and this Brahma-Maya is represented in the pictorial arts so as to indicate its double nature, not only by its hermaphroditic figures but also by the fact that on the one side the foot is drawn up halfway to the mouth to indicate brooding Brahma and on the other side the dancing movements of creative, butterfly-like Maya.

is comparable to no other being and that is why, in another place, we hear,

> The highest godhead, without beginning, is not non-being, nor being.
>
> (XIII, 12)

which is the same thought as that contained in the preceding quoted line, only taken from another side.

Non-being is taken in still another sense when it is meant to indicate the opposite of being here taken as real being, as intrinsic essence. It is then opposed (XVII, 28) to virtue and to truth.

> The creatures are in God.
>
> (VII, 12)

> Devotion, Partha, strives for the highest Spirit, steadily looking at him
> In whom all creatures dwell, who has unfolded this universe.
>
> (VIII, 22)

> Having your nature for its abode, O Ruler of the senses, the world is glad to obey you.
>
> (XI, 36)

He, however, is not in them (VII, 12; IX, 4). By this is meant only that he is independent of them. He contains them in his infinite nature but is not himself contained in their finite one. For in those respects in which it does not restrict him, he is indeed in them; he enters into their bodies and leaves their bodies and lives in the heart of every man (XV, 7–11; XIII, 15, 17). Only his being-in-them is not taken, as is their being-in-him, as absolute and real but only restrictedly, as a sort of dwelling place of his (XIII, 16). For this teaching guards carefully against the possibility that the existence of finite beings might drag down the nature of the infinite creator. In one place the dictum that the creatures are in God is immediately followed by its direct negation. And special attention is drawn to this simultaneity of being and non-being, as containing the highest miracle-working power of the divine nature. Through analogy elsewhere, we may understand this as that tension of the divine Spirit by which he relates all creatures to himself and yet cancels out the restrictive consequences of this relationship (IX, 4, 5). Poetically, the contradiction is dissolved in a metaphor.

> Consider the sum total of creatures dwelling within me
> Like the vast, all-penetrant air filling the space of the ether.
>
> (IX, 6)

That which relates the creatures to God is their spiritual nature. It is one and the same in all of them. In fact, God is the Spirit animating all (X, 20). Hence everyone may recognize in himself all other creatures and them in God.

> Not to blind delusion, son of Pandu, need you return, when you recognize
> First in yourself the sum total of beings, then in me.
>
> (IV, 35)

> Whoever in each creature sees himself, and all the creatures in himself,
> With devoutly immersed Spirit, one and the same everywhere,
> Whoever sees only me, and only in me sees all,
> In him I do not sink from sight, and he does not sink from mine.
> Who honors me, dwelling in creatures, steadfast maintaining oneness,
> He, wherever he may wander, wanders but immersed in me.
> Whoever in the Self's sameness sees the same, Arjuna,
> Whenever he feels pleasure or pain, he is immersed most deeply.
>
> (VI, 29–32)

The miraculous creative power of God, above alluded to, is called a magic, a semblance-producing power, and by this is meant that the only true being is after all only that which is imperishable and everlasting. Everything else, subject as it is to change, is only a semblance produced by the godhead. But since it is difficult to realize that God is not restricted by his share in finiteness and to tell his true invisible being from that being-in-semblance (VII, 25), his magic power has a deceptive effect on men. The Lord of creatures, another line tells us, sits in the region of the heart and confuses with his magic those who are fastened to the rolling wheel of finiteness. But whoever reaches God, overcomes this magic (VII, 14, 15; XVIII, 61).

For he not only recognizes the double nature which, according to this system, must be God's, but is not deceived about the relationship between God's two aspects.

> Earth, water, blazing flame, air, ether, mind and reason,
> Ego—for into these eight parts is my nature divided—
> My lower, that is, for divided from it is my higher nature,
> That life-breathing nature, Great-Armed One, by which this world endures;
> For as germinating from this womb consider all things.
>
> (VII, 4–6a)

In elucidation of these lines I must note that the three spiritual capacities of man in Hindu philosophy are treated as part of God's lower nature; they are counted as the equals of the senses.

Mind (*Gemüth—manas:* etymologically the Latin *mens*) is that function which in the soul corresponds to perception and action in the body. For the Hindus assume, beside the instruments of the five senses, five instruments of action, and put these ten, plus *manas* as eleventh, into one class.

Ego (*Selbstgefühl—ahankara,* literally that which forms the ego) applies outer and inner impressions to the personality and therefore includes self-consciousness as well as self-centeredness.

Reason (*Vernunft—buddhi*) makes decisions.

Above these three stands the pure Spirit, related to the nature of the godhead (*atman,* whence our *atmen* [breathe]).

We see from this that human nature is but an imitation, a particularization, of the divine model, and when the latter creates bodies or permits them to be destroyed it enters them or leaves them and makes use of the instruments which relate the soul to the outside world.

> For in the world's life, life-breathing, my eternal aspect attracts to itself

From nature's womb mind and senses, six in number.
Wherever the ruler enters the body or leaves it,
He combines into one, wrenching them loose, as the wind does the
fragrance of blossoms,
Hearing, Sight, Feeling, Taste, Smell and Mind,
Thus ruling, thus penetrating and working the stuff of the senses.

(XV, 7–9)

Thus God joins himself to mortal bodies and performs actions
by bringing them forth and founding human institutions. It is in
fact necessary for him to act if the world is not to stand still. But
his union with finiteness does not taint him, nor does action restrict
him; he merely lets nature rule. Now we see the return of the teaching, this time expressed of the godhead, which was urged upon
man: that action there must be, but that it is only the clinging to
results which binds the Spirit's freedom and disturbs its peace.
Utter equanimity on the other hand dissolves even real action into
non-action (IX, 8, 9).

Nothing, Partha, is left for me to do in the three worlds,
Nothing to be reached that is not already reached, and yet I visibly
act.
If for a moment I ceased in my tireless weaving of actions—
For, Partha, everywhere do men follow in my footsteps—
These worlds would sink into nothingness, if I did not keep working.
And I should be responsible for the confusion and be the murderer of
this race.

(III, 22–24)

I instituted the four castes, distinguished by quality, by calling;
Yet see in me, who acts thus, the Eternal, the Non-acting.
For action does not taint me; I have no desire for action's fruit.
Who knows me thus, in the Spirit, is likewise not bound by action.

(IV, 13, 14)

Below me nature begets what moves and what does not move.
For this reason, Kaunteya, the world keeps rolling and turning.

(IX, 10)

For without beginning, free of nature's materials, the everlasting Spirit
Abiding in bodies, Kaunteya, does not act, is not tainted.
As the ether's subtlety, all-penetrant, is not tainted,
So the Spirit, dwelling everywhere in the body, is not tainted.

(XIII, 31, 32)

In finiteness not only that which now exists must sink from
sight, but that which has sunk from sight must be reborn. This
we have seen above. The world cycle repeats itself at intervals of
certain millennia, which are called Brahma's Day and Brahma's
Night, and it is God who creates and destroys the cycle.

For he who knows Brahma's day, comprising a thousand ages,
And the night, comprising a thousand, his Spirit knows day and night.
From invisible germinates the visible, when day arrives;
When night falls, it disappears into what is called the invisible.
The organization of creatures, once made, disappears again
When night falls; by itself, Partha, it rises when day returns.

(VIII, 17–19)

All creatures, Kaunteya, return into my nature
When a world-cycle sinks from sight; when one begins, I let them
go again.
For, collecting my own nature, I let go, forever creative,
The organization of creatures by itself, as nature commands.

(IX, 7, 8)

I am the origin of this whole world, and its destruction too.
Loftier than myself there is nothing anywhere, oh Despiser of Gold.
Threaded upon me is this universe, like pearls on their chain.

(VII, 6b, 7)

This last metaphor philosophy seems to have borrowed from
mythology, unless the latter borrowed this poetic-philosophical expression for its aims. For in the plastic arts as well, the series of
created things are represented as a string of pearls. It is interesting
to see a hieroglyph thus deciphered in poetry, or poetry translated
into hieroglyphics. In this connection we must remember the re-

peated appearances of the divine essence which constantly regenerates itself. Indeed it is true that thought, and everything spiritual, cannot exist through rest but only through spontaneous activity, in other words through constant self-regeneration.

> Many births, O Arjuna, were already before this time, your time and
> mine;
> And I in spirit know them, but you, Foe-Vanquisher, do not.
> Though imperishable I am, without beginning, and Lord of all creatures,
> Yet do I collect my own nature within my magic's semblance.
> Whenever justice begins to flag here, O Bharata,
> And injustice starts, I again create myself.
> For the devout's protection, for the destruction of the godless,
> For the steadying of everlasting justice, I arise new from time to time.
> Who thus knows in pure truth my divine doings and becomings,
> He goes, in birth, in death, nowhere but to me, Arjuna.
>
> (IV, 5-9)

The origin of creatures is also described in the following way. Instead of the usual expression for the body the poet uses *kshetra* (field) which one may translate with earthliness but which we may call, more generally, matter, materiality. As constituent parts of it he numbers the five elements, the five sense objects, the eleven instruments of the body, ego, reason, pleasure and pain, desire and revulsion, manifoldness, thinking power, resoluteness, and—very notably—that which is invisible (XIII, 1–7). To this changeable matter he opposes the Knower of Matter. This Krishna calls one with himself. All creativity consists of his relationship with matter.

> Whatever is created, whether fast, whether mobile,
> Is jointly through matter and Knower; know this, Bharata.
>
> (XIII, 26)

> Just as a single sun, sending forth splendor, irradiates this world,
> So irradiates all of matter the Knower, Bharata.
>
> (XIII, 33)

No essential gap in the system of our poem is left, if one leaves out this entire reinterpretation, which is given only in the thirteenth canto, and I confess that it is by no means entirely clear to me. I am most bothered by the enumerations of the constituent parts, among which are numbered, to be sure, the twenty-five usually occurring basic elements of Hindu philosophical systems (Colebrooke, *loc. cit.,* pp. 30–31) but which also contain some already contained in others, such as desire and revulsion in mind, and others which seem alien to earthly matter. I should, for example, have taken the invisible as synonymous with the Knower. In Manu's Code (XII, 12–15) in a likewise obscure passage the same expression occurs in another, more subordinate sense.

God only looks at the heart. He accepts everything which is offered him with devotion: water, a flower, a leaf. He shows an equal disposition toward all. Whoever turns to him, Brahmin or slave, may choose the highest path. But those who are well-intentioned toward all creatures, the virtuous ones who have equanimity and devoutness, are most dear to him (IX, 26, 32, 33; XII, 13–20).

God is the true object of all genuine insight. He is, in an absolute sense, that which is to be recognized. Whereas the poet carries out this theme and briefly summarizes the qualities of God, God's true being presents a paradox which can be resolved only by reference to his intrinsic nature. God includes all finiteness and yet, being infinite, is free of all infiniteness (XIII, 12–17).

In representing a system that is not dogmatically presented, but woven into a conversation, a system which, aside from its intention to be a set of ethical religious instructions about the attainment of the highest consummation, proceeds from a definite situation within a poem, it seemed to me doubly necessary to choose as simple a path as possible. I have therefore carefully collected only those lines above which definitely had as their subject the highest godhead, or rather the absolute concept of divinity. I have all the more used the simple expression "God" in translating these lines, since Krishna speaks in most of the passages about himself, as a personal being. Whatever might for the moment obscure or seemingly confuse this notion I have removed, and shall return to now.

The most important concept to be elucidated is that of Brahma, or divine substance. To prevent misunderstanding I must note immediately that this word, ending with a short "a" is the neuter form of the word "Brahman" and must be differentiated, by ending and gender, from the masculine word "Brahmā" [which represents an individual god of creation].

The neuter form was doubtless chosen significantly. For in our poem as elsewhere, wherever Krishna, the God, and Brahma, the godhead do not coincide, there seems to be the difference between a general divine substance and a personal divine being. There is some talk, furthermore, of the whole Brahma (VII, 29), and this expression is often accompanied by the qualification "the highest" (VIII, 3; XIII, 12) as though the concept were capable of extension and degrees.

Many passages undoubtedly establish that Brahma (neuter) and God are the same concept. It penetrates all (III, 15); the above mentioned description of the godhead as the object of our insight uses the expression "the highest Brahma" and none other (XIII, 11–17); final consummation is the passing over into Brahma (neuter), i.e., into the godhead (II, 72).

Krishna is the same as Brahma (X, 12); he is the highest Brahma itself.

But one cannot reverse the equation, and herein lies the difference. Brahma is the divine primordial power as such, resting as it were upon its everlastingness; in God, i.e., Krishna in this poem, personality is added. Hence Krishna is named alongside with Brahma.

> Whoever saying Om * with the monotone names the godhead, thinking of me,
> Lets the body depart, he walks upon the highest path.
>
> (VIII, 13)

* I shall discuss this word below.

In another passage there is even indicated, with some plainness, a difference in level upon the path to consummation between Brahma and Krishna. After a detailed description of a devout wise man, it reads, he who is of such disposition

> gains strength to become like the godhead;
> Having become godhead, breathing peacefulness, he desires not nor mourns;
> With equanimity toward all creatures, he reaches my highest service;
> Through serving me he recognizes me in truth, how great I am, and who;
> Then, recognizing me in truth he enters into me without hesitation.

(XVIII, 53b–55)

The going over into Krishna is thus represented in this passage as the ultimate and the highest goal, after man has previously become a creature of divine nature.

An even more definite difference between the two is mentioned in a passage which describes them as begetting and as receptive godhead.

> My womb is the great godhead into which I lay my fruit,
> And the origin of all creatures flows only from it, O Bharata.
> For wherever bodies are born of a womb, O Son of Kunti,
> There the great womb is the godhead; I the semen-giving father.

(XIV, 3, 4)

This accords completely with the oriental concepts of the splitting of divine power, emanation from it and return into it. Somewhat alien to the rest of the poem, on the other hand, is this above image which occurs only in this one passage.

Just as in the above lines there is assumed a universal receptive primordial power above and beyond all the individual receptive powers, there is also an absolute action (*karma*) beyond simple action (*akshara*); and there are essences which are beyond spirit, beyond creatures, beyond the gods, beyond sacrificial rites (*adhyatman, adhibhuta, adhideiva, adhiyajna*). It appears, hence, that Hindu philosophy, wherever it perceives individually parceled-out powers or qualities in beings, understands the conceptualization of them in all their purity. It extends them into unlimited universality, not even stopping with Spirit but positing them as true and real archetypal materials. Two things follow: one, that these basic or archetypal materials are the origin of the individually divided powers, and two, that in their purity and infinity they belong wholly or in part to the nature of the godhead.

Absolute action (VIII, 3) is by special definition called the "letting go" or "creating" of creatures which effectuates their existence. For the language combines these two concepts in the same verb (*srij*) and therein remains faithful to the philosophical doctrine that each effect is already contained in its cause and need only be "let go" in order to exist. The concept of action is therefore taken at the primordial point of action, creation itself. It comprises within itself the various separate acts, particularly, with double justification, the rites of sacrifice (III, 14), but it springs from the divine nature (III, 15) which is the primordial mover of all things. In this connection it is no longer strange when we see it said, in immediate context with the godhead and the super-spiritual sphere, that one knows them, and all of action, when one turns toward Krishna in order to free oneself from old age and death. (VII, 29).

The super-spiritual is explained by Krishna with an expression (VIII, 3) which means, literally, "individuated being" and which usually designates that which is intrinsic to a creature, its nature, character, personality (as in V, 14; XVIII, 60). This concept, in other words, is here intensified to that absolute universality that befits a divine being which contains all the causes of its being in itself and which is archetypal personality as such. But we must distinguish this concept from that of the "highest spirit" the expression for which (*paramatman*) also occurs in our poem (XIII, 31).

That which is above creatures, Krishna calls "divided being" (VIII, 4). The individuality of finite beings rests upon their separate personality, in other words upon independence and segregation. The above mentioned concept applied to the former, the present one to the latter. But there must be available a universal basic matter which contains the possibility of dividing itself into segregated parts, since in a system such as this one all beings, regardless of their separateness, are one.

That which is simple and invisible forms the contrast to divided being. It is one and the same with the godhead and Krishna, for both are themselves that which is simple (VIII, 3; XI, 37). But the simple is the highest, as it were, and the most universal divine primordial material. For it is the origin of the godhead itself; the godhead, according to the frequently mentioned concept of the peculiar relationship between cause and effect, is *with and of it,* which the language expresses precisely and completely in a single word (*samudbhawan*) (III, 15).

The question is also raised as to who are the most devoutly immersed; those who worship Krishna in general, or those who worship him as the Simple. The answer is that both attain consummation, but the task demanded of the latter is more difficult, because man, gifted with a body, can only with difficulty raise himself to imagine the invisible (XII, 1–6). From the intention, presumably, to express the simplicity of the godhead even more significantly, arose the sacred mystic name of the godhead: *Om.* In it three tones, "a," "u," and a nasal are interwoven into a single letter, since "a" and "u" here flow together into a nasal "o."

As standing beyond the sacrificial rites, Krishna in a dark and mystic passage names himself (VII, 2, 4) in this, i.e., in his human body, and the same expression occurs in other passages which shed no further light (See VII, 30). Perhaps it is his incarnation which is supposed to be looked upon as sacrifice, and consequently he as the highest archetype of sacrifice, containing all others.

The gods (*deva*) are, in the philosophic systems of the Hindus, merely beings of a higher sort, the foremost and highest (XVII, 4) of creatures, but still created and therefore not comparable with the true divine being, the primordial source of all creation (Colebrooke, *loc. cit.,* p. 33). They are subordinate, just as men are, to the limiting qualities of nature (XVIII, 40), and dwell, together with all other creatures, within Krishna (X, 14, 15). Only those men offer sacrifice to them who are not as pure in their nature as the devotees of the highest God, those who cling to the results of their actions (IV, 12). But these do not return to the highest godhead upon their death, but merely to the gods whom they worshipped (VII, 23).

Brahmā too is to be found within Krishna. Krishna says of himself,

For dwelling place I am of Brahmā and of the everlasting gods' banquet,
Of never-aging justice, and immeasurable bliss.

(XIV, 27)

and Arjuna says of him,

In your body I see the gods, O God, and the hosts of the animal kingdom,
Brahmā in the lotus seat, the ruler, and all the wise devout and the godly serpents.

(XI, 15)

Krishna is greater than he (XI, 37). The first and the last of the here quoted passages, however, are some of those which leave one in doubt as to whether the grammatically neuter divine substance is meant, or the god Brahmā.

What lies beyond the gods is usually called the Spirit (*purusha*), and since the concept attached to this expression plays an important role in one part of our poem, it must here be briefly elucidated.

The exact and intrinsic meaning of the word is masculinity. It means "man" therefore, in both senses [*Mann; Mensch*]. But its customary usage designates man originally only in that aspect in which he is related to higher beings and all things spiritual. For it is actually applied to the creator. In two passages above translated (VIII, 22; XV, 4), where the Spirit has created the world-cycle, containing all creatures within himself, and where Krishna directs himself toward the Spirit, the word is used in the text. Krishna is also called this by Arjuna (X, 12; XI, 18, 38). In this sense *purusha* usually occurs with qualifying adjectives, the highest (VIII, 22), the eternal, the divine (X, 12), the ancient (XI, 38), the primordial

(XV, 4), but it also stands absolute, meaning the Spirit (XI, 18). From this alone one can see that it is not merely a different name for the godhead, and careful examination reveals that it has a wider extension in usage, and shows within the godhead, as well, a certain definite quality or, better, sphere of effectiveness. For it is the working principle of nature, resting within nature but always spiritual, ruling, and subordinating all else to itself. It enters upon relationships with the finite aspect of nature and, as a result, begets and creates earthly things. In Hindu philosophy, even the godhead cannot refrain from doing this. It stems from the idea that God and the creatures are in this sense one, that man can see God and all the creatures within himself, and from this idea, from the divine penetration of nature for purposes of creation, the use of the word comes to apply, so far as I can make out, to divinity as such. Generally speaking therefore, it is the spiritual element which begets upon nature, and when Krishna (VII, 8) calls himself the noblest and finest of every classification among things, he calls himself, among men (males) their *purusha*-power, which the Hindu language expresses merely by a neuter ending and the modification of the stem vowel (*paurushan*). In the Code of Manu there is a very peculiar passage (XII, 118–125) wherein it is stated that the Brahmin can see the whole universe in himself. With playful imagination (of which, incidentally, our poem is entirely free) the gods and the natural beings are divided up among the various parts of the human body. Then, the passage continues, they are all ruled over by the highest spirit, by him who is subtler than an atom (a designation which occurs also in our poem in a passage about to be cited), and whom some call the eternal godhead (Brahma). But when his creativity is described, it agrees perfectly with the kind just described.

> He, penetrating all beings with five times divided matter,
> Like a flame wheel, turns them and rolls them in birth, growth, destruction.
>
> (Manu's Code, XII, 124)

194

From our poem I shall offer two passages in proof, although certain concepts occur in them which will not be discussed until later. In one, the godhead is designated by the word for poet. In the youthful vigor of a nation flowering toward science and knowledge, poetic creation does not seem like a human art but like genuine creation. And manifold, many-shaped, many-colored creation, evoked by the magic of the godhead, standing like a miracle before the youthful mind of man, may well be compared with a poem swishing through the imagination.

> By incessantly directing his aim, unerringly immersing himself,
> Man attains to the Spirit, the highest, godlike One, Partha.
> Whoever thinks of the old high-ruling wise poet, subtler than atom,
> The world-cycle's nourisher, unthinkably manifold, the sun-like luminous One, remote from darkness,
> Whoever devoutly at the hour of death, with the strength of rigid immersion serves him,
> Collecting his breath to the place between his eyebrows, he goes into the god-like, the highest Spirit.
>
> (VIII, 8–10)

> Know both spirit and Nature to be without beginning and everlasting.
> Qualities and transformations know to be nature's companions.
> Cause of the workings of that which is to occur is called Nature;
> Spirit is called the cause of feelings of pleasure and pain.
> Spirit, standing in Nature, takes joy in Nature's qualities.
> His desire for them makes for his begetting, upon good or inferior wombs.
> He the guide, the observer, the enjoyer, the nourisher, the high lord,
> Is also called Primordial Spirit, this highest Spirit, in this body.
> Who knows Nature and knows Spirit, and knows also the qualities,
> He, wherever he may tarry, shall henceforth not be born.
>
> (XIII, 19–23)

The Spirit which pervades the universe permits himself to be thought of in degrees according to his various limiting functions.

Krishna differentiates between a threefold spirit, the divisible spirit who is identical with all creatures, the indivisible one standing at the summit, and a third one, called highest, or primordial, archetypal, who, penetrating the three worlds, nourishes and rules them. Because, he adds, he is higher than the divisible one and superior to the indivisible one, he is called the highest in the world and in the sacred writings (XV, 16–18). One may again here recognize the method of positing universal concepts as real. To the spiritual being which is divided into creatures, and which is defined as their capacity to be thus divided, is opposed another being, of an opposite and higher nature; but for the consummation of the concept both of these together must be contained in a still greater being who can combine their opposed qualities. Manu (I, 19) lets the universe consist of the subtle bodily parts of seven immeasurably strong spirits, *purushas* (the five elements, the ego, and the great soul according to the scholiasts), and adds: the perishable as it comes from the imperishable. Thus the word is here used of archetypal powers generally, but the concepts, above given as its critical ones, of creativity and transcendence over finite nature, are in it.

Nature, as we have just seen, is according to Krishna's teaching as everlasting as the godhead (XIII, 19). It possesses three qualities, *gunas,* which are binding upon spirit as it joins itself to nature. By their binding characteristic is meant all involvement in earthly and worldly things which draw man away from directing his thoughts solely upon the godhead and therefore prevent him from attaining his ultimate goal, perfect peace. In this sense, even the noblest capacities, insight for example, may be binding. The qualities of nature, also called, in an absolute sense, the quality-triad, are in fact different according to the degree to which their binding element is more or less noble.

The first and noblest quality is *sattwa,* literally the quality of being, but being in the sense in which it is completely real, free from all lack, or non-being; as, in other words, being becomes truth for insight and virtue for action. For the word which is originally merely an abstract one, formed from the participle of the verb "to be," is used for both these concepts. I translate this quality of nature, in order to retain as well as may be the connection between all its meanings, with essence [*Wesenheit*].

The second quality is *rajas*. This word actually means "dust" but it comes from a root (*ranj*) which means "stick to," "cling to," and, by a closely connected association, "to color." A noun derived from it is *raga*, which means both color and desire or greed. All these expressions in their imagery and their conceptualization, are closely related.

For the second nature-quality to be designated by this name, several associations of the above complex of meanings no doubt were joined together: the easily excitable violence of crumbled, whirling, dust-like matter; the shimmering, fiery nature of color displays; the nature of dust, belonging to the earth and easily clinging and soiling what it touches. According to how these concepts are considered, there are more or less noble varieties of this quality. Resolute energy, fire of passion, quickness in making up one's mind are part of it; kings and heroes are supplied with it, but always there is in it an admixture of something which drags toward reality and toward earth, and which differentiates it from the quiet and pure grandeur of essence. Those moved by *rajas* love everything great, powerful, and splendid, but they also pursue semblance and are caught in the bright manifold nature of the world. They are even called "unclean" (XVIII, 27) which calls attention to the fact that the worldly mind is not able to escape taint. Even though stormy violence is the main characteristic of this quality, it must be related to the notion of an inferior point of view, not attaining the grandeur and purity of essence, and which may lead to downright taint. I have attempted to combine the various branchings of this concept with the word "earthiness" [*Irdischheit*]. This expression contains simultaneously the striving toward diversity and the clinging to individuality. But I feel quite clearly that, compared with the Hindu word, it is too abstract, too far removed from the concrete application.

The third and lowest nature-quality is *tamas* (related to our

Dämmerung [twilight]), darkness, obscurity, which needs no further explanation.

The differences between these three degrees of finite involvement with nature is shown most philosophically in the above mentioned levels of insight (XVIII, 20–22). The essential man sees in all creatures only the one, in the divided ones, undivided being. To the earthy man there appears in all creatures only their manifold individual separateness. Those enshrouded by darkness cling to individual objects and, without inquiring into deeper levels, in a limited restricted way which fails to realize the nature of things, take the individual objects for the whole. Thus real and undivided being is recognized only by the first group, overlooked by the second, and misinterpreted by the third.

Krishna gives Arjuna the following general explanation of the three qualities:

> Essence, earthiness, darkness are the three qualities of nature;
> They bind, oh Great-armed One, the Spirit, the eternal one, to the body.
> Here now essence radiates forthright, untainted;
> It binds the striving toward insight, O Pure One, with striving of sweet joy.
> Earthiness, breathing hot desire, you shall know by the thirst of passion;
> Through striving for deeds, Kaunteya, it binds the Spirit in the body.
> Darkness breeds lack of insight; it dully paralyzes mortals
> Till they heedlessly sleep in inertia. Thus does it bind them, Bharata.
> (XIV, 5–8)

Afterward, in cantos seventeen and eighteen, Krishna distinguishes a whole series of objects: acts, sacrifices, gifts, beliefs, reason, etc. by the difference imparted to them by those who are gifted with the various qualities; one may easily imagine what these are. Whatever is done with pure motivation, with self-control and equanimity, whatever is directed at the highest, partakes of essence; whatever is done for the wrong reasons, for the sake of passing enjoyment, for the quieting of momentary desire, in unbridled fashion, and directed toward individual, limited objects, partakes of earthiness; whatever is hopelessly bound up in error, wrongheadedness and inert rigidity, of darkness.

An undeniably correct and philosophical view of nature lies in this classification, which first differentiates the genuine, the real from the defective, the faulty, the merely glittering; which seeks the sources of faultiness in the two limitations of all finiteness, the lack of power and the lack of balance, and, in addition, sees even the genuine itself, being after all only finitely real, as a limitation upon nature.

According to a commentator of one of the philosophical works cited by Colebrooke (*loc. cit.,* p. 40) one might be led to believe that the three nature-qualities are divided, according to their degree of worth, among gods, men, and animals, and hence all men partake of the quality of earthiness. This is by no means the opinion expressed in our poem, however. The plain conclusion to be reached from the last two cantos is that all three qualities are divided variously among men. Whether they are what determine the caste differences is a question harder to decide. It is stated, to be sure, that the castes are differentiated according to the qualities, *guna,* of their specific nature, (XVIII, 41; IV, 13), and essence could be made to serve as the mark of the Brahmin, earthiness of the warrior. But it would mean, since there are four castes, that two must serve under the same concept and, in any event, the word *guna* in this connection might easily have a more general meaning.

Actions spring from these three qualities, and when a man considers himself as the cause of his actions, it is really the qualities which enter upon their actualization (III, 27–29).

Likewise it is in God. All being of the three qualities stems from him; his above-mentioned magic power is composed of them and deludes men just by veiling from them the realization that God is higher than the qualities and imperishable (VII, 12–14). But they are in him only because nature is in him, for immediately speaking they belong to nature (XIII, 21); they bind his freedom just as little as nature and his own actions bind him. That is why he is referred to as being at the same time devoid of qualities and enjoyer of qualities (XIII, 14).

The overcoming of these qualities leads to immortality (XIV, 20), and although there is no creature, neither on earth nor in heaven, neither among gods nor among men, in whom they are not present, nonetheless one's effort must go to liberate oneself from them (II, 45). One may be looked upon as liberated from them as soon as one can dedicate oneself to thought of the godhead and its service, in perfect equanimity about all earthly success or failure, observing the rule of the qualities in oneself as though one were a stranger, without participating in their workings (XIV, 22-26).

The system of Hindu philosophy of which the doctrines of Krishna as developed in the conversation comprising this poem are a part of the *sankhya* system, on the whole, whose theoretical dicta I have here tried to present. This is the one which endeavors to bring arithmetical completeness and exactness into the investigation of the nature of things by enumerating its principles. There exist several branches of it but they all share the basic principle that certain work must be done to avoid future evil and that clear insight into pure, discriminating truth is the way to this. One doctrine within the system rests with the application of the rational understanding and denies any proofs of the existence of God as an infinite being. Another doctrine, that of *yoga,* not only places God in his independent infinitude at the summit of all things but sees the true means for reaching eternal bliss in the deepest and most withdrawn concentration upon God's being (Colebrooke, *loc. cit.,* pp. 20, 24-26, 37, 38).

Krishna definitely distinguishes between these two doctrines by telling Arjuna as early as the second canto that what has up to now been demonstrated to him for rational reasons (*sankhya*) he shall now hear by attuning his spirit to the spirit of *yoga* (II, 39). And in all his remaining lecture, he visibly adheres to the latter. His teaching, in other words, is *yoga*-teaching. He had already revealed it once, he says, and it had been handed down by tradition among the wise men of yore, but in the course of time it had sunk from sight and that is why he will explain it anew to Arjuna (IV, 1–3). But it is an esoteric teaching which may only be communicated to one who is worthy of it (XVIII, 67–69). Whether and in how far our poem here agrees with the work of Patandshali cannot be decided from Colebrooke's brief remarks. An exact comparison of the two would be highly interesting, and I should have put off my present paper if it did not seem likely that the English scholar has not much intention of returning to this subject. The concept of *yoga* is one of the differentiating marks of this philosophy and, according to our way of thinking, is part of its practice. I shall therefore proceed to develop that part of the doctrine which has to do with the *summum bonum* and the means for attaining it and conclude with this practical part my entire presentation of Krishna's teachings.

Yoga is a noun derived from the root *yuj,* to unite, to bind together—Latin *jungere* [Engl. yoke]—and signifies the union of one object with another. All the many derivations of the word lead back to this basic meaning. In a philosophical sense *yoga* is the steadfast orientation of the mind toward the godhead, withdrawing from all other objects, even from inward thoughts, halting if possible all movements and bodily actions, immersing itself alone and exclusively into the nature of godhead, and seeking to unite with it. I shall express the word by "immersion" [*Vertiefung*] and have already done so above, several times (VIII, 8–10). For even though any translation of an expression in a language that has developed from a wholly individual point of view with a single word of one's own language is faulty, it is the inward turning which is the main characteristic of the *yogi* (the one devoted to the teaching of *yoga*). Also there lies in the word "immersion" the mystic mood characteristic of the *yogi,* the mood most naturally experienced in connection with ultimate things. Through its orientation toward the godhead the concept adds to itself that of devoutness (II, 61; VI, 47; IX, 14); because of the exclusive yielding of the human being to one object, it approaches also the ideas of consecration, dedication. In this sense the Latin expression *devotio* is a good one for it, and the words derived from *devotio* in the modern languages. But the original meaning of combining, unifying, gets lost in such a translation and the whole meaning of the word presumably narrows down too far. For according to a passage in Colebrooke (p. 36) where he speaks explicitly about "meditation on special topics" it seems possible that the rigid concentration of the *yogi* may be directed to objects other than the godhead. Also *devotio* affords no usefulness whatever in those places, as we shall see further on, where *yoga* is described as an active energy and a characteristic of the godhead itself. When used for effort, or occupation, the word contains the concepts of attuning oneself to something, to settle upon something, to practice or exercise something, and in such various meanings it leads to combinations in various compounds, depending on whether the aim or the means to be applied are to be further defined.

The first demand of immersion is the repression of all passions, the withdrawing from the violence of the senses, and even from the outer objects that stimulate them. Only when spirituality is in control, can immersion attain its power.

> The immersed ones, upon striving, see Him * as they rest in themselves,
> But, though likewise striving, the not perfectly spiritual ones do not.
>
> (XV, 11)

In this way we arrive here too at the destruction of action through indifference toward its result, so much so, that as we saw earlier (II, 47, 48), equanimity and immersion are looked upon as synonymous. When in such fashion all movement of passion, in fact of slightest inclination, is silenced, and the soul is attuned to perfect unwillingness to take sides (VI, 9), then reflection and withdrawn meditation can assume control. Thus the spirit must immerse itself into the thought of the godhead, disturbed by nothing alien, collected solely in itself, and must cling with unerringly stead-

* The reference is to the highest ruler.

fast perseverance to archetypal truth. But at this point, as we have seen upon other occasions as well, this system turns its dogma at the very summit into its opposite. Now even inward thought is to be suppressed; all inner and outer change is to be nullified, as being disturbing to consummate peace, to the eternal selfsame existence of the imperishable. This is expressed as an extinguishing, a wafting away of the earthly spirit. One is inclined now to interpret nonthinking as merely the suppression of all thinking of earthly thoughts. In the Code of Manu (XII, 122) it is said of the highest Spirit that one may reach it only with slumbering thought. But the scholiast declares that this is true only of the closing off of the outward senses. I doubt, however, that this way of explaining which constitutes the explaining away of unusual concepts into quite ordinary ones accords with the true content of this system.

A main passage about immersion in our poem is the following one:

Like a lamp which does not flicker in the breeze is a man
When immersed, steadfast, immersed in self-immersion.
There where the spirit's thinking lies controlled through the practice of immersion,
Where through Self alone, seeing his Self in himself, man is glad,
Knowing endless bliss, felt only by spirit, super-sensual bliss,
Where, steadfast persevering, he never deviates from eternal truth,
Where, having attained this, he prefers it to all other attainments,
And where misfortune, even severe, no longer shocks the steadfast—
This, this dissolving of pain, you must know, is called immersion.
In immersion a man must so immerse himself, alienated from his senses,
Rooting out all desire's striving, the result of stubborn willfulness,
Taming with the mind completely the essence of all the senses.
Striving thus, he gradually comes to rest, winning steadfastness of spirit,
Concentrating his mind upon his Self and thinking of nothing.
Wherever, wherever may roam the unsteady easily mobile element,
Wherever it is, he shall lead it back to lie in control of the inward Self.

Then shall the highest of blessings be visited upon the immersed one,
the quiet one,
Whose peace is no longer disturbed by earthiness, this pure one who
has become God.

(VI, 19–27)

Other passages (V, 27, 28; VI, 10–15; VIII, 10–14) add more
mystical and superstitiously playful prescriptions to this, but they
too always rest upon the foundations of the dogma here indicated.
The man practicing immersion is supposed to sit in a clean place,
far from people, in a seat not too high and not too low and covered
with animal hides and sacrificial grass. He is to hold his throat and
neck rigid, his body in balance, withdraw his breath high into his
head, breathe regularly in and out through the nostrils, look at no
external object but fix his gaze between the middle of his eyebrows
and upon the tip of his nose. And he is to intone the above mentioned mysterious name of the godhead, Om.

This doctrine and this school undoubtedly produced the *yogis*
which are even today common in India. Governor Warren Hastings
describes a noteworthy instance in a letter written in 1784 and published as a preface to Wilkins' translation of our poem. The man
whom he had seen in the performance of such a spiritual exercise
made such an impression on him, that he considers it quite possible,
he writes, that this separation of the soul and the senses, practiced
as a schooled discipline, might well have produced "new tracks and
combinations of sentiment," and that truths comparable to our
simplest ones may well have arisen from it. It is difficult, however,
to see in such extremes, even if they are true and not feigned, anything other than that same rapturous mysticism which turns up in
different guises in many regions, systems, and religions.

So far as our poem is concerned, at least it does not favor this
exercise as a lasting and steady one, or as comprising man's entire
contemplative life. We saw above how much emphasis is placed on
action, and the most violent and liveliest action of all, that of the
turmoil of battle; how it is depicted as an illusion to wish to stop
the efforts of earthly powers toward action and change by non-

action; how each man must solve the problem for himself by acting according to the duties of his caste but, disregarding results, maintaining himself spiritually above his action.

So far as reflection and investigation into what is truth is concerned, Krishna's teaching proceeds clearly from the principle that pure truth—that which yields insight or intuition (*tattwa*) into things as they are—cannot be found by way of discursive or rationalizing reason; that to find it one must prepare the mind, purify it of all taint and pettiness, allow insight to assume control over it, and then animate an inner feeling for truth within it, directing the spirit to that point in which the self is connected with things as such, as part of them. Through its insight into the oneness of all spirituality and its recognition of individuality (*prithaktawa*) as the real limitation of man, this doctrine very definitely and carefully discriminates between the finite and the infinite.

It even appears as though truth might originally have been placed into man and only gradually have sunk into the slumber of forgetfulness. In any event, Arjuna's answer, when Krishna at the end of their conversation asks him whether he has now reached steadfast insight, may indicate as much.

> Disappeared has my error; my memory through you has returned. Now I am rid of doubt, am steadfast, and shall accomplish what you say.
>
> (XVIII, 73)

Since this doctrine means to reach direct insight through inner perception, its main demand of the spirit is firmness and steadfastness, upon whose utmost exertion and persevering orientation toward the point to be investigated success necessarily depends. Hence it makes character building the means for investigation of truth, and collects and focuses all the powers of the mind upon this single point. But the frame of mind thus brought forth is always only one possibility among many, since there are countless dispositions and opinions which divide on various points; those, for example, who proceed in accordance with reason, with rationality, and those who follow certain inclinations and motives in their actions (II, 41–44). Therefore there is nothing so hostile to this teaching as doubt, which is treated like a crime.

> Devoid of insight and without faith, the doubt-breather perishes;
> Not this world, not that one, can bring joy to the doubt-breather.
> Whoever acts, while immersed, renounces; he destroys doubt through insight;
> Actions cannot bind the spiritual one, O Despiser of Gold.
>
> (IV, 40, 41)

By the contrast in the last verse one can see in what sense "spirit" is here taken: not as mere ability to think, which is a main characteristic of a doubter, but as a source of immediate knowledge.

The necessary step which leads to immersion is insight. For in order to attain immersion, a man must have got as far as the highest of the nature-qualities, the one referred to as "essence" (XVIII, 33–35). But to do this he needs insight.

> When insight moves into all the gates of this body, filling them with splendor,
> Then for ripeness—you must know—essence is enough.
>
> (XIV, 11)

By insight is understood the faculty which ties together the strings of all individual investigation, which discriminates between the perishable and the imperishable, which knows the field (matter) from the knower of the field, and which knows the way to ultimate consummation (XIII, 27, 2; XVIII, 50). Insofar as insight simultaneously affects spirit and character, all the virtues of both the wise man and the saint are included in its description (XIII, 7–11). It is recommended and praised as the fire which turns the binding actions of man into ashes, as the sun which illumines the highest path, as the purification which the wise man experiences within himself. Krishna says of him who has it that he, Krishna, looks upon him as though he were his own Self (IV, 33–38; V, 16, 17; VII, 15–20).

Freedom from all stirrings of the senses is its basis; as soon as insight controls a man, ever-flowing from a joyous stillness within him, Spirit takes him over and fills him completely (II, 65).

Faith likewise must necessarily proceed from immediate insight and a frame of mind which is described of the state of immersion (VI, 47; XII, 2). Faith can save from perdition even a man who has been seduced by desire to give up the steady search for what is highest (VI, 37–45). It is presented as preceding insight and leading to it; an inner feeling of truth is described as a state over which insight then pours its full light (IV, 39). Faith is three-fold in accordance with the three nature-qualities, since it springs from man's character. Character and the object of faith stand in an immediate relation to each other within every man. For faith is the image of character, and the faithful believer is like that in which he believes (XVII, 2, 3).

Faith, insight, immersion and all other spiritual exercises have as their highest aim the liberation from the necessity of being reborn after earthly death (IV, 9; XIII, 23). Man may be transformed by reincarnation into a nobler and happier being (VI, 41, 42); he may in the interval between world-cycles enjoy heavenly bliss (IX, 20, 21), but his final aim is his total removal from the forever rolling wheel of returning birth, the loosening of all the birth bonds (II, 51). In a philosophy which looks upon all actions, all sense stirrings, even the most unavoidable bodily functions, as disturbing to the spirit, as binding and soiling, earthly life can only appear unsteady and joyless (IX, 33). The world is looked upon as a forever rolling machine which all who are born into it are forced to mount (XVIII, 61). Therefore the highest happiness must lie in rest, in peace (II, 66). But since death, within the confines of finiteness, must be inevitably followed by birth, (II, 27) there is no way of attaining perfect peace other than going over into the godhead, as the seat of all imperishability and changelessness (VI, 15; XIII, 30; XVIII, 55). This is made possible by the interrelationship of all purely spiritual forces whose discrimination from all corporeality is the aim of immersion. Thus do the various parts of the system cohere firmly and precisely.

The attainment of the ultimate goal is promised to the devout and the faithful several times on almost every page of our book; it has already been attained by saints and sages (XIV, 1). It is simply called the highest (III, 19), the liberation (III, 31; IV, 15), or the highest way (VI, 45), the eternal way (XVIII, 56), the never-returning way (V, 17), the consummation (XII, 10), although in another passage (XVIII, 50) consummation is distinguished from attainment to the godhead which is considered an even higher step; further it is called highest peace (IV, 39), going to God, to Krishna, to the godhead, to Brahma (IV, 9, 24), contact with the godhead (VI, 28), entry into God's existence (IV, 10), the wafting away (*nirwana* from *wa,* to waft) into the godhead (II, 72), the ability to become the godhead (XIV, 26), the transformation into godhead (V, 24).

To it shall attain those who exclusively devote themselves to the highest, who serve no inferior being, who orient their thoughts solely upon the godhead. For the object of man's devotion is his destination after death (VIII, 13; IX, 25; XVI, 19). Particularly decisive in this is the direction of his thoughts during the hour of death (VIII, 5, 6). Those who turn upon the right path also liberate themselves thereby from the upheavals of the world-cycles; they are not reborn when the world is recreated; they do not perish when the world is destroyed (XIV, 2).

The world of Brahmā is the borderline of reincarnation.

The worlds up to Brahmā's world are subject to return, Arjuna;
Who goes to me, Kaunteya, shall not experience rebirth.

(VIII, 16)

But this is one of those above-mentioned passages in which there is some doubt whether the neuter Brahma, divine substance, or the personal God Brahmā is meant. Judging from context, I assume the latter.

Precise as the grammatical definition of Sanskrit words is, nonetheless the declension of masculine and neuter nouns coincides in several of the cases (VIII, 17; XI, 37; XIV, 27), and the language thus has some peculiarities which do not permit distinction as to gender in several instances. Such is the case when masculine and neuter, or as sometimes happens, all three genders have the same basic form, and this basic form becomes an element in compound words (II, 72; III, 15; IV, 24, 25; VIII, 16; XIII, 4; XVIII, 53, 54; also in the Code of Manu, I, 97), and when therefore a case of vocalic contraction arises through the last vowel, either long or short, of one word being the same as the initial vowel of the next (IV, 24; Manu, I, 11). Out of all the passages above cited there seem to me but four instances (VIII, 16–17; XI, 37; XIV, 27), using compounds such as Brahma's seat, Brahma's day, Brahma's world, etc., where the god is meant; in all the rest, particularly those where the transition or transformation of man into God is referred to, the neuter Brahma is meant, the divine substance. Schlegel's very exact translation agrees with this except in one instance (XIV, 27). It expresses the neuter by the word *numen* or another substantive, the god by his name.

Anyone, however, who wishes to attain to the highest abode of peace, here in an image called Brahmā's world, must at some earlier time have purified his nature by means of several incarnations (VI, 45; VII, 19). This destiny which comes upon man after his death takes several forms, according to the three nature-qualities. Those who depart in darkness sink into the depths and are reborn from dull, sluggish creatures; those who die in earthiness maintain themselves in the middle regions and see the light once more among those eager for deeds; those who leave life with matured essence are raised upward toward the untainted worlds of those who know the highest (XIV, 14, 15, 18). This destination seems to be the same as that offered the faithful but not quite consummate ones, who, before they must be reborn, may spend an infinite number of years in the worlds of those who led pure lives (VI, 41, 42). The enjoyment of heavenly bliss in the world of Indra (opposed to the world of Brahma) is perhaps connected with this; it too is but a passing reward, for when the credit earned on earth is used up, those who have shared the world of Indra must return to this world of death (IX, 20–22). This is described as being the lot of those who with limited minds have clung to the sacred writings and to the rituals prescribed in them.

Our poem too inveighs against the teachings of the Vedas and against scientific theology, not precisely condemning them but representing them as believed in by those who do not investigate the ultimate grounds, who do not possess the true purity of spirit, and who do not attain the highest goal (II, 41–53).

Since the ultimate aim of immersion is the transformation of human nature into godly nature, it cannot be merely an intellectual exercise. A genuine energy which produces action must lie in it, an energy of such a sort that it can bring forth what is outside the course of nature, changing the ways and the barriers of existence itself. This is readily understood, considering the required mental effort which rests, preferably, on a steadfast and tenacious will, and for which the mind is prepared by the vanquishing of the passions, the suppression of the sense-stirrings, and the removal of all outer impressions, even to the cessation of bodily functions.

Patandshali's *yoga* doctrine contains a whole chapter about this energy, *wibhuti,* literally "becoming otherwise," in other words, transformation. He posits it in all sorts of magical powers: thought-reading, gaining the strength of an elephant, flying through the air, viewing all worlds simultaneously, etc. *Yogi* and magician are therefore synonymous among the common people of India (Colebrooke, *loc. cit.,* p. 36).

Superstitious games or tricks of this sort are mentioned by no syllable of our poem which is quite pure in this respect; the expression *wibhuti* is not used in it by any mortal, and the energy of *yoga* is not explicitly thought of at all, except in connection with man's becoming god, and insofar as it spreads over the mind when doubts are cut off and the senses are vanquished. In this connection the immersion directed toward self-control is likened to a fire kindled at the flame of insight (IV, 27), a most significant metaphor which accords with the nature of immersion as seizing the entire human being.

But the magic power (*wibhuti*) is, in our poem, ascribed to the godhead, as we have already seen, and since the godhead cannot transform divine nature into something higher, it refers instead to the opposite, to the entering of infinity into the finite, a process which is opposed to the nature of creatures, as well. It is, in other words, the capacity of the godhead for creativity (X, 6, 7), for assuming a shape and form (XI, 47); for permitting creatures to rest in itself and simultaneously not rest in itself (IX, 5). This occurs through the connection of godhead with nature, and here again we see the original archetypal concept of connectedness.

In the course of the conversation Krishna also mentions other means for attaining blessedness, especially sacrifice and penitence. He enumerates several kinds of sacrifices and rituals, but gives preference to the sacrifice of insight (IV, 25-33). Whoever reads his sacred conversation with Arjuna, says Krishna, can worship him with that sacrifice (XVIII, 70). For insight must, as we have seen, prepare the mind for immersion.

Penitence is subordinate to immersion (VI, 46). Krishna inveighs strongly against tortures which are inflicted upon themselves by penitents for reasons of hypocrisy, foolish delusion, or in order to harm others—as continues to be the custom in India today. He classifies such people with those among whom the nature-quality of darkness is predominant (XVII, 5, 6, 19).

Yoga is an ethical doctrine, taking for its basis the vanquishing of the passions and the disinterestedness of actions, insisting everywhere upon removal of sense stimuli, upon control by insight, upon orientation of the mind toward godhead. In many individual passages as well, purity of action and virtue are woven into the system. The man who is immersed hates no one; he is the friend of all creatures; he considers the welfare of all (XII, 4, 13). Whoever acknowledges the godhead working in all things and creatures, does no violence to himself (XIII, 28). Evil men do not reach God (VII, 15); no one who has done right, even though he did not reach consummate purity, shall be lost (VI, 40). Noteworthy is the admonition for each man to fulfill his duty according to his caste, even if guilt is involved in so doing, and likewise the immediately following explanation:

> For all doing is shrouded in guilt, like the blaze of the flame in smoke.

(XVIII, 48b)

In this line there is, to be sure, a deep universal truth, particularly considering the concept of action peculiar to this system, but one must also remember that according to the ideas lying at the bottom of the division into castes many things were considered to be subject to guilt which do not seem so to more universal ethical ideas. It was forbidden, for example, to kill animals, to wound any sort of sentient creature; even sacrificial rites, since such things were done as part of them, were not considered to be absolutely pure (Colebrooke, *loc. cit.,* p. 28).

In the notion, however, that man is by birth condemned, as it were, to a specific mental disposition by virtue of his caste, lies a doctrine of fatalism, a predestination independent of the will, and this is stressed especially where the difference is described between those men who are born to a divine fate and those who are born to a demonic fate. To the former are ascribed all virtues, to the latter all vices; after their death Krishna returns them over and over into demonic begetting and birth, and they finally sink down to the lowest path (XVII, 5, 6). The combination of ethical freedom with the concatenation of mutually determinative natural events and actions is, closely examined, an insoluble task for any philosophic system. Freedom can only be felt and demanded; it cannot be proved in experience; it can be placed at the summit of the course of nature as the first and basic ground; it cannot be sought or found in the midst of natural events. From this point of view we must also look upon the passages in this poem which seemingly contradict one another. From an absolute point of view, ethical freedom is completely safe. The godhead participates causally in no action of man, whether good or evil; all actions originate in the character of the one who performs them. Passion and error shroud insight; that is why the human race sins. But these enemies can and must be overcome; the rule of insight can and must be secured (III, 37–43; V, 14, 15). When, as we saw above, man is contrariwise described on the one hand as an instrument of the godhead which truly performs all action, and on the other hand as being overcome by the torrent of natural events, this is said in connection with the concatenation of all nature in its totality, whereas, when freedom is stipulated, it is said of individual actions and the disposition of those performing them. *Yoga* doctrine is, in fact more than any other philosophy founded on the necessity of ethical freedom, since the nature-transforming perseverance and steadfastness of the will which is its final aim can spring only from absolute freedom which opposes itself to all the stirrings of finite nature.

Krishna counsels to honor him alone and leave all other precepts regarded as holy (XVIII, 66). He therefore raises his doctrine to be the only true one and the only one leading to consummation. But he does not reject wholly the practice of sacrificing to other and inferior gods. Those who do so, he says, really simultaneously address themselves to him, though not in the proper way. He remains the lord and the enjoyer of all sacrifices; only they do not recognize him in his truth (IX, 23, 24). Likewise he does not always judge other philosophic systems with rigid severity, but instead permits them to remain (V, 2), not as preferential or mediating functions, because this would directly oppose the nature of immersion which is undeviatingly oriented toward one goal, but because the godhead, which is the final aim of his teachings, may be reached from all sides and by many different paths. Thus there is spread throughout this whole poem a gentle and beneficent spirit of forbearance. [V, 190–232]

Art in society:

All poetry stems from a world view

Every true poet's poetry is always at the same time a world view. It originates in the way in which his individuality confronts phenomena and is in turn determined by them, both in such intimate interrelationship that no one can tell whether the first impulse comes from the individual or from the objects. Even minor works rightly make this claim; the task to be solved by the poet is the same in a small particular framework as in his over-all life's work: to comprehend and represent his object as a living phenomenon, with all its manifold and necessary interrelationships. [VI, 538]

On untimely works of art

I have just seen a performance of *Don Carlos* with a great deal of pleasure, dear Li. Aside from the pleasure of the drama itself, it meant for me a return to our early youth. I read it several times with you. . . . There is no one left today who could write such a play; even its faults show too much greatness for people nowadays. The titanic quality in idea as well as expression that was so typical of Schiller is not found elsewhere. . . . With Schiller we lost the greatest mind that ever lived among us. I have often wanted to write about it and would enjoy doing this more than anything else, but I never quite know how to go about it. Besides, the time seems entirely wrong; I don't believe there exists any feeling or understanding for Schiller just now. [To Caroline v. Humboldt, June 1817]

The objective portrayal of subjectivity is the artist's hardest task

The most difficult subject for an artist to undertake is the portrayal of the individuality of a delicate, sensitive soul. To describe it, one must sense it; to wholly sense it, possess one oneself, and only with the happiest juxtaposition of balance of powers within and a gentle and considerate fate without, does one succeed in developing one's sensitivity and with it one's character so freely and nobly that it is not merely ready to respect truth and right, to practice goodness and love, but that truth, right, goodness and love emanate from it, appearing as so many different expressions of its all-encompassing strength. An artist who works in this field makes indeed high demands on himself. [II, 335]

*   *   *

If the reader is to forget his own person, he must not be reminded of the person of the author. [II, 164]

What morality may learn from art

How would it be possible . . . to picture vividly the period of youth without there being present, in the imagination, the child from which the youth grew, the man toward whom his strength is maturing, the old age in which the last sparks of his blaze die down! How could one paint the hero on the field of battle, commanding death itself, though in the midst of corpses, and ordering planned destruction, without evoking at the same time in one's soul the quiet thinker who, within his lonely walls, far from all participating activity and alienated from the events of the moment, espies truths which will perhaps bear fruit only in centuries to come, as well as the quiet plowman who takes care only of the needs of the day, who confronts only the forever same, forever changing seasons, and who thinks only of this year's harvest!

One condition invariably, by just being, evokes all other conditions; single men, like humanity itself, can subsist only in community. This is the great gain which creative imagination presents to moral man: it teaches him to unite all the epochs of life, to continue the past, to start on the future, without being any less real a part of the present. [II, 139 f.]

On the literary arts:

The precarious position of literature among the arts

No art is as severely tempted to displace its unique beauty with borrowed feathers as the art of literature. It shares with every other art the possibility of merely filling the imagination with pleasant and entertaining images, of swamping it with bright, meaningless fireworks, instead of preserving it free and active, of requiring it to produce a definite object of its own. In addition, however, literature has another bypath to fear, which is uniquely its own. Since it operates through language . . . it easily invades the fields of philosophy and tries to interest the mind and the heart instead of just the imagination. Since it is thus in a better position to operate through something which is not art at all, it has the greatest number of devotees, whereas music, painting, and sculpture . . . are able to fascinate only the more rarely met with genuine esthetic sense.

On such byways it is easy for literature to degenerate, to try to please by means of picturesque images, to astonish and move by splendid and touching phrases. Thus it sinks from being the off-spring of genius to a mere work of talent. It is still capable of great effects in the hands of certain masters (whom one must not under-rate for this); it can still set imagination in motion while it gains control over the mind and heart; it can still stimulate admiration and emotion by flashes of genius, but what will be missing is a certain luminous and warming flame. There will be lacking that certain intimate inspiration, that high and harmonious serenity which tells us surely that we are in the presence of a genuine work of art.

For unless imagination works freely and alone, it cannot transfer us beyond the circle of reality into the realm of ideality. But this alone, regardless of what means are used, makes for the genuine esthetic effect. [II, 143 f.]

The art of the stage

To leave a truly great dramatic work is the highest achievement in life, measured against all fame and all greatness. In no other form does the spirit live on so creatively and effectively; in none other does it so move all humanity in the breast of each, nor such a variety of human beings. Whoever has accomplished this has accomplished the best. [To Caroline v. Humboldt, August 1819]

* * *

For an actor it is always essential that he does not separate the poetic from the pictorial elements of his art, and especially that he does not give the latter preference, for then he would not only sink from the summit of his true art but actually block his return to it. No art is as closely related, in a certain way, to acting as is the dance. Now just as a good dancer is never content to exhibit various separate beauties but instead strives for beauty and harmony of the whole, just as he does not wish to show several distinguished and graceful motions but instead a body which is incapable of moving other than with distinction and grace, just as he finally persuades the spectator to admire nothing so much as the inner, organic form which develops in a thousand different shapes, ruling them all, and esthetically harmonious in all—so must the actor focus the entire imagination of his spectator upon the soul which animates him, which shines forth from his voice, his expressions, his gestures. . . .

But how can an actor objectify what by its very nature is unobjectifiable? Of course he can show only utterances, but there is undeniably a mood of man in which he feels his own individual nature wholly and purely, a mood in which all his sensations and feelings and attitudes are intimately bound up with one another. When the actor assumes such a mood, when his voice, expressions, and gestures all flow out of it, then he stirs a similar mood in his spectators. And now there can arise in reality what always arises wherever art holds genuine sway: the spectator sees more than the artist objectifies.

It is truly an enormous task to stir all the feelings of mankind, to conjure up the profoundest and mightiest forces of nature, and to retain them in the realm of art, to subject them to esthetic control. And yet this is what we demand of an actor whose medium, if

I may say so, is the entirety of human sensation, speech, and action. A study of the art of acting thus leads to the utmost subtleties of psychological insight. [II, 394 f.]

Poetry and prose

Linguistic usage in everyday life must of course be different from linguistic usage in inward life, representing ideas and feelings, since the speaker in either case partakes of a wholly different mood. For the sharper and purer a thought hovers before his mind, the less it can be endured if the form of speech in which it will be cast is inappropriate. This is the origin of prose—and one should not call everything prose which is not verse. For their fields diverge only where careful attention is given to the form of presentation. The only true view of prose is that it is derived from poetry which always comes first when any language is treated as an art form. For rhythm is the lifeblood of prose as well, and it is not even free of meter, being rather an extension of the narrowly binding meter of poetry. The characteristic difference between poetry and prose, however, is that prose declares by its form that it wishes to accompany and serve thought. Poetry cannot do without at least appearing to control thought or actually bringing it forth. [V, 343]

*   *   *

There are two phenomena of language in which [all the individual aspects of the mutual influences of the character and the language of nations] not only most decisively coincide, but which so reveal the influence of their wholeness that all concepts of particularity disappear from them. These are poetry and prose. We must call them phenomena of language, since even the original structure of a language tends to direct it to one or the other, or, where its form is truly a great one, to the proportionate development of both, and since they in turn react back upon the structure of the language. Truly, however, they are first of all the developmental track of intellectuality itself and must, when its structure is not deficient and its orbit not disturbed, necessarily unwind themselves along it. Poetry and prose therefore require most careful study, not only in relation to each other, but particularly in connection with their relative time of origin.

If we look at both from their most concrete as well as their most ideal side simultaneously, we see that they take separate paths to attain similar goals. For both move from reality toward something which does not belong to reality. Poetry conceives of reality in its sensuous phenomenality, as it is externally and internally perceived by us, but it is unperturbed about whatever makes reality be what it is. In fact poetry specifically rejects anything of a reasoning or causal character. It relates the sensuous phenomena in creative imagination, and guides us through them to a view of an artistically ideal wholeness. Prose looks precisely for the roots of reality which connect it to existence in all the vast network of its connections. It then intellectually combines facts with facts and concepts with concepts, striving for an objective connection of them all within an idea. The difference between poetry and prose as just outlined is drawn only as it expresses itself in their true essence, to be sure. If one looks only at any given piece of poetry or prose as it is actually found in a given language . . . one finds that the inner direction here called prose may be executed in metrical or rhythmic language and that of poetry in unmetrical and arhythmic language, but only at some cost to both. For prose expressed in poetic form has neither the character of poetry nor wholly that of prose, and likewise with poetry disguised as prose. Poetic contents perforce bring about poetic garments, and there are many instances of poets who, feeling this power, have completed in verse something they began in prose.

What both poetry and prose have in common—to return now to their intrinsic nature—is the tension and the comprehensiveness of soul that is necessitated by full penetration of reality coupled with attainment of an ideal relationship of infinite variety, plus the ability to recollect the mind to a consistent pursuit of a once decided upon path. Yet this too must be rightly understood to mean that such a path never excludes its opposite within the spiritual economy of a nation and its language, but actually furthers it as well as itself. Both, the mood of poetry and that of prose, must complement each other to form the communal spirit which permits men to sink their roots deep into reality, keeping always in mind that the deeper the roots, the more joyous the towering into a freer element. The poetry of a people has not reached its summit until by its variety and its free flexibility it announces the possibility of an equivalent development of prose. Since the human spirit, as we conceive of it in strength and freedom, needs to attain both configurations, we know one by the other, just as we can tell from a fragment of sculpture that it once was part of a grouping.

Prose however may be used in another sense as well. It can stop at the mere presentation of facts and at totally external purposes. It may be used for the mere communication of things, rather than the awakening of ideas and feelings. In such a case it does not depart from ordinary speech and never reaches the true heights of what we have been calling prose. Prose in this wider sense then cannot be considered a developmental track of intellectuality; its references are not to form but to matter alone. But wherever prose pursues its higher path it needs, just like poetry, certain special means for reaching deeply into the human psyche. It has to raise itself to that ennobled form of speech of which alone we may speak if we wish to consider it the true mate of poetry. Prose in this intrinsic sense demands a comprehension of its object which requires all the combined capacities of the total psychic constitution. This means a treatment of the object which shows it as radiating toward all the receptive subjects upon which it works. Discriminating rationality is not active by itself; all the other powers of mind aid it, thus forming the point of view properly known as "spirited," "inspired." In such a union of powers, the spirit carries in addition to its work upon a given object, the imprint of its mood over into speech. Language, elevated by the verve of thought, shows forth its advantages but subordinates them to purposes of the whole spirit. It is the moral feeling-life that imparts itself to the language; the soul that shines through the style. In a manner wholly individual and peculiar to itself, there reveals itself in prose, through the subordination and the dialectic of its sentences, the logical eurythmy which corresponds to thought development. This is the internal command which ordinary speech obeys when it becomes elevated by a special purpose. If an author yields too far to it, he produces a mixture of poetry and rhetoric prose. But in "spirited," "inspired" prose, all the details here listed singly act together, thereby sketching out the whole living birth of a thought, the whole process of spirit's wrestling with an object. Wherever permitted, the thought shapes up like a free spontaneous inspiration and performs in the realm of truth what spontaneous beauty performs in the realm of poetry.

From all this we may see that poetry and prose are conditioned by similar general demands. In both there must be an inward and spontaneous verve which lifts and carries the spirit. Man in his whole individuatedness must move with his thought toward both outer and inner world and, understanding particulars, leave to them that form which relates them to the whole. In their directions, however, and their means for achieving their effects, poetry and prose are different and can really never be mingled. In reference to language we should particularly note that poetry's true nature is inseparable from that of music, whereas prose entrusts itself to language alone. How intrinsically Greek poetry was bound up with instrumental music, is well-known, and the same is true of Hebrew lyric poetry. . . . However poetic a thought and even its language seems to be, if the musical element is missing, we do not feel we are on the genuine ground of poetry. Hence the natural alliance between great poets and composers, although the tendency of music to develop in absolute independence sometimes intentionally casts poetry into the shade.

Carefully considered, it can never be claimed that prose stems from poetry. Even where, as in Greek literature, it seems to have been that way historically, this can only be explained correctly by pointing out that Greek prose originated in the spirit and the language most carefully worked upon for centuries by genuine and various forms of poetry. But these are two different matters. The germ of Greek prose lay, like that of Greek poetry, originally in the Greek spirit, a part of whose individuality it is that they complement each other as they do, neither harming the nature of the other. Greek poetry already shows the wide bold soaring of the spirit which brings about the psychic need for prose. The development of both was a completely natural one from a common origin and an intellectual urge which embraced both. Only adverse external circumstances could have kept it from flowering. Still less can prose (in the sense in which it is parallel to poetry) be explained as originating in the admixture, however refined by special purpose and good taste, of poetical elements in the language. The differences between their natures naturally exert an effect in the language itself, and both poetic speech and prosaic speech have their peculiarities as to choice of expression, grammatical forms, and arrangements. But the basic difference between prose and poetry is maintained far deeper than through these details through the fundamentally different tone which resounds throughout their deeper nature. The sphere of poetry, however infinite and inexhaustible in its most inward nature, is nonetheless always a closed circle which does not accept everything into itself or does not leave what it does accept its original nature; prose, on the other hand, being thought not bound by external form, may develop more freely toward all sides, both as regards the particulars within it, as well as the constituency of the universal idea.

Seen from this point of view, the psychic need for the development of prose lies in the abundance and the freedom of intellectuality and makes prose the proper expression for certain periods of spiritual development. But prose has another side as well, through which it may fascinate and insinuate itself into the feeling life: its close relationship with the conditions of ordinary life which may be intensified by refinement with prose's spiritedness without thereby losing truth and natural simplicity. Along these lines, poetry may actually choose the garment of prose in order to represent sensations in all their purity and sincerity. Just as human beings are sometimes hostile to all language, as too confining to the psyche and as distorting its pure utterance, and long for a life of thought and feeling without this medium, just so we may in the highest mood of poetry take refuge in the simplicity of prose, by divesting language of all ornament. Poetry always bears an external art-form which accords with its nature. But the soul may be attuned to a feeling for nature in opposition to art, though reserving for nature a completely ideal-oriented character nonetheless. This in fact seems to be a general mood of modern nations with old cultures. At least —and it is of course connected with the relatively nonsensuous tendency of our language which nonetheless retains profundity —this seems to be true of the German psychic disposition. The poet in such a case may intentionally stay close to the conditions of real life and execute a genuine work of poetry in prose garments—if the power of his genius is sufficient to produce the necessary tension. One need only recall Goethe's *Werther,* of which every reader will agree that the outer form has a most necessary relationship to the inner content. I mention it only to show how from all sorts of psychic moods there may arise juxtapositions of poetry and prose and combinations of their outer and inner natures, all of which influence the character of a language, and all of which—this being more readily visible to us—experience the reaction of language upon them.

But both poetry and prose retain a certain color of their own when they are quite separate. In Greek poetry the predominant color of poetry, as it was of the whole realm of Greek spiritual productivity, was its emphasis on outward artistic form. It was due to poetry's close and complete alliance with music, but also to the delicate sense of tact and timing with which the Greeks were able to weigh and balance inner psychic effects. Thus the ancient comedy was dressed in the richest and most various rhythmic garments. The lower into the realm of the ordinary and even the common it dipped in its descriptions and expressions, the more it felt the necessity to gain balanced stance and verve through self-limitations upon its outward form. This combination, now, of high poetic tone

with absolutely practical, old-fashioned maxims directed at simplicity of morals and civic virtue seizes the soul with a profound
sense for union of the opposites (as we can check for ourselves by
the reading of Aristophanes). A mixture of poetry and prose such
as we find in Shakespeare and also in the Hindus was foreign to
the Greeks. The need, which they also felt, of approaching a conversational style on the stage, and the correct feeling that the most
detailed narrative told by a player is always different from the epic
recital of a rhapsodist (though one is always reminiscent of the
other), gave rise to unique syllabic measures for these parts of a
drama which form a mediation, as it were, between the art form
of poetry and the natural simplicity of prose. But upon prose, as
well, the general disposition had its own effect and gave even to it
an externally artful configuration. The national character of the
Greeks shows up uniquely in the critical judgment upon the great
prose writers. The reasons for their superiority are sought where
we should never seek them, in the subtleties of number, in artful
figures of speech, and in externals of periodic structure. The total
effect of the whole, the perception of inner thought development,
of which the style is but the outward reflection, seems to us to disappear in the reading of such writings as, for example, the pertinent
books of Dionysius of Halicarnassus. It cannot be denied, on the
other hand, that, leaving out such one-sidednesses and sophistries
of prose criticism, the beauty of the great Greek models does rest
upon all of its details, including these, and the careful study of this
view leads us deep into the characteristics of Greek character. For
the works of genius only exert their effect as they are understood
and accepted by the nations. . . .

The progressive development of the spirit leads to a level
where it ceases to intuit and to suppose, and strives instead to put
foundations under its insights and to relate their essences into a
single wholeness. This is the era of developing science and of the
scholarship which follows in its wake, and this moment cannot be
other than of utmost influence upon a language. I have elsewhere
discussed the school terminology of the sciences. But the general

import of such an epoch must here be mentioned, since science demands prose, and poetry can only incidentally fall to its share. In this field the spirit deals with objectivities exclusively, or rather with subjectivities only insofar as they contain necessity; it seeks truth and the separation of all outer and inner appearance from intrinsic nature. Thus only through the working impact of science does language get its final acuity in the isolation and definition of concepts and the purest weighing out of paragraphs, sentences, and parts of speech. Since, however, an entirely new vista is opened to the spirit by the scientific form of the structure of insight, and by the definition of the relation of insight to the capacities which produce it, a vista, moreover which excels in sublimity all the details which went into its opening out, this too has its effect upon language. It gives to language the character of high seriousness and a strength which brings all concepts into clearest focus. On the other side, linguistic usage in this realm demands coldness and sobriety and complete lack of entanglement, in short whatever aids the understanding and is appropriate to a simple presentation of its object and nothing more. Hence the scientific tone of prose is quite different from that previously described.

Now language, dispensing with all show of independence, is supposed to accompany and represent thought as closely and faithfully as possible. In that part of the human spirit's orbit that is visible to us, Aristotle may justly be called the founder of science and of the scientific spirit. Although the striving for science came, naturally, much earlier and its progress was gradual, it congealed into conceptuality only with him. As though it must have burst forth with a clarity never dreamed of, there is between his methodology and that of his most direct predecessors a decisive gap, not to be filled in with evolutionary steps. He investigated facts, collected them, and tried to guide them toward universal ideas. He tested the systems he found, showed them to be untenable, and endeavored to give to his own a sound epistemological basis. At the same time he sought with his gigantic intellect to bring all knowledge into a single conceptual order. From such an attempt, going deep and wide simultaneously, oriented equally strictly toward form as toward matter, and in which investigation of truth was marked most notably by a sharp segregation of all seductive appearance, there had to develop a language which presents a most remarkable contrast with that of his predecessor and contemporary, Plato. Indeed, one cannot place the language of these two into the same developmental period. One must consider Plato's diction the peak of something never to rise again, Aristotle's the beginning of a new epoch. And what is most notable is the effect of the characteristic treatment of philosophical insight on the part of both men. One would surely be quite wrong if one were to ascribe Aristotle's less graceful, bare, and undeniably often harsh language to a natural pedantry or meagerness of spirit, as it were. Much of his study was taken up with music and poetry. Their effect had made a deep impression on him, as one may see by the few judgments remaining to us on these subjects, and only a natural inclination could have led him to this branch of literature. We still have a hymn of great poetic verve written by him, and if his exoteric writings, particularly his dialogues, had come down to us, we should probably be able to form quite a different judgment about the comprehensiveness of his style. Isolated passages, particularly in his *Ethics,* show us to what heights he could rise. A truly profound and abstract philosophy also has its ways of attaining great diction. The soundness and even the tight definition of concepts, wherever the doctrine proceeds out of a genuinely creative spirit, impart to language a sublimity quite befitting its inner profundity.

The formation of a philosophical style of quite unique beauty meets us also in the pursuit of certain abstract concepts in the writings of Fichte and of Schelling and, if only now and then, yet all the more moving, in Kant. The results of factual, scientific investigations are not merely capable of a prose which is well worked out and informed by a deep and universal view of nature's wholeness, but the existence of such a prose furthers scientific investigation by kindling the spirit which alone can lead to great discoveries.

If I mention here the works of my brother, I know I am only repeating a universal, often expressed judgment.

The fields of knowledge, coming together from all directions, may form an arching vault of universality, and this elevation is most intimately connected with the most precise and complete working out of all the factual bases. Only where scholarship and the endeavor to expand it are not imbued by the genuine spirit, does language, too, suffer, and in that case it is one of the aspects which threatens prose with deterioration, as does the sinking of cultivated, idea-oriented conversation to everyday or conventional talk. The works of language can only prosper as long as the vitality of spirit, aiming at its own extension and completion and at the relating of the world to itself, carries it along. This vitality appears in numerous gradations and configurations, but its ultimate striving, whether the individual human being in whom it has its abode is conscious of it or not, is always toward ultimate relatedness. Wherever the intellectual character of a nation is not strong enough, or where language is being abandoned by spirit to which alone it owes its strength and its blossoming because of the intellectual deterioration of a cultivated nation, no prose in the grand style can arise, or it crumbles as soon as arisen because of the flattening and leveling effect of mere learned accumulating which is put in place of creativity.

Poetry can belong only to certain moments of life and certain moods of the spirit; prose accompanies the human being everywhere and constantly, in all utterances of his spirit's activities. It clings to every thought and every feeling, and when it has perfected its ability within a language to raise itself from any point at all to the realm of free striving—by its definiteness, bright clarity, flexible liveliness, euphony and harmony—and when simultaneously it has developed the subtle tact necessary to determine where and how far this self-elevation is appropriate, then it both reveals and furthers an equally free, easy, ever smoothly progressing development of the spirit. This is the highest summit which language may reach in the development of its character. It is therefore the point which, beginning with the very first germs of external form, needs the broadest and securest base.

If prose is to achieve such heights, poetry cannot have remained backward, since both flow from a common source. But poetry can attain a high degree of excellence without prose attaining a similar development in the language. The complete circle of language can be rounded out only by both. Greek literature preserves for us, even with some regrettable lacunae, this process of language development more completely and purely than we know it anywhere else. Without recognizable influence of foreign works (which does not exclude the influence of foreign ideas, to be sure) the Greek language develops from Homer to the Byzantine authors through all phases of growth, a development grounded in its own nature and in the transformations of the national spirit through inner and outer historical upheavals. The characteristic of the various Greek nations consisted in a certain popular mobility which made them strive for freedom and superior power, but which usually gladly reserved at least a semblance of the former even for the vanquished enemy. Like the waves of the inland sea that surrounded them, their mobility was moderated and limited but brought with it constant changes, nonetheless, changes of habitation, of number of population and of rule, and afforded constant new nourishment for the spirit, and stimulus to try itself in all sorts of activities. Where the Greek influence reached beyond their borders, such as in the cities they colonized, the same popular spirit ruled. As long as this condition lasted, this inward, national principle imbued their language and their works. In this period one has a lively feeling of the inner progressive connection between all psychic products, of the living interaction of poetry and prose, in all their many genres. But since Alexander, when Greek language and literature were spread by conquest, and afterward, when they joined with the world-ruling conqueror, as part of the conquered nation's resources, we can still find excellent brains and poetic talents but the soul had died out, and with it the living creativity, springing from the fullness of its own strength. Now only became revealed the natural lore of a great part of the earth; scientific observation and systematic work on the whole field of knowledge for the first time became clear to man's spirit through the truly world-historical connection between an extraordinary man of action and ideas, and the teaching and example of Aristotle. The world of objects confronted with predominance the subjective world of creativity, and this latter world was further depressed by its own earlier literature which, since the principle of freedom which had animated it was gone, now looked like a great power which at most one might try to imitate but whose superiority no one could contest. This is the period, then, which starts a general gradual deterioration of language and literature. But now scientific preoccupation with language and literature as they had been during their period of flowering began and—incidentally—furnished us with a large part of the works themselves. It told us how these works were ever reflected in the conscious appraisal of subsequent generations of this people who always remained the same but who were suppressed by outer conditions beyond their control.

As to Sanskrit, we cannot judge with certainty considering our present fragmentary knowledge of its literature, how far and how broadly its prose was developed. The conditions of civic and social life in India hardly placed the language in an equally favorable position. The Greek spirit and character had a tendency more than perhaps any other to arrive at combinations in which conversation if it was not the sole aim was nonetheless the main ingredient. Lawsuits and public assemblies demanded convincing and guiding eloquence. To such factors we may ascribe the probability that we never shall find in Hindu literature anything which one could stylistically compare to the Greek historians, rhetoricians, and philosophers. But the rich, flexible Sanskrit language, endowed with all manner of means which may impart soundness, dignity, and grace to speech, visibly contains all the germs of an equally great development and would have developed many more superior characteristics than we now know, had it been vouchsafed a period of higher prose. . . .

Roman prose stood in a relation to Roman poetry quite completely unlike that of Greek. The whole Roman language was equally strongly influenced by its imitation of Greek models and by its own originality, everywhere emerging. For the Romans imprinted their language and their style visibly with the stamp of their inner and outer political development. Their literary development taking place at a relatively much later time, there could be no original natural growth, such as we can follow in the literary progress of the Greeks from Homer on down, and particularly through the permanent influence of those earliest of songs. . . .

A look at the prose of modern languages would lead us into even more complicated relationships, since the moderns . . . were variously attracted by both Greek and Roman literature but at the same time produced entirely new conditions and a type of originality hitherto completely unknown. . . .

One more relationship between poetry and prose must be taken up, and that is the relationship of both to writing. Since Wolf's masterly investigations into the origins of Homeric song it has been generally acknowledged that the poetry of a people may remain unwritten for a long period after the invention of writing, and that both these periods by no means necessarily coincide. Meant to magnify the presence of a moment, and to contribute to ritual celebrations, poetry in earliest times was too intimately bound up with life, found its way too freely simultaneously out of the imagination of author and listeners to be friendly toward the cold purposiveness of recording it in writing. It streamed forth from the lips of the poet or the schooled singers who had accepted his poetry as part of themselves; it was a living recital accompanied by song and instrumental music. The words formed but a part of it and were inseparable from the rest. The entire recital was handed down to posterity and the thought could not easily rise of separating this whole and recording only some of it. In fact the thought of recording poetry in writing could hardly have risen in the entire period of poetry's flourishing. Written records presuppose reflection, and reflection always develops toward the end of a period which simply and naturally practices an art. They also presuppose a greater unfolding of civic life with its resultant demand for separating and specializing and repeating successes in the interest of their permanence. Only at such a time could the connection of poetry with recital and with living ritual celebrations become somewhat more loose. As for aiding the memory by recording, this is hardly necessary in the case of poetry with its poetical word order and meter.

In the case of prose all this is entirely different. Even here, I am convinced, the main difficulty is not that writing is required as an aid to memorization. There is much national prose among all peoples which is merely handed down by oral tradition and in which the expressions are quite obviously not accidental or arbitrary ones. We find in the tales of those nations which possess no writing at all a use of language, a kind of style, which makes it evident that they have come down from narrator to narrator with only small, if any, alterations. Children too tend to use the same expressions quite conscientiously when they retell stories which they have only experienced through the ear. . . . And yet the impulse to record in writing, lacking in early poetry, lies necessarily and directly in the spirit of prose, even before its full artistic development. Facts are to be investigated or presented, concepts to be developed and related; something objective, in other words, is to be made out. The mood which brings this about is a sober one, investigation-minded, discriminatory as to truth and error, and tending to turn its business over to reason. It first rejects meter, not because it makes for difficulties, but because the human demand for it is not founded in its other demands, because the many-faceted inquiries of an investigating and combining reason do not care for the form which would force them into a single feeling mood. Recording now becomes desirable, in fact indispensible, because the investigated parts and even the process of the investigation itself must stand secure in all their countless detail. The aim is the greatest possible permanence. History is now to retain what would otherwise vanish in the course of time; doctrine is to be handed on from one generation to the next so that the same ground need not be covered over and over. Now prose founds and confirms the single, named author who steps out of the earlier mass of general creativity. Investigation brings with itself personal research, visits to foreign countries, personally worked out methods of combination. Truth, especially when other proofs are lacking, needs a bondsman, and the historian, unlike the poet, cannot derive his certification from Olympus. The mood within a nation which leads to prose must therefore seek the easing of its tasks in recorded writing and, if writing is already available, may in turn be stimulated by it.

By a natural development of national growth there arise in poetry two different genres, characterized by poetry's use or lack of use respectively of writing. That characterized by its lack of use of writing seems a more natural type of poetry, seemingly flowing from the source of inspiration without intention and without artfulness. The other is a later, perhaps more derived type, but nonetheless belonging to the profound and genuine spirit of true poetry. In the case of prose the same thing cannot happen in this fashion, and still less in the same respective periods. But in another way it happens to it also. When opportunity arises within a people equally endowed for prose and poetry to make use of freely flowing eloquence in their lives, we find a relationship of prose to life similar to that which we found for poetry. Prose too, as long as it lasts without consciousness of artful intent, rejects the cold and dead record. This was surely the case during the time of Athens' greatness between the Persian and the Peloponnesian wars and even later. Speakers such as Themistocles, Pericles, and Alcibiades surely developed mighty prose talents; it is specifically remembered of the latter two. And yet none of their speeches came down to us . . . and even ancient times seemed to have possessed no record of them. At the time of Alcibiades there were already written speeches, even some which were intended to be recited by people other than their authors, but it was nonetheless intrinsic to the conditions of public life at that time that the men who were the true leaders of the state saw no reason for writing down their speeches, neither before nor after they were given. And yet their natural eloquence, just like that of unwritten poetry, not only preserved the germ of what was to come but in many cases served as the unsurpassed model of later, more artful prose. . . . And something very similar must have happened with the living dialogue in the schools of the philosophers. [VII, 193–209]

Philosophical poetry

Poetry and philosophy grow out of the same soil; they come from the highest and deepest levels of mankind, and the difference between a genuine philosophical poem and one which does not deserve the name lies in the question whether the two sources are represented as truly joint or whether they have been mechanically superimposed upon one another.

It is a prerogative of poetry to claim man's total undivided nature and to lead him to the point where his finite nature loses itself in intuitions of infinity. Poetry deserves its name only when it achieves this. Therefore nothing is excluded from its proper field—no object, no genre, not the plainest elegiac, not the most lightheartedly joyous nor the more irrepressibly or capriciously comic verse. For feeling itself, partly in its own movements, but especially when it is purified by the esthetic sense whose activity is always stimulated in man at the first musical note, carries a relationship to infinity. An art form knows no barriers except those placed by its own definition. But the true secret lies in the creative imagination within which all art operates and which it controls. By its magic power in a mode very much like that described [in the Bhagavad-Gita] it so destroys finite nature in its substance and so preserves it in its forms that, living in the midst of sense involvements, it dissolves all sentient emotion into pure, ideal-oriented perception, just as the dogma of renunciation and immersion dissolves the liveliest action into nonaction. What Krishna says of creatures, namely that they meet but remain unknown to one another, like sudden apparitions ([Bhagavad-Gita] II, 29) is also and characteristically true of any genuine poem. It stands before us, and no footprints tell us whence it came. It requires certification from elsewhere, therefore, and the invocation to a higher power is a need felt as natural by every poet, insofar as he is not—as is the author here under consideration—imbued with the feeling that he is carrying such certification from on high within himself.

If poetry, then, is to combine with philosophic ideas in a worthy manner, the latter must be of the sort that they too could not have come about without an invisible capacity for inner inspiration. The fire and the loftiness of poetry must look necessary for calling forth truth from the depths of the spirit; philosophic dogma must not seek a poetic garment like a borrowed ornament but must pour itself out in voluntary, free rhythms, moved by an inner urge; it must move within poetry as though in a natural, indigenous form. But this can only be the case if the philosophic ideas go back to the point where the rationalizing intellect has to give up its effort to develop effects from causes; the point where truth flames forth by the mere purification and orientation of spirit, by the removal of all dialectic semblance, from an intensification of pure self-awareness. In this realm, where the poet feels strong enough to maintain the nature of truth even in the midst of ardent poetic imagination—here alone is found the true philosophical poem. [V, 334–36]

MAN'S INTRINSIC HUMANITY: HIS LANGUAGE

All understanding is also a misunderstanding

No one when he uses a word has in mind exactly the same thing that another has, and the difference, however tiny, sends its tremors throughout language, if one may compare language with the most volatile element. With each thought, each feeling, this difference returns, thanks to the element of unvarying identity in individuality, and finally forms a mass of elements which singly went unnoticed. All understanding, therefore, is always at the same time a misunderstanding—this being a truth which it is most useful to know in practical life—and all agreement of feelings and thoughts is at the same time a means for growing apart. [V, 396]

Language is the great mediator

Language everywhere mediates, first between infinite and finite nature, then between one individual

235

and another. Simultaneously and through the same act it makes union possible and itself originates from it. The whole of its nature never lies in singularity but must always simultaneously be guessed or intuited from otherness. But neither can it be fully explained from oneness and otherness together; it simply is (like everything in the presence of which true mediation occurs) something individuated, unique, incomprehensible. It is something which is given by the idea of union, of the reconciliation of what for us and our way of thinking must always be opposites, and it is a something which is given only in this connection. Linguistic study—which must, in order to avoid becoming chimerical, always begin with the totally dry, pedantic, in fact mechanical analysis of the corporeal, constructible elements of language—thus leads to the depths of humanity. Only one must free oneself of the notions that language can be separated from that which it designates as, for example, the name of a person from the person, and that it is a product of reflection and agreement, an agreed-upon code, as it were, or in fact that it is any work of man at all (in the common sense in which one takes that phrase), not to mention the work of some individual. A true, inexplicable miracle, it breaks loose from the mouth of a nation, and—no less marvellous, though seen by us every day with indifference—it breaks daily through the gurgle of any baby. It is the brightest trace and the surest proof of the fact (leaving out for the moment the celestial relatives of mankind) that man does not possess an absolute, segregated individuality, that "I" and "Thou" are not merely interrelated but—if one could go back to the point of their separation—truly identical concepts, and that there exist, therefore, only concentric circles of individuality, beginning with the weak, frail single person who is in need of support and widening out to the primordial trunk of humanity itself. Otherwise all understanding would be impossible into all eternity. [III, 296–97]

The individuality of languages lies in their tone

In the nature of tone as such lies the true individuality of each language. Whatever one may do or try to do in order to describe the peculiarity of a language, all one succeeds in defining ever more closely is the genre to which it belongs. As *this* language, however, and no other, it expresses itself only before the listening ear. Although the alphabet of the whole human race is enclosed by certain not even very wide limits, each people with a language of their own have their own tonal system which excludes certain tones altogether, demonstrates strong preference for others, uses different ones to designate different classes of concepts, treats tone combinations in certain ways, etc. One may compare this with the various screeches and tonal varieties of the various animal species. [V, 379]

Linguistic groups must not be mistaken for racial groups

A difficult and important question is whether the racial physical differences within the human species which now—whatever their origin—are handed on and altered exclusively through heredity exert an influence on the constitution and structure of language. It is one more question which cannot be settled completely, since the original conditions may have been altered by so many subsequent events that nothing can be proved by the present state of a language. Yet inner probability and present experience are definitely against such an assumption. However different man may be as to size, color, build, and facial features, his spiritual-intellectual predisposition is the same. The opposite contention is disproved by manifold experience and is surely never made seriously and with unbiased conviction, but only advanced in connection with the commerce of slavery or an absurd pride of color. [VI-1, 196]

Grammar is the unconscious of language

Grammar, more than any other aspect of language, is contained invisibly in the modes of thinking of a speaker. Everyone adds to a foreign language his own grammatical opinions and, if they are more complete and explicit, he projects them also upon the foreign tongue. For in each language, each word of a sentence may be classified under a grammatical form, if one considers all the factors involved in its use. But it is a totally different matter whether or not the speaker who knows only the language in question shares this view; and all grammar thus projected upon a language must be carefully distinguished from whatever grammar is contained in it naturally. Actually in a language itself lies only that grammar which is either expressly signified by inflection, grammatical terms, or prescribed word order, or what reveals itself beyond all doubt as silently present in the cast of a sentence or the form of a spoken word. [V, 311]

On logical and practical definitions

All words designating moral qualities can accord only to a certain degree, never wholly, with the things which they designate. Like all words, in fact, they express only concepts, with their relatively firm and definite boundaries, since the things for which the words stand, due to the indissoluble interrelationship of all parts of the moral universe, flow over one into the other without any boundaries that can be noted. Language helps us out of this embarrassment by subjecting the usage of a word to the dicta of practiced feeling, rather than bothering about exact logical definition. Therefore all such words operate in a double sphere: a logical one, bordered by the defined concept which they designate, and a practical one, determined by custom and usage. The true difference between these two spheres ought to rest on the difference which always exists between the concept of an object produced by reason and the image of it formed by sensation and feeling. These, since we sense and feel more, and more subtly than we think, never coincide. The factual difference, however, in most languages rests much more on accident and prejudice. One need only compare the extent of actual usage with the extent of the best and subtlest definitions of such words as "wit," for example, or "delicacy" or "rapture," to convince oneself that one is frequently much greater and just as frequently much smaller than the other.

That is why the beginner in any language expresses himself so unidiomatically without actually making mistakes; that is why the number of synonyms always decreases with the degree of linguistic development; and that is why the linguist always recognizes more of the latter than does the finest, most cultivated author. Now if a word is newly formed, or its meaning freshly defined, then it occupies at first only the logical sphere which coincides with the concept for which it was meant. It therefore presents itself only to our understanding, leaving our imagination and our feelings untouched. . . . This is why neologisms, made in great numbers and intentionally, are advisable only in the completely speculative or technical sciences where only pure rational concepts are dealt with, not real things, or where it suffices to differentiate things by certain singled-out characteristics alone. But in the field of practical philosophy, where everything depends on not merely thinking the moral objects given in experience but on representing them in their total natural endowment, one must avail oneself of the help of neologisms much more sparingly and cautiously. Else one runs the danger of taking all the spirit and all the fruitfulness out of one's line of reasoning. [II, 73-75]

Language is a human archetype

Language, I am fully convinced, must be looked upon as being an immediate given in mankind. Taken as a work of man's reason, undertaken in clarity of consciousness, it is wholly inexplicable. Nor does it help to supply man with millennia upon millennia for the "invention" of language. Language could not be invented or come upon if its archetype were not already present in the human mind. For man to understand but a single word truly, not as a mere sensuous stimulus (such as an animal understands a command or the sound of the whip) but as an articulated sound designating a concept, all language, in all its connections, must already lie prepared within him. There are no single, separate facts of language. Each of its elements announces itself as part of a whole. As natural as the supposition of the gradual development of languages is, yet the "invention" of language could only happen all at once. Man is man only through language; to invent language, he would have to be man already. As soon as one imagines that it happened gradually . . . , that by means of a bit more invented language, man became more human, and being more human, thus was enabled to invent a little more language, one fails to recognize the indivisibility of human consciousness and human speech, and the nature of the intellectual act which is necessary to comprehend but a single word, but which then suffices to comprehend all of language.

Naturally this does not mean that one is to think of language as a given that is complete and finished, for then one could not comprehend how a man could understand or use any single given language. It necessarily grows out of an individual, gradually growing up with him, but in such a way that its organization does not lie, like an inert mass, in the dark of a man's soul till it is brought forth, but instead that its laws condition the functions of thought. Thus the very first word gives the hint of and presupposes the whole rest of the language. If one seeks an analogy for this—and there is really nothing comparable to it in the whole realm of the mind—one might remember the natural instincts of animals and call language an intellectual instinct of the mind. [IV, 14 f.]

*   *   *

Nor can the articulation of tones, that enormous difference between the dumbness of the beast and the speech of man, be explained by physical means. Only the strength of self-consciousness forces upon material, physical nature that sharp division and definite boundary line that we call articulation. [IV, 4]

*　　*　　*

Everything that has once been expressed in words shapes that which has not, or prepares the way for it. [IV, 4]

On translations

But if translation is to assimilate to the language and the *Geist* of a nation something which that nation does not itself possess or possesses differently, then the first demand we must make of translation is that it be simply faithful. Its faithfulness must be oriented toward the true character of the original, not toward accidental properties. . . . Every good translation both proceeds from and results in a simple and unassuming love for the original and the study that springs from such love. This view entails, to be sure, that the translation will carry a certain color of strangeness, of peculiarity, but the border line after which this becomes an undeniable mistake is easily drawn. As long as the strangeness itself is not felt, but only that we are in the presence of something strange, the translation has fulfilled its highest purpose. But where the strangeness itself is felt, possibly even to the point of obscuring the knowledge that this is after all something unfamiliar to us, there the translator reveals that he is no match for the original. [VIII, 132]

*　　*　　*

One might even assert that a translation departs from the original to the same degree to which it strives to be painfully faithful. For in so doing it seeks to imitate the more subtle characteristics, avoiding mere generality, and yet finds that it can only confront one peculiarity with another. But this must not frighten us away from translating. For translation, especially of the work of poets, is one of the most necessary labors of any literature. Partly because it introduces certain forms of art and of humanity to those who do not know the foreign language and would otherwise remain entirely ignorant of them. Every nation has considerable to gain from the performance of this task. But, more important, translations must be made because the effort to make them broadens the significance and extends the expressiveness of the language into which the translation is made. [VIII, 130]

*　　　*　　　*

Translations: These may serve a threefold purpose as to the author translated. 1) To make those who are unable to read him in the original acquainted with him. 2) To serve as a commentary for the better understanding of those who can read the original. 3) To acquaint those who are about to read him in the original with his manner and to initiate them into his spirit. If we are to label these three purposes in accordance with their usefulness, we shall find that purpose one is the least useful and most inferior, purpose two somewhat more important but still not very useful because translations are not a particularly good means to this end, and purpose three the really important one, since the translation will stimulate one's reading of the original and even support it in a higher sense than purpose number two, not by making individual passages clear but by attuning the spirit of the reader to that of the author. In addition, an author will be ever more clearly understood if he can be read in the medium of several languages. The achievement of this final purpose ends in the supreme valuing of the original, and so we may say that the highest useful purpose served by a translation is that it destroys itself. [I, 280]

On language learning

The main difficulty in the learning process is to orient oneself at the proper time, to aid one's memory by the right rules. Nowhere does one feel this need so urgently as when learning languages. The present method of language-learning lands one in a forest of words which are not connected by any associations; in grammar we have a little more order, but there too we are fatigued by a pile of forms with no insight into any reason for their existence. And yet we feel that these signs cannot be as disconnected in nature as they seem to be in the language lessons. When we have studied a language for a length of time, we see clearly the reasons we could not see at the beginning, and we gain a sort of tact and rhythm, not for guessing, but for intuiting, as it were, that which is still unknown. Anyone who has learned a number of languages, and who has observed himself as he learned, can remember how in each one, almost, he came upon facts which suddenly cast a bright light over all that had gone before and which would have saved him a great deal of trouble if someone had told him of them earlier. Whoever has the courage, then, to learn a language by himself without a tutor will always start by reading its entire grammar quite carefully and often paging through its dictionary as well. He will work over in his imagination as many forms as he can thus remember, and then leave it to his own linguistic intuition to construct for himself a sort of general type-form of the language in question. Everyone when he learns a language, most notably children who create far more than they memorize, proceeds by darkly felt analogies which allow him to enter the language actively, as it were, instead of just receptively. The critical point is to find the moving spirit of the analogical process; only after that do the benefits and the pleasures begin that are to be had from learning a new language. [VII, 599 f.]

*   *   *

Once the pleasure in language as language is awakened, it does away with the arrogant revulsion which is still today frequently felt against dialect and conversational idiom, a feeling which carries the seed of death for all strength and vigor in a language and a nation. But loving language for what it is, in its live state, would cause a rapport between the upper classes and the masses; culture would gain a more wholesome direction, and one's care for the refinement of language would be more fruitful if one first loved it in its freshness, intimacy, and crudity. [VII, 626]

*   *   *

First and foremost, spiritual striving must awaken in an individual and grow into maturity; the laws according to which this happens might be called the physiology of spirit. There must be similar laws for a nation. Explanations of certain events, of which language is the most notable, cannot even be approached without the concept of nationality, applied in addition to that of nature and that of a community of individuals. Nationality is defined in part by communal living and communal origin, but it is certainly neither exhausted with these nor is its true nature represented. The nation is a being, just as the individual is. The connection between the two through a common predisposition will probably never be riddled out as such, but its influence becomes evident wherever the national aspect is active within the individual without any consciousness on the part of the individual that this is so, as is the case with the origin of language. . . .

The study of the various languages of the earth misses its point if it does not continually keep its eye on the development and organizational forms through which the human spirit educates itself and sees its true aim therein. The painstaking sifting of the tiniest elements in the languages and the noting of differences among them, indispensable as it is to a recognition of language in its peculiar influence on the history of ideas, becomes petty without the larger view and sinks to the level of mere curiosity seeking. Neither can the study of languages be separated from that of their literatures, since grammar and lexicon yield only their dead skeleton. Their living structure is visible only in their works. [V, 32 f.]

The relationship of language to the functions of the mind

Every language sets certain limits to the spirit of those who speak it; it assumes a certain direction and, by doing so, excludes many others. [VII, 621]

* * *

Thinking is not merely dependent on language in general but, up to a certain degree, on each specific language. People have wished, to be sure, to replace the words of the various languages by universally valid signs, as lines, numbers and algebraic symbols serve in mathematics. But only a tiny part of that which is thinkable can be designated that way, because such symbols by their very nature fit only those concepts which can be produced by mere synthetic construction or are otherwise formed by rationality alone. But where the raw materials of inner perception and sensation are to be imprinted with conceptualization, everything depends on the individual way of looking at things of an individual human being whose language is an inseparable part of him. All attempts to cancel out the many unique signs for eye and ear and replace them with a few general ones are but methods of abbreviated translation. It would be folly and delusion to imagine that such methods might transport one beyond the circumscribed limits of one's own language—not to mention all language. Of course a central point at which languages might meet may be sought for, and even found, and it is necessary when doing comparative studies of language (grammatical as well as lexical) to keep one's eye directed toward such a center. For . . . there is a number of things which can be determined and defined a priori and hence separated from all conditionalities of a given language. But on the other hand, there is a far greater number of concepts, and grammatical peculiarities as well, which are woven so indissolubly into the individuality of their language that they can neither be held by a thread of inner perception as hovering above all languages, nor translated from one language into another. A most significant part of the content of each language stands in a relation of such undoubted dependency on it that its specific utterance cannot be a matter of no consequence. [IV, 21 ff.]

*　　*　　*

The mutual interdependence of thought and word illuminates clearly the truth that languages are not really means for representing already known truths but are rather instruments for discovering previously unrecognized ones. The differences between languages are not those of sounds and signs but those of differing world views. Herein is contained the reason for and the final aim of all linguistic study. The sum of the knowable, that soil which the human spirit must till, lies between all the languages and independent of them, at their center. But man cannot approach this purely objective realm other than through his own modes of cognition and feeling, in other words: subjectively. Just where study and research touch the highest and deepest point, just there does the mechanical, logical use of reason—whatever in us can most easily be separated from our uniqueness as individual human beings—find itself at the end of its rope. From here on we need a process of inner perception and creation. And all that we can plainly know about this is its result, namely, that objective truth always rises from the entire energy of subjective individuality. [IV, 27]

*　　*　　*

In no two languages do we find completely equivalent words designating incorporeal objects; we find words whose meaning is related, to be sure, but none whose is the same. . . . An extremely interesting demonstration of this might be given in connection with *psyche, anima, âme, alma, Seele, soul,* etc. . . . Such comparison can usually be made only between languages that have a literature. To make such studies would demand profound absorption in each language considered, and yet all language is so rich and fruitful in its eternal youthfulness, its eternal mobility, that the true sense, the sum total of all the connotations of such a word taken as a totality, could never be defined or completed, never be designated in all its grandeur. Time subtracts from it, changes it, adds to it; words grow richer or poorer in content; they are construed sometimes sharply, sometimes loosely. In language, the creative archetypal energies of humanity are active— that deep reservoir of capacity in us whose existence and nature can neither be understood nor denied. [IV, 248 f.]

*   *   *

As little as a word is an image of the thing which it designates, so little is it a mere intimation that this thing is supposed to be thought by reason or represented in imagination. It is differentiated from an image by the possibility inherent in it and in us to imagine the thing according to the most various points of view and in the most various ways; it is different from a mere intimation in that it has its own definite, sensuous form. If you utter the word *Wolke* (cloud) you neither think of its definition nor do you see a single definite image of the natural phenomenon. All its different concepts and images, all the sensations and feelings which have been joined to its perception, everything—finally—which is related in some fashion to it, within us or without us: all these may represent themselves to the mind simultaneously and yet run no danger of confusion because the single sound of the word fastens and secures them. But the sound does even more: it brings back sometimes this, sometimes that association and if, as in the case of *Wolke,* the associative material is rich in itself (*Woge* billow, *Welle* wave, *wälzen* rolling, *Wind* wind, *wehen* blowing, *Wald* woods, etc.) then the sound of the word attunes the soul in a manner befitting the object, partly through itself, partly through recollection and associative analogies. Thus a word reveals itself as an individual with a nature of its own which bears resemblance to an object of art in that, with a sensuous form borrowed from nature, it makes possible an idea which is beyond all nature. Here however the resemblance stops, since the differences leap to the eye. For this idea which lies beyond all nature is precisely that which alone renders the objects in the world capable of being used as materials for thinking and feeling. It is the lack of definition of objects which ever and again provides new transitions to other objects (since that which is each time represented or imagined need neither be completely filled in as to detail, nor preserved); the lack of definition without which the independent action of thought would be impossible—and the sensuous vividness which is a result of the spiritual energy that is expended when a language is used. Thinking never treats of an object as isolated and never uses the sum total of its reality. It always skims off its surface relationships, conditions, points of view, and combines these. But a word is by no means merely an empty substratum into which certain details may be placed, but it is a sensuous form which by its incisive simplicity spontaneously indicates that the expressed object, too, should be represented only according to the needs of thought, and, by its origin in an independent psychic act, reorders the merely perceptive psychic capacities back into their boundaries. Moreover, by its capacity for change and its analogic relationship to other linguistic elements, it prepares the connectedness which thinking tries to find out in the world and bring out in its own products. Finally, by its transitoriness it bids us tarry at no point but hurry on to whatever end itself and all the other words are tending. In all these respects, the kind of sensuous form a word has . . . is in no way a matter of indifference, and it may be justly asserted that even when words of different languages designate the same, completely sensuous, object, they are by no means perfect synonyms. Whoever utters *hippos, equus,* or *Pferd,* by no means says completely the same thing three times. [III, 169 f.]

Languages as objective expressions of human subjectivities

The least advantageous influence on any sort of interesting treatment of linguistic studies is exerted by the narrow notion that language originated as a convention and that words are nothing but signs for things or concepts which are independent of them. This view up to a point is certainly correct but beyond this point it is deadly because as soon as it begins to predominate it kills all mental activity and exiles all life. To it we owe the constantly reiterated commonplaces that linguistic study is necessary only for external purposes or for the discipline of as yet unpracticed mentalities; that the best method for learning a language is the one that leads most quickly to the mechanical, automatic understanding and use of it; that any language, if one only knows it well, is about as useful as any other; that it would be best if all nations could agree on the use of a single one—and whatever other prejudices of this sort there are.

A more careful examination demonstrates precisely the opposite of all these notions.

Naturally, a word is a sign insofar as it is used to stand for a thing or a concept, but in its particular past development and its particular effectiveness it is a particular and independent creature—an individual. The sum of all words—language—is a universe which lies midway between the external, phenomenal one and our own inwardly active one. Naturally it is based upon convention, insofar as all the members of a linguistic group understand one another, but the individual words were first formed out of the natural feeling of the speaker and understood by the similar natural feeling of the hearer. Hence, linguistic study teaches, in addition to the use of a particular language, the analogical relation between man and the world in general, and each individual nation in particular, which is expressed by language. And since the spirit which constantly reveals itself in the world can never be exhaustively known through any given number of views or opinions, but is always discovered to contain something new, it would be far better to multiply the languages on earth as many times as the number of earth's inhabitants might permit. [III, 167 f.]

*   *   *

The Spanish call those who enter hermitages, *gente retirada y desengañada,* retired people who have returned from the deceptions or illusions of worldly living. The Spanish *desengañar* corresponds to the French *désabuser.* But it is worth noting how the different cultural levels at which the two nations stand have influenced the usage of these two words. The Spanish *desengaño* almost always has a ring of pathos; it is the solemn word of the poet when the deceptive veil of love is rent, or when a rapturous mood impels the soul toward heaven, away from the vanity of earthly pleasures. The French *désabuser,* on the other hand (in its most modern usage to be sure—that of the last ten or fifteen years) indicates a concept which is possible only in the greatest turmoil of society. It is the death of all poetic, or any sort of elevated, mood, expressing the emotional state of complete frigidity, caused by incessant involvement in complicated external conditions.

We Germans have no word for the returning from an illusion or infatuation in either of the above-mentioned senses, a lack which might be explained by our lack of both the super-refinement of French social manners and the passionate infatuation possible to the Spanish character. On the other hand, it would be hard to find in any language an equally beautiful word for the basic condition, namely our *nüchtern* [sober]. A *sober* mind indicates a freedom from illusion and infatuation which is not bought at the price of a new illusion, nor of a total freezing of feeling. Rather, it always combines strength and wisdom and—by its derivation alone (from *Nacht* [night])—designates that freshness and freedom of one's feeling-life with which one wakes in the morning after the quiet and solitude of a night's rest, as yet unburdened by the day's impressions. [III, 56–57]

* * *

Language, being the creation of a nation and of primordial time, is something alien to the individual human being. On the one side he is limited by it; on the other, however, he is enriched, strengthened, and stimulated by the deposits of countless generations. Language is subjective seen from the point of view of the realm of the knowable; it is objective seen from the individual human point of view. For each language is an echo of the general nature of humanity and, although the essence of language may at no time become a complete expression of human subjectivity, yet all the languages approach forever this goal. But the subjectivity of all humanity is again something objective. The original correspondence between the world and man, upon which all recognition of truth rests, is regained bit by bit and progressively by the phenomenality of the universe. The objective always remains what must be striven for, and as man approaches it through the subjective orbit of his particular language, his other effort is always to shed subjectivity (even if only by replacing one language-subjectivity with another) and to separate the objective from himself as purely as possible. [IV, 27 f.]

A general introduction to language

The present introduction * should, I believe, be devoted to general considerations which will more adequately prepare the transition to the specific facts and the historical investigations. The distribution of the human race into nations and races and the differences of its languages and dialects are directly related to each other, to be sure, but also stand in a direct relationship of dependence on a third, higher phenomenon, namely the

* To Humboldt's work on the Kawi language of Java. *Tr.*

production of human spiritual energy in ever new and often intensified configurations. Within this relationship the nations and their languages find their proper valuation but also, insofar as research can penetrate them and grasp their connections, their explanation. The manifestation of human spiritual energy over the course of millennia and the space of the earth, ever diverse in degree and kind, is the highest aim of all movement of the spirit. It is the ultimate idea which world history must strive to enunciate clearly. For this elevation or extension of inner existence is the only thing which an individual, so far as he shares in it, may look upon as his own inalienable property. For a nation, it is the only thing from which will unfailingly be born again more great individualities. Comparative linguistics, the precise investigation into the diversity with which countless peoples solve the task of language imparted to them by human nature, loses all interest when it does not proceed from the point at which language is connected to the general configuration of the national spirit. But even one's insight into the unique character of a nation and the inner relationships of a language, as well as its relationship to linguistic considerations in general, depends entirely upon one's consideration of the sum total of spiritual characteristics. For only by these, as nature has given them and given situations have affected them, does a national character attain coherence. Upon them, and upon what they produce by way of deeds, institutions, and thoughts, does national character rest, and in it lie all the energies and values which are then handed on to individuals. Seen from its other side, language is the organ of inner existence; in fact it is inner existence as it gradually attains first to self-consciousness and then to utterance. It sinks all its finest multitudinous root fibers into the spiritual energy of the nation, therefore, and the more appropriately the latter reacts back on it, the more lawful and rich is its development. Since in its web of connected elements it is only an effect of the national linguistic sense, the very questions which concern the core of linguistic formation and from which spring the most significant linguistic differences cannot be answered thoroughly unless one assumes the foregoing elevated point of view toward linguistic studies. Of course this elevation yields no materials for linguistic comparisons, which can be had only from a historical consideration, but it does yield the only insight into the original relationships between the various facts, and the realization that language is an inwardly connected organism. This done, it will further even a correct evaluation of the historical details. . . .

General considerations of human development

A careful consideration of our current status so far as political, artistic, and scientific development is concerned, leads us to a long concatenation running through many centuries of mutually determined causes and effects. In following it, we soon become aware that two different kinds of elements hold sway over it and that investigation does not solve them both with equal felicity. For whereas we may explain causally a number of events, from time to time, as every attempt at a cultural history of the human race has amply demonstrated, we hit knots, as it were, which resist all further historical untangling. The reason for this is to be found within that spiritual energy which cannot be wholly penetrated in its nature by us, nor calculated in advance. It acts together with what is prior to it and current with it, but treats and forms all such elements in accordance with its own unique character. Any great individual of any period could provide the starting point for all world history; one could show against what background he arose, and how the work of all the centuries before him had contributed to this background. And yet the way in which the background made his thus conditioned and supported activity what it was, what stamped it with his uniqueness, may be described, perhaps represented, surely felt, but never derived from anything outside itself. This is the natural, everywhere recurring phenomenon of human functioning. Originally, everything in the human being is inside him—sensation, feeling, desire, thought, decision, language, and deeds. But as the inside comes into contact with the outside world, it begins to operate independently and determines by its own unique configuration the inner and outer functions of others. In time there grow up security measures for what at first had but fleeting effects, and less and less of the work of prior centuries is lost to future ones. Here is the field in which investigation can examine one level after another. But it is at the same time so crisscrossed by the operations of fresh and incalculable inner powers, and without a proper separation of and deliberation upon this double element the material of one can become so overpowering that it threatens to choke out the energy of the other, that no true appreciation is possible of the noblest products which the history of all times offers us.

The deeper we go into the earliest times, of course, the faster melts the mass of materials transmitted from one generation to the next. But then we meet with another phenomenon which transplants our investigation onto another field of difficulty, as it were. Individuals delineated with certainty become rarer and rarer; we no longer know them in their life situations; their fates, even their very names become uncertain; even whether a given work ascribed to a certain person is truly his, or whether a name has simply become the rallying point for the work of many. Individuals get lost in a collectivity of shadow figures. In Greece this is the case with Orpheus and Homer, in India with Manu, Vyasa, Valmiki, and with so many other celebrated names of antiquity. And as we go still further back, the roundedness of individuality disappears even further. A language as polished as Homer's must for a long time have passed up and down on the waves of song, throughout whole cycles of history of which we have no lore. Even more plainly this is seen in the original forms of language itself. Language is deeply enmeshed in the spiritual development of mankind. It accompanies it on every level of its current progress or lag, and each cultural step is recognizable in it. But there is an epoch in which we see only language; it does not accompany spiritual development but entirely occupies its place. Language, to be sure, emanates from a depth of collective humanity which downright forbids us to locate it as a proper product, as a creation even, of nations. It possesses a force of spontaneity which is perfectly evident to us, though inexplicable, and therefore cannot, with this in mind, be called the product of an activity, but must be considered an unconscious, involuntary emanation of the spirit; not a work of nations but a gift given to them by their inner fate. They make use of it without knowing how they come by it.

Nonetheless it must be true that languages have always developed alongside of and within flourishing national groups, and been spun out of their spiritual character, retaining various of its special limitations. It is no empty play with words if we say that *language* has its spontaneous origin in itself, in divine freedom, but that *languages* are bound to and dependent on the national groups which speak them. For languages have entered upon the field of deterministic limitation. While speech and song flowed free, language formed itself in accordance with the measure of the inspiration and the freedom and the strength of the spiritual energies involved. But this could only emanate from all individuals at once; each single individual had to be carried by all the others, since inspiration attains vitality only from the certainty of being understood and felt. Here opens up, however dimly and weakly, a vista into those times when individuals for us are lost in collectivity, and when language itself is the work of intellectually active energy.

In every survey of world history there lies an advance, here also indicated. But it is by no means my intention to set up a system of teleology or infinite perfectibility; on the contrary, I am on quite another tack here. Peoples and individuals grow lushly like plants, spreading all over the face of the earth, enjoying their existence in happiness and activity. This life which dies with each individual goes on undisturbed at what effects it will produce centuries hence. Nature decrees that all who draw breath shall finish their course to their last breath; the aim of a beneficent and orderly providence that each creature should enjoy its life is attained, and each new generation runs through the same circle of joyful and painful existence, of successful or blocked activity. But wherever man enters the stage, he functions humanly. He socializes with his fellows; he arranges institutions, and gives himself laws. And where these things happen in too imperfect a manner, individuals or groups import or transplant what has been more successful elsewhere. Thus with the very origin of man, the seed of morality is given, and grows together with him. This humanization we can watch constantly advancing; it is partly due to nature itself, and partly to the extent to which it has already advanced, that its further perfectibility can hardly be substantially disturbed.

In the points here mentioned there lies a not to be ignored element of planning; it is no doubt present elsewhere as well, where it may be less obvious. But it must never be assumed; if we look for it we are immediately led astray in our evaluation of facts. The thing of which we are here speaking can least of all be subordinated to the assumption of planning. The appearance of human spiritual energy in its diverse configurations is not bound to progress in time or to the heaping up of what is already accomplished. Its origin is to be explained as little as its effect is to be calculated, and its highest attainments lie not at all necessarily in its latest manifestations. If, therefore, one wishes to investigate these natural formations, one must not project ideas upon them but take them as they are. In all nature's creations she brings forth a certain number of forms which express what has attained reality in any given species and what therefore suffices for the perfectibility of the idea of it. We cannot ask why there are no more forms, or no other forms. There are no others right now: this is nature's only "natural" answer. But this view permits us to consider whatever exists in physical and spiritual nature as the functioning of a basic energy which is developing according to principles unknown to us. If we do not wish to relinquish all possibility of discovering inner connections for the outward phenomena of human life, we must come back to some sort of independent and original cause which is not itself determined and which does not pass away. But the most natural candidate for this is an inner life principle, freely developing in all its aspects, whose various unfoldings are not unrelated just because its outer manifestations seem to stand in isolation. This view is totally different from a teleological one, since it does not aim at an end but only at an origin which is instantly recognized to be unfathomable. It is the only one which seems to me to be applicable to the diverse configurations of human spiritual energy. The ordinary claims of humanity seem to me to be satisfactorily answered by the functioning of natural forces and the somewhat mechanical continuity of human activity. But—assuming this division is a proper one—these forces do not seem to explain by any sufficient derivation the emergence of great individualities, either as individuals or as groups, which suddenly and incalculably intervene in the old ways that are more visibly determined by causally explicable operations.

This view is equally applicable, of course, to the main functions of human spiritual energy, especially to the one to which we limit ourselves here: language. The differences among languages may be considered the result of the striving with which the universal human power of speech breaks through into reality, more or less felicitously, helped or hindered by the spiritual power of a given nation.

For if we examine languages genetically, as a spiritual labor directed toward a definite end, it is obvious that whatever end is stipulated may be attained to a greater or lesser degree of success. In fact the main points appear, in which the unevenness of attainment will consist. A greater success can, for example, be attributed to the strength and fullness of the general spiritual energy which acts upon the language; it may also lie in the degree of special adaptation of the spirit to linguistic formations, for example, in the special clarity and plasticity of its archetypal ideas, or in the depth to which it can penetrate the nature of concepts in order to find instantly their major characterizing element, or in the ready mobility and creative strength of its imagination, or in the properly felt pleasure in harmony and rhythm of tone, to which therefore belong elasticity and mobility of the organs of articulation plus acuteness and subtlety of ear. Further to be observed are the quality of the traditional materials and the historical position in which a nation finds itself during an epoch of significant linguistic change or renewal, midway between its past and the as yet dormant germs of its future development. There are elements, too, in languages which really can be judged only by the effort directed toward them, not by the success of such effort. For languages do not always succeed in following through on a certain effort, however obviously marked. I am thinking here, for example, of such questions as that of inflections versus agglutination, about which much misunderstanding has been current and still is. That nations of happier gifts and under more favored conditions have more excellent languages lies in the very nature of the thing. But we are led to a deeper-lying cause, as well, the one we have just touched upon. The production of language is an inner need of mankind, not merely an external vehicle for the maintenance of communication, but an indispensable one which lies in human nature, necessary for the development of its spiritual energies and for the growth of a Weltanschauung which man can attain only by bringing his thinking to clarity and definition by communal contact with the thinking of others. If one now looks upon each language as an attempt to do this—and it is difficult to look at it otherwise—and upon all languages together as a contribution to the fulfillment of this basic human need, it may well be assumed that the language-creating energy in mankind will not rest until it has brought forth, whether in one place or everywhere, whatever accords most perfectly with its demands. In other words, there may be, even among languages and language groups which show no historical connection, various levels of advance as to this principle of their development. But when such is the case, such connectibility of outwardly unconnected phenomena must be founded on a universal inner cause which can only be the development of the operative energies. Language is one of the aspects from which collective human spiritual energy constantly proceeds into active manifestation. To express it in another way, one can see in language the striving of the archetypal idea of linguistic perfection to win existence in reality. To follow up this striving, and to depict it, is the business in its ultimate simplest analysis of the linguist.

Linguistic studies, incidentally, by no means require this perhaps too hypothetical sounding view for their foundation. But they can and should use it as a stimulus to try to find out whether such a step-by-step approach to perfectibility can be discovered in the various languages. There could be a series of languages, both of simple and of more complex structure, which do reveal to comparative study an advance in the direction of perfect structure. The organism of such languages would have to carry, even in complex forms, a certain order and simplicity which would make their striving for linguistic perfection more easily visible. Progress along this line would be found first in the isolation and perfect articulation of its sounds, hence in the syllabification dependent on it, in the pure segregation of its various elements, and in the structure of its simplest words. Further, we should be able to trace it in the treatment of words as sound units in order to obtain true word units which correspond to conceptual units, and finally, in the proper separation of what should appear independently in language and what should appear as a dependent form which adheres to an independent entity, which of course demands a method that can differentiate between additive compounds and symbolic fusions. For the reasons given above, I do not go into this in any detail, but merely wish my readers to recognize among the various points of view under discussion those which have guided me in my placement of the Kawi language among the Malayan language group. In the consideration of languages to follow, I separate all the changes which can be developed out of each language completely from their forms which to us look like original ones. The sphere of primordial linguistic forms now seems to be closed; the situational development in which we find human energies now does not seem to have the power to repeat itself. For however inward a phenomenon language is, it nonetheless has an independent external force of existence which compels man under its sway. The growth of primordial forms would therefore assume a separation of the peoples in the world which is now no longer thinkable . . . if, indeed—and this is a likelier explanation—there is not a definite period for linguistic breakthrough provided for the human race, as there is for the human individual.

Extraordinary spiritual energy:
Civilization, culture, Bildung

The power of the spirit which out of all its inward profundity and abundance intervenes in the course of the world is the truly creative principle in the hidden, mysterious evolution of mankind. . . . It is the noteworthy spiritual characteristic which broadens the concept of human intellectuality and shows itself unexpectedly and, so far as its depths are concerned, inexplicably. Its most characteristic mark is that its operations do not merely form the bases of our activities, but at the same time carry the kindling flame which generates and regenerates them. They reproduce life because they emerge from the fullness of life. For the power which starts these operations works in the tension of its total endeavor and its full unity. At the same time it acts creatively, looking upon its creativity as an inexplicable natural process. It does not merely accidentally add to something already known. Such was the origin, for example, of Egyptian art. It succeeded in building the human figure outward and upward from the organic center of its situation, and hence stamped its works with the imprint of genuine art. In this setting, we can see the significant difference, no matter what their relatedness, between Hindu poetry and philosophy and classical antiquity, and between Greek and Roman thought and art. Likewise, in later time, the life suddenly springing from Romance poetry, developing with the decline of the Latin language, in the European Occident now become independent, and from it the mainspring of modern culture. Where such grand operations did not take place, or where they were choked out by unfavorable outward circumstance, there even the noblest heritage, once hindered in its natural course, could not recreate its grandeur and originality.

We can see this sad fate as it befell the Greek language and the remains of Greek art. For centuries they languished, through no fault of their own, in a nation held down to barbarism. The old forms of language break up and mingle with foreign elements; its organic structure crumbles, and the powers of resistance against this process are not strong enough to transform and transport it into a new orbit, to breathe into it a new breath of life. By way of explaining the failures, we can always demonstrate favorable or unfavorable conditions, preparatory or retarding factors. It is part of human nature to begin with a *fait accompli*. Each idea whose discovery or execution gives humanity a new vitality permits of careful and painstaking analysis. We can always show how it grew gradually in countless minds before it burst forth in one. But take away the puff of genius, individual or national, and the chiaroscuro of these glowing coals never flames up. However little the nature of this sort of creative power permits of analysis, we do see this much clearly: there is an ability in it to rule any given materials from the inside out, to transform them into ideas or subordinate them to ideas. Even in his earliest days, man went beyond the moment and beyond sensual pleasure with his spirit. In the crudest human hordes we find expressed love for ornament, dance, music and song, as well as intimations of immortality, together with the hopes and cares man founds on such intimations. We find traditions and fairy tales which descend all the way down to the origins of mankind and its original home. The stronger and brighter this independent spiritual power, which proceeds in accordance with its own laws and its own forms of perception, casts its light into the worlds of prehistory and things-to-come with which man surrounds his existence of the moment, the purer and more varied does all materiality take on form. Thus arise science and art; and the everlasting goal of humanity is therefore the blending of inward independent creativity with all the outward givens of the world, each field taken in all its purity and completeness and each related to the other in all its organic functions.

We have portrayed the individuation of the spirit here as something most excellent and superior as well as most extraordinary. Yet even when it has reached its highest conceivable level, we must look upon it, too, as a limitation of universal nature. An individual creature is forced into certain limits by this activity of the spirit, because each individual character can be what it is only through principles of predomination and exclusion. But a narrowing down also heightens and intensifies strength, and exclusion, too, can be guided by a still higher principle of wholeness so that several unique characteristics, formed by exclusiveness, can make up a new whole. Here lie the deepest inner reasons for every sort of higher human cooperation, be it that of friendship, of love, or the grander association for the sake of the well-being of the nation or of humanity itself. Without further analysis of just how limitation of individuality opens for human beings the only road on which they may approach (though never attain) wholeness, I content myself here with merely calling attention to one thing. The powers which make man truly human (and therefore constitute the simple definition of his nature) manifest themselves and their diverse endeavors in new concept-broadening configurations when they come into contact with the world, with the—if I may be permitted to say it—vegetative life of the human race that somewhat mechanically tends to keep evolving along its ancient lines. The invention of algebra was an example of such a new configuration of the human spirit, at least of its mathematical direction. And similar instances can be cited from every science and every art. How it occurs in language we shall discuss at greater length below.

Such configurations of spiritual energy do not limit themselves to the thinking and representational functions of man, but are found notably in the formation of his character. For whatever rises from the wholeness of human energy may not rest until it returns to it. The totality of the inner appearance of a person, his sensations, his sentiments, are joined to his outer appearance which radiates them. This inward-outward appearance must allow us to perceive that it manifests all of human nature in broadened, and heightened form, being wholly imbued by the workings of all its individual efforts. Here arises a character's universal effectiveness; that in it which most worthily elevates the entire human race by being what it is. And language, the mid-point in which the most diverse individualities may come together through communication of their external plans and their internal perceptions, stands in the closest and liveliest interrelationship with character. The strongest and the most sensitive, the most penetrating and far-reaching, and the most fertile and withdrawn minds, all pour into language their strength and their tenderness, their depth and their inwardness, and language re-echoes them, sending up its sounds from its womb to further develop all the moods of character that sank down into it. The more character disciplines and refines itself, the more it levels and unifies the various sides of the mind and, like sculpture, gives to its object a configuration which may be grasped as a whole but which at the same time shows its contours ever more faithfully enclosing its inner substance. Language is particularly suited for transmitting and representing this configuration through its fine subtle harmonies, invisible in detail, but wondrously woven into its whole symbolic network. Only the effects of character formation are much harder to calculate than those of merely intellectual progress, since they so largely rest on those very mysterious links between one generation and the next.

There are steps in the progressive evolution of the human race, in other words, which are attained only because an unusual, extraordinary power has unexpectedly leapt to them. There are cases where, instead of our customary cause and effect explanations, we must assume the unprecedented expenditure of sudden, extraordinary energy. All spiritual progress can only emanate from expressions of inward power and thus always has a hidden cause which is inexplicable simply because it is self-moving. But whenever the inner power holds forth so sudden and mighty a creation that the prior course of things couldn't possibly be considered a preparation for it, then all possibility of explanation simply ceases. I hope I have made this convincing, because its applications are important. For it now follows that wherever intensified efforts within a certain direction take place, unless facts very clearly indicate otherwise, we must not assume a gradual evolution. For every sharp significant rise in energy is the result of a unique creative power. . . . If we fail to distinguish quite clearly between calculable, evolutionary and direct, creative progress of human spiritual energies, we simply ban from the history of the world the phenomenon of genius—as it shows up both in individuals and at certain moments in nations.

We also incur the danger of improperly evaluating the various conditions of human society. Certain things are often ascribed to civilization or to culture which cannot possibly be their result but which are rather created by the same basic power which also created them.

It is a commonplace, when dealing with languages, to ascribe all their excellences and advances to their being higher in the scale of cultural evolution, as though the only important difference between one language and another was its degree of relative progress. But if we consult history, such power of civilization and culture over language by no means asserts itself. Java obviously received a higher civilization and culture from India, both to a high degree, but this did not cause the indigenous Javanese dialect to perfect its less perfect linguistic forms, far less adapted to the needs of thought. On the contrary, it robbed the more refined Sanskrit of its forms, and stuffed them into its own. And India itself, regardless of how early and how indigenously it was civilized, did not receive its language at the hand of its civilization, but the deep creative principle of its linguistic sense flowed, as did its civilization, out of the genial spiritual direction of its people. That is why language and civilization by no means stand in a two-way relation to each other. Peru was easily the most civilized country in the Americas, no matter which of its Inca institutions one may regard, but no connoisseur of languages will put Peruvian at the peak of American languages, though special effort was made to spread it far and wide through war and conquest. To my mind, Peruvian is far inferior to Mexican, in particular. So-called crude and uncivilized languages are quite capable of excellences of structure, and often contain them in reality, and it would be by no means impossible to consider them quite superior to so-called civilized ones. . . .

This matter is too important not to discuss at some length. Insofar as civilization and culture import certain concepts hitherto unknown to a nation, or for that matter develop them out of their own nature, the point of view attacked above is from one aspect undoubtedly correct. The need for a concept and its resultant amplification does precede the word for it, which is merely the expression of its perfected clarification. But if one stops with this observation, thinking to discover the qualitative differences between languages by this fact alone, one falls into error which is most disadvantageous to proper evaluation of language. It is unfortunate to try to judge the sphere of concepts of a certain people at a certain time by consulting word lists. Quite aside from the uselessness of such procedure in the case of most non-European languages for which we have only very deficient word lists, it should be self-evident that, even where such a list is complete, a great number of nonsensuous concepts might easily be expressed by metaphors considered unusual by us or totally unknown to us, or even by paraphrase. What should be far more decisive is that there lie in the concepts, as well as in the rest of the language of a people, however undeveloped, a certain wholeness which corresponds to the wholeness of limitless human developmental capacity. . . . The progress of language development can proceed only within the limits prescribed by the original constitution of the language in question. A nation may use a less perfect language as a tool for ideas, as an impetus for whose birth it would not have sufficed, but it cannot cancel out the inner limitations which are deeply founded in its structure. Here, even the highest degree of educational development remains unfruitful. Even what subsequent times add by way of externals is taken over by the original language which modifies it in accordance with its own structural principles.

From the point of view of inner spiritual values, one cannot look upon civilization and culture as the summits to which the human spirit may rise. Both have flourished in our time to an unprecedentedly high level and extent. But whether therefore the inner structure of human nature (as we see it for example in certain periods of antiquity) has grown as varied or as mighty, or is even growing at all, is a very doubtful question. And even more doubtful is it in the case of those nations which were most responsible for the modern spread of civilization and a certain culture.

Civilization is the humanization of nations in their external institutions and customs and the inner sentiments referring to these. Culture adds to this the refinement of social conditions, science, and art. But when we say *Bildung* in German, we mean something at once higher and more inward, namely, the disposition which harmoniously imparts itself to feelings and character and which stems from insight into and feeling for man's whole spiritual and moral striving.

Civilization can come from the inner constitution of a people and then testifies to that not always explicable spiritual movement of which we spoke. If it is transplanted into a nation from the outside, it spreads faster, possibly penetrates more branches of social life, but does not have an equally energetic reaction back upon the spirit and character of the people. It is a high privilege granted to us moderns, to carry civilization to the remotest parts of the earth, to join this effort to all sorts of others, and to spend time and money on it quite apart from any secondary considerations. The principle of universal humanity here operating is a unique sign of progress in our time. All the great inventions of the last few centuries unite to make it increasingly possible. The Greek and Roman colonies were far less effectual. To be sure they had not the means of communication nor the extensive institutions of civilization itself. But they lacked, besides these, the inner principle as well, which alone can bring such attempts to true life. They possessed a clear concept, deeply interwoven with all their feelings and sentiments, of high, noble human individuality. But the thought of respecting a human being just for his humanness had not yet gained validity among them, much less a feeling for resultant human rights and obligations. This important aspect of universal morality had remained a stranger to them, their development being much more narrowly national. . . . All the individual social efforts were far less separated and isolated from each other in the ancients than they are in us, and so they were far less able to communicate what they had, without activating the spirit which had created it. With us this has become quite different. A power active in our own civilization keeps driving us forward in a straight course, and the nations whose development comes under our influence get a much more uniform shape from us; any development in them of an original character, even where it might have occurred had they been left alone, is now suppressed at an early stage.

Cooperation among individuals and among nations

The effectiveness of an individual's effort is always fragmentary. But it seems to share, and up to a certain point it truly does share, a certain similarity of direction with that of the entire human race. For every individual's direction is conditioned by and in turn helps to condition the intrinsic connectedness of the course of time, past, present, and future. From another and profounder point of view, however, the direction of any individual diverges from that of the race, these two types of movement, crossing and recrossing and tangling with each other, constituting the web of world history insofar as it is connected with inward man. The divergence is readily seen by the fact that the fate of the human race seems to proceed, and, so far as we can judge, proceed with increasing perfectibility, quite independently of the ever-recurring disappearance of one gen-eration of men after another, whereas the single individual has to depart from the scene not only suddenly and often in the midst of his most significant contributions, but with the utmost inner con-viction and intuitive certainty that his departure does not constitute an absolute end to all his activity. In other words, the individual looks upon his own activities as separate from the course of human events and he forms, even during his lifetime, a sense of opposi-tion between development of self and the shaping of the world, armed with which he intervenes in reality. The general internal constitution of human nature sees to it that this opposition will not spoil either the evolution of the race or the self-education of the individual. For development of self can only proceed in step with shaping of the world; and far beyond the confines of his life, certain requirements and needs of the heart and certain images of the imagination bind man to the fates from which he eventually departs: family ties, striving for fame, joyous prospects for the future development of seeds he has planted. Nonetheless an opposition is felt and through it there grows . . . a certain inward quality of the mind upon which are founded the mightiest and holiest feelings. This inward-turning of the mind is all the more effective because man considers not only himself but all other beings like him equally destined for a solitary self-development, far beyond the confines of life, and the bonds, therefore, which join mind to mind assume another and higher significance. From the various degrees to which that inward-turning reaches, separating the self from reality in spite of all connections, and from its more or less exclusive predominance, spring the nuances significant for all human development. India offers a notable example for the purity to which it may be refined, but also for the glaring contrasts to which it may degenerate; Hindu antiquity is best explained from this point of view, in fact. This mood of the soul exercises a special influence upon language. It goes one way in a people which likes to follow out the solitary paths of abstract thought, quite another in one which needs thought mainly as a mediation between outward activities. The symbolic elements are quite differently comprehended by the one type; whole large segments of linguistic possibilities remain dormant in the other. For language must first be introduced by a dim and undeveloped feeling to the sphere over which it is to pour its light. How the breaking off of the life of individuals is to be harmonized with the continuing development of the race—perhaps in a region unknown to us—remains an impenetrable mystery. But the feeling for this impenetrability is a most important factor in man's inner development toward individuation, because it awakens a reverence for something unrecognized remaining after everything recognizable has been disposed of. It is comparable to the impression that night makes on us, where the scattered sparkle of bodies unknown to us takes the place of all the things ordinarily within visibility.

Another great significance of the continuousness of the fate of the race and the breaking off of the separate generations lies in the different investment each generation has in its own past. The later generations find themselves . . . observing a stage, as it were, which unfolds a richer and more brightly illumined drama. The stream of events also seems to place certain generations at random into darker and more weighty or brighter and more easily livable periods. For the reality-bound, living individual, this difference looks less great than it seems to be when seen from the vantage point of history. One lacks many means for comparison; one experiences at any given moment only a small segment of the total development; one intervenes with pleasure in activity, and the rights of the moment carry one over the unevennesses. Like clouds precipitating out of fog, an epoch takes on its visible limits only when seen from a distance. But the influence of each generation upon the next makes plain what it has itself received from the preceding ones. Our modern cultural development, for example, rests in large part on the opposition with which antiquity confronts us. It would be difficult and saddening to say what might be left of us if we should have to part from everything that antiquity has been and is to us. And if we investigate the condition of the peoples who constituted what we call antiquity, in all its historical detail, we find that they by no means accord with the image we have of them in our soul. What is so powerfully effective for us is our own understanding of antiquity, our own view which proceeds from the center of their greatest and purest endeavors, emphasizing the spirit far more than the reality of their institutions, leaving out of consideration their contradictions, and making no claims on them which would be incompatible with our idea of them. But it is not random willfulness that leads us to such a view of the nature of antiquity. The ancients themselves justify it; we could not hold it about any other epoch. The deep feeling for their intrinsic nature is what lends us the capacity to elevate ourselves that we might reach their level. Because reality in them always passed over with felicitous ease into idea and creative imagination, and because they were able to use them to influence reality in turn, we have the right to look upon the ancients as exclusive inhabitants of this whole spiritual territory. For according to the spirit hovering over their writings, their works of art, and their practical ambitions, they described the full free circle—regardless of whether their reality lagged behind in certain respects—of humanity in its consummate purity, wholeness and harmony, thus leaving us with an ideal image, the image of human nature intensified and raised. As between sunny and clouded skies, their superiority over us lies not so much in their lifelike figures themselves, as in the wondrous light poured all around their living configurations. The Greeks themselves, however great an influence of earlier peoples upon them one may assume, seemed to have been completely devoid of such a light shining upon them from the far distances of other peoples and other lands. Within their own past, however, they did have a similar experience: in the Homeric and other heroic songs. Just as they are inexplicable for us as to their nature and the reasons for their existence, just as they are models and sources for a great number of enrichments of our spirit, so the Homeric times were for them: dark, and yet radiant with unique luminous images. For the Romans, on the other hand, they were by no means what they are for us. Their effect upon the Romans was that of a contemporary, highly cultivated nation which had the advantage of an older literary tradition. India lies too darkly in the distance for us to be able to judge of its primordial past. Its influence upon the Occident was not centered upon the individuality of its spirit—such an influence, had it existed, could not have disappeared without a trace— but at most operated through separate opinions, inventions, and legends. . . . Their own antiquity probably appeared to the Hindus as the Greeks' did to them, we should guess. At any rate, this is very plainly true of China, and the influence and contrast of their older style and the philosophical teachings it contained upon their later periods.

Since languages or at least their elements (a difference not to be ignored) are transmitted from one epoch to the next, and since we may speak of the beginnings of a language only by completely transgressing the field of experience, the relationship between past and present leaves the deepest marks here. But the difference to a language by reason of its placement among other more familiar ones, is an infinitely strong one, even in the case of an already formed language, because language is also a way of looking at a nation's total thinking and feeling processes, and these, coming to a people from remote times, cannot operate without also being influential on the language. Thus our languages today would have had a different configuration in several respects if, for example, Hindu antiquity had had as insistent and lasting an effect on them as did Greek classical antiquity.

The single human individual is ever connected with a whole —with his nation, the race to which it belongs, the human race itself. His life, regardless of what aspect one looks at, is necessarily bound to sociality, and an external, shallower view of this fact leads to exactly the same point as a more spiritual and higher view. . . . In the merely vegetative existence of human beings on the earth, the helplessness and need of the individual drive him to union with others, demanding communication through language as the prerequisite for cooperative undertakings of mutual aid. But consummate spiritual development, even in the loneliest abstractedness of a single soul, is no less dependent on language, and language demands to be addressed toward an outer, other being who understands it. Articulated sound wrenches itself loose from the breast, in order to awaken in another an echo leading back to the ear. Simultaneously man discovers that there are other creatures of similar inner needs, capable of meeting the diverse yearnings present in his own inward sentiments. For an intuition of wholeness and a striving to reach it is given directly with the feeling of individuality and intensifies in proportion to the latter's acuteness, since each individual carries the whole nature of humanity, but within a single developmental orbit. We have not the remotest realistic inkling of a consciousness which is not self-consciousness. But that striving and that germ of inextinguishable yearning, planted in us by the intrinsic nature of humanity itself, do not permit the conviction to perish that our isolated individuality is but a phenomenon in the field of the merely determined aspects of existence, their common spirit being the reality.

The connection between the individual and a whole, strengthening his power and providing him with constant stimulus, is too important a point in the spiritual economy—if I may be permitted this expression—not to be elucidated further at this point. The union (which invariably simultaneously evokes separation) of nations and races depends, to be sure, first of all on historical events, largely even on the quality of their homeland or migratory territory. But even if (and I should not precisely like to justify this view) one desired to separate from this external situation all influence of an inner, even an instinctual, attraction or repulsion, every nation nonetheless can and must also be viewed as quite separate from its outer situation, much like a human individuality which is following an inward characteristic orbit of the spirit. The more one realizes that the individual's effectiveness, regardless of the degree of his genius, endures and operates only to the extent to which it can be supported by the spirit of his nation, and the latter in turn receives new vitality from the creative individual, the more it becomes obviously necessary to seek an explanation for our present cultural level in these national individualities of the spirit. And history gives them to us, wherever it transmits to us the data for a judgment upon the inner development of peoples, in certain well-defined forms. Civilization and culture gradually cancel out the glaring contrasts between peoples, and even more successful is the striving for more universal moral forms on the part of a deep, refined feeling for education. The advances of science and art, too, fall in with this, for they strive toward ever more universal ideals, unfettered by national prejudice. But though we seek for equality, we can attain it only each in his own way, and the diversity with which human individuality, without falling into one-sidedness, can express itself reaches infinite proportions. And it is just this diversity upon which the successful striving for universals solely depends. For this striving demands the whole unsegregated union of powers which can never be explained in their completeness but which necessarily operate only by means of the most acute individuality. A nation therefore intervenes most fruitfully and powerfully in the course of universal culture not only by succeeding in various particular scientific endeavors, but especially by a total exertion of that which makes out the center of human nature. It expresses itself most clearly and completely in philosophy, poetry and art, and from these pours itself out over the whole ways of thinking and feeling of a people.

As a result of the connection between the individual and the collectivity surrounding him, every significant spiritual activity of the individual belongs also—but only indirectly and in a certain special sense—to the collectivity. The existence of languages proves, however, that there are also spiritual creations which by no means originate with any individual, to be handed on to other individuals, but which come forth out of the simultaneous, spontaneous activity of all. In languages, in other words, the nations (since a language is that which defines a nation) as such are the true and direct creators.

Yet we must beware of assuming this view without the proper reservations. Since languages are inextricably entangled in the inmost nature of man and break forth spontaneously to a much greater degree than they can be produced at will, one might just as well consider the intellectual characteristics of a nation the product of its language, as the other way around. The truth is that both simultaneously and in mutual agreement emerge from unfathomable depths of human psychic constitution. We know no such language creation from experience, nor are we anywhere offered an analogy for consideration. When we speak of an original language, this only refers to our ignorance of its earlier components. A connected chain of languages had rolled on for millennia before it got to the point which our sparse lore designates as the oldest. And not only the primitive forms of a truly original language, but also the secondary forms of later stages which we know quite well how to analyze are inexplicable, in so far as their moment of birth is concerned. All process of becoming in nature, most particularly its organic and living aspects, slips beyond the grasp of our observation. However carefully we investigate a previous and obviously preparatory condition, the gap between the new creation and its preparation always remains the barrier between something and nothing, and the same thing is true of the moment of cessation. All human comprehension occupies only the territory between birth and death. So far as languages are concerned, we have a notable example in a creation period which lies well within the reach of our history. We can follow the manifold changes which the Roman language underwent during its decline; we can add the mixtures due to immigrant hordes: none of it explains the origin of the living germ which in diverse forms meanwhile unfolded into the organisms of new languages. An inner and original principle, different in each of the modern languages, rebuilt in its own way the ancient crumbling structure. We, who are forever bound to the field of effects, become aware of alterations only when they have become massive. It may seem preferable, therefore, to leave this point out of consideration entirely. But this is impossible if one wants to sketch the developmental road of the human spirit in even its broadest outlines, since the formation of languages—even of a single language in all its derivations and recompositions—is one of the facts which most intrinsically defines the human spirit, and moreover shows the cooperation of individuals in forms not occurring elsewhere. While confessing, therefore, that we stand at a border line beyond which neither historical investigation nor free thought are able to lead us, we must nonetheless faithfully record the fact itself as well as its most immediate consequences.

The first and most natural of these is that this connection of the individual with his nation rests exactly in the center from which the total spiritual energy controls all thinking, feeling, and willing. For language is related to the whole of man's spiritual energy, to the sum total as well as the parts; nothing in it is or ever remains a stranger to language. It simultaneously is not only massive, receptive of impressions, but also follows out of the infinite diversity of possible intellectual directions one single definite one, modifying with inner spontaneity every external operation directed toward it. But it cannot be regarded as anything externally separated from spiritual character and can therefore not be taught (though at first glance this may seem otherwise), but only awakened in the psyche. One can only give it the clue along which it will develop of itself. While languages are thus creations . . . of nations, they also remain self-creations of individuals in that they can reproduce themselves only in individuals, but only in such a way that each individual assumes the understanding of all others, and all satisfy this assumption of any one. Whether we look upon language as a world-view, then, or as a thought-relation, one thing is certain: it always rests necessarily upon the whole energy of man, and nothing can be excluded from it since it comprises all.

This energy now varies individually in the various nations, both absolutely as well as during certain periods, according to degree and according to individual methods within the general direction open to all. The difference must become visible in the product, language, and does so, of course, primarily by its greater proportion of either external influence or internal spontaneity. We therefore frequently meet cases in comparative linguistics where an explanation of the structure of one language leads more or less easily to the understanding of another. Still, there are those which look separated from the others by a genuine gap. Individuals by the energy of their individuality may impart to the human spirit a push into hitherto undiscovered directions; nations may do the same to the processes of linguistic development. But between linguistic structure and the success of all other kinds of intellectual activity, there exists an undeniable connection. It lies first and foremost (and we here look upon it from this side alone) in the breath of inspired enthusiasm which the language-building energy in its act of transforming the world into thought imparts to language in such a way that it harmoniously spreads throughout the whole. If one can think out the possibility that a given nation's language might originate just as a given word develops most significantly and plainly out of a total world view, rendering it back most purely and forming itself in such a way that it can slip most easily and incorporeally into any and every arrangement of thoughts—then such a language, as long as its life principle holds out, must evoke the same energy in the same direction with equal success in each single individual. The entry of such a language (or one approaching it) into world history must therefore found an important epoch in human development, especially in its highest and most marvellous products. Certain orbits of the spirit and a certain verve which carries it in its orbits, are unthinkable until such languages have arisen. They form a true turning point in the inner history of the human race. We may look upon them as the peaks of linguistic development, but such peaks are at the same time the starting point for soul-inspired and imaginative human spiritual development. Insofar it is quite correct to assert that the work of nations must precede the work of individuals, although as soon as one has said it, one has demonstrated unfailingly once again how inextricably and simultaneously the creative activity of the two is interconnected.

Transition to a more specific consideration of language

We have now reached the point at which we recognize languages as the first necessary step in the primitive development of the human race, and from where the nations can begin to pursue any higher human direction. Languages grow together with growing spiritual energy, under the same conditions, and at the same time constitute the enlivening and stimulating principle of the latter. But the growth of language and the growth of the spirit do not proceed parallel to one another, but absolutely and indivisibly as the same activity of the same intellectual capacity. As each people creates an area of freedom coming from within for its developing language, a freedom which is the instrument of all human activities, it searches and attains the thing itself, as well. In other words, by developing language it reaches something higher than and different from language, and by reaching toward this on the paths of poetic creation and meditative intuition, it simultaneously reacts back on its language. If one calls even the very first, crude, and formless experiments of an intellectual effort literature, then one observes language pursuing its single path, forever inseparably bound up with creativity.

The spiritual characteristics and the linguistic structure of a people stand in a relationship of such indissoluble fusion that, given one, we should be able to derive the other from it entirely. For intellectuality and language permit and further only mutually agreeable forms. Language is the external manifestation, as it were, of the spirit of a nation. Its language is its spirit and its spirit its language: one can hardly think of them as sufficiently identical. How they join together in truth, at a source which remains hidden from our comprehension, remains inexplicable and unrevealed to us. But without wishing to decide the priority of one or the other, we must look upon the spiritual energy of a nation as the real explanatory principle and as the true cause of the differences to be found in various languages, because this spirit alone stands alive and independent in our world; its language but clings to it. For insofar as language likewise reveals itself to us in its creative spontaneity and independence, it transcends the field of empirical reality and loses itself in ideal being. Historically speaking, we always deal with a real speaker—though this should not mean that we therefore leave the true relationships out of account. We may divide intellectuality and language; such division does not therefore exist in truth. If language justly appears to us as something higher, something beyond the work of mere humans, unlike other human spiritual creations, this would hardly be so if it were not for the fact that human spiritual energy only confronts us in separate phenomena.

If instead its basic nature itself shed its light on us from its un-fathomable depths, and we could therefore have insight into the collective unity beneath human individuality, then we should see clearly that language, too, goes far back beyond our separation into individuals. So far as practical linguistics is concerned, it is only important not to rest satisfied with any shallow explanatory prin-ciple, but really to elevate oneself to this high and ultimate one; to accept as the firm center of this whole spiritual structure the propo-sition that linguistic structure varies within the human race only as national spiritual characteristics vary.

But once we look closely (as we cannot stop from doing) at the various types of method employed by the various linguistic structures, we can no longer wish to apply to any given language the result of our investigation into the national character, of and by itself. In those early epochs into which our present investigations place us, we know the nations only through their languages; often we do not know exactly what nation we are to think of—by way of history or origins—in connection with any given language. Thus Zend is for us the language of a nation which we can only guess at. But among all the utterances in which spirit and character may be recognized, language is the only one suited for revealing both, in their inmost secret byways. If one looks upon languages, therefore, as an explanatory principle for progressive spiritual development, one must consider them as originating in intellectual character, but one must seek the type of their individual characteristics in the structure of each separate one. Thus, if the considerations thus far introduced are to be carried out with some completeness, it is now necessary to look more closely at the nature of languages and at the possibility of their reactive differences, in order to join comparative linguistics to its ultimate and highest point of reference.

The form of language

It takes a special direction of linguistic investigation, to be sure, to follow successfully the path outlined above. One must look upon language not so much as a dead product, but much more as a productivity. One must abstract it somewhat from its functions of designating objects and communicating understanding, and instead explore rather carefully its origin, closely interwoven with its inner spiritual activity, and the relation between these two. The advances which linguistic study owes to the successful efforts of the last few decades make an over-all view of it much easier. Now we can move up on our aim of designating the various diverse methods by which the business of linguistic development flourishes throughout the great divided, isolated, but also related collectivity of the human race. But herein lies both the cause of the varieties of human linguistic structure as well as its influence upon the development of the spirit—in other words, the entire object which interests us here.

As soon as we enter upon our investigation, we meet with a major difficulty, to be sure. Language offers us an infinitude of details by way of words, rules, analogies, and exceptions of all kinds, and we are at a loss as to how to bring this chaotic looking mass—which has already been ordered and classified a good deal, at that—into a proper comparative parallel with our unified single image of human spiritual energy. Even if one is in possession of all necessary lexicographical and grammatical detail of, let us say two important language groups such as Sanskrit and Semitic, one is not very far along with one's attempt to draw the character of each in such a clear compelling outline that a fruitful comparison and placement of each . . . becomes possible. This demands an additional search for the common sources of the various characteristics, a fusion of the dispersed traits into the image of an organic whole. Only by this method can one gain a handhold which enables one to hold fast to the details. In order to successfully compare various languages in reference to their characteristic structure, we need therefore to explore the form of each most painstakingly. In that way we may ascertain how each language solves the major problems which lie as the task to be fulfilled by all language. But since the expression "form" in connection with linguistic research is used in several senses, I shall need to develop more extensively the way in which I shall use it here. This seems all the more essential since we are not speaking here of language in general but of the various languages of various peoples, and it is therefore important to know what is meant by language in contrast to cognate language group on the one hand and dialect on the other, and what is meant by one language where such a one has gone through considerable alterations.

Language, taken as real, is something which constantly and in every moment passes away. Even its preservation in writing is only an incomplete mummified depository which needs, for full understanding, an imaginative oral reconstitution. Language is not a work (*ergon*) but an activity (*energeia*). Its true definition can therefore only be a genetic one. For it is the ever-repetitive work of the spirit to make articulated sound capable of expressing thought. Taken directly and strictly, this is the definition of each act of speaking, but in a true and intrinsic sense one can look upon language as but the totality of all spoken utterance. For in the scattered chaos of words and rules which we customarily call language, the only thing present in reality is whatever particulars are brought forth by individual acts of speaking, and this is never complete. It needs another type of work performed on it in order for us to recognize in it the type of living speech that it is, in other words to yield a true image of a living language. Just the highest and subtlest aspects of language cannot be recognized in its separate elements; they can only be perceived or intuited in connected speech (which demonstrates all the more that language intrinsically lies in the act of its production in reality). Connected speech is what we must hold before our inner ear as the true and foremost manifestation of language, if we are to be successful in any of our investigations into the living essence of language. Beating it down into words and rules is only a dead artifice of scientific analysis.

To designate languages as works of the spirit is a completely correct and adequate expression, if only because the existence of the spirit can only be imagined in the form of activity. The analysis essential to the study of linguistic structure compels us, in fact, to look upon language as a method which pursues certain aims by certain means, and hence to consider it truly a creative formation of a given nation. (I have tried above to prevent the misinterpretations possible at this point. . . .)

I have also drawn attention to the fact that our linguistic studies place us—if I may thus express it—into a historical center, and that neither a nation nor a language now known to us may be considered original or primordial. Since each has already received some of its materials from previous generations in times unknown to us, the spiritual activity above explained as bringing forth thought is always directed at something already given. The bringing forth which is here meant is not so much a purely creative, as a transformative activity.

This activity, now, operates in a constant and uniform manner. For it is the same spiritual power which keeps exerting itself, and it diverges only within rather narrow limits. Understanding is its aim. No one, in other words, may speak to another in a way in which, under similar circumstances, he might not himself be spoken to. And finally, the materials transmitted are not only whatever they are—miscellaneous materials transmitted—but, since they too had a similar origin, they are most closely related to the general spiritual direction. Those elements, in this endeavor of the spirit to lift articulated sound into expression of thought, which are constant and uniform, represented as completely and systematically as possible with full comprehension of their inner connections—constitute the form of language.

In this definition the form appears to be a scientific abstraction. But it would be totally incorrect to look upon it solely as such an existenceless figment of thought. In reality it is the quite individuated urge by means of which a nation creates validity in language for its thoughts and its feelings. Only because it is never given to us to see this urge in the undivided totality of its striving, but merely in its invariably isolated effects, all we can successfully do is comprehend the identical nature of its manifestations with a dead general concept. In itself, the urge is a living whole.

The difficulty facing just the most significant and subtlest linguistic investigations frequently lies in the fact that something which flows through the total impression a language yields is perceived with the clearest feeling of conviction, but is wrecked by all attempts to present it with sufficient completeness of detail and to define it by limited concepts. This is a difficulty which we must also face here. The characteristic form of language depends on each single one of its tiniest elements; each is somehow determined by it, however unnoticeable in detail. On the other hand, it is hardly possible to find certain points of which, taken individually, it could be asserted that the form of the language is specifically and decisively contained in them. Whenever one goes through any given language, therefore, one finds many things in it which one can imagine might be quite different, without their altering the form. To see the form purely differentiated, we are willy-nilly led back to a total impression. And here the opposite instantly takes place. The most decisive individuality lies clear before our eyes, unmistakably convincing to our feeling. Perhaps the least incorrect analogy to languages in this respect is our experience with human physiognomy. Individuality confronts us undeniably; similarities are recognized; but no amount of measuring or describing of the parts, either alone or in relationship to the whole, can weld the evident characteristics into a concept. It rests upon the whole and upon each individual reception of that whole; no doubt, therefore, each physiognomy appears different to each observer. Since language, however we look at it, is always the spiritual exhalation of a nationally characteristic life, the same applies to it. However much we stuff into it or embody in it, however much we abstract and analyze out of it: something unknown is always left over and this, slipping out of the grasp of all direct attack upon the problems language raises, is exactly that wherein it is a unity and the breath of a living entity. Since such is the constitution of languages, then, the representation of their form can never be complete in the sense here indicated, but can only be successful up to a point—which point, however, should suffice us for an over-all view. But this awareness of ultimate failure on the part of the linguist should not render his path any less definite by which he must explore the mysteries of language and seek to reveal its nature. If he loses his way, he will unfailingly miss a large number of investigative clues and must leave unexplained a good many points which are perfectly explicable, for he will take for isolated detail what is in reality joined in a living relationship.

The above introduction makes self-evident that by form in language we do not here mean its so-called grammatical form. The difference that we are in the habit of observing between grammar and vocabulary can only serve practical purposes in connection with learning a new language; it surely prescribes no limits or rules for genuine linguistic research. The concept of form in languages stretches far beyond the rules of syntax and word formation, insofar as one means by the latter the application of certain general logical categories of function, effectuation, substance, quality, etc. upon the roots or bases of words. Form is intrinsically applicable to the formation of roots and bases themselves and must, in fact, be reserved to them as much as possible, in order to clarify the intrinsic nature of language.

Form is opposed, to be sure, to substance. But in order to find the substance of language form, we must pass beyond the boundaries of language. Within them, the only substance that can be found is something which may be only relatively opposed to something else, such as bases, for example, in relationship to declension. A language may borrow words from another and treat them like substances. But again, such words will be substances only in relation to the language that borrowed them, not in themselves. Taken absolutely, there can be no unformed substance—no raw materiality —within language, since everything in it is directed toward a certain aim, namely the expression of thought, and this task already begins with the first element of language: articulated sound. In fact, sound *is* articulated by formal activation. The true material substance of language is on the one hand sound as such, and on the other hand the totality of sense impressions and spontaneous spiritual movements which precede, by the help of language, the formation of concepts.

It is therefore self-evident that the realistic quality of the sounds must be particularly noted, in order to get a notion of the form of a language. Investigation into form begins with the alphabet and this is treated as its major foundation throughout all parts of our investigation. Generally speaking, nothing factual or particular is excluded from our concept of form; on the contrary, all that which can be explained only historically, the most individual aspects possible, are just what is contained in this concept. All the details of language, in fact, if one pursues the method here designated, can only thus be secured for investigation, since they can all too easily be otherwise overlooked. This leads to painstaking and often petty elementary research, to be sure; but it simply is the vast quantity of petty details upon which one's total impression of a language rests. Nothing is as incompatible with linguistic study as the ambition to look only for great things, for spirituality, and predominant factors. Careful search of each grammatical subtlety, painstaking dismemberment of words into their component parts, are absolute necessities if error in all one's judgments is to be avoided. It is likewise self-evident, however, that no detail is taken up into the concept of form as a mere isolated fact, but only insofar as a method of linguistic structure can be recognized in it. By representing to oneself the form, one must recognize the specific way that a language (and with it a nation) has taken in order to express its thoughts. One must be in a position to have an over-all view of its relationship to other languages, both as to its aim and theirs, as well as its reaction and theirs, back upon the spiritual activity of the nations involved. . . .

Whatever identity or relationship two languages may have must rest on the identity or relationship of their forms. . . . Form alone decides the relationship among language groups. This applies to Kawi, for example, which does not stop being a Malayan language just because it contains a great many Sanskrit words. The forms of several languages may be collected under a still more general concept of form, and this in fact happens as soon as one looks only at the most general characteristics, such as the interrelationships of the ideas necessary for the designation of concepts and the exigencies of syntax, the sameness of the organs of articulation whose extent and nature permit of only a certain number of articulated sounds, the relationships, finally, between certain consonants and vowels to certain sense impressions, from all of which springs identity of form without necessarily cognate relationship. For the individuation of languages, within a most universal sameness is so marvellously great that one might say with equal propriety that the entire human race has but one language, or that each human being has his own. Among the linguistic analogical similarities, however, first and foremost is that which is due to the family relationship among nations. How great and of what quality such similarity must be in order to justify the assumption of cognation when it is not otherwise historically vouched for, we cannot examine here. We are concerned here only with the application of our concept of linguistic form to cognate languages. It should be clear by now that the form of various cognate languages must be found in the form of the entire linguistic family. Nothing may be contained in them which is not in harmony with the more general, generic form; as a rule one will find each special characteristic of the individual language at least hinted at in the generic form. And there will usually be one or more languages in each family which will contain the original form more purely and completely. For we are speaking here of languages one of which has grown out of the other, where, in other words, a given material substance (always taken, as above specified, in a relative sense only) passes over from one nation to another and is transformed in passing. This happens in a definite sequence and order, which can usually not be accurately determined, however. But the transformations themselves, given the similar ideational complexes and directions of the operative spiritual energy, the sameness of the speech organs and the transmitted speech habits, and finally the many similar historical influences, can only be closely related.

The nature and attributes of language in general

Since the difference in languages rests upon their form, and this form is related to the spiritual constitution of the nations and the particular energy coursing through them at the moment of their creation or transformation, it now becomes necessary to develop the concepts underlying these in greater detail and to pursue at least several of the main directions of language. For this purpose I shall pick out the most consequential ones which clearly show how basic inner energy reacts upon language and language in turn upon it.

Two principles come to light as one reflects upon language in general and the analysis of specific differences among languages in particular: phonetic form and the uses made of it for the designation of objects and the interrelation of thoughts. The latter is founded on the demands made upon language by thought, from which originate the general rules of language, and this aspect is therefore the same among all peoples, within the limits of their national characteristics or its subsequent developments. The phonetic form itself, on the other hand, is the truly constitutive and guiding principle of the diversity among languages, both in itself as well as in the helping or hindering effect it has on the inmost tendency of language. It is of course likewise closely related and dependent upon the total constituent characteristics of a nation, being a part of the human organism that is closely connected with the sum total of inner spiritual energy, but the types of connection and the reasons for them are shrouded in an obscurity which hardly permits of any clarification. These two principles now (phonetic form and its application), in all the intimacy of their mutual interpenetration, yield the individual form of every language. They form the points of reference which linguistic analysis must investigate and attempt to represent in all their connectedness. The indispensable ingredient in such investigation is that the undertaking be founded on a correct and worthy estimate of language as a whole, of the depth of its origin, and the vastness of its extent. We shall therefore need to tarry once more in order to ascertain that we are working with these requirements well in mind.

I am taking the linguistic process in its widest sense, not merely in its reference to speech or to the accumulation of its verbal elements as the immediate products of speech, but also in its relationship toward our thinking and feeling functions. Under consideration, therefore, is language's entire path, emanating from spirit, reacting upon spirit.

Language is the formative organ of thought. Intellectual activity which is totally spiritual, totally inward, which passes without a trace, as it were, becomes externalized and perceptible to the senses by means of the sounds of speech. It and speech are therefore one and indivisible. But aside from this, intellectual activity has a reason implicit in itself for entering into relationship with the sound of speech; if it did not, thinking could not reach clarification; imaginative representation could not be conceptualized. The indivisible connection between thought, the organs of speech and the organs of hearing lie unalterable and intrinsic in the arrangement of human nature, to be explained no further than to state that it is so. The harmony of sound with thought presents a clear enough image. Just as thought, comparable to a flash of lightning or a blow, collects all imaginative representation into a single point which excludes everything not belonging to it, so does sound resound with incisive acuity and singleness of purpose. Just as thought seizes the entire psychic constitution, so does sound possess a power which penetrates and shivers every nerve. What makes sound different from and unique among all sensuous impressions is that the ear (which is not true or not equally true of the other sense organs) receives the impression of actual movement, of an action in the case of the sounds of voice, and that this movement or action emanates from the inmost core of a living creature—a thinking creature in the case of articulated sound, a feeling creature in the case of unarticulated sound. Just as thinking in its most intimately human aspects is a yearning from darkness to see the light, from restrictedness and constraint toward infinity, so sound streams outward from the depths of the breast and finds in air a wonderfully appropriate mediating material, the subtlest and most mobile of all elements, whose seeming incorporeality accords with even the sensuous conception of spirit. The incisive acuity of speech sounds is indispensable to the understanding as it grapples with a conceptualization of objects. The objects of external nature as well as the internally stimulated activity press in upon man all at once, with a multitude of distinguishing marks. But he strives for comparison, analysis, synthesis, and—in his loftier moments—for the development of an ever more comprehensive organic development into unity. He demands, therefore, to conceive even of separate objects in a well-defined form, forcing the unity and clear definition of sound to replace the object. But such sound never displaces any of the other impressions made by objects on man's outer or inner senses, but instead becomes their carrier, adding a new significance which is the joint result of its own individual nature and the individual reception the object impressions have received from the speaker. At the same time the acuity of the sound permits an undefined number of modifications which are cleanly separable from the original imaginative representation and which are equally separable from each other. This is nowhere nearly as true in any of the other sense impressions. Since intellectual endeavor does not only occupy the understanding but stimulates the entire human being, this fact too is reflected by the sound of the human voice. As living sound, like the breath of life itself, it comes forth from the human breast, accompanying, even without language, his pains and joys, his loathings and his desires, thereby breathing the life which produces it into the sense which accepts it as part of itself, just as language itself always reproduces the represented object together with the feeling which it stimulates, thereby relating over and over again in repeated separate acts the world with humanity or—in a different formulation—man's spontaneous activity with his receptivity. Finally man's upright posture, denied to the animals, is a singularly fitting accompaniment to the sound of speech which evokes it, as it were. For speech does not care to die away along the ground; it longs to pour forth from the lips of the speaker directly toward the recipient, to be accompanied by the expression of his eyes and countenance as well as the gesture of his hands, thus being surrounded by all the typically human aspects of human beings.

After this preliminary consideration of the appropriateness of sound for the operations of spirit we may now have a closer look at the connections between thinking and language. In thinking, a subjective activity forms itself an object. For no type of imaginative representation may be considered a merely receptive apperception of an already existent object. The activity of the senses must be synthetically joined with the inner action of the spirit. From their connection the imaginative representation tears itself loose, becomes objective in relation to the subjective energy, and then returns to it, having first been perceived in its new, objective form. For this process language is indispensable. For while the spiritual endeavor expresses itself through the lips, its products return through the very ears of the speaker. The representation is therefore truly transformed into actual objectivity without therefore being withdrawn from subjectivity. Only language can accomplish this, and without this constant transformation and retransformation in which language plays the decisive part even in silence, no conceptualization and therefore no true thinking is possible. Without reference, therefore, to the communication between persons, the act of speaking is a necessary condition of thinking even in a single individual in complete solitude. So far as actual reality is concerned, of course, language develops only socially and man understands himself only by having tested the understandability of his words on others. For the objectivity is intensified when the word which one has formed oneself re-echoes from someone else's mouth. And yet nothing is robbed from the simultaneous subjectivity because every human being feels humanly allied to other human beings; it is, in fact, likewise intensified since the representation now transformed into language no longer belongs exclusively to a single subject. By being imparted to others, it joins the collectivity of the entire human race, of which each individual carries a single modification which longs for the wholeness which can only come through the others. The greater and more varied the social operations on language, the more it gains, other conditions being equal. What makes language necessary in the simple act of thought production, is repeated over and over in man's spiritual life; social communication through language affords man conviction and stimulation. The thinking function requires something like itself and yet separated from itself. It is kindled by the sameness; the separateness gives it a touchstone for the validity of its inner products. Although the epistemological ground for truth, for absolute permanence, can only lie within the human being, his spiritual efforts to attain it are ever accompanied by the danger of delusion. Immediately feeling as he does only his ephemerality and his limitations, man must actually look upon this epistemological ground as something lying outside himself. And one of the most powerful means for drawing near it, for measuring its distance from himself, is social communion with others. All speech, beginning with the simplest, is a relating of that which is separately sensed and felt to the common nature of mankind.

It is no different so far as understanding is concerned. It is present in the psyche only by its own activity. Understanding and speaking are but different operations of the same linguistic capacity. Communal speech is never to be compared with the handing on of a given material. The materials of speech must be developed by the intrinsic capacity of listener as well as speaker; what the listener receives is only the stimulus that attunes him harmoniously to the other. It is very natural for human beings to give out immediately with what they have just heard. Thus the whole of language lies within each human being, which only means that each of us contains a striving, regulated by a definitely modified capacity, which both stimulates and restricts, gradually to produce the entire language, as inner or outer demands dictate, and to understand it as it is produced by others.

Understanding as we have just discussed it, however, could not rest upon inner spontaneous activity, and communal speaking would have to be something other than merely mutual awakening of the linguistic capacity of the listeners, if human nature did not lie in the diversity of its individuals, split off from the basic unity of nature, as they are. The comprehension of words is something quite different from the understanding of unarticulated sounds, and comprises a great deal more than the mere mutual evocation of sounds and the objects they signify. Words, to be sure, may also be taken as indivisible wholes, just as in writing one sometimes recognizes the sense of a word group without as yet being certain of its alphabetical composition. It is possible that the child's psyche operates like that when it first begins to understand. But just as not merely the sensory understanding which we share with animals but also the specific human linguistic capacity is stimulated (and it is far more probable that even in an infant there is no moment when this does not hold true, in however small a degree), so the word, too, is perceived as articulated. Now that which is added to the mere evocation of a word's significance by the articulation is that it presents it directly through its form as part of an infinite whole—that of a language. For it is a language that gives us the possibility, even if we know only individual words of it, to form from its elements a truly unlimited number of other words, in accordance with feelings and rules which define them, and thereby to create a relationship among concepts. But our psyche would lack all comprehension of this artful mechanism, it would comprehend articulation no better than a blind man color, if it did not contain an intrinsic capacity to realize that latent possibility. For language simply cannot be looked upon as though it were a collection of materials lying visible and gradually communicable before us, but must be considered forever in process, where the laws of generation are constant but the extent and in a sense even the kind of product remain wholly indefinite. When infants learn to speak, the process cannot be described in terms of the simple addition of words of vocabulary, their retention in memory, and the subsequent attempts at repetitive babbling, but only as a growth of the child's linguistic capacity, judged by age and practice. What has been heard does more than merely communicate itself; it imparts skill to understand more easily what hasn't yet been heard; it casts sudden light upon what was heard long ago but not understood at the time; it sharpens the urge and the capacity to draw more and more of what is heard into memory and to let less and less of it roll by as mere sound. Progress in linguistic capacity is therefore not measurable in even advances, as is progress in—say—vocabulary learning . . . but is constantly intensified and stepped up by the mutual interaction of the material and the child's ability to handle it. A further proof that children do not mechanically learn their native language but undergo a development of linguistic capacity is afforded by the fact that all children, in the most different imaginable circumstances of life, learn to speak within a fairly narrow and definite time span, just as they develop all their main capacities at certain definite growth stages. But how could the listener master the spoken word just by the developmental process of a separate isolated capacity growing in him if there did not underlie speaker and listener alike the same nature, merely divided into mutually corresponding individuality, so that a signal as subtle but as profoundly rooted in nature as is articulated sound is sufficient to stimulate both and mediate a harmony between them!

An objection to this argument might be found by pointing out that if children are transplanted before they learn their native tongue, they develop their linguistic capacity in the foreign one. This undeniable fact, it might be said, clearly shows that language is the mere reproduction of what is heard, depending entirely on social intercourse without consideration of the unity or diversity of the people involved. In the first place, however, it has by no means been determined by exact tests that the inclination toward such children's native speech did not have to be overcome at some cost to the finest nuances of skill in the adopted language. But even disregarding this possibility, the most natural explanation is simply that human beings are everywhere human and the development of linguistic capacity may therefore take place with the aid of any given individual. That doesn't mean that it comes any less from the individual's innate nature; only, since it always needs outer stimulus as well, it must become analogous to whatever stimulus it receives. This it can do, since all human languages are interrelated in some sense. Nonetheless the binding force of closely related origins is plain enough to behold in the division of nations. Nor is it difficult to understand, since national origins are so predominantly powerful in their effect on individuality, and the various languages so intimately related with these origins. If language were not truly connected through its origins in the depths of human nature with even the physical hereditary processes, how then could one's native tongue have so much power and intimacy for the ear of the uneducated and educated alike, that after a long separation from it it greets one like the sound of magic and creates deep yearning for itself during one's separation from it? This obviously is not a matter of the spiritual content of any language, of its expressed thoughts or feelings, but of the most inexplicable and individual element in it: the sound. When we hear the sound of our native tongue it is as though we heard a part of our self.

And even when we consider the products of language, the notion that it consists but of the designation of perceived objects is not confirmed. With this function alone, the profound and full contents of language can never be exhausted. Just as no concept is possible without language, so no object is possible without it for the psyche, since even external ones receive their intrinsic substance only through language. But the entire method of subjective perception of objects goes necessarily into the development and use of language. For words are born of the subjective perception of objects; they are not a copy of the object itself but of the image of it produced in the psyche by its perception. And since subjectivity is unavoidably mingled with all objective perception, one may—quite independently of language—look upon each human individuality as a singular unique standpoint for a world-view. But it becomes far more so through language, since words when confronted with psyche turn themselves into objects, an intrinsic significance being added to them, and thus produce a new characteristic quality. This, being one which characterizes the sound of speech, presents thoroughgoing analogies within a language, and since the language of a given nation is already characterized by a similar subjectivity, each language therefore contains a characteristic world view. As individual sound mediates between object and person, so the whole of language mediates between human beings and the internal and external nature that affects them. Man surrounds himself by a world of sounds in order to take into himself the world of objects and operate on them. What I am here saying outdistances in no way the simple truth. Man lives with objects mainly, in fact exclusively, since feeling and acting depend on his mental images, as language turns them over to him. The same act which enables him to spin language out of himself enables him to spin himself into language, and each language draws a circle around the people to whom it adheres which it is possible for the individual to escape only by stepping into a different one. The learning of a foreign language should therefore mean the gaining of a new standpoint toward one's world-view, and it does this in fact to a considerable degree, because each language contains the entire conceptual web and mental images of a part of humanity. If it is not always purely felt as such, the reason is only that one so frequently projects one's own world-view, in fact one's own speech habits, onto a foreign language.

One must not think of even the earliest origins of language being limited to a sparse number of words, as one frequently does if one thinks of language not originating in free human sociality, but rather as limited to acts of mutual assistance—a point of view facilitated by the reduction of early humanity to an imaginary status of "children of nature." These notions are among the most erroneous views one could possibly form regarding language. Man is not as helpless as all that, and besides, inarticulated sounds would suffice for the purpose of mere mutual aid in trouble. Language is human even in its very beginnings, and extends broadly without special purposes to all objects of random sensory perception or inner operation. Even (and especially in fact) the languages of so-called savages, who after all should be fairly close to a state of nature as we think of the phrase, show a fullness and diversity of expression which far exceeds simple needs. Words well up from the breast of their own free will, without need or intention, and there doubtless never was a wild wandering horde in any of the earth's desolate places which did not already have its songs. For man, as an animal species, is a singing creature, though one who joins thoughts to the tones.

But language does not merely transplant an undefined number of material elements from nature into the psyche. It also acquaints it with the aspects of form which come to us from the whole complex. Nature unfolds before us a bright many-colored diversity, rich with configurations affecting all our senses, and irradiated by a luminous clarity. Our power of reflection discovers in this richness a regularity or conformity to law which suits our spirit form. Quite apart from the corporeal existence of things there clings to their outlines a magic haze of outward beauty, as though it were made for man's sake alone, in which the conformity to law is wedded to the sensory material in a way which moves and overwhelms us but which we cannot explain. All these things we find again in the analogical echoes of language, for language can represent the state of affairs as we find it. For by entering the world of sound with the aid of language, we do not leave the real world that surrounds us. The conformity to law found in nature is related to that found in linguistic structure, and by stimulating man to perform his loftiest, most human activities, it furthers his understanding of the formal impression that nature makes, since it too cannot be considered other than a development of spiritual energies, however inexplicable. Through the rhythmic and musical form inherent in related sounds, language—affecting yet another human field—heightens the impression of natural beauty in man, but even independent of this, affects the psyche's mood by just the accents of speech.

Language, being the mass of its products, is different from whatever fragment is spoken at a given time. And before we leave this chapter we must tarry awhile at that difference. A language as a whole contains everything transformed by it into sounds. But just as the materials of thought and the infinitude of its connections can never be exhausted, neither can the number of things to be designated and related by language. A language therefore consists of not only its already formed elements but above all of a methodology for continuing the spiritual labor for which it designates the orbits and the forms. The firmly composed elements form a certain kind of dead mass of language, but this mass carries the living germ of never-ending definability. At each given point and in each given epoch, therefore, language just like nature appears to man as an inexhaustible reservoir, in contrast to all he has already thought and known, a reservoir in which his spirit may still discover the unknown, and his inward sensation may still become aware of things not felt this way before. Each time language is used by a truly original and great genius, that is what happens. And the human race needs for the inspiration of its constantly advancing intellectual efforts and the unfolding of its spiritual life-stuff, the ever open vista beyond what has already been achieved, the assurance that the infinite entanglements yet remaining may gradually be dissolved. But language contains a dark unrevealed depth, as well, and a depth which reaches in two directions. For backwards as well as forwards, it flows out of (or into) an unknown wealth of materials which may be recognized only up to a point and then vanishes from view, leaving the feeling of unfathomable mystery. Language has this infinity, with neither end nor beginning except for a very brief past, in common, so far as our view is concerned, with the whole existence of the human race. But we feel and intuit in language plainly and vividly how even the remote past is related to the feeling of the present, since it has passed through the human sensations of former generations and has retained their living breath. But these same generations are nationally and familially related to us in the same sounds of their native tongue which becomes the expression of our own feelings.

This double aspect of language, partly firm and partly fluid, produces a unique relationship between it and the generations that speak it. They produce within it a depository of words and a system of rules by which it grows in the course of the centuries into an independent power. Our attention was earlier focused on the fact that a thought taken up by language becomes an object for the psyche and thus exerts an effect upon it from the outside. But we have been looking at this object mainly as it has developed from the subject, at the effect, in other words, as emanating from that upon which it reacts. Now we must also look at the process from the opposite point of view, according to which language is truly a foreign object, its effect actually emanating from something quite other than that upon which it reacts. For language must necessarily belong to a twosome and at the same time it is truly the property of the entire human race. Since in writing, too, it holds out slumbering thought to be awakened by the spirit, it builds for itself a unique existence which can only attain validity in any given act of thought, but which in its totality is nonetheless independent of thought. The two contradictory views here suggested—that language is both extrinsic to the psyche and a part of it, that it is both independent from it and dependent on it—pertain to it in reality and make out the individuality of its nature. Nor must we seek to solve the contradiction by saying that language is in part extrinsic and independent, and in part neither. For language is objective and independent to precisely the same degree that it is subjective and dependent. For it has no abiding place anywhere, not even in writing; what we called its dead part must always be newly generated in thought; it must always transfer itself alive into speech or understanding, in other words become wholly transferred to the subject. But this same act of regeneration is what makes it also into an object. To be sure, it experiences the entire operative influence of the human individual, but this same operative influence is bound by what it is and has been. The true solution of the paradox lies in the unity of human nature. Whatever originates with what is one and the same with myself, dissolves the concepts of object and subject, of dependence and independence. Language is mine because I produce it as I do. And because the reason I produce it as I do lies in the speaking and having spoken of all the generations of men, insofar as uninterrupted linguistic communication reaches, it is the language itself that gives me my restrictions. But that which restricts and confines me came into language by human nature of which I am a part, and whatever is strange in language for me is therefore strange only for my individual momentary nature, not for my original, true nature as a human being. [VII, 13–64]

There is a realm of the invisible beyond the reach of language

Man thinks, feels, and lives within language alone and must be formed by it, in order—to mention only one aspect—to understand art, which by no means acts through language. But he senses and knows that language is only a means for him; that there is an invisible realm outside it in which he seeks to feel at home and that it is for this reason that he needs the aid of language. The most commonplace observation and the profoundest thought, both lament the inadequacy of language. Both look upon that other realm as a distant country toward which only language leads—and *it* never really. All higher forms of speech are a wrestling with this thought, in which sometimes our power, sometimes our longing, is more keenly felt. [IV, 432]

THE WISDOM OF HUMAN LIFE

The role of insight

One must trust nothing so little and work on nothing so incessantly as one's strength of soul and self-control, both of which are the only sure foundations for happiness on earth. [To C. Diede, September 1829]

*　　*　　*

We consider psychology necessary only in our dealings with people, and we call our knowledge psychological when we have observed a number of individuals and have gained some skill at guessing their motives from their actions or, conversely, at inducing certain actions by artfully suggesting certain motives. In a certain political sense this may be correct. But philosophically speaking, psychology (insight into man in general and into individuals in particular) can be nothing less than insight into the various intellectual, sensate, and moral human capacities and functions, into the modifications they undergo through inter-

299

action with one another, into their possible correct and incorrect interrelationships, into the influence of external conditions upon them, into what they may accomplish in certain combinations and what they will never accomplish, in short: insight into the laws of inward necessity and outward transformations. This insight, or rather our effort to achieve it since this is all that is possible, leads to true psychology. And this knowledge, in various degrees of extension and intensity, is indispensable to every human being just because he is one, even if he were to live completely isolated from his fellows. [I, 257]

*   *   *

The art of full practical knowledge of human nature [psychology] rests upon three points: Making correct, complete, individual observations. Abstracting, properly and completely, from these the essence of a character, which essence can appear only partially in any single utterance. Moving with perfect ease and familiarity from concept to observation and back again, constantly correcting one with the other. Whoever has the talent to undertake all three of these tasks as independently of each other as possible, and yet can bring them so close that, as he performs one he prepares the next—he alone has the genuine genius for psychology [*Menschenkenntnis*]. [II, 77]

*   *   *

Every person needs a serious look into his inner nature; it must precede any decision to act and purify it. Besides, there is no other object which one has so completely and neatly available in a single bundle for examination and judgment. This can of course be very deceptive; one explains away one's weaknesses or enlarges, in a different context of vanity, upon the guilt of one's failings, for it is naturally true that judgment is difficult when the object of judgment is one's ego. But if one undertakes an examination with straightforward simplicity of heart, in order to get straightened out with oneself and one's conscience, one need not fear the dangers. Each of us must make for himself a living image of what goes on inside him. In a way it is the point of reference for everything else. And one must not stop with an examination of one's morality or duty but take one's inner person in its whole extension and from all sides. The concept of sitting in judgment on oneself, asking oneself "guilty" or "not guilty" is far too narrowly limited. The entire enrichment and ennoblement of one's nature, the elevating of one's spirit, the greatest extensions of one's inner effort, are all tasks which one must solve just as much as the problem of purity of one's actions.

In morality too there are things which cannot be encompassed within the concepts of duty or nonduty but which demand a higher point of view. There is a moral beauty which like beauty of countenance demands a blending of all dispositions and feelings, a voluntary self-relating of them into spiritual wholeness. This alone visibly shows that all the details and all the particulars well from an urge of one's inmost nature up toward heavenly perfection, and that the soul has before it an image of infinite grandeur, goodness, and beauty which it can never attain but which—since this image always remains the inspiration—renders the soul worthy for transformation to a higher level of existence. Even the development of one's intellectual capacities belongs, up to a degree, to one's general enrichment and ennoblement. [To C. Diede, March 1832]

*　　　*　　　*

Not to subordinate oneself to another's individuality is a characteristic of any considerable mental and emotional stature, but to have insight into another's individuality, as being different from one's own, to value it in all its parts, to derive from one's admiration of it the power to direct one's own more decisively and appropriately toward *its* aims: this is a quality that very few possess. [VI, 512]

*　　　*　　　*

How deeply and in what manner a human being grows roots in reality, forms the original and characteristic mark of his individuality. [VII, 179]

* * *

One must always sacrifice one's inner life to the outer law and yet, by sacrificing it, save it. [To Caroline v. Humboldt, November 1813]

* * *

One of the truly greatest difficulties that beset man is to establish the proper connectedness between one's sympathy with ideas and one's interest in the world. Most people think they find the right combination if they moderate and modify each by the other, balancing themselves and becoming a sort of middle ground between theory and practice. But few feel and hardly anyone practices what really ought to be: to live in each part with equal purity, to be equally at home in each, and to be equally just and strict with the claims of each. [To Caroline v. Humboldt, August 1814]

* * *

A better name for physiognomic studies might perhaps be physiognomic dreams. No one can deny the fact, however, that there sometimes is so obvious a resemblance between certain facial features, right down to the bony structure, and certain characters that everyone notices it. Physiognomy has become so suspect only because it has deteriorated to an attempt to read a man's inner life from his outer aspect and thereby avoid the expenditure of time spent in effort and in waiting for suitable occasion. It is indeed a strange proposal to exchange the dependable and plain language of acts and even words for the ambiguous, obscure cipher of a few bumpy outlines curving one way or another. On the contrary, knowledge of the inner character, gained in other ways, is necessary to even begin to decipher or understand facial structure. In any event, the study of face and character must go hand in hand, and true physiognomy is as useless for ordinary practical psychology as it is indispensable for the highest forms thereof. . . . For the ordinary observer, the language of physiognomy is far too subtle . . . but two kinds of observers can and should make high and worthy use of it. These are the philosophers and the artists. [II, 346 f.]

*   *   *

The term "character" is in ordinary usage limited almost exclusively to the customs and opinions or the general disposition of a man and is regarded as a standard for judging his morality. If one extends it to the qualities of his mind or taste, one prefers to call it "intellectual character" or "esthetic character." In yet another sense one indicates with the word a certain enduring tenacity of any way of thinking or acting. "To have character" then means to show consistency. In this sense one denies character to a great many people. Neither of these definitions is proper to a philosophical theory of the knowledge of human nature, the first principles of which we are here trying to establish. For such purposes, character is understood as all those peculiarities and individual traits which designate one man (taken as a physical, intellectual, and moral being) absolutely, and which distinguish him from all other men. And since a man cannot even be thought of except with all the traits which are exclusively his, and since all these traits lie scattered over his whole nature as an individual, we can neither declare a man to "have no character" nor can we limit the word to some single quality in him. [II, 55]

*   *   *

Men were truly born to represent two types: those who take life and themselves as though life and themselves were the only reality, the only goal, the only thing that mattered, and the others: as though life were only a form which humanity experiments with as the artist does with a lump of clay. For them life could perish, if only thought leave its traces. There is no complete and true reconciliation between the two types, just as one cannot simultaneously be an actor and a spectator of the same drama. Whoever is wholly involved can see only rarely and imperfectly beyond his own fortunes, and whoever has the need to see an over-all view, only rarely submerges deeply in the scene before him. [To Caroline v. Humboldt, May 1809]

*   *   *

The formal component parts, as it were, of our vocation as human beings are these: correct relationship between receptivity and spontaneous activity; close intimate blending of everything pertaining to the senses and everything pertaining to the spirit; preservation of balance and symmetry in the sum of all endeavors; ultimate reduction of everything else to real, active, human life; creative representation of each sublime type among individuals, nations, and the whole human race. And it is just these ingredients in all their well-defined outlines, in all their wealth of form, in all their variety of motion, their strength and vividness of hue, that are the most characteristic marks of the ancient Greeks.

But there is such a thing, afterward, as pursuing the individual formulations of these extremely general universal strivings. This had to remain alien to the spirit of the ancients. Their sole aim was the light, happy conjunction which contradicts, at least apparently and for the moment, all separate and isolated considerations. The absolute must also be fathomed as an abstraction; reality must be investigated by learnedness; moral cooperation among men must be led to even greater and more difficult achievements, and these at first glance contradict the development of individuation.

In these other matters, then, we moderns can outdo the ancients, and it shall surely be reserved for our descendents to find the new connections and the new totality which must come after our work of segregation and isolation. And this will be a more difficult but also a greater achievement still than was the original unity prior to separation. [VII, 613 f.]

* * *

A man may perhaps collect sufficient materials and contents for individual single purposes or periods of his life, but never for himself and his life as a whole. The more matter he transforms into form, the more variety into unity, the richer, more alive, more energetic, more fruitful he becomes. Such variety is vouchsafed him if he comes under the influence of complicated situations. The more he opens himself toward them, the more strings in him are vibrated, and the more alert must his inward activity be, to form and develop each single one, and to organize them into a whole. Improper and pernicious is always the lazy, inert yielding of oneself to a single condition. From this arise the dull national and family stereotypes which we constantly meet in reality; it is inner slackness and indolence that is always responsible for them, never outer complexity. [I, 385]

* * *

Character is but the result of the constantly repeated activities of certain thoughts and feelings. The fact that certain functions are incessantly occupied and others never or rarely, develops some functions and supresses others, so that gradually a definite character form emerges. By virtue of this thoroughgoing correspondence between what we are and what we believe, our practical and our theoretical make-up, we are enabled to exert influence upon ourselves, both of a theoretical and practical sort, through ideas and through spiritual activity. We can comprehend nothing with our rationality that has not in some way been prepared for in the senses and the feelings, nor can we accept anything as part of ourselves that is not somewhat organized by conceptualization. We can have no insight where we do not have a feeling for something . . . but neither can we be something of which we have no concept whatever.

Attentiveness to character accomplishes even more. On the one hand it takes each object first and foremost in its relation to the inner being; on the other hand it awakens character and activates it. Now as soon as character has once been awakened, it accepts of all the many things which work on it only those which are homogeneous with it. In other words, matter and nourishment coming from many and various sources are all focused on a single point. One can see this quite easily in those characters who are by nature violent, passionate, and one-sided. One says quite justly of them that they see themselves everywhere, project themselves on everything, and thus progress at double speed in their one-sidedness. Their fault lies not in too much individuality, but in the fact that their individuality is based solely on passion and natural predisposition. If it were stimulated by activity and mood of the spirit, by the endeavor, for example, to render itself beautiful, it would show entirely different results. Such a person too would let everything influence him characteristically and he would treat everything characteristically. But he would neither overlook nor discard the elements heterogeneous to him; he would use them in his own way and for his own purposes. He would accept all objects quite objectively and seemingly naïvely; the whole difference would lie in the degree and the manner of his assimilation—but here lies the very crux. [I, 386 f.]

*　　*　　*

Do not become impatient or restless. One must never send forth doves from the ark until green Ararat has risen from the waters. [To Caroline v. Humboldt, May 1809]

*　　*　　*

There are ideas which a wise man would never think of trying to put into practice. In fact reality is never, in any epoch, ripe for the loveliest, ripest fruits of the spirit;

the ideal must merely hover before the soul of the artist—of whatever medium—as a model never to be attained or reproduced. [I, 237]

*   *   *

However carefully and deeply one may have gone into the nature of human capacities, for . . . any scientific purpose the resultant insight can only be a general one. But every human action is a result of the total qualities of all the capacities underlying it in their absolutely determined individuality. All history bears witness to the revolutions that a single act of a single person may produce. [I, 91 f.]

*   *   *

All we need, in order to comprehend the most extraordinary and the simplest phenomena as part of the same human sphere, is to be genuinely attuned to humaneness. Only someone who lacks . . . wealth and variety of inner experience feels certain directions that sensation sometimes takes to lie beyond the barriers of natural truth; only someone . . . who lacks high humane simplicity of mind will fail to accord universally valid utterance to the rare and the unusual. [II, 213]

The role of feeling

For me it is a firm, incontrovertible dictum: nothing good and great that a human being ever truly was, will ever perish, even if it were only the feeling of a single moment, not recognized consciously by anyone. But it imprints itself on his nature, on his *Gestalt;* it passes from him over to others, and if others did not exist, it stamps dead nature herself with his image. Life always conquers death, penetrating it and creating for itself life again, and light. Works and deeds perish, but dispositions and feelings are eternal and regenerate themselves with incomprehensible adaptation. [To Caroline v. Humboldt, May 1797]

*　　*　　*

Nothing perishes by outer fate. Man dies from within; it is his feelings that destroy him. When no way is left open for feelings, when they have exhausted all their powers, then they wrench themselves loose from a thankless existence. Or when they have exhausted the sphere of possible human enjoyment, possible human developments, they pass on to higher regions, to new life. . . . [To Caroline v. Humboldt, May 1791]

*　　*　　*

Everything you say about remorse . . . I too feel to be true. A remorseful justifying of everything one has done I find unbearable, and whenever I myself fall into it, it is only for a brief moment. A short interval of solitary tranquillity drives it away. To do no wrong, even if one is sensitive and hence strict with oneself, is beautiful as an idea, but in reality is seldom related to spontaneity, warmth, or profundity. The highest and best of life always takes place on the precarious ladder of feeling, and who could assert that his footing there is always firm! Sadness at what one has done is one of the most salutary, cleansing sensations of the soul, and whoever is not well acquainted with it, is alienated from himself. The inner life of his psychic constitution has touched him only superficially; not everything in him that should be quickened by psychic awareness, has been. Without remorse, there could not be that mutual forgiving, either, which makes love so beautiful and enchanting, so deeply moving. Man has himself under control only up to a certain point. Whenever he pursues anything far enough, he runs the danger of losing his way, and whoever feels that the inner life is the only true life for him, must forever walk in paths on which he is bound to stumble and on many a step of which he looks back upon with grief. Where, then, could be found

consolation except in the long-suffering love which accepts and forgives, which does not even ask that one leave the dangerous path
that leads to the highest values, which knows an inexhaustible
treasure of forgiveness and reconciliation and which, never itself
failing, is yet imbued with the recognition that its own failing is
entirely within the bounds of possibility.

It is terrible that so few people live with an acceptance of their
own feelings and fewer still with those of another. To most people
only their youth, with its first upwelling of feelings which cannot
be ignored only because they are like the germination of a plant
or the spring-stirring of the sap, gives to their love its humanity.
After they outgrow their youth, they only know how to separate
from one another or to walk side by side the cold streets of life,
without ever touching each other again. Few have seen the feelings
of youth grow throughout all their years, have seen them unfold,
and have felt with wonder that they remain as mysterious, as
deep, and as infinite as ever they were. For most people the heart's
youthfulness in the midst of life's transitoriness remains forever
a riddle. Nor can it be denied that it must usually be bought at
the price of sacrificing one's peace of mind. One must intervene more
deeply in one's inner life and make one's heart sorer than even
the world's rough handling prepares it for.

But joy mingled with sadness, even with grief, is the deepest
human joy. It winds itself about the soul with indescribable sweetness, with a dim but unerring sense for what will some day be
born of it. [To Caroline v. Humboldt, August 1809]

*   *   *

When I think how happiness is
found by such different roads . . . it seems to me like a cocoon into
which each person spins himself in his own fashion. A certain
condition becomes happiness for him because he wanted it that
way, because it crept gradually into all his doings and thoughts
so that the inhabitant of the cocoon now believes it all his innermost nature. Nothing is more erroneous, for this reason, than to

measure happiness according to the number of positive joys there might be. Happiness is so nonsynonymous with joy or pleasure that it is not infrequently sought and felt in grief and deprivation. It depends not nearly so much on the things to which one ascribes it as on the ability and tendency of the soul to transform its outer condition into its inner destination, to seize its own particular circumstances with a sort of yearning desire and to cling to them. That is why I have always maintained, and still do, that man may be assured of happiness to a high degree by simply wanting it and that whoever can feel this acutely within himself has little to fear from unhappiness. [To Caroline v. Humboldt, August 1823]

*   *   *

There is an immediate given in human nature which is a profound and invincible mood of melancholy. It is by no means always destructive of human happiness. On the contrary, it is frequently a great, sweet happiness in itself. The deeper and more humane the psychic constitution, the more easily does melancholy well up in it and suffuse it. It is the gentlest and loveliest reminder of the disharmony between the constraints of reality and the freedom within. In a purely attuned soul it touches upon this disproportion and then dissolves it, passing over into a gentle harmony. Often, to be sure, it can be painful as well. Memories of unhappiness tend to cling to it, intuitions of misfortune arise in connection with it, and it ends with an oppressive feeling that human existence is, after all, meant to be a painful trial.

One can, of course, say that all existence consists of a struggle to preserve and maintain, to stand independent against oppressive superior force, to rise from the unyielding inert mass of mere dead nature. And all existence, also, is a feeling of isolation, of loneliness, of longing for union with another accompanied by the feeling that no union will be close enough, no means of communication clear and intelligible. What is usually called happiness, therefore, or peace, is mostly only a living on those levels which never touch upon the depths of humanity. The happiness which is truly desirable can only be the culmination of that profound mood when we feel true inner being in its intimate connection with all that is great in the world, so that all sensation of opposition and strife disappears. And this can be true only of brief moments. But whoever is surrounded by the element of pain, grief, and melancholy in its unclouded purity, he feels at home in it and feels a sense of well-being. For, unnoticed, there increase in him the powers of inward humanity. He embraces nature more intimately, penetrates it more powerfully, and in moderation and renunciation leads a rich and infinite life which he would exchange for no other. [To Caroline v. Humboldt, July 1810]

*   •   *

Everything profound by its very nature has feelings of grief and pain at its core. But ordinary people do not sense it. They rise up in arrogance against trouble and grief instead of seeking them out to be their faithful companions. [To Caroline v. Humboldt, May 1814]

*   *   *

Suffering, like vice, is really only partial. Whoever has wholeness before his eyes sees that whatever ascends in one place, beats down in another. [I, 261]

*   *   *

Man is never more beautiful than when he makes that which he has gained exclusively by his own capacities his own in such a way that it looks to us like a universal quality of humanity. [II, 288]

*   *   *

A strength-infusing sense of peace is never lacking where man has a total over-all view of his relationship to the world and to fate. Only when he ceases functioning just at the point where outward force threatens to overcome his inward capacities, or inner violence to upset his outward balance, then there arises his mood of desperation. But so favorable is our human position as a whole that harmony and peace invariably return to us as soon as we fulfill ourselves within the circle of phenomena that imagination presents to us in those moments of serious feeling-response when we have demanded an accounting from our fate. [II, 135]

*　　*　　*

It is and remains true that nothing turns out well in life when the heart does not retain a certain inner warmth and the spirit a secret, solitary depth in which it is understood by few and by itself only in its best moments. It is the inner voluntary activity of man's original strength of character which draws upon his total life experience but without which, on the other hand, even the widest life experience remains lifeless and the fullest knowledge empty verbiage. It is man's only link with a higher power and the only mark by which one can distinguish others as conceivable sympathetic companions. [To Caroline v. Humboldt, March 1804]

The role of the unconscious

[We may by certain means] collect expressions of character, divide the insignicant from the significant, order the latter under certain points of view, and thereby supply the imagination with a complete and definite image which suffices for practical everyday use. We may even thereby help bring about a stricter, more philosophical consideration of character, but we shall always leave something out, something unknown and unexpressed, and we cannot hide from ourselves the knowledge that this something is precisely the important thing. It is the true self, the individual personality. [II, 93 f.]

*　　*　　*

Life would be of an incredibly boring uniformity if event were to develop from event, if sudden incalculable accidents did not constantly break the chain. Through such accidents, through the fact that a great part of our soul's activities lies with all its details outside the sphere of our consciousness, so that our thoughts and feelings shoot upward from unknown depths . . . through the interaction of these forces there arise those surprises which, according to the constitution of our imagination, we to a greater or lesser degree interpret as miracles. [II, 200 f.]

*　　*　　*

The thought of an evil power pursuing us would always be a thought alien to me. I have never been able to go along with those notions which assume the existence of a being who is hostile to the good and finds pleasure in evil. The passages of the New Testament which lean in that direction I consider to be imaginative ones, containing expressions current among the Jews of the time, to indicate that evil which man must always struggle with inside himself, even when he is good and even when he believes himself wholly innocent. Undeniably, there are persons who meet with more misfortune than good fortune and even the very fortunate and happy ones know shorter or longer intervals when the course of events does not accord with them and they are forced to swim against the current. But this—where it is not due to their own guilt or is not merely a consequence of incorrectly calculated behavior—is given in the natural concatenation of circumstance where what is generally necessary or unavoidable may run counter to the interests of individuals. Very often—and this seems much more probable than assuming the devil—it may be due to arrangements of the ever wise and ever benevolent sternness of a healthily disciplinary providence which tests us from time to time. For discipline coming from superearthly and superhuman wisdom does not necessarily assume guilt in us. There may be ways and paths of insight reaching far beyond human reason which discipline the guiltless without thereby rendering them guilty, only to lead them back to wholeness. Besides, even the best of men, if he conducts his self-examination with appropriate strictness, is not free from taint. Also there may be traits unconscious to him which would lead him into guilt but for a wholesome discipline which prevents this. Man himself is too myopic and his eye too dull to see this, but the powers on high see it and know how to guide it and arrange it for the best. [To C. Diede, October 1826]

*   *   *

In the psychic constitution of man the predispositions to every sort of capacity and function are related to one another, and each individual one develops more freely and fully if it is supported by the corresponding organic development of all the others. [II, 117]

*   *   *

There is something wondrous about dreams, infinite power and lack of substance simultaneously. The fact that one so rarely dreams of what one loves most always seems to me to be an inward shyness of the soul, unconscious to itself; a hesitancy to alienate itself from the reality of life entirely by investing its dreams with too much happiness. [To Caroline v. Humboldt, June 1818]

*   *   *

What you say in your last letter, dear Charlotte, about self-knowledge and self-delusion interested me very much. But I confess that I cannot quite share your opinion. I consider self-knowledge extremely difficult and rare, self-delusion very easy and usual. Perhaps there are those who have attained their aim and so I would not wish to dissuade you from believing that you understand yourself correctly and thoroughly. I however should not claim such a thing with equal confidence. At first glance it seems indeed easier to know oneself than to know another, since one has an immediate, direct feeling of oneself, but merely perceives utterances of others from which one must first deduce the cause, thus doubling the possibility of error. Nonetheless the one who makes the judgments is forever isolated from the one that is judged and can always retain a cold neutrality and quiet discernment. He is not necessarily bribed or overwhelmed by the object of his judgment, nor necessarily prejudiced against it or distrustful of it. But in self-examination one faces all these dangers. The judging power is forever affected by its object. Both carry the same color and mood. One is at times just as inclined to invent failings or magnify existing ones as to do just the opposite. Also one judges oneself differently in different circumstances. The errors which often occur by no means always stem from a disregard for truth or from conceit but often from the purest intentions and the most sincere will, for the errors were there before one started, creeping into all one's views and one's feelings. So the case seems by no means as simple as you say, that all one need fear is falsification through vanity. For that matter, vanity itself is so complex an emotion that there is probably no one who could really claim to be free of it. One may be free of this or that kind of vanity, scarcely of all kinds. A little easier to judge in oneself are perhaps certain definite acts and their motivations. But the closer such investigation comes to complexes of actions and the totality of one's character, the less certain the judgment becomes. That is why autobiographies are really instructive only when they contain a great number of facts. Self-analyses too easily lead astray. [To C. Diede, December 1834]

*   *   *

The accidents which happen to people originate far more than one might think in the people themselves. There is a secret and unnoticed influence of people upon things. One cannot ascribe guilt because of it, because it does not lie within consciousness, but it comes from within all the same. When the inner mood is unfavorable, gloomy, far from gaiety, it produces appropriate outward events; if one does not carry life lightly or at least quietly and equably with a certain coldness toward fortune and misfortune, life becomes oppressive and burdensome, not merely because one feels that it is, but—within my experience at least—because actual misfortunes start to happen. Perhaps—and I might be willing to subscribe to this—this does not apply to major happenings, but of the smaller ones, which after all life is full of, it is undeniable. [To C. Diede, January 1827]

*   *   *

[Upon his wife's worry whether their son Wilhelm's death might have been prevented:] Human beings must have no standard for their acts other than the necessity of the moment; we must not bother about the conceivable consequences. When fate, after an action of ours, directs its outcome toward great good fortune or toward great calamity, our grief or joy will lead us to hitherto unfamiliar regions. Only then can we acknowledge a power forever beyond us, yet related to us. Only then can we discover truly untapped energies in ourselves for relating what formerly seemed irreconcilable, for feeling certainty where formerly we allowed ourselves no more than a dim intuition. This is how we grow, how that in us grows on which all inner greatness and inner happiness rests. We find in ourselves at last an irresistible urge to seek our essential being only where reality, felt through to its deepest layers, dissolves in infinity. In our active life we find, at last, that tranquillity and presence of mind which in any situation orient themselves toward the dictates of the moment and of good sense. From such steadfastness in action and such tranquillity in being springs the strength which even the happy man needs to endure life, an ability to make the contradiction between fate and the wishes of the heart into a new wellspring—if not of happiness, then at least of a sort of joyousness even in grief—of an ever greater and deeper capacity to feel. No one can escape his own remorse if he acts as he should not, but a man cannot properly call himself the causal agency of any given consequence, and this is truly one of the greatest benefits which heaven has conferred on us. It has made our actions of no consequence in the course of the world, and has left them important only for our inner perspective and our inner sense of responsibility. [To Caroline v. Humboldt, September 1804]

*　　*　　*

Much might be said on the subject of misfortune. I am convinced that it sometimes lovingly pursues great souls in order to glorify itself in them and them in itself. For everything divine—and there is nothing more divine than fortune and misfortune—pursues as its aim always and solely the creation of the great and the beautiful. Everything else doesn't matter. [To Caroline v. Humboldt, February 1814]

*　　*　　*

It is possible, and necessary, that the epitome of humanity, its depth dimension within its limitations, eventually and gradually should reach the light of consciousness, and that the mind should accept . . . the archetypal idea of humanity and of divinity, i.e., of absolute energy and natural order (like the "thou" given through the existence of the "I"). But if this is the use of human history, it is not the purpose of individual human destiny. Such purpose, whatever one may call it, does not exist. The destinies of the human race roll on, as the streams roll down the mountains toward the sea, as the fields sprout grasses and weeds, as insects spin cocoons and become butterflies, as nations push and are pushed, destroy and are destroyed. The energy of the universe, seen from the standpoint of time from which we are forced to see it, is simply an irresistible onward-rolling. Hence we must recognize the energy of nature and of humanity in world history, not as the imagined superimposed intentions of an alien, imperfectly felt and still less perfectly understood being. . . . [III, 357]

*　　*　　*

Man is more than and something other than his words and his deeds. He is more, also, than his feelings and his thoughts. However well one may know an individual, one understands only some of his isolated utterances and is never satisfied by any attempt to put them all together and make them spell out all at once what the individual really is. Up to a point, all the plans and rationalizations of a person may be developed and analyzed without great difficulty. But as soon as one gets to the point where his thought or his decision first comes up, one finds oneself suddenly at the border of an unknown world. Some single apparitions, devoid of context, seem to leap forth but the landscape itself is shrouded in impenetrable darkness. And yet it is just here that the springs, the inner powers which make up the true nature of an individual and originally set everything in motion, where that which most ennobles man: greatness of soul, virtue, heroism —have their home. And it is only here that there originates every great deed and every genial thought.

From the annals of history as well as from one's own private life almost everyone can recall people who seemingly never revealed any special capacity or energy until they suddenly, in a critical and dangerous situation, show an enduring tenacity or a courageous decisiveness which seems to lift them far beyond themselves and their ordinary mediocrity. Who could not recall more than one example of this sort from the frightful scenes of the French Revolution alone? Vainly, then, we try to explain their self-transcending character by some known principle or maxim that they are supposed to have had. Nowhere, however far we search, do we find anything to justify an expectation of their sudden greatness. We usually help ourselves by saying that it was the unusual situation that awakened and kindled their spirit, but that only means that we must start looking for a capacity which is capable of such awakening. No, it is simply the inward, hidden part of character which is not measurable by concepts that have reached the plain light of day, nor by its own ordinary sensations.

It slumbers long, perhaps, but when its opportunity comes, it suddenly wakes and appears in all its force. This part of character is so little a mere result of the precepts of a man, or a work of his ratiocination—it is so much mere, original nature—that the converse of what is usually thought about it is true. It does not arise from the maxims of the known part of character, but these instead stand under its influence, so much so that the likelihood of its emergence usually stands in an inverse ratio to the development of reason and the amassing of knowledge. Thus it is more likely to be seen in females than in males, among less rather than more civilized nations, in the lower rather than in the upper classes. Culture seems to weaken it, though it should be obvious that this is a disadvantage that merely usually accompanies culture; it is hardly an integral part of it. Constant investigation into relationships of cause and effect, constant search for ends in acts and events, easily weakens the energy with which one loves or abhors an object without any reference to its ends, merely for its own sake. . . . Besides, man's moral inclinations are originally instinctual, so that it may easily happen that culture, with its emphasis on reason (which ought only to prevent their remaining merely instinctual) adulterates and dirties them. It is undeniable that we frequently meet with things in people which we are in no position to understand, no matter how carefully we have observed other expressions and utterances of theirs. Still less can we explain these things, and this fact necessarily leads us to stipulate an inward, original reservoir of powers in man which makes out his real self, his true character. . . .

It is an absolutely vain endeavor to attempt to reconstruct or even comprehend the nature of a human being by simply knowing the forces which have acted upon him. However deeply we should like to penetrate, however close we seem to be drawing to truth, one unknown quantity eludes us: man's primordial energy, his original self, that personality which was given him with the gift of life itself. On it rests man's true freedom; it alone determines his real character. [II, 88–90]

The preparation for death

I strongly believe that one does not die until one lets go of life from an inner motive—which, to be sure, is not under one's conscious control. . . . [To Caroline v. Humboldt, May 1817]

*　　*　　*

This afternoon at Goethe's house I saw Schiller's skull. Goethe and I—Riemer was also there—sat before it a long time; it is a strangely moving sight. What one has seen while it was yet alive so great, so close to one, so stirred by thoughts and sentiments now lies before one stiff and dead like a stone image. Goethe is keeping the skull and showing it to no one. I am the only one to have seen it and he asked me very urgently to tell no one here.

First of all you must know that they did not purposely remove the skull from the rest of the skeleton. The upper coffins in the vault where Schiller had been temporarily placed had crushed the lower ones and the vault had been damp, besides. Thus the bones of several of the bodies had fallen apart and lay uncovered. Schiller's were searched out and, with the exception of some, found. Goethe took only the skull and had the other remains placed in a casket in his library. There they are to rest until he himself dies. . . . Then he wishes to be buried with them. Whether or not the skull shall accompany them, he is leaving up to his executors. Meanwhile it lies on a blue velvet cushion with a glass bell over it which can be removed. One can really not gaze enough at the form of this head. We placed a reproduction of Raphael's skull side by side with it. The latter is more regular, more evenly rounded. But Schiller's head has something greater about it, something more encompassing; some areas are seemingly stretched and unfolded, others smooth or sunken. It is an infinitely moving sight, though a very odd one. [To Caroline v. Humboldt, December 1826]

*   *   *

Old age really does not make such a division in one's life that anything which was formerly there is now no longer there. Inner and outer life is a whole, all transitions are very gradual, and one thing so flows into another that one really has nothing to mourn and nothing whose absence one regrets. Truly—one can never marvel enough what infinite, ever self-renewing fullness flows out of a single life, how thinking and feeling and willing and doing find ever new stimulation, if one preserves oneself from earth-bound dullness and earth-bound irresponsibility, if one embraces grief and joy with equal love, dissolving both in a feeling of humanity, and if one seizes only that in everything which leads to a renewal of one's inner life. But there is one thing which belongs to old age alone, and there comes a moment in which one is surprised by it, not having felt its slow growth. That is the awareness that it is a slow gentle preparation for death. As the Bhagavad-Gita says very beautifully, suddenly that which is night for others grows light for one. One looks at the stars, the heavens, the blue air in a different way, and if it was human and earthlike to take pleasure in forms, now there arises within one a wondering gaze at formlessness, a certain longing for it, for dissolution into higher, less limited powers, a pleasure in solitude—there being nothing which looks more solitary than the cloudless depth of the sky. [To Caroline v. Humboldt, November 1824]

*   *   *

Looking through your letter again, I see what you say about grief: that there is much of it, and that the older one grows, the more easily hurt and sympathetic one becomes, though at the same time stronger. That is wonderfully true and lovely. People who are advanced in years really can endure more, and when their feelings are delicate and tender they hope especially that youth will be spared the all too heavy hand of fate, for youth needs that considerateness. But growing accustomed to grief and pain makes one's feelings more sensitive, one's nerves more quivering. The tears that flow are not the impatient tears of youth but the quiet ones, the ones that dissolve the whole soul. It is no longer the sort of pain that seems unnatural and therefore short in duration which gains control of all one's powers, dulling and paralyzing them, but the quiet melancholy which suffuses the whole psychic constitution, making itself at home there and, intending to stay forever, leaves the human being a good measure of peace and reflectiveness. But this deeper rooted mournfulness of one's maturer years bears lovelier and nobler fruits and winds about the heart with bonds at which one cannot be angry. More than this: grief and compassion and all that belongs to so-called unhappiness always seems to me to comprise an enormous world of its own, like the night-side of the Homeric world tablet where there are guiding stars as well, though one must, to be sure, do without the sun. But to try to escape them with averted eyes seems inhuman to me; on the contrary, this world attracts one with a wonderful mysterious power, so that, just to see those shapes in the dark more clearly, just to immerse oneself in the human depths, one sometimes draws suffering close to one, like a friendly power, staying with it and living in it. [To Caroline v. Humboldt, January 1818]

*   *   *

It depends solely upon the individual human being to grow ever more tender and beautiful, more pure and filled with inward peace. Old age is not to blame if this does not happen. Age never hinders maturity but is always beatified by it. I truly love it and know no greater goddess than Time. One could write a book about how she gives all to her devotees and takes only from those who do not understand her. [To Caroline v. Humboldt, February 1815]

*   *   *

I cannot quite share your ideas about death in its relation to life. No one can fear death less than I do, nor am I very attached to my life, and yet I have no longing for death, although I agree that it is nobler than simply being tired of life. Nonetheless it must be disapproved. Life must, as long as providence so decrees, be enjoyed and suffered—worked through, in a word—and this with complete humility and devotion, without complaints, laments, or bad feelings. It must be tested and tasted to the end. It is an important law of nature which one may not lose sight of, the law, I mean, of ripeness for death. Death is not a conclusion of life but an interval, a transition from one form of finiteness to another. Both forms—here and yonder—are closely related, in fact indivisibly joined, and the first moment of *yonder* will follow properly only when the moment of departure from *here* was truly the last one in the free development of the individual being. No human cleverness can calculate, no inner feeling can designate the moment of ripeness for death, the moment, in other words, at which it becomes impossible to continue to develop here. [To C. Diede, June 1832]

*   *   *

All of life must be a preparation for death, just as all of life, from its first moment, is a gradual approach to death. . . . A number of things might be said, however, in favor of a foreseen death which happens while one is conscious. There is always something violent about sudden death, even if it is only due to a stroke and in reality is quite gentle. Still, there is something very human in the wish not to withdraw from death, to make its acquaintance, to observe in oneself up to one's last breath one's departing life. [To C. Diede, June 1827]

*   *   *

To take away a vivid, live image of the world, properly organized, is perhaps the best thing man can do when he dies. . . . Whatever can happen or appear in the world may be rediscovered in primordial and archetypal ideas, as though in eternal, preconstructed images. There is no amount of study that could weary one of observing how multiplicity proceeds out of unity and, enriched, returns to it. The spontaneous, unmediated intervention of the ideal in the real, the true seeing of the spirit in the body, is common enough in certain easy instances. But in its entire range, in its deepest nature, it is so rare that it seems a ridiculous or mystical matter to most. And yet a true comprehension of the world which is made up of these two entities is possible only when one makes this kind of sense of it. Likewise the comprehension of character and of individuality. [To Caroline v. Humboldt, April 1809]

*   *   *

In your last letter you used the expression "setting one's house in order." That has always seemed such an appropriate and substantial figure of speech to me. It is an old-fashioned, truly Biblical expression, like many others of this sort taken from deep levels of life and again reaching the soul at a deep level. Even long before I approached those years when setting one's house in order becomes a truly urgent matter, I used to use it to divide my life into perceptible epochs and always found it very helpful. But in the soul too there is a setting of one's house in order. This is done by contracting the mind into a small focus of feelings, giving up all the others to the reservoir of what is forgotten, and being happy in the peace of one's chosen limitations. If one does this right, one does it only once. One does not again leave the space thus outlined and fenced in. [To C. Diede, December 1832]

*   *   *

You ask in your last letter that I explain more fully what I meant by inwardly setting one's house in order. I meant something very simple and quite in accordance with the usual meaning of the expression. It is said that one's house has been set in order when one has taken care to correct whatever has thus far been left uncorrected, in the event of one's death. The expression further implies that one has made disposition of one's possessions. To set one's house in order therefore means cutting entanglements, cutting off uncertainty and unrest, and promoting order, clarity, and peace of soul. That is how it is understood in external life. But a similar thing may take place, only on a much higher and nobler level, in the spiritual realm. There too we find things of greater and those of lesser importance, things tied more or less to earth-bound existence, things related directly or indirectly to the highest human possibilities. I don't exactly mean, at least not exclusively, religious ideas. What I am here talking about are matters having little to do with religion. It cannot in fact be decided, generally, what is the highest or most important thing. Everyone has the same experience: whatever seems profoundest and most significant to him is what he does not have time for, and lets himself be robbed of by inferior and time-consuming other matters. This is what one puts a stop to when one sets one's house in order; one renounces the disturbing "other matters" and zealously devotes oneself to the important ones. Even more, however, this self-recollection in the short stretch of life that may be left to one applies to the sphere of feelings. Here, however, one meets with a great and significant difference. Resolution, conscious decision, has great power over the intellect and over all matters of reflection. We can and must intentionally direct our thoughts and our thinking capacity toward certain points. In our feeling life this is not only impossible, it would be harmful. In sentiments, there can be nothing forced, nothing felt against or because of one's will. There, any change can come about only of its own accord and can only be likened to the ripening of a fruit. It proceeds by itself as soon as the whole disposition of the soul lets it be known that the "letting go" of its earthly existence is complete. The change consists in a simplification of feeling and a withdrawn psyche, but here also, even more than in the realm of thought, no generalizations can be made. In myself it happened very simply: my mind was concentrated so closely upon a single object of sensation and feeling that it has become unavailable to any other, at least in the sense that it can no longer receive from any other. For I have not grown colder or less sympathetic, I think, only less self-centered and demanding, not only toward people but toward fate itself. I should feel tribulations like anyone else; this cannot be rooted out of the soul. Deprivation will always be deprivation, and pain and grief remain pain and grief. But the peace of my soul: this they can no longer take from me . . . [To C. Diede, February 1833]

*   *   *

The certainty that I am in the last stages of life admonishes me to complete an endeavor oriented toward life. I mean the endeavor to round off life, to make an inward whole of it. To be in a position to work on this, by not being torn away out of the midst of activities but to experience a time of contemplation and peace, is a blessing of providence which one must not waste. I do not mean that I wish to *do* anything or to complete anything still undone. What I have in mind can really be done by anyone at any time. I mean working on one's soul, bringing one's feelings into harmony, rendering oneself more independent of outer influences, trying to shape oneself in the image which is seen by one's quietest and peacefulest moments. Everyone, no matter what he may have done in this respect, has much still to do. To do it probably takes longer than anyone's lifetime. But it remains what I call the true aim of life. [To C. Diede, December 1829]

Part II

SECOND PERSON
SINGULAR

THE DIALECTICS OF EXISTENCE

Mankind seeks to settle its internal opposites without destruction of either side

The basic endeavor of mankind goes toward the unlimited extension of its combined energies involved in both receptivity and spontaneous action. And since mankind comprises both visible and invisible elements, it seeks to settle its internal opposites without destruction of either side. [VII, 612]

Individuality and unity

Insofar as character can be described in accordance with its utterances and even its qualities, such description never reveals true individuality. This always remains inexplicable and incomprehensible. It is the life of an individual, and the part of it that appears in a statement about him is always the least important part.

In a certain way, individuality can nonetheless be recognized, as being the consequence of a certain striving which excludes a number of other strivings: it is something which individuates itself against, and through, restraint.

Such restraint leads, due to our inherent mental organization, to an archetype (*Ideal*) which stands above the individual.

The comparison of several individuals both among themselves and with their archetype makes the view possible that the mutual complementation of various individuals depicts the archetype. And there are certain individuals who explicitly point to its reality.

The most obvious example of this is the difference between the sexes. Those whose feeling-life is attentively oriented toward this phenomenon may best learn from it the relationship between an individual and an archetype. Beginning with sex, they may most easily find all the other, similar, cases of such relationship occurring in creation. . . .

But since every creature can only be something by not being something else, there is a true, not-to-be-reconciled conflict, and an unbridgeable gap between each individual and the next, no matter how close their relationship, as well as between each individual and his own ideal type. The command, to reach the ideal within the bounds of individuality, is impossible of fulfillment.

And yet we may not be absolved from it.

Therefore the conflict must be but a seeming one and, indeed, it arises only when we separate incorrectly that which to truer feeling is one and the same.

Nothing living, and therefore no energy of any sort, may be looked upon as a substance which is either static in itself or within which something static lies. Rather it is a kind of energy which solely and singly depends upon the activity which it is exerting at any given moment. The longest stretch of past exists only in the present moment, and the entire universe would be destroyed if the activity of any given moment could be destroyed.

No energy is completed by its prior activity. With each action it grows; it has an unknown and never-to-be-known plus beyond any specific activity, and its future products cannot be calculated from its past. New things can and must forever come to pass.

It would therefore be a monstrosity to imagine a divine, self-sufficient and unchangeable being. For it is not merely incomprehensible for us, bound as we are to the limitations of time, but, as a static energy, it would contain a contradiction in itself, and, in escaping time, it would base itself upon wrongly applied concepts of space and substance. The true infinity of divine energy rests upon the capacity, inherent in all creation, to re-form itself forever new and forever greater. But it cannot be hypostatized apart from creation.

The individual energy of the one is the same as that of all the others and of nature in general. For otherwise there could be no understanding, no love, no hatred. And everywhere one can recognize the same form.

Wherein, then, consists the separateness of individuals? It is very difficult to comprehend and perhaps inexplicable. Is it possible, since man can become meaningful to himself only through reflection—and this is feasible only by confronting a subject with an object—is it possible that the energy of the universe, as well, at the stage at which we know it, must split itself into multiplicity in order to become meaningful to itself?

From such a viewpoint, the above-mentioned conflict looks entirely different. We are here talking not even of definite substances, circumscribed by unalterable boundary lines, but of forever changing energies. Further, it is everywhere a similar—perhaps a single—energy, which yields different views of the same result rather than different results and, finally, the archetype is only a mental image which can have the universality of an idea precisely because it lacks the particular definiteness of an individual.

For in order to completely imagine individual energy, one must think of it, in addition to being limited to existence in the present moment, in connection with two other things: one, its hidden and unfathomable capacities, only a tiny part of which is revealed at this given moment, and two, the ideas which are the immediate reflection of these capacities but all of which the individual never has the power to effectuate, i.e., make operable as part of his life. Hence there is between life and idea forever a distance but also forever a contest. Life is lifted to the idea, and idea is transformed into life.

To come back to our initial problem, then: the form of individuality, as it is meant to be, is the emergence of an energy, suffused by a living consciousness that it is connected with the mysterious, unfathomable but also infinite reservoir of nature's capacities, and the orientation of this energy, within the boundaries of a definite, particular reality, toward that which corresponds to those hidden capacities but which can be comprehended only with intuition and represented only as idea. [III, 138–40]

Form and matter

Upon mutual interaction alone rests the secret of nature. Dissimilar materials relate themselves to one another; the resultant relationship again becomes part of a greater whole and up to infinity each new union comprises a richer content, each new manifoldness serves a lovelier unity. Material and form, involved with one another in a thousand ways, exchange their nature with one another, and nowhere is there anything which only organizes or only is organized. Thus nature maintains both unity and richness, two seemingly opposed but closely related qualities, either one of which will afford the spirit blessed peace when the other has made it exert itself in active reflection.

Astonished by the magical working of these countless powers, the human spirit despairs of ever penetrating this sacred darkness. Yet human nature calls upon us to try. [I, 312 f.]

*   *   *

The purest form with the lightest covering is what we call "idea"; the matter least gifted with configurative powers we call "sensation." Form rises from interrelationships between materials. The greater the abundance and variety of the materials, the loftier the form. A divine child is but the fruit of immortal parents. Form becomes the material in turn for even more beautiful form. Thus the blossom grows into the fruit, and from the seed of the fruit comes the new stem, bearing new blossoms. The greater the increase in variety and subtlety in matter, the greater the energy, for the more intimate the connectedness between them. Form seems blended into matter and matter into form or, to give up the image, the more ideas there are in man's feelings, and the more feeling there is in his ideas, the more he approaches godliness. [I, 108]

Sense and spirit

Sensuousness and nonsensuousness are related by a mysterious link, and if our eyes are denied sight of it, our feelings are not denied intuition of it. To the twofold nature of the visible and the invisible world, to the congenital longing for the latter and the feeling of sweet indispensability of the former, we owe all our philosophic systems which have grown truly out of man's intrinsic nature, as well as our most senseless sentimentalities. The everlasting endeavor to unite the two in such a way that one robs the other as little as possible, always seemed to me the true aim of what is humanly wise. Everywhere unfailingly we recognize the esthetic feeling by which sensuousness is known to be the outside surface of the spirit, and the spirit the animating principle in sensuousness. The everlasting study of this physiognomy of nature is what develops our intrinsic humaneness. [I, 169]

Generation and growth

Whatever comes into being through development or growth is a part of the being from which it stems. It receives its animating power from outside itself. But whatever comes to be born, to be generated, is a being in itself,

itself possessing life and organization and the ability to generate and bear. And even though this ability is spread widely throughout nature, there is no power that can form life and organization mechanically, and there is no wisdom that tells how to do it. That is why generation is different from development and can be likened only to an awakening. The growth that follows it does not belong to the parent but to the offspring. We know what precedes begetting and conception. We know the creature that follows them. But what relates the process with the result is shrouded in impenetrable veils. Generation seen from the parent's side is awakening; from the offspring's side it is but a momentary configuration, characterized not only by the greatest exertion of the energies alive in it, but also by their complete unitedness. [I, 316]

Duality

The concept of duality . . . belongs to the double realm of the visible and the invisible. By presenting itself in a lively and stimulating manner to sensuous viewing and external observation, it predominates, at the same time, in the laws of thinking, in the striving of emotion, and in the—in its profoundest depths unfathomable—organic structure of the human race and of nature.

First of all—to start with the easiest and most superficial level of observation—a group of two objects stands out all by itself between a single object and a group of several, as being visible at a glance and possessing a certain compactness. Next, our perception of and sense for duality in human beings passes to our division into two sexes and all our concepts and feelings as regards this division. It further accompanies us in the form of the human (and animal) body, with its two equal halves and its pairs of limbs and sense organs. Finally, several of the mightiest and greatest phenomena of nature which surround us as well as primitive man at all times represent themselves as, or in any event are interpreted to be, dualities: the two great heavenly bodies by which we reckon time, day and night, the earth and the overarching heavens, the land and the water, etc. What shows itself so ever-present to the view, the living mind transfers naturally and expressively to a linguistic form especially dedicated to it.

In the invisible organism of the spirit, however, in the laws of thinking and the classification of its categories, the concept of duality roots in a much deeper and more original way in thesis and antithesis, in positing and negating, in being and not-being, in the I and the world. Even where concepts divide into three's or more, the third term stems from an original dichotomy or at any rate our thinking likes to reduce it to one.

The origin and the end of all divided being is unity. Perhaps that is why the first and simplest division, where the whole divides only to reunite immediately, only this time containing an organizing principle, is the predominant one in nature, the most illuminating for man's thought, and the most gratifying for his sensate life.

It is especially decisive for language that duality occupies a more important position in it than anywhere else. All speaking is founded on dialogue in which, even when more than two are present, the speaker always opposes the ones spoken to as a unit other than himself. Even in his thoughts man speaks to an "other," or to himself as though he were an "other," and draws his circles of spiritual relationship accordingly, separating those who speak "his language" from those who do not. This first separation of the human race into two classes, natives and strangers, is the basis of all primordial social intercourse.

We might have noted earlier that the duality appearing outwardly in nature may be taken more superficially and in more intimate interpenetration of thought and feeling. It will be sufficient to bring to mind just a few examples. How deeply the bilateral symmetry of the human and animal body penetrates our imagination and feeling and becomes one of the major sources of the architectonics of art, has recently been demonstrated . . . by A. W.

von Schlegel. The sexual difference, taken in its most general and spiritual configuration, guides our awareness of one-sidedness which can be healed only through mutual complementation, through all the interrelationships of human thinking and feeling. But I purposely mention this two-fold, superficial and profound, sensuous and spiritual view only now, since it plays its part just at the point where language rests on the duality of dialogue. We have so far mentioned only the simple empirical phenomenon. But there lies in the primordial nature of language an unalterable dualism, and the very possibility of speech is conditioned by address and response. Even thinking is essentially accompanied by the inclination toward social existence, and man—quite aside from all bodily and sensate relationships—for the sake of his mere thinking longs for a *thou* which will correspond to his *I*. Concepts seem to attain definition and certainty for him only when they are reflected by a thinking power other than his own. Concepts are generated when they are torn loose from the moving fabric of representations and form themselves into objects, in opposition to a subject. But their objectivity seems more complete when this division does not occur in the subject alone, but when the representor really sees the thought outside himself, which is possible only in another being that, like himself, represents and thinks. But between one thinking power and another there is no mediator other than language.

Words in themselves are not objects. Viewed as over against objects, they are something subjective. Yet they are supposed to become objects in the mind of the thinker, generated by him and reacting upon him. There remains between a word and its object such an alienating chasm; a word, born singly in a single individual, resembles so much a merely illusory object! And language cannot be brought into reality by a single individual, but only socially, by the joining of one daring experiment to another. In other words, the word must gain thing-hood; language must gain extension in a listener and a responder.

This archetype of all languages is expressed by the pronoun in its differentiation of the second person from the third. *I* and *he* are really different objects and all things are actually exhausted by them because they are *I* and *not-I*. But *thou* is a *he* placed in opposition to an *I*. While *I* and *he* are based on inner and outer observation, there lies in *thou* the spontaneity of choice. It is also a *not-I* but not, like the *he,* in the sphere of all beings, but in another sphere, that of activity dependent on mutual interaction. In the *he* there lies, in addition to the *not-I,* also a *not-thou;* it is opposed not only to one but to both. Traces of this can be seen in the fact . . . that in many languages the designation and the grammatical formation of the third person pronoun diverges in all its aspects from the first and the second persons. . . .

Only through the joining, effected in language, of an "other" to an "I" do there arise all the profounder and nobler feelings which motivate the whole man, which in friendship and in love and in every communion of mind make the connection between two beings the loftiest and the most intimate of all connections. [VI, 24–27]

Active power and receptive power

The power that begets is more attuned to action, the power that conceives, more to reaction. What animates the first we call masculine, the second, feminine. Everything masculine shows more spontaneous activity, everything feminine more passive receptivity. The difference consists not in the capacity but in the direction. For however the active power of a being is constituted, so is the passive, and vice versa. Something which is only passive and nothing else is not thinkable. Part of all passivity (the sensing of activity not originating in oneself) is touch, to say the very least. But if something possesses no capacity for activity whatever, it is nothing; it may be wholly penetrated, but it cannot be touched. Therefore passivity and reaction are everywhere equal. Active power, on the other hand (keeping in mind that we are here talking only of the finite sort) is subject to the conditions of time and matter, hence bound to passivity. Without going into any deeper proofs, we may everywhere see activity and receptivity mutually interact and accord with one another when we look at a human being. The active spirit is also the sensitive spirit, and the receptive heart is also the heart which returns each impression with the liveliest energy. Only the difference in direction, as we have said, distinguishes masculine capacities from feminine ones. The masculine begins, due to its spontaneity of action, by exerting its influence but then accepts, due to its own corresponding receptivity, the reaction of the other upon itself. The feminine takes the opposite direction. With its receptivity it accepts the active influence and then responds to it with its own spontaneity and activity.

This twofold character is likewise shown by the condition of the masculine and the feminine power just prior to their union. Both experience the feeling of overflowing power coupled with that of painful privation. Where masculinity holds sway, the power is the life-force, devoid of matter, and the yearning, the feeling of privation, is directed toward a being who can give to his energy the necessary material for action, and who can alleviate the burning violence by the reaction of her receptivity which has a diverting effect upon him. Where femininity holds sway, the power is a lush overabundance, too rich to enliven itself with its own energy, and the yearning is for a being who can awaken the inner materials and impart to her own energy a greater strength by forcing her to respond. In masculinity, therefore, there is a strength which is collected at a single point and seeks to get out. Outside itself it looks for materiality, being unable to find enough occupation for activity within itself. In femininity, there is an abundance of materiality which longs to accept a foreign object inside its own being, in order to receive its own oneness from it. Thus each power satisfies the yearning of the other, and both entwine to make a harmonious whole. [I, 319 f.]

*　　　*　　　*

Character best develops with purity and individuality when it comes into social connection with other pure and individual characters. It is not alone their similarity which provides the education, it is also their contrast, their opposition. For there is indwelling in moral organization, as there is in physiological organization, an urge to assimilation. But this aims, once a character has established the beginnings of individuality, not at similarity but at some appropriate relatedness between two separate individualities. Thus the masculine character becomes more purely masculine when it is confronted and opposed by the feminine, and vice versa. [I, 387]

*   *   *

Nature, who pursues with finite means infinite aims, founds its structures on a conflict of powers. Everything limited is aimed at destruction; heavenly peace dwells only within the confines of self-sufficiency. The destructive activity of one must therefore be opposed by the destructive activity of another, and while both prevent each other's final aim they fulfill the unlimited plan of nature. . . .

The power of masculinity, meant to infuse life, collects itself spontaneously, self-moved. All the materiality that it possesses is urged to collect in undivided union. The richer and more manifold it is, the more fatiguing the effort but the greater the effect. The material must not be already self-related within its own nature. It must receive its entire orientation from the masculine principle and be under its control. Thus focused, it exerts a powerful effect by just shooting forth. Animated by a violent urge toward activity, it wishes to find an object it can penetrate but, being mere spontaneous activity, it is closed off at this moment from all receptivity. The effort, however, is soon followed by fatigue; it was like a breath which powerfully enlivens but soon vanishes. With the feeling of flagging strength there awakens, however, the longing for receptivity and, giving up pure creativeness, it would now gladly come to rest. Thus it is what it is through itself and its unique form.

The man whose breast is inspired by active, bold courage feels himself tense and shut up within himself. With observant spirit he has collected many experiences during the course of life; he has created high ideals out of his inmost self; various feelings now move him, partly the worth of the new creation for which he longs, partly sympathetic fellow-feeling with the objects he seeks to enrich. But his breast is not wide enough to contain all these sublime images; an ardent thirst for activity drives him on. He is looking for a world that corresponds to his yearning. With no thought of himself or his own pleasure he fructifies it with the impact of his strength. Now at last the new creation stands before him and happily he rests, gazing upon his children.

The power of femininity, meant for reaction rather than action, collects itself upon an alien object and through alien stimuli. Since the materiality which she possesses in rich profusion relates itself by its own peculiar nature, it works more by virtue of a passive rather than an active-spontaneous force. With the degree of variety grows the beauty of its effects, but not the effort. This, in fact, is eased by being so variously in contact with a variety of forces; its degree determined solely by the intimacy of the enclosure which is dependent on mutual harmony. The materials of the feminine principle need not so much the control of a unifying power; they easily relate themselves to each other by their natural affinity. Within her unity of relatedness she responds to outside influence with ever increasing ardor until finally her whole activity is exerted as well. But since her unique nature renders her more capable of resistance and since she is free of the hectic violence which consumes the male, she makes up for her slower effectiveness by more endurance and greater tenacity. Thus she owes to the nature of her materiality part of her effectiveness which is prepared and supported by it. A heart moved by many and various feelings and sensations, animated by lofty strivings, feeling rich within itself but lacking the bold courage to give itself direction, is tormented by restless yearning. Not understanding itself, poor in the lap of plenty, it wishes to find a being who can gently untie the cramped knots of its feelings. The deeper and more hidden the sources of this mood of confusion, the harder it is to meet up with its fulfillment, but the more intimate the closure when it is finally found. The longer her counterpart stays with her, the more points of contact he can find, and he does not leave her until the germ has ripened into its perfect fruit. [I, 322–25]

*   *   *

Only physiological effects penetrate our coarse minds. Meanwhile the subtle but powerful influence which emanates from everything living just because it is living slips away from us like an invisible breath of air. Likewise, our capacities for begetting and conceiving have had entrusted to them far more than the reproduction of our species or the act of intercourse which occurs before our eyes. Preservation, too, is part of its work, and since preservation of the infinite means incessant death to which then ever-returning life relates itself, rebirth too, though it is hidden from our eyes, is a work of sex. Even if nature might attain its aim of reproduction by some other method, it could never do without that interaction of forces with which the sexes complement one another. [I, 322]

WOMEN AND MEN

The study of women is essential for men

Where two beings are separated by a total chasm, no bridge of understanding leads from one to the other, for in order to understand one another we must, in another sense, already have understood one another. [IV, 47]

*　　*　　*

All in all, I've immersed myself more deeply than ever . . . in the study of women's lives and have learned to honor and respect them even more, as my compassion for them has grown. It isn't so much that women are unhappy— what touches me most about them is that they so often imagine they are much happier than they really are. I think one can have no deep knowledge of either human beings or of the human heart if one has not often and in all seriousness studied this aspect of women's inner life. However much I am otherwise occupied . . . I nonetheless cannot keep from seizing any opportunity that permits

me to devote myself to this quiet, hidden world. [To Caroline
v. Humboldt, December 1809]

*   *   *

The first difference among indi-
viduals within a nation is the natural one of sex. . . . Feminine
peculiarity which is so vivid and visible in matters of the mind, as
well, naturally extends to language. Women generally express
themselves more naturally, delicately, and yet more forcefully than
men. Their speech is a more faithful mirror of their thoughts and
feelings and—even if this has been rarely recognized or said—they
preserve especially the richness, strength, and naturalness of language in the midst of a culture which ever robs language of these
qualities. This, although women progress culturally at an even pace
with men. Women in their handling of language lessen the disadvantage of the split which culture always produces between the
common people and the rest of the nation. Truly more closely
bound to nature by their own nature; placed on a more nearly equal
footing with other members of their sex because of the importance
of the most common events of their lives; occupied in tasks which
demand the most natural feelings or at any rate afford full opportunity to the inner life of thoughts and feelings; free from the
compulsions of business and even science that press the mind into a
lopsided mold; frequently involved in a conflict between external
constraint and inner longing, a conflict which, although painful,
yet reacts fruitfully upon the psychic constitution; often in need of
persuasion and themselves inclined toward verbal communication
by inner liveliness and alertness: women refine and beautify the
naturalness of language without robbing or violating it. [VI, 204–
05]

*   *   *

Women are very fortunate in that
the daily tasks they have to perform are, if not entirely, yet in large
part, of a mechanical nature, requiring little head and no feeling at

all. Thus they free women to use all their better, subtler, and higher aspects of humanity for their own development, much more than is available to men. Men so easily become one-sided, pedantic, wooden, just through their daily work; women never, not even when through adverse circumstances they are forced to earn a living. . . . [To C. Diede, May 1823]

*   *   *

One-sidedness is something very relative. In men, who are supposed to turn toward a great variety of objects, it may well be feared. But women have the good fortune —and one must call it that—of not needing to know a great many things which are alien to them or lie outside them. Usually they gain by contracting the circle of their knowledge and their sentiments to a smaller circumference and a correspondingly greater depth. One-sidedness of the sort found in men is therefore not harmful to them. I remember knowing two women in my youth who were equipped with all the means for living the most varied and socially mobile lives. But from pure preference, without any pressure from misfortune, they preserved themselves in such solitude that it was actually difficult for anyone, even a single individual, to approach them. But this did not in the least diminish their quality of being interesting. [To C. Diede, Summer 1826]

*   *   *

The disproportion between thinking and knowing, especially when it is found in women, stimulates very unpleasant reactions. Since my earliest youth, even before I went to the university, I knew a woman of this sort, and have known her ever since, throughout many different stages of her life. She knows ancient languages thoroughly and well and most of the modern ones besides; she is free of all vanity and affectation; she never neglects her household for her studies; but none of her knowledge has ever made her in the least interesting to anyone. She may have read the greatest and most difficult authors of the

345

world, but she cannot write a letter worth reading. [To C. Diede, March 1832]

*   *   *

We usually reproach the feminine sex for looking at the world with too much subjectivity; instead of comprehending it objectively and simply, they project themselves into it, we tell them. We must grant that this is not infrequently the case. For however faithfully women seem to gaze upon the face of nature, true objectivity—that mood which comprehends first the dry and dead letter, completely separated from spirit and essence—is to a high degree alien to them. They too easily hurry on to results; they make combinations before all the particulars are duly collected, and they like to relate even the most direct and simple observation—if not quite to individual, at any rate to subjective values: to what is pleasing or displeasing, beautiful or ugly, and so forth. Hence they follow only with an effort an abstract line of reasoning which proceeds with a chain of conclusions without immediately showing the ultimate end; they believe only with difficulty in any convictions which are forced by reason on logical grounds; they seldom distrust their feelings and opinions and they decide against their inclinations, on the basis of reason alone, only with great difficulty. Such a strong admixture of feeling-sensations in the activities of the other psychic functions is incompatible with perfect clarity, to be sure. Clarity is somewhat missing in women anyway because their feelings possess such a high degree of intimacy, force, and profundity. But from the lack of clarity genuine mistakes and failures do sometimes spring (in various degrees, according to various situations and persons). Worse, lack of clarity may give rise to those unfruitful inner griefs and tensions with which the soul torments itself in vain, without external cause, only because it cannot find the way to wholeness within itself. Now, tempted by this fault of the opposite sex and its harmful consequences, we have tried to save women once and for all by taking away from them all possibilities of a finer cultivation of their sensate capacities, by cutting off all the things which might nourish their excessive rapturousness and—despairing of being able to support them boldly on the heights—by denying them instead the right to raise themselves. Only a confusion of what is accidental and what essential in the character of the different sexes could lead us into such an error. To be sure, a certain leaning toward subjectivity is necessarily a concomitant of receptivity. Hence fantasy and feeling will always exert a greater influence upon the other sex. But we must not forget that sensation as well as receptivity is completely satisfied only by the greatest degree of reality, and one may approach truth equally well by preparing the feelings for its unfalsified reception as by the ordering and collecting of its separate materials, coupled with a more active participation in the process. The necessary difference, in other words, lies not in the success of the effort, but only in the means thereto, in the purposes and the objects for which and in which it is expressed. Furthermore, we may see more men going astray by falsely assumed concepts than women by arbitrary mixing of the figments of their imagination. But it is true that women achieve their final aim with greater difficulty and more rarely, just because it really is more difficult to attune one's entire being to a certain level of performance than it is to function one-sidedly with several separate capacities, as men do. But to make up for this, women can achieve incomparably more, because at the moment at which they observe reality they are already making it into their own.

This only, then, is an essential quality of the feminine character: the predominant effort to relate external observation directly and at once to inward individuality; to accept truth into itself by sensing, tact, and feeling, more than by espying it through reason and the ability to abstract; to balance and adjust toward each other inclination and duty in a peaceful harmoniousness. Merely accidental in individual female persons, on the other hand, is the total loss of object in a subject, the total rout of truth by fantasy, the total rule of conviction by personal inclination. [II, 100–02]

*   *   *

Let us look at the various natural traits of women in comparison with those of men, and we shall find the following:

1) Their bodily structure is smaller, weaker, and more delicate; their bones more delicate and flexible; their muscular strength more adapted for long endurance than for sudden exertion; their figure limited by soft, flowing contours, full and graceful; their expressions both in rest and in movement more varied, expressive, and gentle, less straightforward, firm, and definite; their beauty in general more notable for the graceful freedom of its materiality rather than the rule of form in well-defined features; their physical organization, finally, characterized by predominant sensitivity and activity of the nervous system plus a certain passivity which combination enables them to resist disease longer and suffer great physical changes more readily.

2) In respect to their intellectual capacities, they are characterized by a decided inclination for observation of nature and of everything which possesses a direct value and substance, bound up with an almost equally strong disinclination against everything merely mediated or symbolic; an admirable capacity for investigating that aspect of truth which demands lively and mobile sensitivity, easy and rapid understanding and combining; on the other hand a no less notable weakness for and an almost stronger resistance against anything that demands spontaneous activity and discriminating analysis. That is why it is so characteristic of women that they always direct their efforts to the true essence of things but so rarely attain it in its objective purity. They treat an object not as arbitrarily as a man often does but with such considerate indulgence that it becomes impossible for them to properly see through and penetrate it. Faithful to the spirit of truth, they fail to observe its letter. Thus they always turn directly to reality itself for their observations, but since they yield themselves more to the impressions which reality sends out to them rather than uncovering them, analyzing them, or experimenting with them, they seldom succeed in fathoming reality in spite of all observation. Mostly they join

their own subjective way of looking at things to the things themselves, and thus only continue to live their own inner lives through things, as though it were the most natural element in the world. Likewise they surely take a given line of reasoning from its most significant and fruitful side, and join it to all their other concepts in one interacting system, but they are usually not careful enough to support it with an initially secure foundation. For similar reasons they feel an urgent need to know the last results of the most abstract philosophies, since their nature does not allow them to rest until they have combined all their thought masses into a single whole, but since all abstraction forever contradicts their sense of individuality, they remain strangers to true speculation, nonetheless. A sense for truth exists in them quite literally as a sense: their nature impels them to love it and do homage to it, but their nature also contains a lack or a failing of analytic capacity which draws a strict line of demarcation between ego and world; therefore, they will not come as close to the ultimate investigation of truth as man.

The difference in intellectual peculiarities of men and women, then, is largely founded on the vividness and sensitivity of women's imagination which does not permit the other psychic capacities, particularly those of reason and understanding, to act independently, nor, on the other hand, as arbitrarily as is often the case with men. Instead, their reason remains more faithful to their senses and their feelings.

We should not therefore expect a cash deposit of factual knowledge or separate truths from women; their spirit can do far more and is meant for nobler and higher pursuits. Nature itself has given to women the highest and best spiritual activity: the comprehending of manifold abundance, faithfulness to nature and to immediate substance, the striving to make connections everywhere and relationships between all things, the inner need to relate them not merely to the ego and the world but to weld them absolutely into a single whole. The only thing lacking is the ability to attend to and secure those particulars which stand alone.

This is also why the feminine character has such a salutary effect upon the masculine. Where the latter falls into doubt through arbitrary notions and speculative abstraction, the wholesome and natural point of view of the feminine character calms and reassures him; where women, on the other hand, overlook or have little respect for facts which run contrary to opinions of theirs which were stabilized too soon, man invites them to doubt. But a man can always see the infinite path which he knows he must walk slowly step by step represented in the spirit of woman as though it were but a leap, and thereby he is forever reminded of the ultimate and the highest goal of his striving, and the fact that he is supposed to reach it without being disturbed in his natural way of working, being on the contrary encouraged to work even more in typically male fashion by seeing the faults and lacks in the female way.

3) The esthetic sense of women. If the sense for beauty is to be lively and mobile, the spiritual energy of a human being must be kept in a certain middle region between sense activity and pure reason. No object must be seen solely from the side of its practical use nor solely from its conceptual side; rather it is necessary to take both aspects together and interchange them, as it were, treating both the substance and the concept as *Gestalt,* i.e., something sensuous but incorporeal. Now the whole intellectual disposition of women is highly suited to this combination of heterogeneous psychic capacities, this hovering between reality and pure spirituality. Given an equal cultural level with men, women are far more strongly directed toward high ideals (partly because they strive for unity of any sort, partly because the creative imagination of which they hold such a large share has the same direction, and partly because they are less acquainted with a low level, business-type occupation of their time) and yet do not care to depart very far from sensuous reality. . . . Nothing can be more welcome to them, therefore, than a type of judgment which carries as much universality and necessity with it as any imaginable, but which is nonetheless not formed mechanically in accordance with plainly recognized, totally expressed basic principles. To this is added the outward grace and beauty possessed by the feminine figure, both as a given and as a

latent capacity, the correctly apportioned fullness and fineness of structure and feature, the grace of movements, the euphonious power and gentleness of voice. For aside from the fact that these indigenous charms constantly surround the senses, they react back upon the nature and the rhythm of women's feelings and sensations, or, more correctly perhaps, are founded upon them. Finally there is their external situation in which the most serious business is just that which is spiritually least demanding; it allows looking upon everything else as play and recreation and generally permits a maximum of leisureliness of spirit and free roaming of the imagination. That is why a sense for beauty is so incessantly active in women and to such an admirable degree; that is why they judge everything in accordance with its qualities of being pleasing or displeasing, and seek to weave esthetic taste into the smallest details of their lives. This much is genuine sexual predisposition and must unavoidably occur wherever human culture and feminine character combine. Whether this type of sense of beauty is correct and pure, however, whether it does not frequently mistake the merely pleasing for the truly beautiful, are questions which must be asked of the individual female person.

But from such an indefinite sense for beauty there is a long way yet to go to genuine esthetic feeling and a still longer way to artistic genius. In the whole realm of art everything technical which rests simply on logical rules may be divided from faithfulness in the imitation of nature, and this again from the genuine artistic or poetic factor, the pure productivity of spontaneous imagination. The correctness of judgment as to the first, the technical aspect, depends totally upon the conventions of a certain cultural level. The feminine mind will not be too particular as to this; on the contrary it tends to forgive even significant technical faults if there are significant beauties also present within a work. As to the second aspect, that of faithfulness to nature, women will be excellent judges, because of the subtlety of their observations and the reliability of their tact and timing. Being so near nature themselves, no feature borrowed from it is very alien to them; being so highly sensitive and mobile, no tone awakened in them by a poet will fail to find a response within them. Thus their understanding will be deeper and closer, but their judgment will also be stricter. For since they follow their own natural feelings, free of preconceptions (which so often lead men astray), the unnatural and uncharacteristic will be less able to deceive them. The only danger which threatens them here is that their judgment may be too one-sided, basing itself on an experience which leans too heavily on their own individuality, but even this danger is not a considerable one because their character comprises a large circle which encloses many things. Feminine nature in and of itself is more poetic than masculine nature and it is small wonder that women are more open and receptive for the highest and ultimate aspects of art, as well. The feminine spirit does not easily immerse itself too deeply in reality, and only very rarely lifts itself completely to the realm of pure ideas. The only thing here which women might lack would be the strength of the active imagination to hold its product freely hovering midway between nature and idea, completely individual and completely ideal at one and the same time. From this point of view, the feminine judgment is indeed not always a pure one; often it is determined more by the truth than by the art of a work of art; no less often bribed by subjective references, agreements, or differences. The sexual differences make an art judgment easier and more possible with greater frequency for women, but also places greater obstacles in their path by limiting its freedom and purity (through too close a connection between sensations, feelings, and imagination; in fact too close a connection between all psychic functions). Meanwhile, however, such obstacles are never so great that they cannot be overcome, at least so far as judgment is concerned, without any of the individuality inherent in them getting lost.

Far more difficult, to be sure, is actual artistic creativity, the question of artistic genius. Genius, being the freest and highest vibration of the human spirit, can only exist within individuality and must find in all generic character greater or lesser obstacles. The question is only, does it find more obstacles in men or in women? Women are undeniably successful, and to a high degree, in certain aspects of artistic achievements. Their productions tend to have lightness and grace; they are lovely and pleasing, and, at least in certain individual features, are truly and deeply taken from nature. Whether, however, women are capable of representing a *Gestalt* in such a way that it both rises high above nature and yet remains entirely nature, whether their imagination has sufficient strength, or at least authority for being a law unto itself, whether their spirit simply does not lack the necessary objectivity—those are other questions. This much is certain: the feminine character because of its great receptivity will require a proportionately far greater amount of independent, spontaneous activity in order to keep the balance necessary for productions of genius. To what extent any given individual might triumph over these difficulties, cannot be answered in general. Only experience teaches us that women do not easily try those artistic genres whose success rest purely on their artistic form, such as epic and dramatic poetry or sculpture, but almost exclusively only those with relatively more surface, as it were, those which leave more room for charm and for abundance of material, such as music, painting, the novel, and lyric poetry. It may also be that the others demand more skill and enduring diligence than women usually exhibit.

Femininity in general must have undergone considerable refinement before scientific or poetic productivity becomes possible. Without it, even the most superior feminine individuals lack sufficient clarity and peace, and even more the strength and even the inclination to separate a whole series of thoughts or feelings from their kind and work on them in isolation.

4) Their feeling capacity and their will. To see the feminine sex from its most characteristic side, one must look at its moral character. As spirit is most mobile and active in man, so is disposition in women. Whatever they find, from any source, is transformed into it; everything goes over into it and everything comes forth from it again. That is why such a decided and constant orientation toward reality is so characteristic of them. For whereas

spirit, at least measured by its ultimate goals, always tarries in the realm of universality and necessity, and imagination in the realm of possibility, feeling and disposition belong only to individual, particular presentness.

The first and original reason for this lies in the natural purpose of sex. In order to give life and existence and to nourish and preserve them, the female sex must remain faithful to nature and to reality and bind itself strictly to them. This rests first of all on physical organization, to be sure, but its influence spreads directly to the moral character as well. For since the needs of nature and the most humane and spiritual feelings are inextricably bound together in love, this feeling spreads throughout the entire being and imparts its characteristics to everything it touches. The same thing is equally true of men, but the important difference is that women are the receptive, the nourishing, and the preserving part, that motherhood is theirs peculiarly, and that their whole sexual character is somehow more intimately bound up with their individual personalities.

Feminine sensation is characterized by a greater sensitivity than masculine sensation, but even more by greater intimacy. It isn't that a single feeling could not penetrate so deeply into the soul of a man that it exercises all his powers and all his motivations at once; this in fact is a characteristic peculiar to man. But in the souls of women there sound (if I may be permitted the image) all the strings when one is vibrated; woman's mind is like a still and clear water in which the slightest wave movement spreads, trembling, to the outermost shores. Hence her communications of intimacy are more likely to be accompanied by lightness and warmth, those of a man more by violence, fire, and effort.

From the communication of intimacy springs feminine modesty; from it in turn feminine chastity. The sensation of modesty always arises when one has been immersed in oneself and has not cold bloodedly enough separated reflection and intellect from feeling and inclination, and then suddenly becomes aware of someone else's opposite and contrasting condition. Because a man is by nature more cold and reflective, feminine modesty is most visible when it is related to the opposite sex. The physical organization of woman is just as inclined toward acceptance and receptivity as her moral nature is toward reflecting everything back to its own inner condition. When these two oppose each other we have the phenomenon known as virginal modesty, which we may take to be the source from which this feeling pours out over the entire organization of the female and over all its various conditions, in various amounts and guises.

Entirely characteristic of women is their maternal feeling, particularly during the prenatal period. It is a love brought about by no impression of individuatedness (for her affection for the father of the unborn child may strengthen and alter the feeling, but not produce it), and yet is bound up with the most unconditional self-sacrifice which rests on the fact that an alien being is in such absolute communication, such intimate contact with a woman that it forms a true part of the mother and yet is known to be a living and human creature who is bound for only a short time to the mother and who is destined for separate, independent existence. This kind of love, which moreover is implanted even in those who never experience it in the flesh, surely does not merely fulfill a physical purpose but spreads its influence over the entire character. It reveals to women a wholly different sense of "ownership" and teaches them a wholly unique way of relating external objects to themselves, to preserve and nourish them, and to let them go again, than is ever vouchsafed a man even in concept. No wonder that any deep sensation or feeling, any characteristic idea, becomes a true part of a woman's soul from which she can unwind herself only with pain and travail, and that she can know a joy in deprivation and even in painful self-sacrifice, which man may sense only very rarely and only in highly individuated passionate moments.

Lively sensitivity and affection for an opinion once formed, naturally bring forth a passionate, easily excitable and violent character. Since intellectual culture diminishes the one-sidedness of rationality, however, and esthetic culture diminishes the materiality of sensation, the passionate nature of women at a high cultural level may disappear to the vanishing point. Their psychic constitution experiences less often those uneven stormy affects which we call passions, but it attains in place of them a condition of enduring even tension. When a passion does seize them, it is usually for an object which, at least in the opinion of the subject, is worthy of all imaginable efforts of the soul. . . . In the sway of such a passion, beautiful femininity loses its habitual shyness; suddenly free, it steps forth, declares itself aloud in favor of the beloved object and casts off the yoke of external and conventional considerations.

Nothing is as repulsive to femininity as moral indifference. In rather common natures this trait announces itself by harshness and intolerance; the better and higher natures show a free and beautiful liberality, to be sure, but when they deal with people or things, an aspect of which insults their feelings, their depreciation of that aspect is not raised a whit by some estimable aspect which may also be present in the same object. Here they are different from men who easily err in the other direction, by sharing the fault he believes he merely wishes to be tolerant of. Women in general are far stricter in their judgment of principles than of their application to individual cases, and it is a feminine trait to exaggerate mildness or illogic (both are frequently the case) in application.

If one raises the question as to which is predominant in women, sensuous, esthetic, or moral sense, not one of these can be given preference over any other. As a rule, overpowering and violent sensuality is so little characteristic of women with normal upbringing, that the well-known dispute as to whether women are more cold or more passionate as a sex would surely have to be decided, in connection with this point, in favor of coldness. Their esthetic sense will, where matters of feeling and character are involved, never victoriously oppose their moral sense. And the dry and threadbare earnestness of the moral sense by itself will never suffice the superior woman, though it may satisfy the common conventionality of many. Where the psychic constitution of a truly beautiful feminine character is to be kindled to true and intense passion, all three senses must meet; but then each one will burn with such a bright flame that the inexperienced observer will easily be led astray by seeing overemphasis of one or the other. Excess of sensual passion is not foreign to natural femininity in the raw, as it were, but it originates not in a positive strength of sensuality but rather comes from a certain emptiness of the sensate life, and from the lack of an opposing power which would hold it in check. That is why it is toned down by advancing culture more than is man's.

The harmony which women demand of the sum total of their senses and feelings, the totality which they insist upon in any object to which they devote themselves with some warmth, and the depth and intimacy of their feelings must all together produce a high degree of that which we call a steady and permanent disposition, opposing it on the one hand to changing whim and on the other hand to the intentional acts of will. Hence feminine morality rests more on nature than on reflection and strength of character, the feminine psyche often affording us the beautiful drama of a voluntary rule of noble sentiments, as over against the masculine which offers us the sublimity of single victories. That the female sex has similar strength to win such victories over itself is shown by frequent examples, the difference being that their steady affection for a pure morality stems more from sentiments which have become second nature than from direct explicit respect for law. [I, 400–10]

Some female and male archetypes

In [Goethe's] Dorothea we see above all two main qualities: *helpful active industry* and *discreet versatility*. Any other qualities she may possess are either shown briefly, as the occasion arises, or else remain hidden in her inmost soul. But these two are the clue to her life. . . .

At no level of class, in no situation, can there be a lovely feminine character without this psychic climate, this wholehearted readiness to perform any helpful service. For without it, no deep intimate feeling for domestic virtues is possible; all feminine loveliness and greatness must blossom forth from this main trunk. The female sex is meant for the loveliest and worthiest rule, the rule over that part of the human soul that contains the feeling values. Women's consciousness of this destiny, together with their consciousness that this moral force may be won only with the total sacrifice of all physical force, make out the feminine character and produce the psychic climate we have named. Without the last, the rule of females is outrageous and repulsive; without the former their servility is slavish and contemptible. [II, 308 f.]

*   *   *

To find pure types of masculinity and femininity is infinitely difficult and, in experience, downright impossible. In experience, the unique characteristics of an individual always get in the way and partly distort the universal sexual characteristics, partly hinder them . . . from reaching perfection. The characteristics alien to sex must therefore be separated out, and the limitations of the individuals be removed, before pure sexual character can be represented. But this is a rational process and rationality can give us only bare abstractions, whereas in this case we are particularly interested in obtaining a complete sensuous image because the true spirit of sexual characteristics can be expressed only in the living cooperation of all its particular, separate traits.

Here we are saved by creative imagination which transforms experience into ideality, separates out all accidental overflow and accidental limitations, and clothes the infinity of types with forms as many and as various as are ordinarily formed by the accidents of time and birth. With this marvellous capacity extraordinarily developed in their nature, the Greeks peopled their Olympus with ideal figures. When they sought pure individuatedness and beauty, they turned to the gods and found in their circle what they failed to find on earth. No one in the centuries to follow has ever outdone the Greeks in the art of plucking the secret character of a being before it was so much as unfolded in its bud and then giving it a definite shape and form while leaving it in its incredibly tender state of promise. Only the Greek artist succeeded in making the ideal itself into an individual. . . .

Among the goddesses the ideal of femininity first approaches us in the person of Dione's daughter [Aphrodite]. The small delicate build which holds every flattering charm, the lush curves, the moist melting eyes, the yearning mouth a little open, the charming air of prudence which reveals more virginal bashfulness than stern remoteness, and the heavenly grace which, like a breath, is poured over the whole figure—all communicate the sex which founds its power on its weakness. Whoever approaches her draws in love and pleasure with every breath, and her sweet look invites him. It was a great far-reaching idea that was represented in the Greek *Venus:* the power which brings everything forth and the power which flows through all living things. No happier symbol could have been found than the ideal figure of woman as she first blossoms forth, the most beautiful of all the creatures who bring forth, at the very moment when her first desires, still only partly known to her, swell her bosom.

In this first youthful flush, femininity appears purer and may be perceived more clearly because it has not yet adapted itself to the rest of nature; it does not so much consist in character as in the moment's mood, the moment's inclination. Feminine characteristics may, to be sure, be visible in the soulful countenance, in the living utterance of the moral and even the intellectual character of a woman, but their most faithful revelation lies in the bodily shape and the expression of sensuousness and this, lifted into ideality, is what radiates from the goddess of beauty. What our darkest feelings expect of the feminine figure we may find most easily in her, and if we examine the impression she makes on us, we find that it rests on the lush abundance of charm supported by marvellous beauty of build and moderated by a subtle grace. This is why she seems so human to us and although she in no way denies her divinity, we nonetheless approach her with trusting hope.

What the goddess of love says loudly and unmistakably to us, rests slumbering and not yet unfolded in the figure of *Diana.* Gifted with every charm of her sex, she scorns love's sweet joys and takes her sole pleasure in masculine occupations. Accompanied by a flock of playmates of like mind she roams through the depths of the forests pursuing the deer with cruel bow and metes out harsh punishment to any sinful man who approaches her with unchaste eyes. By virtue of her virgin modesty she is related to *Minerva,* but their characters are essentially quite different nonetheless. Every feminine weakness has been rooted out in Jupiter's awesome daughter by the earnestness of wisdom; this is shown most of all by her quiet, pensive, downcast eyes. Diana's eyes cling with lively desire to the object of her endeavors; she has merely substituted one affection for another. Femininity is not alien to her; nowhere does she exhibit masculine strength; she is simply unconscious of it with a sort of joyous innocence. She does not represent a generic ideal anyway, but an individual mood or rather a certain period before maturity. That delicate yearning which attracts one sex to the other needs for its development a period of quiet introversion. But the first welling up of youthful feeling roams, like Diana's eyes, the distances. That is why the first years of young womanhood are not infrequently characterized by a certain lack of feeling, in fact harshness, since the development of feminine mildness and sweetness depends on the development of feelings for the opposite sex. Some character types slip past this growth stage so rapidly that it is hardly noticeable; others remain in it much longer. This latter situation is the one which produced the characteristics of Latona's daughter in the hand of the artist. Feminine charm does not flow from her in melting beauty but is still enclosed within itself and hidden from itself. The limbs have more firmness and slender mobility and the entire expression tells us that the soul has not yet turned toward the inside but still turns outward upon foreign objects. But the main characteristic of divine femininity, grace supported by dignity, represents itself so powerfully that it overwhelms the more it withdraws. And the creative imagination of poets has somewhat softened Diana's harshness. When nocturnal solitude and the silence after the wild chase have recalled the goddess somewhat to her inward self, she is touched by Endymion's charms. But in serious Pallas Athene no such weakness may be found.

If we now compare Aphrodite's grace with the dignity of *Juno,* we see femininity placed in a new and extended sphere. In the former it is mobile and active, in the latter it has imbued the entire being with its calm flow and does not appear by itself, nor in a single moment of affection or affect, but, intimately interwoven with the divine personality, it has become true character. If one reads the poets, to be sure, it may be somewhat difficult to find these features in a goddess who pursues her enemies breathing vengeance and jealousy and who sighs her satisfaction at the smoking ruins of Ilium. But we must distinguish the archetypal character of the gods from the fables about them. . . . As little as Jupiter's lasciviousness is intrinsic to the nature of the father of the gods, so little is Juno's jealousy and vengefulness characteristic of the queen of heaven. But not even in the poets' fables can the character of sublimity and mildness be denied the goddess, and only at moments can the might of her affects darken it. To be sure, at the hand of the sculptor, who for obvious reasons has to hold the arbitrary aspects of his imagination more in check than does the poet, she appears clothed in the highest feminine grace and dignity. Here too an awesome sublimity draws a sacred circle around the goddess. But if her silent admirer succeeds in drawing near it with devoted heart, she too dazzles him with breath-taking beauty. . . .

In this divinity we have another image of true femininity, only this time on a more elevated level. Femininity is not emphasized in any single trait or feature, but seems to surround the entire figure with a delicate veil through which her divinity shines free and unobstructed. She is therefore not shown in the limitation of any certain temporal condition, but comprises every attitude and disposition, developed or not, giving to reason and to imagination an infinite scope. Juno reveals the woman in her not, like Venus, by inviting yearning nor like Diana by youthful innocence, but by a serene fullness which is poured out over her entire being. Even the shadow of unsated desire disappears, and an inner self-sufficiency lifts her far beyond the earthly sphere of limitations. Her tall figure, her wide open eyes, the sublime expression of her mouth give her a dignity which does away with the slightest trace of neediness. But although her femininity is in a way denied by these characteristics, it is all the more expressive in the beauty of her person as a whole. Feminine is her fullness and roundedness, feminine her slowly, gradually streaming, beneficent power, and feminine her lovely grace in all the flower of its youth. For all divinity enjoys the privilege of enjoying and suffering everything human as well as triumphing over the changes of time, and Juno too returns to Zeus' embrace forever as his young bride.

And yet she does not portray femininity as it comes from the creative hand of nature, untouched by personality. Nature in her is wedded to divinity and is carried upward with it. That is why she towers tall, her great eyes wide open, her mouth curved proudly in command. She is free from the limitations of her sex and gifted only with its excellences. The expressions of divine and of female nature gently blend in her, each heightened or moderated by the other. The lush fullness of femininity which easily loses stature is transformed into self-controlled abundance; the strength of femininity which depends on external necessity seems in her bound to inner necessity instead. But wherever the awesome greatness of divine nature might cause terror, it is checked by gentle womanliness. In her, the firm decisiveness which the divine brow announces does not seem dependent on feminine whim, but related to high objective order. And the solemn seriousness which surrounds the goddess loses all sense of harshness since it emanates from womanly chastity and prudence.

Here, then, we meet femininity in a new configuration. It is not really the ideal of femininity at all, not a figure intended to show its excellences and its limits, but it is really an archetype of spiritual nature as such. In order to assume a bodily shape it had to assume sexual characteristics, and chose the feminine. There must be some pure archetype of humanity, (or of divinity, in the sense of the ancients) independent of the forms of sex, to which either sex may aspire. The difficulty with such entrance into foreign territory is not to leave one's own, but instead to widen it to ideal proportions. This demand is fulfilled in the figure of Juno since her divinity destroys the character of femininity as a natural character and portrays it instead as a voluntary one. . . . Each characteristic of this sublime configuration is feminine and divine at one and the same time, a living image of the truth that in goddesses as well as in women, humanity and divinity increase in the same degree in which femininity animates their entire being. . . .

Femininity, as we have seen, is readily recognizable everywhere by its greater gracefulness than is to be expected from mere humanity. Now, in masculine beauty there should be apparent an equivalent character of masculinity. But there is the peculiar difference that masculinity is not so much observed as such when it is present, but rather missed when it is not. Intrinsic sexual characteristics are less obvious in the masculine figure, and it is hardly possible to *single out* an ideal of pure masculinity in an individual configuration, such as can be done for femininity in the figure of Venus. A first glance at the male and female body shows us that the specific sexual characteristics of the male are less dispersed, less closely connected with the rest of the bodily structures. In the case of the female body, nature with unmistakable care has poured all the parts, whether they designate its sex or not, into a single mold and even made its beauty dependent upon this arrangement. In the male body, nature permitted herself a greater freedom; it allowed its beauty considerable independence of its sex, and was content to indicate sex with a single stroke, as it were, not bothering about its harmonious union with the rest of the body. Perhaps, on the other hand, the masculine character is simply expressed with greater subtlety elsewhere, by an over-all expression of greater strength, alertness and tension, and less mass. This special characteristic cannot be accounted for by sex, however; since it in no way contradicts the character of pure humanity, it may be an inherent human rather than masculine—as opposed to feminine—characteristic. Hence it remains true that a greater independence of purely sexual characteristics is an intrinsic part of masculinity.

The more strength and freedom the masculine figure reveals, the more masculine it is deemed, even by everyday judgment. Even more than is true of feminine beauty, power must have overcome mass, and we shall forgive the infringement of grace by too much energy more readily than the infringement of power by too much mass. Therefore masculine beauty is always heightened to the degree that its expression of power is strengthened, and lessened by portrayal of its inertia. Even the method by which the growth of strength is furthered is not a matter of indifference; and masculinity diminishes wherever strength seems to come from nourishment rather than exercise. The *Bacchus* of the ancients is an example of this. A rich abundance characterizes him; in joyous frenzy he moved about the earth, conquering remote and mighty nations more through the abundant might of his nature, than the exertion of his will. And his figure is more delicate and youthful than that of the other gods; his hips have an almost feminine roundness; all his limbs are fuller and rounder. Though armed with the strength of virility and expressing the characteristics of male sexuality, he approaches the borders of the feminine. Like Venus, he symbolizes a power of nature, and like her, and unlike some of the more spiritual divinities, he is closely related to nature. But Venus is the most faithful image of utter femininity and Bacchus a deviation of pure masculinity, illustrating the deep truth that the more a man is ruled exclusively by his sexuality, the greater his actual loss of masculinity. Although in the long run this is also true of women, the loveliest features of femininity becoming extinguished in the utmost violence of sexual affects, their limits are nonetheless farther off. Women seem to be permitted to a very high degree to give in to their sexual natures, whereas men must at a very early stage sacrifice a great deal of theirs to other human values. But this too is affirmed by the great freedom his figure shows from the limitations of sexuality. For the male body can reveal the highest degree of masculinity without reminding one of the exigencies of sex, whereas the careful observer of the female body is always made conscious of it, however delicately the femininity seems to be contained and spread out. The male bodily structure seems to accord with one's expectations of the human body, and it isn't partiality on the part of men toward men that makes the male body the rule, as it were, from which the female deviates. Even the least prejudiced observer must admit that the female body more closely incorporates the specific ends of nature, namely to reproduce her kind, but the male more the universal aim of all life, namely to conquer mass by form.

But in the male figure, too, there remain enough traces of sexual characteristics which must lose themselves in pure humanity, if the greatest possible beauty is to prevail. If the female body offers us a soft and gentle surface, closed off by wave-shaped contours, the energy and abruptness characteristic of the male raises sinews on his body, and his sturdier build, less clothed by flesh, shows all its outlines plainly. Angularities stand out, whether the eye is prepared for them or not; the entire body is divided into rather well-defined segments and looks like a drawing made by a bold hand with sternly correct lines but little care for resultant grace. . . . The male body, even at its highest refinement, continues to exhibit a definiteness which borders on hardness. This ideal is . . . represented in the Farnesian *Hercules*. He is shown resting after his long labors, supported by the instrument of his strength. He has vanquished giants and monsters, but not with the easy power of the gods who can destroy their opponent with a word of their mouth or a wave of their hand, but he has battled with the efforts exerted by mortals; with painful sweat he has accomplished his victories. . . .

Everything in the nature of divinity strives toward the purity and the perfection of the archetypes of the species. Sexual character, too, begins to disappear, and in the youthful figures of the gods the sharp delineation of the male body loses itself in a milder grace which takes away the hardness without sacrificing the definiteness. When Hercules has at last reached Olympus and in Hebe's arms forgets his laborious life on earth, his bodily structure, too, is irradiated by a more refined beauty, and his uncramped limbs move again with a youthful ease. Man too may seek to approach this ideal, and only the blending of human with manly beauty can perfect the latter. . . . Such an ideal of genuine masculinity we see in the Vatican *Apollo*. The greatest possible masculine energy and definiteness is there clothed in the figure of a beautiful divine youth; all his features are drawn gently and some are perceptible only to our feelings. If the bow in his hand and the quiver over his shoulder strike terror to our hearts, the quiet sublimity of the god nonetheless immerses us in a feeling of profound reverence. [I, 336 ff.]

*   *   *

It is sad that the great qualities in women which are formed by the interaction between themselves and the world should die unacknowledged, in a way. They are seldom recognized by more than one person in all their depth and grandeur; for everyone else they remain either hidden or, at best, dimly intuited. And many women experience the fate that even the one person with whom their destiny connects them most closely never gains a clear picture of their qualities. But there is something good and lovely about all this, too. Perhaps humanity's most precious and best should remain, like gold in the shaft, solitary and obscure. For, seen or not, it exerts a beneficent influence all around. I am utterly convinced that the power which women wield is infinitely greater than that which men exert. Without even wishing to, women imprint with their image the psychic constitution of everyone around them, in all their relationships. [To Caroline v. Humboldt, March 1810]

The treatment of women

Carl [an old mutual friend] writes me, "Why don't you send for your wife now? . . . A wife should always be at her husband's side." You can see that he is still the same old Carl. The same sternness, the same constraint, the same judging of everything according to certain general precepts. The morality which kills true morality by looking at circumstances in place of people, by failing to recognize deepest inner stature, by having no respect for another's freedom. The result is that even in tender and softhearted souls—and Carl is such a one—the tenderness and softheartedness are finally destroyed. I should "send for" my darling! Just the words horrify me: like sending for a book or a bust!

There are women, to be sure, whom perhaps one must treat that way. They can be very good and very nice, but they can only exist as the possession of a man which their nature seems to intend them to be. If fate had blinded me into marrying one of them, I too would treat her like that. Only he who is capable of holding the lesser at its own proper level and treating it according to the demands of its own nature, can have genuinely deep respect for the greater. But whoever is truly fortunate, to whomever the very best of humanity has given herself, he must not want to own her like a base ordinary possession. He must honor his own freedom in hers and hers in his. The saving thing about Carl is, of course, that he does not do what he says. It is only the concepts "duty" and "obedience" that rise so quickly to his lips. [To Caroline v. Humboldt, November 1809]

*   *   *

[In connection with two friends he writes:] It would be better if he told her straight out that he does not love her. Because then he would really let her see the inside of his soul and she would have the happiness of that, at least, and the knowledge that he was carrying her feelings, if not in a loving, yet in a warm and sympathetic heart. In unrequited love there is no consolation except the sight of the lofty beauty of the beloved object. Only this can raise the soul and make the feeling which is consuming it all the dearer. [To Caroline v. Humboldt, November 1790]

*   *   *

If man's happiness in almost any situation is founded on his own will, woman's happiness is primarily dependent on—how shall I say it?—whatever it is in a man's character that is *not* his will, that exists apart from it; whatever lies more in his nature than in his convictions or intentions, more in his whole manner of being than in any specific action of his. [XVI, 37]

*　　*　　*

Women, with an infinitely more easily wounded nature than men, are always in a position where it is hardly possible to prevent their hurts. For their entire way of life always excites and makes claims on their emotional nature. The whole happiness and peace of their existence hovers forever in unavoidable danger. Certain characters to be sure are even more prey to these dangers than others. . . . One can say of men that only in their very best moments is there a complete balance in them between their tenderness and their strength. And in no man are his best moments his predominant ones. Hence, if his strength even just slightly outweighs his tenderness, then the tenderness in his inmost and best nature must suffer. I know quite well that there are many moments when women make men suffer injustice. But it isn't the same thing. In good women it always springs from a source which a man honors and loves (either for its own sake or for the sake of certain qualities connected with it), and so the effect is that it never really hurts him. He may feel deprived, or annoyed, but he feels such a constantly, visibly flowing treasure of love emanating from the feminine heart that a certain gentleness is imparted to a woman's every utterance, even to those which a man might have expected to be quite different from what they turned out to be. . . . This psychic situation of women inspires a compassion in men which is one of the loveliest sensations in life and upon which one might construct a whole universe of poetry. [To Caroline v. Humboldt, November 1817]

*　　*　　*

Very few people understand how infinitely important is solitude, especially for a woman. If she is married and has children, her family circle constitutes her solitude; if not, she has absolute solitude available, in which she really lives alone and sees few people.

Fortune passes and hardly leaves a trace in the soul and often can hardly be even called fortune because one gains nothing lasting from it. Misfortune also passes (and that is a great consolation), but it leaves deep traces, healing ones, if one knows how to use it well, and thus frequently brings great happiness because one has been purified and strengthened. For it is a peculiar thing in life that when one doesn't in the least think of happiness or unhappiness but only of strictly fulfilling one's duty without saving oneself, happiness suddenly appears of its own accord, even if one's life is deprived and painful. I have often seen this in women who lived in extremely unhappy marriages but who would rather have died than give up their task. [To C. Diede, July 1822]

Suprasexual personality

Since man is a mixed creature who contains both freedom and natural necessity bound up together, he attains the ideal of pure humanity only by a consummately harmonious balance of both. If moral worth is to be upheld, the will should be in control, to be sure, yet it should not control a resistant, but an agreeable nature. And even external appearance should communicate such harmony. But here reality is left far behind the imagination. It nowhere supplies us with the figure of a pure being who is beyond all sex peculiarities; in fact it is difficult to even imagine such a one. For as imagination seeks to erase the character of one sex it runs the danger of simply substituting that of the other or, avoiding this pitfall, weakening all characteristic marks to the point of obscurity.

Yet undeniably it happens sometimes, even in reality, that a few isolated traits of a certain individual shine through and seem purely human, midway between masculine and feminine. And because we all carry a dark image of this in our soul, we do not fail to recognize it when we see it. Here and there we find something superwomanly (if I may be permitted the expression) which no one would therefore call unwomanly or masculine, and in men, too, we occasionally meet traits which do not seem colored by sex. An example of such traits is a certain quiet greatness of soul which rises not from nature but from self-control. It never seems unwomanly when it is met in a woman and likewise in a man, it seems always more human than masculine. [I, 349 f.]

On love

What is the purpose—understood or not—of human beings in their every imaginable mode of action? All of us serve the one and only Goddess: the Enhancement of the Human Race, the Growth of Human Energy and Human Capacity for Enjoyment. This striving is visible only dimly where cares for the necessities of existence limit the horizon, but it is visible even there. All care, physical or otherwise, is only the effort to reach the condition of the possibility of the one and only good. Where mind rises and cares for mind, the striving is more nearly to the point, but even there it is often—even mostly—far off from the true goal. So many things that enter the human soul remain forever alien to it. They do not become the soul's own; the soul *possesses,* but it does not *become.* The only difference, then, between the people of articulate mind and the others is that the former possess moral, intellectual goods instead of physical ones. But the true divinity is glimpsed only by him who immediately and directly, and with the giving of all that he is, acts upon himself and upon others. But to act thus upon another may be done upon only *one* other, and to receive thus from another may be done only with *one.*

Many things may be taken from many people. But true becoming, true growth, one can only achieve by passing oneself over to one other human being. [To Caroline v. Humboldt, March 1791]

*   *   *

How infinitely true it is that there is no greater torment than to feel homeless within oneself, to be without an inner abiding place to which one may return peacefully when outer fate crowds one back on oneself, to feel destructiveness in the only place from which peace and steadfastness can really spring. And equally true is it that circumstance and accident lead us slowly, step by step, and unnoticed, into entanglements so that in the end we suddenly find ourselves doing what we had believed ourselves to be utterly remote from. . . .

It is just the best, most feeling people who find themselves entangled this way. Inner artlessness, the consciousness of pure and guiltless feelings, noble enthusiasm for the good: all these so naturally lead away from the paths of the conventional, and man becomes so helpless as soon as he feels himself abandoned by the regular course of events. But there must be a double standard, an external and conventional one for the condition of mere reason and coolness, an inner one for those who are worthy of it, for the moments of inmost awareness of existence in its totality, for the state of inspiration that can spring only from such awareness. The first standard is that of right and wrong, the proper measuring stick for external action; the second is the standard of love, the just appreciation accorded to the inner and truest life.

The standard of love is no less strict than the standard of right and wrong, but it is more just and less one-sided. It is just as clumsy for judging separate acts as the other is for appreciating the value of the whole man. It may never be applied when the moment of acting is at hand, but it is indispensable when that moment has echoed away, when the step has been irrevocably taken. What is there to revive and comfort the sick heart, what can restore peace to the wrecked feeling-life, if it is not that suddenly the horizon grows larger, that suddenly in the wondrous workings of fate itself lies the answer to transgression, and that through the strict but impartial contemplation of the whole being, the feeling-life regains courage and confidence in itself once more. Everyone who has insight into himself must unfailingly find himself two persons: one, who commands fate and shapes his own destiny; another, who succumbs to fate and is ruled by it. Woe to a man who has never felt the latter; he could never be other than cold and feelingless —worse—intolerant and harsh. But to see others and even—and especially—oneself succumb to an alien power, the power of feeling opposed to the voice of duty and the needs of a given situation, to see them (and oneself) as guilty and at the same time as pure in spirit and guiltless: this is possible only in the deepest and inmost self-oriented moods or in the moments which only the highest friendship or true love can evoke.

A conviction which cannot be effectuated by individual facts nor by plainly articulated reason, which cannot be founded on what appears to be the case at any given moment, but only on what is truly, really unique (and therefore never appears in any specific connection but only when the totality of the human being is considered): such a conviction can appear with certainty and at the same time with genuine modesty and humility only where soul immediately passes over into soul, where the life of the feelings is sufficiently moved and inspired to be receptive with all its powers as well as active with all its powers. That is why it is so true that love forgives all, and at the same time that only love can be strict and just. That is why it is not a sentimental feeling but a natural and true one that one so easily excuses a person whom one loves from the conventional judgment and prefers to withdraw into one's own quiet unshakable conviction. [To Caroline v. Humboldt, May 1797]

*   *   *

What a lovely thought it is, my Li, that all growth toward perfection is but a returning to original existence. It has often seemed so to me. Through all the veils which conceal within a narrow human life the archetype of the human soul's beauty, we glimpse, in moments of inspiration, its characteristic form. And we intuit with lofty, firm certainty that a time will come when the veils shall be lifted. The joy we partake of at such moments is always twofold. For one senses oneself, too, as vaster and more beautiful a being, because it takes the joint striving of the noblest and best powers to comprehend what eludes most eyes. That is why one is so often wrong in estimating human beings: one does not differentiate between what is characteristic for an individual and what rises merely from the combination of outer circumstance or inner disproportion or opposition of energies. But only from the recognition of a person's characteristic *Gestalt* may we judge what he is capable of, and make any sort of certain judgment of his character. Without it, our judgment must fluctuate with every moment, since it can only be arrived at by judging separate ideas, actions, or words, all of which are particularly misleading in the case of people whose minds are nimble and whose trains of ideas run uneven. One should describe a character only in reference to its archetypal *Gestalt,* and only through it can love arise, in any genuine sense. And here, it seems to me, lies the reason why love must always be inseparable from sensuousness, why it always needs the living presence. For only our perception of the total human being, in every possible mode of its utterance, can give us an image of the archetype. The entire body, above all the eyes, is its reproduced impression, the body at rest, and then, especially, the body in motion. The rapidity or slowness, the violent affect or the peacefulness, the ease or clumsiness, the solemnity or the simplicity of its movements, in their smallest degree and subtlest nuance, are most truly that from which one may calculate the nature of a human being's feelings, their spaciousness, depth, vividness. [To Caroline v. Humboldt, September 1790]

* * *

There is no freedom without love, and the measure of love is the greater or lesser degree of unrestricted freedom. [To Caroline v. Humboldt, January 1791]

373

Part III

FIRST PERSON
SINGULAR

PERSONAL EXPRESSIONS
1789–1797

Old age has always been an object of my most intense longing. It is not right to call old age a period of inactivity. The sphere of activity may be more narrow, more restricted, but perhaps it is all the lovelier. And perhaps the good is purer in old age, the good which one gives and the good of which one partakes, and above all: what a perspective old age has on the past! What near prospects for the future! [To Caroline v. Humboldt, May 1789]

*   *   *

I am glad . . . that my sensations, my feeling for friendship, for love, for the union of souls, received none of their direction from books; that only association and my own experience educated me in this respect. It means that no external influence has violated me, that nothing alien was insinuated into or mixed up with my feelings. I am, in this respect, the way nature meant me to be. I have read very little; few people of my age in approximately similar circumstances can have read as little as I have. But I am glad of it. I have thought more, learned to place less value on alien ideas, and more upon experience exclusively. . . . [To Caroline v. Humboldt, May 1789]

*   *   *

Between Duissburg and Krefeld one crosses the Rhine by ferry. One of the workers on this ferry was a girl, extremely ugly, but strong, masculine, and a hard worker. It is incredible how such a sight attracts me—any sight of a physically hard working woman, especially from the lower classes. I find it nearly impossible to turn my eyes away, and nothing else so strongly stimulates my sexual feelings. This is a leftover of the first years of my childhood. When my soul was first occupied with females, I always imagined them as slaves, oppressed by all sorts of toil, tormented with a thousand tortures, and treated with total contempt. I still have some feeling for such notions. I can still, as formerly, imagine whole novels with such contents. Only now they contain somewhat less poor taste and somewhat more probability than when I was younger. It continues to be of great psychological interest to me to go through these unwritten novels in my mind, in chronological order. How this direction first originated in me, remains a mystery. On the one hand such harshness, on the other hand such voluptuous indulgence. But I am sure that it has been the basis, coupled with the situations that came my way, for my whole present character. I derived from it the solitary preoccupation with the life of the imagination, a distaste for society and social intercourse, my strong voluptuousness (which still bears unmistakable traces of these notions), and from voluptuousness love, friendship with women, preoccupation with women in general, from this the study of all character, the effort to participate in the ideas of others, to adapt to the modes of action of others, in short my whole superrefined skill in social intercourse which finally led me to be to others whatever I feel like being (a great deal to some, nothing to myself). This has so ground down my own original sensibilities that none has remained. I am left finally with that indifference and emptiness which now characterizes my diseased state. How plain and clear all this seems! Only a few weeks application, and I would have described myself so that not the slightest feeling would any longer be obscure. Everything in me would be developed with my single clue! But that would also be the moment at which I should no longer be what I am, not to myself, not to anyone else! [XIV, 79 f.]

*   *   *

Home until after twelve. Wrote in my journal. Felt what I so often feel when I am absorbed in writing or talking. As long as the fire lasts, I am enchanted by what I bring forth. As soon as it is done, it seems idle chatter and the words *parturiunt montes, nascetur ridiculus mus* ring forever in my head. Also I imagine myself most often in the image of a tinkling cymbal. [XIV, 89]

*   *   *

To be something to many people, to communicate myself to many, is not possible for me. In fact it is very difficult for me to let anything of myself pass over into others. All my ideas, even on perfectly general subjects, are so intimately woven into everything that is dear to me, that they take on a very great value for me. Any uttered form that I might give them seems not perfect enough. I can hardly ask you to conceive the hurt that I feel when I must tell some idea which is valuable to me, and do not have the power to develop it or at least to state it so precisely that others may accord it equal worth. And I feel that this is not vanity in me, but the effect of the love which I have for whatever the idea is. I have lived so much inside myself, have in part constructed for myself such a universe of ideas, that I sometimes fear I will be swamped by sentimentality for it. That is why I very much long for an older, experienced, not exactly colder (for often it seems to me that I myself am very cold, too cold to be really good or even really happy) but more reality-oriented man for a friend. But such a one is hard to find, if one seeks at the same time a good mind and a reservoir of at least former warm feelings. . . . I am talking about myself again. But it is my failing to talk a great deal about myself and to like others best when they talk about themselves. [To Caroline v. Humboldt, April 1790]

*   *   *

My early youth was so sad. People tormented me, I had no one who meant anything to me or, if I idealized someone into such a role, I could not associate with him. This produced in me a genuine love for books, and admixed with the most pedantic studies was a sort of feeling of attachment and affection that sprang from bitterness toward people and often had me in tears. I felt it most when I was studying Greek because they always scolded me for spending too much time on Greek, and I really suffered a good deal from this. Forgive all this stuff. But the memory of it so often becomes vivid in me, and basically I find very little difference between what I was then and what I am now. [To Caroline v. Humboldt, April 1790]

*   *   *

The work [of being a judge] as such affords me no joy either. I do not use it to strive for external advantages—I could never become ambitious—and the quality of the work itself does not please me. For on the one hand I know only too well what performing such a task could ideally mean to be ever satisfied with my own performance, and on the other hand those talents which would be necessary to perform it well have no inner value for me. The most interesting cases, to be sure, are the criminal cases and I work on those almost exclusively. But it necessitates talking and rationalizing about the character of some unfortunate, that he was or was not thus or so, hence he is now guilty in such and such a way. And I appear to myself like a child who sits in judgment on the action of a man. I am supposed to imagine, from reading some clumsy document, that I know a certain human being, how he thinks and how he feels, and usually a human being, at that, who, even if I lived side by side with him, would cost me hard and long study to appreciate properly. Next, I am supposed to adapt the result of my observations—a very subtle thing often—to an inflexible positive law and then, to bridge the gap, take recourse to ingenious, often hairsplitting ratiocinations.

The part that pains me the most in all this is just this type of argumentative reasoning about a human character. For it surely must be far more painful to have imputed to oneself the wrong motives than to endure even the harshest punishment. The business about which I wrote you the other day was of this sort. A woman had killed her five-month old child because she was unable to place it and saw no way of supporting it herself. It cost me a much greater effort to pronounce that she did it from indifference to the child's life, from cowardly unwillingness to try supporting it, than to sentence her to a lifetime in prison. Of course I know quite well that it is my own feelings which are this way, not those of the people I am talking about. I know that I do not hurt them nearly as much by imputing to them false motives as by sentencing them to too severe a punishment. But nonetheless it is how my imagination presents the case to me, and to be truly decent toward others one surely has to stipulate for them, feelings as delicate as one thinks one would have in similar circumstances. [To Caroline v. Humboldt, October 1790]

*   *   *

I 've always been a crazy creature, always had ideas and feelings that so warmed me, that got so intimately bound up with my whole nature, that I concealed them in myself like holy objects. I blushed and trembled as though I were guilty whenever I had to utter them. Even now, even just in my thoughts, it costs me much, alas much too much, to bring them to the light of day. To endow a thought that is dear to me with utterance, still casts my soul on the waves and tosses it between highest pain and highest bliss. That is why I cannot tell anyone anything that is very dear to me. The burning glow which it kindles in me! And the wretchedness and coldness in which it stands revealed and with which it is comprehended! [To Caroline v. Humboldt, November 1790]

*   *   *

These [Leibnitzian] monads are simple. Nothing can come from them and nothing can enter them. So there is no immediate interaction of one being with another. Each lives alone, only in itself and its ideas, and if there is a mutual effect, it is merely due to the arrangements of the Creator who placed the ideas of each in such harmonious relationship that if a certain idea arises in the first, a corresponding one arises simultaneously but independently in the other. Can you imagine anything more sophisticated and more contrary to all natural feeling? And yet I remember very well what warmth this system generated in me. Especially one night [at home] in Tegel. I sat that night, under a starry sky, in a small acacia grove. And as I imagined more and more vividly how everything around me was a separate being, like myself, each leaf that rustled in my ear, each crumb of earth I stepped on, and that the sleeping powers of these beings would one day waken and be heightened, a nameless enthusiasm overcame me. I can still feel how it was, how I knelt and cried from joy, and how I prayed so devoutly to the star-sown heavens. Oh—that's how devout I always was and still am. . . . [To Caroline v. Humboldt, November 1790]

*   *   *

Strange—as sacred as the simple truth of the heart is to me, as surely as my slightest inner feeling never violates it, there are . . . circles where I am taken to represent almost the opposite. And this among people who are worth more in my eyes than many others, and who, at the same time, don't mind associating with me in spite of their opinion of me. A very good and sensitive girl told me to my face, not long ago, that she simply could not trust me and always had to be on guard, not to be deceived by my honest face. . . . I feel very well how such a suspicion could arise in all seriousness and could last a long time. I really do appear in very different guises sometimes, and I hardly ever take pains to let others see my inner consistency or at least whatever truth the seeming contradictions contain. Besides, there is rarely anything in my ideas and feelings which excludes anything else. Even when I feel most deeply for some species of objects, its complete opposite never appears to me in a totally hateful or unbearable guise. I always retain some sense for *its* charming side, and whatever I consider truly mine becomes greater and loftier, the greater and loftier I am able to consider its opposite. [To Caroline v. Humboldt, November 1790]

*   *   *

Today we had a terrible rain storm. I rode out at twilight. The waves of the Spree rolled so darkly against the banks. Black clouds had piled all around the wide open sky. In the pine tops the storm raged. Then I felt better. How marvellously we impart our inner moods to the nature outside us! The wildness of the raging elements transformed itself within me to an aching melancholy. Slowly I rode along between the woods and the stream, in a wretched but calm mood. "How dare you lament," something cried to me, "the joys now gone. Like a sunbeam they gladden the poor heart of a mortal but a storm blows them away. Obey the fate that rules!" It wasn't courage that was poured into my heart but a yielding to a stronger force. I often feel it, but never so strongly as when nature itself shows such powerful evidence of its might all around me. I am a strange creature. But the sight of a force which nothing can resist has always attracted me most powerfully—and I don't care if I myself or my last and dearest joys get drawn into its whirlpool. When I was a child—I remember it clearly—I saw a coach rolling through a crowded

street, pedestrians scattering right and left, and the coach uncon-
cerned, not diminishing its speed. That made my heart beat so
strangely. Don't laugh at me, Li, and my childish memories. I cannot help it that so many of my views are still what they were in
my childhood, and that it is so characteristic of me to see shapes of
the spirit in the forms of sense objects. Everything I look at transforms itself so readily, not into signs *of* something, but into the expressed reality itself, and because this lies deep in me, because it
rises from my feelings and not from the rationalizing of a hairsplitting intellect, I like to let myself go and do not stop what
comes up in me. [To Caroline v. Humboldt, December 1790]

*   *   *

The nights? Oh Li, at night, feel-
ings flood through me which I wouldn't imagine possible in the
frightful monotony of the tortured days. With the light my joy dies
away and a heavy oppressive feeling smothers me. Often I cannot
go to bed. I wander aimlessly, roam the streets, salute the Dipper
and all the others, stand on a bridge, perhaps, and see them sparkling,
the forever youthfully shining ones, in the bright water. . . . I cannot part with my nights, and like living, participating beings, the
constellations move over my head. [To Caroline v. Humboldt,
January 1791]

*   *   *

I am dissatisfied with many sepa-
rate things [in myself] but I do feel a fervent gratitude toward fate for
orienting me so, that ever since I can remember two things and two
things only have occupied me: first, a love for certain ideas which have
modified themselves in me many times, to be sure, but which have
nonetheless remained essentially the same; and second, the need for
finding a being between whom and myself there would be intimate
understanding, a being whose happiness would become my dearest
care and whose love my only existence. [To Caroline v. Humboldt,
May 1797]

PERSONAL EXPRESSIONS
1804-1814

            I well know that our life can no longer be as happy as it was. It has been disturbed once and for all at its core [by the death of their son Wilhelm at the age of ten]. But, dear, it isn't the most important thing to live happily, but to complete one's destiny, to exhaust, in one's own way, all the human possibilities that are latent in one. The isolated existence which is all that we now feel cannot be everything, and it cannot last forever. However incomprehensible it may be, the individual is only the outpouring stream of a single power, of which he senses only a part. But he must spin it out, and spin it out fully, purely, in order to regain the truth, the true complete level of existence where there will no longer be a new opposition to be reconciled, but where there is a true sensation of wholeness, where fate ceases to show itself as the constant opponent of feeling, where grief and loss and separation dissolve, showing up as errors in our comprehension, and dispersing, like dreams after a long oppressive night. All we need do is hold fast to that inner identity. We must take hold of our life with a sort of relentless boldness and live it out. For that in us which seeks to do this is our truth, our pure primordial selfhood; everything else must perish. . . . [To Caroline v. Humboldt, March 1804]

*   *   *

Since we were children we [my brother Alexander and I] have diverged like two opposite poles, although we have always loved one another and at times have confided in one another. His striving was directed, from an early age, toward the outside world. And I very early chose for myself an inner life alone. Believe me, in that difference is encompassed everything. I never had the talent of stopping at some one point and treating it as though it might be an end or a goal. For that matter, I haven't learned it yet, and often this is to my disadvantage in daily living. My first questions were always: What does it all come to in the end, the real end? What is left over? Why was it ignored? Why must this or that be left out of regard and disappear? Something was thus formed in my basic nature that can never leave me as long as I live. It gives me a deep sense of peace, an enduring self-reliance which lets me find myself and my life and my fate again and again. And if the view should become obscured, a single solitary walk, a single thought of you, of the children, or of the past bring it all up again in all its strength and richness. Believe me, dear Li, it is no credit to me that I have found this. It is a great good fortune to have it. It cannot be taken away, but it is always being given. Nor would it be good if many were this way, because such persons get more enjoyment than they give and that creativity is discouraged through which, after all, the greatest human products come into being.

Man ought really to create for himself *one* limited, definite object in which he may lose himself, for a time at least. You will often have noticed it in Goethe and in Schiller. Of the two, Schiller is somewhat freer, less constricted by his nature, more able to choose an object while remaining independent of it, and more able to look upon it with an impartial eye when his work on it is done and his peace has returned. But both these men can fasten themselves totally to their work, truly forgetting everything but the one, though desiring to represent the all through the one. In the thinking and feeling of ordinary life, someone like me seems to himself to represent a higher point of view, and this is probably correct. But he will always need the others and will hardly ever himself contribute to that which to him seems the highest achievement of all. For one really needs a handhold, as it were, a sensuous shape, for reaching the greatest heights, and what I lack, what nature hasn't granted me, is *one* such handhold. I see things more variously, perhaps, and more purely, because I am never bound to a single mode or form, but I cannot retain or focus my glimpse for long. Only one thing, I think, is peculiar to me, and I mostly have you, dear Li, to thank for it. It is my penchant for recognizing the highest values through the medium of human nature itself, my preference for observing live people in their natural doings and to arrive at values of utmost purity and loftiness through doing just that. In most people, intuition does violence to feeling, creativity to the ability to observe ordinary reality, and vice versa. In this respect only, I think I have found my own proper way. What I like best is to proceed from the plainest most straightforward observation to that which is not seen and scarcely apprehended at all, or to arrive at the same place by beginning with natural, even sensual feelings. I see the same process in others in connection with those objects which in themselves seem to carry the imprint of a pure inner organization, those which seem already formed for and by human imagination. So a love of nature, for example, frequently awakens and lifts the observer to creative effort. But to utilize the least organized of all nature's children, the least pure and ordered, human beings themselves as one finds them in their comings and goings: this is more difficult and yet infinitely more rewarding. For however obscured it may often be, the highest value is still expressed most directly in the human being. Where it has been smudged out of all recognition in a soul, it may often be found in the body's form which often preserves the original purity more surely. In a few individuals one sees it resplendent in all its beauty, but as soon as one has got to the point of feeling that the highest human attainment is but a brightly and purely unfolded manifestation of simple, plain naturalness, then one will see its traces everywhere. Only a similarly constituted person, to be sure, will see its meaning, and thus, the more in life one searches for, and finds, human beings, the richer, more self-sufficient, more independent one becomes oneself. More humanized, more readily touched by all that is human in all the facets of one's nature, and in all aspects of creation. This is the goal, dear Li, to which my nature urges me. This is what I live and breathe. Here for me is the final key to all desire, the harbor out of which I no longer care to set sail. For this is the end for me; this is no longer good *for* something, but has its goal and end in itself. Who, when he dies, can tell himself, "I have comprehended as much world as I was able, and have transformed it into my humanness," has fulfilled his aim. He could not wish to start over in order to accomplish the proper things at last. He has accomplished what "life" in the fullest sense of the word means, and it would be folly to wish to subjugate life to an alien purpose. One spins it out like the silkworm as long as the thread holds—and with that there's an end to it. [To Caroline v. Humboldt, October 1804]

* * *

I thought that I would be able to return to Rome next spring. But I find out, though so far only indirectly, that I have been given an appointment in Berlin. You, my dear Prince, have known every detail of our life in Rome; you know what this unique city has come to mean to me and to my wife. Even the violence of grief, the irreparable losses we have suffered there, have bound us indissolubly to that place. We are making the greatest sacrifice we are capable of making by leaving Rome and transplanting ourselves to Germany. Without the profound misfortune of our native country we could have lived assured that we too would some day rest near the Pyramid next to our children [who are buried there]. [XVI, 74 f.]

*   *   *

The terrible thing is that there is simply no one else beside me whom the King can ask [to fill the chief position in the Ministry for Public Worship and Education], and that everyone else is likewise convinced that this is so. One can hear it said publicly by quite uninformed people. They do need men here. There may be crises approaching—in fact they are just about at hand—when the need will become a truly urgent one. I am more capable than many others. Here they can use me for many, in fact any, purposes; in Rome for very few. To go back to Rome, then, would mean not only leaving the King but backing out of a meaningful task—in fact, any task at all. So I have given up trying to back out. I have told the King, very seriously and somewhat sadly, that if he commands me, I should and would obey, but that I hope he will, in view of my complete subordination, fulfill my own dearest wish also, namely return me to my post as Resident in Rome in four or five years, or earlier if important considerations should warrant it. Conditions other than this I did not care to make. If remain I must, I'd rather remain without petty stipulations.

All this, dear Li, is terribly sad for us. But I do believe that I cannot withdraw right now from the duty to act. We ourselves would be hurt and sorry if we were sitting in Rome and things went badly here [in Prussia] in a way that I might have been able to help prevent. We are a part of this land, I suppose, as are our children, and must not remain entirely passive toward it. [To Caroline v. Humboldt, February 1809]

*   *   *

The will which one exercises in actual activity depends frightfully much on fate and even on those sundry chance happenings which one doesn't care to dignify by even calling them fate. But the will which lies deeper in the soul, which influences one's mode of action and one's way of life, seen as a whole, this will I completely believe in. That is why I gladly leave single events to chance and don't care to exert my will on them, but abide firmly by my over-all direction of willing. I prefer to use circumstances as I find them rather than to try bringing suitable ones about. In this way one exerts a very definite influence on people, because one apparently—and really, too—leaves them much freedom. But in the end one nonetheless has determined one's own fate. [To Caroline v. Humboldt, April 1809]

*　　*　　*

It is quite true that I seldom seem to require the presence of an actual sense object as such in order to enter into a thing even quite deeply, or to get an over-all view of the spirit that moves it, or to become quite intensely interested in it. But I find this neither good nor amiable nor—and this is not a bad standard in such matters—would I wish it on any of my children. One rarely produces anything more with such a constitution than can be predicted and calculated. For it is the natural warmth, the ardor that is generated only by the spontaneous influence of a piece of reality upon the faculty of sensation, with no intervention of thought—it is the very first contact of the imagination with an object that does the work of genius and creates what had hitherto not even been intuited. . . . There are compensations of a beneficial and pleasant sort, of course, for a disposition or a way of thinking such as mine. One has an entirely different sort of recognition of the world and of people; one has a much more manifold feeling for one's own existence; one is not one-sided (which is quite important in my present tasks) and—most important—one stands at an over-all center of things from which all the surroundings may be seen in their true light. If it were not for this, a lack of one-sidedness would be worthless, to be sure. What must be joined to it is the gift of comprehending the true and unique spirit of any individual, specific thing. The point at which I feel that gift is reflected in me comes where my intense and peculiar love for individuality takes over. The new in people and things attracts and interests and pleases me not only for its newness but for its individuality. I do not merely wish to know and feel how anything is different from anything else, but how it forms a whole, and how it is related to the wholeness of all things, and to the wholeness of all the possibilities in all things.

This love for the individual quality in human nature (and all things are, after all, reducible to human nature) lies at the bottom of every feeling, every sensation of mine. The naturally and temperamentally strong ones . . . it tones down and allows to appear in the form of imagination and reflected feeling; the naturally weak ones it strengthens, and it compensates, in certain cases, my sometimes total lack of all sensation. [To Caroline v. Humboldt, May 1809]

*　　　*　　　*

No one can riddle out the future. But—I don't know—I have a kind of courage which may perhaps seem extraordinary to some people; I think it is roughly founded on the proverb: What bends, won't break. . . . [XVI, 170]

*　　　*　　　*

When one is engaged upon a task which must be done, one mustn't let uncertainty irk one. One must work, not only to achieve something useful, but also for form's sake, as it were, in order to solve the problem of a given task with skill. That is my view and that is why I could work today if I knew for sure that some decree would annihilate all work tomorrow. Such a strange view may seem bizarre, but what is much more bizarre is that right now it is useful in practice. In fact it is the only view that permits one to work at all these days. [XVI, 176]

*　　　*　　　*

I rose today earlier than usual, dear Li, and am writing first to you. It is [the anniversary of] the first unhappy day of our life together and all the terrible and sad memories are reliving themselves before my eyes. Our dear good Wilhelm —he would be big and strong now; he would be with you or with me, or even by himself somewhere; he would be a good boy and we would be proud of him. But it is still indescribably wonderful to have had him, even for those few years. Even if his lovely deep nature (that he had though he was a young child) was with us only briefly, yet it *was;* it was generated from us and nourished itself from us. His was a beautiful human form to have been recognized, and we shall surely recognize it again in some human being or other. Whatever raw materials have once been organized into a truly individuated being, are forever wrenched away from formless matter. They have forever passed into that which alone is truly living, and the length of time such a being spent here, on this side, is of lesser consequence. Though everything on the other side of the grave is dark and uncertain, nonetheless the power of love is indissolubly strong, and what has once become one's own shall return through all the byways of transformation. This pure and inward life which must be attuned to the most delicate alertness in order to blossom into deep and real love rules all the dark ununderstood powers of nature. What one has once bound up with it through one's feelings cannot get lost in all eternity. [To Caroline v. Humboldt, August 1809]

*   *   *

I must admit that I have a . . . certain peculiarity which, although I disapprove of it, I cannot divest myself of. It is that I place very little value on any sort of activity, mine or anyone else's, and even less value on my own reputation. It remains a fundamental trait in me that I want to try out any and every possibility I can imagine, for the purpose of getting to know the most heterogeneous objects and placing them in inner or outer relationship to myself and to each other. I accord incredibly low value to results and successes. And I am irresistibly fascinated by any and above all any new activity. I should like to say this to you only, for it really condemns whatever claim I may have to any sort of significant public office, but nonetheless it's true. [XVI, 220]

*   *   *

Wilhelm's death, to which you refer in your letter, has shaken me anew if there can be anything new in it. . . . The holy part of happiness is gone; that pure unsullied beauty, when fate's hand touches us, and ever after, each impulse of happiness is mixed with care and worry. The tribulations of life have started and our destinies cloud over as our hearts have clouded over. Both one's fate and one's inner heart stand in a wondrous relationship of mutual interaction. He who is unreservedly happy grows happier because he is happy already. Grief returns familiarly to the place where it has once been received and—alas—we cannot be angry with it for doing so. Grief fastens onto our hearts with bonds which we could not loosen without tearing ourselves apart. It belongs to our weak and dark human existence more than does joy, and it holds a peacefulness and calm which at last can no longer be overwhelmed by a hostile fate. [To Caroline v. Humboldt, October 1809]

*   *   *

I have always prized only what is individual and unique in a human being, and the ideal incomparably more than the real, and I still do. What for years now has occupied my time [politics] is basically alien to my nature, or, at most, a side issue in me. If I followed my inclination, I should live in a hidden corner somewhere with those whom I love. And this would cause me no qualms of conscience; in these matters I have my own standards and my own judgment. But for another reason I gladly do what I am now doing and am going to continue doing. If I merely occupied myself with ideas I would—for a thousand reasons which I know very well—never accomplish very much. But my meanderings in reality accomplish much more because the reality of public life is a field which is much more rarely seized upon by anyone of some intellect and feeling than the other. Great genius, to be sure, I shall never exhibit in it either. I simply was not made for genuine production or action. To be successful there, one must be able to insist upon one's own opinions and convictions, once formed, with considerable stubbornness and even one-sidedness. Whenever I am faced with multiple choices, I choose several at once; I too clearly always see what is lacking, and I often prefer other people's opinions to my own. . . . The more utterly fascinated I am, as for example just at present, by the spectacle of reality, the less I pay attention to its detailed aspects and the more it transports me to a tranquil and free observation post for a total world view. . . . [To Caroline v. Humboldt, November 1813]

*   *   *

I suddenly remember . . . that to-day is the anniversary of Mama's birthday. . . . A few days ago I had what was for me quite a strange sensation. I was reading in some verses, I have forgotten whose, about those gossamer threads which at home we used to call "summer." You only see them when it's hot, at Indian summer time. And suddenly I was overwhelmed by an image of myself as a child, running through the heat, at home in Tegel, trying to grasp that gossamer. I really ached with longing for that bygone place and time. When such unusual moments well up in the soul it always seems to me there must be good reasons for it. In fact, I often feel as though an infinitely deeper and more nearly omniscient spirit in ourselves than any we know of were sending up messages to us from our depths, and that what we think of as our natural mode of reasoning and thinking only spins on drily in the intervals between those communications. [To Caroline v. Humboldt, December 1813]

*   *   *

FRAGMENTS OF AN
AUTOBIOGRAPHY

It has been a constant plague of my inner life that I go pregnant with ideas for an essay, a book, frequently a major work, but never get it done. The circumstances which have prevented me have not been outer ones; for a long stretch of years my position was one of the most enviable freedom. Rather, they were inner circumstances and the investigation of them that I am about to undertake in these pages will provide the major key to my whole intellectual character. Suffice it here to state the fact. At almost no time, not even during my busiest periods, have I been free from plans of writing. Hundreds of times I would make them, start to write something down, tear it up, make vast collections of data for future works, and give them up too, half-finished. It is not therefore surprising that this lifelong desire is being stimulated once again, during my stay here, where I am enjoying almost total solitude and a great deal of leisure. The fact that I have finished my translation of *Agamemnon* is itself tantalizing bait to start something else. So again I started in my usual fashion and again I failed as always before.

But suddenly I tried a new course. For, feeling keenly that a work of research can hardly be undertaken without a complete library and with only odd hours at my disposal, I resolved to renounce all such plans entirely until fate once more places me into a position of independence. Meanwhile there occurred to me that which I am doing now: attempting an autobiography. For this I can draw entirely on memory and reflection, both of which are always with me and accompany all my activities anyway. And it is more dignified to devote those years of life which may easily be one's last to meditation rather than the mechanical collecting of data. One cannot foretell the possible influence on one's character and one's inner fate of one or two years, looked upon as a period of standstill, which may serve as a vantage point for looking over one's past. I am not thinking, to be sure, of making anything of this that might even resemble a book. But this was not the object, at least not so much, of my inner need referred to above. My main aim is to execute one idea of mine in written form.

By autobiography I certainly do not mean a description of my life, which I should consider highly insignificant, nor a history of my time, which I do not feel qualified to write. Nor do I have in mind one of those indictments plus self-justifications where one stands as though in judgment over one's own corpse. In every person, as in every creature in the realm of reality, there are certain parts which concern only himself and his accidental existence, and which quite properly die with him, unknown to anyone else. But there is also a part which constitutes his connectedness with whatever idea or archetype is best expressed through him in particular, that of which he is the symbol. One might consider as one of the fundamental differences among people the fact that ordinary people are only symbols of man's generic character; higher types imbue the generic character with some kind of individuality which is, however, easily derived from it, but great and extraordinary men symbolize an idea to which we could only have attained through their living exemplification. This difference between what is symbolic in man and that which is solely particular to him, solely a slag of his reality, as it were, shall guide me in my autobiography. I shall pass over the latter entirely, but descend with the greatest thoroughness into the depths of that which can extend our view of the world and of mankind. Whether this will present me in a more favorable light or a more unfavorable light shall not concern me. It is by no means my intention to stop with myself or to go back to myself; what I shall do is to start with myself, as the creature I know best, and proceed on to the world. I shall therefore spread myself considerably in discussing all the things I have observed in my life, or with which I have busied myself: nature, art, science in all its aspects, particularly history and language, countries, nations, outward conditions, state affairs, and people. But, as I said earlier about myself, I shall look at all these objects only in conjunction with the ideas expressed through them, at their connection with the realm of ideas. I shall therefore search out whatever lies symbolically concealed in the world, and judge everything according to my own inner standard, oriented toward my goal of harmonious self-organization and development. But, true to the concept of autobiography, I shall faithfully describe only that which I myself have experienced, in other words only those things of which I have had a full outer or inner view.

For such a task I might easily be particularly well-suited. For, more than anyone, I am a mere observer in the world. Grown independent of fortune and misfortune at an early age by strict exercise of my will, directed by natural bent more toward form than content, more toward activity than its results, more interested in observation than in sensation, nothing has occurred within me or without me without my constantly, with considerable intellectual freedom, observing it. Conscientious historical accuracy has always been a fundamental trait in me, and I have always especially valued the talent of bringing perceptions and ideas, both left in as pure a state as possible, into touch with each other. In this I have had much practice. I remember, since my earliest childhood, paying close incessant attention to the people around me, comparing them with each other and with those who seemed most excellent to me. I always considered it the most desirable of arts to play on people as though on instruments, not for outer purposes which I always despised and often have very little skill in but for the inner purpose that the others should recognize themselves more vividly, express themselves more significantly and freely—in short—because I myself wish to be thus treated by others. Later I entrusted my whole store of observed materials to solitude and to nature, always turning it and comparing it in my mind. For I know no one who has as much inner leisure time as I do. It is really the deep and clear rock bottom of my life, on top of which swims all the rest, all the ballast of business, purposes, affairs without which one would too readily drift hither and yon on the tide of mere sensation. My deep desire to remain inwardly free of the ballast has in time accustomed me to rolling it away from me with ease and never letting it come near to my true nature. And so I have not more experience of the world than anyone else but unquestionably a kind of experience in which simple experiential materials and reflection operate together in a peculiar way.

If now I am peculiarly fitted for this kind of autobiography, in which the description of the world is part of the description of oneself, it could also be said that I am limited to this kind of autobiography by a sort of necessity of my nature. I have, not exactly an inability, but certainly a strong resistance of my intellectual will to segregating subjects from objects, particulars from universals. No matter what object I touch, it grows infinite under my hands; it relates itself to everything else and I do not know where to start or where to stop. Now this is perfectly all right for an autobiography. There is supposed to be nothing purely objective or general in it; everything is supposed to touch on everything else. Only the universal point of reference is the immediate given, and thus one always knows where one will stop and what one will return to. Those people who have had an exact and true judgment of me have always found that I was not meant by nature to do great deeds nor to produce important works of the mind, but that my most characteristic sphere seems to be life itself: accepting it, observing it, judging it, dealing with it and formulating and developing it. And this is what is important here, since the object to be described is my life itself.

Whether or not anyone should in future read these sheets can only be determined, when they are nearly done, by what is in them. But I shall write as though they were meant to be read by everyone who can understand them. Only what is written with such a presupposition may lay claim to clarity, definiteness, and pragmatic universality. One person, however, shall surely read them, one who has shared my life, who has had the most decisive influence on it, and on my views and ideas of it. I shall be mentioning her, or having her in mind, in the course of hundreds of statements in these pages.

I shall start by drawing a brief picture of myself in which, as though in a mirror, my nature is to appear all at one throw.

My predominant traits are: complete control of my self-directive will; a significant and untiring ability to think, but only within certain restrictions and in a certain way; no inclination toward outer, but passionate demand for inner occupation with and in myself—this idealistically oriented in a peculiar way.

In other words, I am a thoroughly inward-oriented person whose entire effort goes to transform the world in its most manifold shapes into his own solitude. Now I shall more closely outline each of the above single traits.

The self-control, which I have practiced since my twelfth year when I started it from a completely autonomous impulse, up to now (since I still do not scorn to practice it), has never had any purpose outside itself. I did not conquer my passions in order to be virtuous; I did not gain control over my outbreaks in order to make my way in life more skillfully; no purpose drove me to pursue one goal exclusive of all others; no enthusiasm elevated one single idea while beating down all others. But I have always had a revulsion against interfering in the world and an urge to stand free of it, observing and examining it. This led me naturally to feel that only the most unconditional self-control might give me the standpoint outside the world that I should need. Besides, for me the essential nobility of man lies in the sobriety which honors the autonomy of the purely inward will. These notions were first awakened in me by antiquity; later they kept me in relation to the ancients forevermore. I started with the pure concept of the Stoics: to will, because one wishes to. But my self-control and my retirement from the world are totally different matters from the ascetic slaying of desire or the hermit's desired distance from worldliness. I do not hesitate to give desire its reins and I acknowledge in sensual pleasure—even in those forms which many people would call excessive—a great, beneficent, and life-giving power. But the other greeds: anger, hatred, vengefulness, whose satiation merely accomplishes relief from their boiling fires for man—they have been partly alien to my nature, in part purposely repressed by me. If they are to be justified at all, or their consequences ever to be considered wholesome, it must either be because a pure concept of justice, separated from hatred and bitterness, is too weak to do its work, or else because they can produce effects for which man's psychic constitution is strong enough only when it borrows their pathological strength. With them, to be sure, man assumes the proportions of a natural force. I admire it, I do not disapprove of it, but I do not care to be one. And so far as the world is concerned, I have never wanted to part from it. On the contrary, I have wanted to know and see as much of it as ever possible. Only I have wanted to be and to remain a stranger in its midst. It is after all my very aim to comprehend the world in its individuality and totality, and this is the fundamental reason for my will-control. One's rule over one's will has a negative and a positive aspect. The conquest of pain, the independence from pleasures and even needs, the taming of desires, all are part of the easier, more customarily practiced, negative aspect. But taken in all its ramifications (and I have never taken it otherwise), self-control demands a never-disturbed reflectivity which always sees soberly and always rules absolutely what sensations it should permit, what external thing it should do next. It consists therefore of the recognition of truth and the doing of right, or at least of that which is consistent.

That is why it is quite wrong to believe that self-control has to do with natural coldness or naturally weak desires. They only ease the lowest aspect, the mere taming of the passions. But reflectiveness, meant to be fruitful for truth and for right, needs its own unique power, one which must flow from the pure part of the soul. Connected with self-control is absence of fear or, in any event, courage. Courage has never been instinctive in me; that is why I may be sure now of possessing any sort of it at any given moment. Upon the positive aspects of self-control I came only late in life. I should like to divide this again into two aspects. One is the ability to solve satisfactorily any given intellectual or practical task which does not lie too far beyond talent or practice. Early in life I had absolutely none of this. I could almost never get anything done just because I wished to; for everything and anything I needed the right mood which could come only of itself. Even writing a letter was hard for me; I should never have been able to produce a verse or a rhyme. It was not until I came to Rome and finished my translation of *Agamemnon,* and later, in transacting various business matters, that I finally learned it, and learned it in a high degree considering that I had to struggle for it in the teeth of my nature. The other aspect of positive self-control has to do with actions, also; with the carrying out of plans that are held over a length of time. To this I was introduced, some years after I was married, by the reading of some biography. At that time, several years before I entered any public office, I made a firm resolve to go into public service and reach therein the highest sphere open to me, and I kept that resolve. Later I was able to make and keep other resolves, both in private and in public life. My method, however, is not that of merely incessant direct pushing. It goes deeper, seeking more to compel the very heart of the situation. Very often I take no visible steps for a long time, but I never lose sight of my purpose; I prepare the soil from which, by the nature of the situation, opportunity must spring; I listen for any promising sounds; I choose the right moment and then act with untiring zeal; I do not let myself be side-tracked by momentary failures but use them to further my aim. Aside from the eye and the skill which are more or less mechanical aids, it is mostly a question of untiring effort coupled with indifference toward failure or success. With this combination one can go incredibly far. Most people do not reach their goals because they care too much about succeeding and this worry relaxes their efforts. Finally, I must determine here whether or not I have what people commonly call "character." The simple answer is: none whatever by nature; a high degree whenever I will it. I have no difficulty whatever in deviating from any conviction, resolve, or plan of mine. Whenever I meet even slight resistance, I tend to give in. In fact I have a general tendency to give in to others, but I know this springs largely from my inward self-confidence. I know that I shall nevertheless be and remain what I want. But once my will has made an inward resolve, there is hardly a more iron stubbornness than mine, for most people rarely have such a deep conviction that any outward consequence must give way and shatter to bits when opposed by the severity of an idea. But I seldom make use of my brass-bound intractability, because I know that in only a very few cases is it a useful weapon. The characteristic quality of my self-control, then, is its flexibility: neither does it stiffly and pedantically serve so-called higher aims, nor do I have trouble controlling it if need be.

Against my mind and the quality of my mental capacities very significant objections might be raised, which would be difficult to refute. I have no quickness, no ease, in grasping various interrelationships between objects and ideas, regardless of whether certain intermediate concepts are available or not. In my business, I improve upon this lack only by diligence, research, and consultation with others. For this reason, attentiveness has become second nature to me. Nor am I any good at guessing, combining possibilities, or making suppositions; I have never learned a single card game even tolerably well, and have never been any good at philological criticism. This lack does me no end of harm in my trade as ambassador. It is not possible to find substitute skills for it; it can only be more or less concealed. I am not in the least inventive. Everything looks more orderly than manifold to me; even in my writing and speaking this shows up as a certain monotonousness which even keeps bringing back the same words. Whatever wealth of ideas I may possess at most shows up piecemeal, in the form of wit, but it never flows easily. I so seldom have any certainty of truth and so easily hover between any two ideas, that I always consider one most excellent when I am at the point of accepting the other. I have never had the conviction, nor have I seen anyone else have it about me, that I have any real capacity for the field of true synthetic metaphysics. Nor was I born to be a poet. My imagination is either overwhelmed by the dryness of my intellect, or else by the sensate materials that roll in on me. Throughout my childhood, until I heard my first philosophical lecture from Engel, and even after that for some time, I was always taken for a slow head, little favored by nature, especially in comparison to my brother Alexander. I still have—only they are fortunately either not noticed or else ascribed to distractions or some other external cause—extremely simpleminded, silly, empty moments, both in social intercourse and in business, moments which are, furthermore, far too long for the sort they are. On the other hand I cannot say that my mental powers have flagged with the passing years; on the contrary, they have grown and improved. But what was formerly true remains so: my head is by nature slow, scanty in variety of content, and not very lively. To this must be added that I impart few outside materials to it. For I have read unbelievably little and still do not enjoy reading; I know very few things with assurance, far fewer than the world thinks, and I have wasted far too much time in mechanical studies which benefitted my mind very little. Thus far the indictments and the faults. [XV, 451–60]

PERSONAL EXPRESSIONS
1817–1818

Bülow [his secretary and youngest daughter's fiancé] proved to me the other day again that he is really in a bad way. He was telling me that a woman from Berlin had come to him looking for a job—she wanted to supervise our laundry arrangements. I asked in all innocence, just as I would have if it had been a man who applied, what she looked like. In spite of his usual extreme courtesy toward me Bülow practically jumped at me and said that he certainly hadn't looked at her! I didn't dare say another word nor bring the subject up again, though the woman might have been very useful to us. But to myself I thought . . . Dear God! God help the poor man! Nowadays they can't even look a chambermaid in the face! To be serious for a moment, I am actually rather fond of such continence in young people, whether its origin lies in religion, morality, or lovesickness, and times are really better in this respect than they were twenty years ago. On the other hand one must admit that such a way of life, practiced by a man, presupposes great moderation in desire, natural delicacy of feeling, and self-control if it is not to prove, at least upon some occasions, a burden to his wife. For such a way of feeling funnels imagination, sensation, appreciation of the beautiful and the individual, everything whatever—into that desire which is not of the spirit and which is always too selfish to be lovingly considerate of the delicate feelings of a wife. However deeply she loves her husband, she sometimes does not want all this—or wants it differently. And even where this is not so, still the tenderest and the best love gets lost in mere unconscious pleasure. It is really true that I look upon these matters totally differently. That which to me is love is never mixed with anything that has to do with want or need; love to me is the pure impact of being on being, and it is accompanied by such infinite pleasure in the beloved, that one cannot do enough to let her develop in complete freedom; one cannot step back quietly enough to steep oneself in her image. And it is just this feeling that produces a sense of security which makes monstrous even the thought of unfaithfulness. There can be no such thing: nothing is comparable to one's love, nothing can get in its way. Whatever else might please or fascinate or attract one does it, like everything else in nature and in art, through its outward shape or inner form of the humanity which adheres to it. But it does not become a part of the innermost being of him who enjoys it; it passes back into the total image of the world. A man may be enriched by it in a number of ways, but he cannot be alienated from himself by it, or from that which truly, inwardly belongs to him. It may play the range of his senses, his imagination, his desires, but it is always possessed. Never does it possess him. That is how I have always looked upon these matters; they have never clouded my heart. On the other hand, not everyone understands them in this way, and I have often quietly admired your free view of them, your consideration for someone else's individuality, your infinite goodness in always having understood me and carried me as I am. Forgive me for this speech, but I've long had it in my heart to talk with you about it. If you had ever wished me otherwise, had I ever had the slightest inkling that you did, I should have become as you wished me to be, in your absence as well as your presence. I know of nothing on earth that I wouldn't do for you, and I could tolerate nothing in myself that would disturb your happiness, even if it were a whim of yours that I didn't approve of. Anyway, the world is rich enough to fulfill and keep one busy, even if one were to give up whole series of things. Only the *one* that one loves one can never give up without perishing oneself.* [To Caroline v. Humboldt, October 1817]

*   *   *

You know Alexander's views. They can never be the same as ours, much as I love him. It is often downright funny when he and I are together. I always let him talk and have his way, for what's the use of contending when the first bases of all our principles are totally different. Alexander has not only unique learning and truly comprehensive views, but an unusually lovely character: warmhearted, helpful, self-sacrificing, unselfish. What he lacks is a quiet contentedness in himself and in thinking— but from these springs everything else. That is why he understands neither people, though he always lives in close association with someone and even by preference concerns himself with people's feelings, nor art, although he readily comprehends all its technical aspects and is a pretty good painter himself, nor—and this a bold and frightful thing to say about him—does he understand nature, though every day he makes important discoveries in natural science. As for religion, it is not visible in him; neither that he has any nor that he lacks it. His mind and his feelings do not seem to reach the borderline at which this gets decided. Moreover, there is nothing flexible left in him about all these main aspects of humanity; every-

---

* It may be of particular interest to the modern reader to see Caroline v. Humboldt's answer to this letter, which is hereby appended. *Tr.*

I had to smile quietly to myself about all that you say in connection with Bülow. Believe me, dear heart, that I can never misunderstand you, in any of your utterances, in any aspect of your nature, and that I am forever deeply suffused by the goodness, the consideration, the love with which you have always carried me, cared for me, loved me, and forborne with me. Only in this recognition and appreciation of you—alas in nothing else—can I never be surpassed. [To Wilhelm v. Humboldt, November 1817.]

407

thing is as though separated and locked in by iron partitions. Right now his hobby is to have all sorts of ideas about constitutions (though nonetheless purely monarchical ones), not in order to get mixed up in anything political, but in order to harmonize with the Liberals in Paris and with the Opposition here [in London]. Every moment he talks about his "basic principles" in this connection. But he has never, in any way, reflected deeply on the matter; the weak and wretched gossip he has heard about them in France suffices him, and if he were ever to ask me for my opinion on these subjects, I wouldn't know at what point even to begin, in order to reach him. But fortunately he doesn't ask me; he looks upon me as someone who both in himself and through his political position is bound to disagree, and this is just as well. He tells me by the hour about Parisians—personal gossip about them—and I sit and listen peacefully and can only reflect that not one of the men or the women that he mentions ever rouses my slightest interest, not even any purely intellectually idle curiosity. When he speaks of his studies, on the other hand, he is highly interesting and always to the point. My final conclusion, whenever we have been together for a long while, is always that it is one of the most astonishing situations in the moral universe that my father and my mother, who had only two children, should have had these two who—although in general they both are similarly oriented, toward the world of thought and the contemplative life—should nonetheless diverge more completely than could be expected if they had been born on different planets. And Alexander didn't change, basically; he was always this way. Living in foreign countries didn't change him; rather he sought foreign countries because he could never truly feel at home in Germany, though he is far superior to most Germans. [To Caroline v. Humboldt, November 1817]

*   *   *

The newspaper stories about convicted criminals here [in London] are often very touching. They are quite strict and harsh here and believe in a totally different kind of justice from that which we would call justice at home. They ask only whether the act was committed and what the law is. There is no digging and wallowing in the morality and the feelings of the poor wretched criminals, and if I were to stray into similar errors, I should prefer the system here. On the other hand, some terrible things can happen within it. For example, a husband was sentenced to a term at Botany Bay several years ago. His wife wanted to be with him and didn't know how to go about it. She was twenty-three years old. She got the idea of committing forgery, in order to be convicted and sent there herself, but she didn't know that the penalty for forgery is death. She forged a single one-pound note and not long ago she was executed. [To Caroline v. Humboldt, February 1818]

* * *

One must never improperly excuse oneself. This much modesty I really do have, and it is true and deep in me. I always know very well, in private life as well as in my business, where I failed, or erred, or did wrong. Remorse is foreign to me because I am convinced that it always rests on the incorrect notion that one's guilt did not lie in one's act but in one's being, in the deep source of one's act. But to be remorseful for being as one is seems to me to lose all hold on one's thought. Nothing has any meaning then. One gets into the grip of depression as to oneself, others, fate itself; but even if one hates oneself one cannot truly wish to be other than one is, for what does that mean: to be other than one is? One cannot lose oneself. But even if I do not, thus, really feel remorse, I do not therefore hide from myself the consequences of my acts or my guilt and I do, as a matter of fact, as though drawn against my will, go over and over the concatenation of circumstances which seem to link the acts with their con- sequences. . . . [To Caroline v. Humboldt, February 1818]

* * *

I understand very well how melancholy and dejected one can be without any apparent outward cause. . . . There are things that occur inside one's bosom of which clear thought has not so much as an intuition. Certain things stand in an immediate relationship of interaction with fate itself, and even if it is nothing other than this, the destiny of all humanity in all its truth and meaningfulness senses itself in our dark depths. There is nothing more simultaneously melancholy and happy. I too, sweetheart, often feel it and not only now and here but far back in my childhood and my youth I remember such days, where a many ton weight seemed to oppress my inner mind, and where together with complete gloominess of one's thoughts there seemed to be an actual pain in one's heart, all the more peculiar because it contains the knowledge that it is not a pain of the body. [To Caroline v. Humboldt, March 1818]

*   *   *

I have always carried a twofold nature within myself, one person who is ever oriented away from the world, toward solitude, and another who lets himself be pushed by circumstances, and sometimes too readily by the simple love for trying out his strength toward the world. This accounts for a curious mixture which frequently people do not understand and which I myself do not wholly approve of but which I have grown so accustomed to that it remains possible to maintain my balance. I had the great good fortune, moreover, to have enjoyed solitude in the two most decisive periods of my life, once in late youth and actually long into maturity (for when we married we were at just that age which seems the best part of youth) and again during my final period of life; my coexistence with the outside world consumed relatively few years and just those in which it does the least harm to individuality and least occupies one's entire time. Looking at the course of my inner development I should say that never has a man been so favored by fate which permitted it to flourish, and

hence there will never be a man who will die so filled with gratitude. There is nothing I should want removed from my life except
the painful loss of the dear children and several periods where I
might have made you happier than you were. But the first must
never prevent one's reconciliation with fate and over the latter
breathes your gentle and sweet forgiveness. [To Caroline v. Humboldt, June 1818]

*   *   *

It is the fate of one's life that
there is always a power which initially carries, lifts, and supports
one, but in the end steps up and claims that one is its property,
that one's freedom is over, that one must renounce one's own feelings, one's inner life. . . . For long now I have felt a longing to
withdraw myself from this power without violating it; it does not
spring from fear or from aversion to the places where it draws one,
but it is the increasing dominance of the inner life which, like a
stream approaching the sea swells ever more mightily the closer it
comes to the outermost beachhead of earthly existence. I am now
at a point where outer circumstances will perhaps permit of it, and
I am therefore stepping delicately in order not to tie any new knots
as I try to loosen the old ones. [To Caroline v. Humboldt, November 1818]

*   *   *

One lives so constantly and solely
within one's imagination. At least that is literally true of me, although no one loses as little of reality as I do. But there is a way
of taking reality which always sees more in it than time and the
barriers of existence permit. In art this is obvious. But in life too it
can be like that. First, everything is what it is, and second, everything is a symbol of what it is in its deep inner nature, in its relationship to everything else, but what it can never wholly be in this
or that moment. Whoever is most capable of taking all things al-

ways and simultaneously both as themselves and as symbols of themselves, whoever can smelt these two aspects into the widest and deepest truth, he best reaches the depths and heights of life; he most enjoys his existence. [To Caroline v. Humboldt, December 1818]

*   *   *

PERSONAL EXPRESSIONS
1822-1832

Speaking of pure fortune, the kind sent to us by the gods through no merit of ours: such fortune I count it that you and I once met, that in you a human image came before my eyes which I always remembered and always shall, with nothing to disturb my peace. For even if it were possible that something were to come over you that I should disapprove of, the image would nonetheless remain forever pure and undefiled in me. Whatever happened to you would be something human, something that could happen to any human being, but it could not attach itself to the features which are drawn upon that inner image. For every person, however good he may be, carries within him a better person who makes up his true self, but to whom he may at times be unfaithful. To this inward and much less changeable self, not the very changeable and everyday person, one must cling, reminding the one of the other's existence, and forgiving oneself many things of which the deepest self is innocent.

I had not the slightest notion what a treasure of love and loyalty you were preserving for me throughout an entire lifetime. How should I not feel fortunate! [To C. Diede, December 1822]

*   *   *

The few hours remaining to me after business correspondence, walking, talking to people, etc. I spend almost exclusively reading Aristotle's *Ethics* and the Bhagavad-Gita which Schlegel has published. Both books are really concerned with the same theme: the aim of all things, the value of life, the highest good, death as the beginning of a new life. In Aristotle one finds the loftiness of a great, almost tremendous spirit and the most cultivated nation in the world; in the Hindu poem the perhaps still more moving greatness of remotest antiquity and a people seemingly created for profound meditation. I never read either of them for long, but each sound moves me with a strength which stimulates my own reflection. I often think how strange it is that Goethe lives so almost exclusively with the products of our time and so clings to what he calls his "paper work" [notes and comments] which can be meant only for current use. If I believed I were so near death as he must be, considering his age and the state of his health, I should find all such work impossible. I should go back solely to prehistoric times, looking, in order to collect and focus myself properly, in all the places where human nature seems to have expressed itself most purely and simply. [To Caroline v. Humboldt, December 1823]

*   *   *

Already when I was young, and throughout my adult years, I imagined and in imagination enjoyed how it would be when old age at last presented me with the proper excuse to withdraw from social intercourse. What I imagined has come to pass. I always thought of old age as fascinating and much more fascinating than the earlier periods and now that I have got there I find my expectations exceeded by reality. For that reason perhaps I am somewhat older psychologically than physiologically or chronologically. I am now fifty-seven years old. . . . Lack of humility and lack of patience are really what magnify whatever evils there are and make them difficult to bear. For these, old age is a real cure, provided one does not have too many ingrained naughty habits which, of course, spread their poison over any age. But the greatest gain from the increased spiritual freedom, from the lessening of greed and passion, from the cloudless sky, as it were, which increased years allow to rise over our psyche is that our reflection becomes purer, stronger, more lasting, and more demanding of our total humanity, that our intellectual horizons open out, that preoccupation with every kind of knowledge and every aspect of truth more exclusively fills out the mind and silences all other needs, all other yearnings. [To C. Diede, July 1824]

*　　　*　　　*

The events of the world hold not the slightest interest for me. They pass by me like apparitions of a moment and are not able to give anything to either spirit or heart. The circle of my acquaintances is ever narrowing; the men with whom I formerly was most pleasantly associated have died, and I have always considered such association a lucky accident to be made use of, not a need whose fulfillment was to be sought. The field of knowledge and investigation, on the other hand, is immeasurable and constantly offers new charms. It fills out the hours and makes one wish only one had more hours to fill. I can truly say, I think, that I live with such inward matters for days at a time, without ever turning any except the most superficial attention away from them. The natural sciences have never attracted me. I never had the mind for attentive observation of external objects. But from an early age I was attracted by the antiquities, and they are what all my studies really deal with. Where man was somewhat closer to his origins, more greatness, more simplicity, more profundity and naturalness show in his thought, in his feelings, as well as in the expressions that he gave to his thoughts and feelings. [To C. Diede, September 1824]

*   *   *

I have never understood how time is supposed to heal the pain of loss.* The loss remains for all time and the healing could only consist of the weakening of memory or of the fact that loneliness may cause one to draw close to some other person. This, I very much hope, will not happen to me—it does not happen to any noble soul, I believe. But I have no objections to my feelings staying exactly as they now are. . . . For many years I have been supremely happy at my wife's side, for the most part solely and wholly because of her, and at the very least in such fashion that the thought of her mingled with all that made me truly happy. This whole happiness has been taken from me forever by the course of nature, the decree of heaven. It has been taken forever and without possibility of return. But my memory of the departed, that in me which was ripened by life and by her—this, no fate can rob me of without at the same time destroying me. Fortunately there is thus something which every man can hold on to if he wishes to, and over which no fate has any power. If I may live for my memory in solitude and retirement, I shall not complain and shall not be unhappy. For one may have great and deep grief and pain and yet not feel unhappy. One may feel it so bound up with one's inmost being that one would not care to part with it. On the contrary, by nourishing it and holding it dear, one helps grief fulfill its true meaning. . . . A new stage of life is thus beginning. What one has lived thus far is finished; one may look it over in its completeness, hold it fast in one's mind through memory, and inwardly continue to live with it. Only one no longer has wishes for the future. Since one constantly enjoys, in a way, a certain spiritual presence, one feels strengthened in all one's powers

---

* His wife, Caroline, had died six weeks prior to the writing of this letter. *Tr.*

and thus it is that life . . . retains its charm. [To C. Diede, May 1829]

*   *   *

If I had a magic wand to bring youthful strength and vigor into the years now remaining to me, I should not choose to do so. Youthful energy and freshness do not go with the feelings of old age and these feelings, earned and attained in the course of a long life, I would not give up for anything on earth. [To C. Diede, March 1830]

*   *   *

It is almost midnight, dearest Gabriele, and the moon shines mild and bright through the window which I always leave unshuttered for it. You won't believe how beautiful the view from my room is even now, facing as it does all the ice-stiffened trees. I have just been reading some of the letters of your dear mother, as I usually do at night, and now must thank you for your lovely cordial letter, dearest child. You must forgive my few and brief letters; you know the reason, and that my thoughts are always with you. There are a few things which are ever present to the soul; one does not cease to think of them when one thinks of something else; the other things roll over them like a brook over its bed. In such thoughts lies one's true inner happiness; they simply do not let one be unhappy. For they grow in strength with their sadness and embrace the soul more closely the more it needs them. Thus you, beloved Gabriele, and your sisters are forever one with your mother in me, each one of you in her own image, all warmed by the breath of her love till the hour of her death, and all so fully and purely and truly within me that I speak to all of you as I speak to myself.

Your new hopes moved me deeply as soon as I first heard of them. I ask the blessings of heaven upon them. Heaven has so often guarded you and your dear children, especially during the dangers to poor little Linchen, that its blessings will continue. What you write, dear Gabriele, about the connection between the unborn and the no longer living is very beautiful and true. It cannot be comprehended, to be sure, nor even intuited by reason, but the intuition of feeling gives us no less assurance. But this far at least we may reach with our thoughts: that the reasons which cause our life to be incomprehensible to *us* as regards its condition before birth and after death, no longer apply to those who have left this part of life. Death surely rends one veil, and if it were not for the fact that the longing for that which one had and now no longer has extinguishes all other feelings and thoughts, one might be downright happy in anticipating death as the revelation of certain secrets of existence. What therefore most gently relates death to life is a quiet, peaceful, but very lively and clear preoccupation with ideas, to which old age quite naturally inclines one. At the same time it contains the sweetest pledge of seeing one's loved ones again and being reunited with them. One can earn or deserve this only through the strength of one's love, whatever else one likes to imagine or tell oneself. . . .

But love grows with quiet inward occupation of the spirit and within it applies everything to itself. That is why—and I have argued this since my earliest youth—the life of women is so much higher and nobler than that of men. With the utmost simplicity they relate, and tie together the strongest and slightest threads of life, and more than this no man can do, by all his countless detours; in fact he seldom succeeds. As I read Mother's letters I often note down to the smallest details how infinitely profound was her effect on us all, and how for that reason alone she is always with us and in us. In myself especially I can trace throughout long periods of time how she developed me in all the things which I still value today, and which without her would be forever closed off from me. And yet her intent, even as regards you children, was hardly ever to teach or to form. It was her nature itself which had a powerful, quiet effectiveness. In her one could get a clear view of every deeper human feeling; one clearly felt that one had never before known it as one saw it in her. And though she took an infinitude away from us when she died, she left us an equal infinitude. Without even counting the sweet poignancy of her memory, one can live in her in one's ideas and never exhaust her unique being. [To Gabriele v. Bülow, Humboldt's youngest daughter, January 1832]

*   *   *

I feel as though I were beginning to reach the point where all my earlier works and studies draw together in one point, much more than used to be the case. I look upon it as a warning not to trust the length of time I have left, but to use the present time well, in order to carry with me and simultaneously leave behind me in ordered fashion those matters which I feel very plainly, but which still lie undeveloped and in part unproven within me. I always think of taking with and leaving behind in the same breath. So far as ideas are concerned, we only possess wholly that which we have represented, placed outside ourselves, allowed to transfer itself to others, and regardless of how obscure the beyond, I cannot consider it a matter of indifference whether or not I have reached true clarity before I leave, in all the ideas I have battled with throughout a lifetime. Individuality cannot get so far lost, and since there are two directions operating in the world which, like warp and woof, form the historical tapestry—one, the life and development of individuals, ever breaking off, the other, the everlasting and permanent concatenation of fate, produced by the operations of these same individuals—I cannot help looking upon individuality as the main thing, from which the course of the world proceeds as a sort of necessary consequence. Thus inward clarity, when I can tell myself that I have not missed too much, remains my most urgent motive for continued work, and I am happy that my work now seems to move in a steadier direction. [To Goethe, January 1832]

BIBLIOGRAPHICAL APPENDIX

The numbers in brackets at the end of most of the selections refer to volume and page of Humboldt's collected works: *Wilhelm von Humboldt's Gesammelte Schriften* (17 vols., Berlin: Königlich Preussische Akademie der Wissenschaften, 1903). A list of the specific works from which the selections were taken follows below. In addition, the following were used:

Wilhelm und Caroline von Humboldt in ihren Briefen. Herausgegeben von Anna von Sydow (7 vols., Berlin: E. S. Mittler, 1907–1919). Selections from these letters are indicated at the end of each passage by the notation "To Caroline v. Humboldt" plus the month and year of writing.

Briefe von Wilhelm von Humboldt an eine Freundin (Leipzig: Brockhaus, 1860). Selections from these letters are indicated by the notation "To C. Diede" plus the date.

Goethes Briefwechsel mit den Gebrüdern von Humboldt. 1795–1832. F. Th. Bratranek (ed.) (Leipzig: Brockhaus, 1876). Selections from these letters are indicated by the notation "To Goethe" plus the date.

List of works from which the selections were made

Volume I (of the above cited edition)

Pp. 1–44. *Sokrates und Platon über die Gottheit, über die Vorsehung und Unsterblichkeit.* (Socrates and Plato on divinity, providence and immortality.) 1785, 1787.

Pp. 45–76. *Über Religion.* (About religion.) 1789.

Pp. 77–85. *Ideen über Staatsverfassung, durch die neue französische Konstitution veranlasst.* (Ideas on government, occasioned by the new French Constitution.) 1791.

Pp. 86–96. *Über die Gesetze der Entwicklung der menschlichen Kräfte.* (On the developmental laws of human energies.) 1791. [Fragment]

Pp. 97–254. *Ideen zu einem Versuch die Grenzen der Wirksamkeit des Staats zu bestimmen.* (An attempt to define the legal limits of government.) 1792.

Pp. 255–281. *Über das Studium des Altertums und des griechischen insbesondere.* (About classical studies, particularly concerning the Greeks.) 1793.

Pp. 311–334. *Über den Geschlechtsunterschied und dessen Einfluss auf die organische Natur.* (About sexual differences and their influence on organic nature.) 1794.

Pp. 335–369. *Über die männliche und weibliche Form.* (On masculine and feminine form.) 1795.

Pp. 377–410. *Plan einer vergleichenden Anthropologie.* (Plan for a comparative anthropology.) 1795.

Pp. 411–429. *Pindar.* (Pindar.) 1795.

Volume II

Pp. 1–112. *Das achtzehnte Jahrhundert.* (The eighteenth century.) 1796–97.

Pp. 113–323. *Ästhetische Versuche. Erster Teil: Über Goethes Hermann und Dorothea.* (Essays on Esthetics. Part I: On Goethe's *Hermann und Dorothea.*) 1797–98.

Pp. 324–334. *Über den Geist der Menschheit.* (On the spirit of humanity.) 1797.

Pp. 335–344. *Rezension der Agnes von Lilien.* (Review of *Agnes von Lilien* [by Humboldt's friend, Caroline von Wolzogen, published anonymously].) 1798. [Fragment]

Pp. 345–376. *Musée des petits Augustins.* [Essays on several French art objects.] 1799.

Pp. 377–400. *Über die gegenwärtige französische tragische Bühne.* (On the contemporary French theater.) 1799.

Volume III

Pp. 30–59. *Der Montserrat bei Barcelona.* (Mt. Montserrat near Barcelona.) 1800.

Pp. 114–135. *Cantabrica.* [Various small essays on Spain.] 1800.

Pp. 136–170. *Latium und Hellas oder Betrachtungen über das classische Altertum.* (Latium and Hellas; Observations about classical antiquity.) 1806.

Pp. 171–218. *Geschichte des Verfalls und Unterganges der griechischen Freistaaten.* (History of the fall and decline of the Greek city states.) 1807–08.

Pp. 288–299. *Ankündigung einer Schrift über die vaskische Sprache und Na-*

tion nebst Angabe des Gesichtspunktes und Inhalts derselben. (Announcement of an essay on the language and nation of the Basques, including the theme and contents thereof.) 1812.

Pp. 342–349. *Über die Bedingungen, unter denen Wissenschaft und Kunst in einem Volke gedeihen.* (On the proper conditions for science and art.) 1814. [Fragment]

Pp. 350–359. *Betrachtungen über die Weltgeschichte.* (Observations on world history.) 1814.

Volume IV

Pp. 1–34. *Über das vergleichende Sprachstudium in Beziehung auf die verschiedenen Epochen der Sprachentwicklung.* (On comparative linguistics with special reference to the various periods of linguistic development.) 1820.

Pp. 35–56. *Über die Aufgabe des Geschichtschreibers.* (On the historian's task.) 1821.

Pp. 233–284. *Versuch einer Analyse der mexikanischen Sprache.* (Attempt at an analysis of the Mexican language.) 1821.

Pp. 420–435. *Über den Nationalcharakter der Sprachen.* (On the national characteristics of languages.) 1822. [Fragment]

Volume V

Pp. 1–30. *Inwiefern lässt sich der ehemalige Kulturzustand der eingeborenen Völker Amerikas aus den Überresten ihrer Sprachen beurteilen?* (To what extent may one judge the cultural level of the American natives from their linguistic remains?) 1823.

Pp. 31–106. *Über den Zusammenhang der Schrift mit der Sprache.* (On the relationship between writing and speech.) 1823–24.

Pp. 190–231. *Über die unter dem Namen Bhagavad-Gita bekannte Episode des Mahabharata.* I. (On the episode from the Mahabharata known as "Bhagavad-Gita." Part I.) 1825. [A speech read before the Prussian Academy of Sciences on June 30, 1825.]

Pp. 309–324. *Über den grammatischen Bau der chinesischen Sprache.* (On the grammatical structure of the Chinese language.) 1826.

Pp. 325–343. *Über die unter dem Namen Bhagavad-Gita bekannte Episode des Mahabharata.* II. (On the episode from the Mahabharata known as "Bhagavad-Gita." Part II.) 1826.

Pp. 364–475. *Grundzüge des allgemeinen Sprachtypus.* (Basic characteristics of linguistic types.) 1824–26.

Volume VI

Pp. 4–30. *Über den Dualis.* (On the dual form.) 1827.

Pp. 111–303. *Über die Verschiedenheiten des menschlichen Sprachbaues.* (On the differences in human linguistic structure.) 1827–29.

Pp. 492–527. *Über Schiller und den Gang seiner Geistesentwicklung.* (On Schiller and the course of his spiritual development.) 1830.

Pp. 528–550. *Rezension von Goethes zweitem römischen Aufenthalt.* (Review of Goethe's *Zweiter Römischer Aufenthalt.*) 1830.

Volume VII

Pp. 1–344. *Über die Verschiedenheit des menschlichen Sprachbaues und ihren Einfluss auf die geistige Entwicklung des Menschengeschlechts.* (On the differences in human linguistic structure and their influence on the spiritual development of the human race.) 1830–35. [The general introduction to Humboldt's work on the Kawi language.]

Pp. 593–608. *Fragmente der Monographie über die Basken.* (Fragments of the monograph on the Basques.) 1801–02.

Pp. 609–618. *Über den Charakter der Griechen, die idealische und historische Ansicht desselben.* (On the Greek character: an ideal and a historical view.) 1807.

Pp. 619–628. *Einleitung in das gesamte Sprachstudium.* (Introduction to general linguistics.) 1810–11.

Volume VIII

Pp. 117–230. *Aeschylos Agamemnon.* ([Introduction to Humboldt's translation of] Aeschylus' *Agamemnon.*) 1797–1816.

Volume X

Pp. 250–260. *Über die innere und äussere Organisation der höheren wissenschaftlichen Anstalten in Berlin.* (On the inner and outer organization of the higher institutions of learning in Berlin.) Ca. 1810.

Volume XIII

Pp. 1–196. *Die Vasken oder Bemerkungen auf einer Reise durch Biscaya und das französische Basquenland im Frühling des Jahrs 1801.* (The Basques: Observations made during a trip through the Spanish and French Basque country in the spring of 1801.)

Volume XIV

Pp. 76–236. *Tagebuch der Reise nach Paris und der Schweiz*. (Diary of a trip to Paris and Switzerland.) 1789.

Volume XV

Pp. 451–460. *Bruchstück einer Selbstbiographie*. (Fragment of an autobiography.) Frankfurt, 29 January 1816.

Pp. 532–549. *Roman*. [An account of Caroline von Humboldt's early life.] Written some time between 1832 and 1835.

Volume XVI

P. 37. Letter to Prince Georg. 1 September 1804.
Pp. 74 f. Letter to Prince Georg. 31 December 1809.
P. 170. Letter to Wolf. 14 July 1809.
P. 176. Letter to Vincke. 18 July 1809.
P. 220. Letter to Wolf. 13 October 1809.

INDEX

Academies of Arts and Sciences, relation to universities, 136–40

Accidents, 315–16

Active power and receptive power, 337–41

Adams, John Quincy, Humboldt's similarity to, 4

Adhibhuta, 190

Adhideiva, 190

Adhiyajna, 190

Adhyatman, 190

Aeschylus, 82, 165

Agamemnon, translation of by Humboldt, 18, 395, 401

Akshara, 190

Alcibiades, 232

Allegory, 97, 98

Amilavaca, 71

Anthropology, comparative, needs methodological approach, 109–14

Aphrodite, 359 *et seq. See also* Venus

Archetypes, 30, 83, 86, 92, 98, 162, 239–41, 247, 258, 317, 330, 336–37, 357, 373. *See also* Ideas and ideals

Aristides, 92

Aristophanes, 82, 224

Aristotle, 225 *et seq.*, 414

Arjuna, 168 *et seq.*

Art: as communication, 160; as organized imagination, 160; as objectification of nature, 161; as transformation into images, 161; in society, 213–15; and morality, 215; and beauty, 162f

Artists, and their works, 164 *et seq.*

Arts: conditions for flowering of the literature, 103, 215–34; painting, 162; music, 221. *See also* Poetry, Prose, Stage, Translations

Astronomy, 102

Athene, 361. *See also* Minerva

Athens, 232

Atman, 178 *et seq.*

Bacchus, 97

Basque, language, 10

Bureaucracy, growth of, 53 *et seq.*

Beauty, in art and in nature, 162f

Berlin Academy of Sciences, 22, 23

The manuscript was prepared for publication by Christine Colditz. The book was designed by S. R. Tenenbaum. The typeface used for the text is Linotype Granjon designed in 1924 by George W. Jones, based on a cutting originally made by Claude Garamond in the 16th century. The display face is Venus Bold Extended cut by Bauersche Giesserei of Germany based on a 19th century revival.

This book was printed on Warren's Olde Style Antique. The book is bound in Joanna Mills' Parchment cloth. Manufactured in the United States of America.

This manuscript was examined for publication by Christine Collins. The book was designed by S. R. Tenenbaum. The typeface used for the text is Linotype Granjon designed in 1924 by George W. Jones based on a face cut by Claude Garamond in 1592. Granjon was named for Robert Granjon a type designer and punch cutter active in France in the sixteenth century. This book was printed on acid-free paper and bound in the United States of America.